WORLD
COIN
ENCYCLOPEDIA

Aes grave, c. 269 B.C.

WORLD COIN ENCYCLOPEDIA

EWALD JUNGE

BARRIE & JENKINS

London Melbourne Sydney Auckland Wellington Johannesburg

Barrie & Jenkins Ltd

An imprint of the Hutchinson Publishing Group

17-21 Conway Street, London W1P 6JD

Hutchinson Group (Australia) Pty Ltd
PO Box 496, 16-22 Church Street, Hawthorne, Melbourne, Victoria 3122
PO Box 151, Broadway, New South Wales 2007

Hutchinson Group (NZ) Ltd
32-34 View Road, PO Box 40-086, Glenfield, Auckland 10

Hutchinson Group (SA) (Pty) Ltd
PO Box 337, Bergvlei 2012, South Africa

First published 1984

Set in Times Roman Compugraphic

Printed in England by
Ebenezer Baylis & Son Ltd, Worcester, and London
and bound by Anchor Brendon Ltd, Tiptree, Essex

British Library Cataloguing in Publication Data

Junge, Ewald
Coin encyclopedia.
1. Coins—Dictionaries
I. Title
737.4'03   CJ89

ISBN 0 09 155140 4

To the memory of
LEONARD STEYNING FORRER 1899-1968
Friend and Mentor

CONTENTS

Declaration type crown
(obverse: enlarged) of Charles I

Clazomenae, tetradrachm, 5th century B.C.

PREFACE

The compiler of any encyclopedia faces, besides the certainty of writer's cramp, almost equally certain charges of plagiarism for what he includes and of ignorance for what he omits. "To be a general numismatist is beyond the powers of one man," wrote Stanley Lane-Poole as long ago as 1885; since when the scope of both general and specialised numismatic knowledge and research has greatly increased.

But, as G. K. Chesterton once remarked, a thing worth doing is worth doing badly. It is a fact—surprising perhaps, but a fact none the less—that there is no reasonably comprehensive A-Z numismatic encyclopedia in English for the general reader or collector. There are dictionaries, certainly, of terms and denominations; there are biographical dictionaries of coinmakers and medallists; there are gazetteers arranged by countries, towns or mints. But you could not look up, before this, in one fairly compact volume and in consecutive alphabetical order, all of the above-mentioned categories—with information on numismatists, collectors and collections thrown in for good measure. And if there is another numismatic reference work with headings under BOSWELL and PUNCH I shall be very much surprised.

Which brings me to the nub of this preface and apologia. Any work of this kind, if it be of this length, must be selective; and the selection had better be personal or it will be deadly dull. Inevitably, therefore, this book is to some extent an exercise in self-indulgence. I have my hobby-horses and one of them is what I like to call "perspectives": the manner in which seemingly unconnected matters may be quite closely related. That is why you will find (for instance) a fairly lengthy entry under PRINTING, not primarily concerned with paper money at all. I also have my *bêtes noirs* (or, if you prefer, blind spots). Take a sentence such as this: "The Bouquet series is without doubt the most interesting of our Canadian coins, and towards the completion of which our collectors should not fail to devote their best energies." (P. N. Breton: *Illustrated History of Coins and Tokens relating to Canada.* Montreal, 1894). I regard this as arrant—even dangerous—nonsense; and though you will find an entry under BOUQUET SOU none the less, please do not expect me to aid and abet Breton in ruining your eyesight while searching for what are to my mind totally insignificant detail changes. Of course one must learn to look at a coin carefully; but that is to note differences which are deliberate rather than accidental.

Finally, to my debts. They will be largely apparent from the extent of the bibliography. I have tried to check my facts against the best available printed authorities in various specialised fields. But my chief indebtedness must be to a handful of contemporary numismatic authors who have themselves achieved remarkable feats of scholarship and synthesis combined: R. A. G. Carson in

Coins, Elvira Clain-Stefanelli in *Numismatics, an Ancient Science*, John Porteous in *Coins in History*. Terminological and denominational coin dictionaries such as Schrötter and Frey have been constantly at my side; but I doubt if any proved as useful, by way of constant reminder of how much can be instructively and interestingly said in a brief compass, as did C. C. Chamberlain's *Guide to Numismatics* in the English Universities Press "Teach Yourself" series. By the same premise, I have shamelessly and gratefully used the index to Dr Sutherland's *Art in Coinage* to remind me of the nucleus of essential names among great artists and craftsmen from Kimon to the Wyons, adding more of my own choosing as I went along, without in any sense attempting even a précis of entries as found in the *Biographical Dictionary of Medallists* (which alone would make two volumes of this size!).

A special word of thanks is due to Peter Clayton who not only took the majority of photographs but also read the entire manuscript in proof and made many valuable suggestions.

My greatest debt is best expressed in the dedication (posthumous, alas) of this book. The late Leonard Steyning Forrer's *The Art of Collecting Coins* first opened my eyes to what numismatics is all about; his unfailing kindness to a very "green" beginner determined me to try and do better; his friendship was the inspiration behind this book, plans for which he actively encouraged. It would have been the better for being submitted to his critical eye stage by stage; as it is, I can only hope that I have not let him down too badly.

I do not think that much is needed by way of "Notes to the Reader" or "How to use this book". An asterisk (*) placed immediately in front of a word indicates where a cross-reference to another entry seems particularly necessary or desirable.

The black-and-white photographs of coins appearing in the margins are not separately listed. They are placed as close as possible to the relevant entry; where not, they are captioned to avoid confusion. The photographs are reproduced at the actual size of the coin unless otherwise stated.

A Most frequently seen as a distinguishing mark on coins to denote the principal mint of a country (e.g. Berlin, Paris, Vienna). It may, however, also stand for the initial letter of a town (e.g. Ancona, Arles, Avila). The private mint of Ackroyd & Best used it on certain coins struck for British East Africa in 1920.

A.A.A.F.F. An abbreviation for *auro argento aere flando feriundo*, found on many Roman coins, often in association with the name of a moneyer and almost without exception preceded by the abbreviation *III VIRI*. These *triumviri monetales* were minor magistrates responsible for the coinage, and the inscription refers to the gold, silver and copper contained in the coins, and to the process of manufacture.

AACHEN A city in north-east Germany, not far from the present Dutch frontier. It was a regal mint from Carolingian times, and became an Imperial mint during the Hohenstauffen dynasty from 1166. Later it operated also as a mint of the Dukes Jülich-Cleves, and from the 16th century onwards as an *autonomous free city. There are siege coins of 1597, and it is also noted for one of the earliest modern coins (1422) to bear a date.

ABACIS A silver coin formerly in use in the Portuguese possessions of India and East Africa.

ABBASI Base metal Persian coin of the 18th and 19th centuries; also a silver coin of Georgia worth 2 Persian abbasi. In Afghanistan, it circulated at one-third of a *rupee.

ABBEY CROWN A gold piece in the coinage of James V of Scotland, struck in 1526 to the value of 20 shillings. Its name derives from the fact that it was struck in Holyrood Abbey.

ABBO A *Merovingian moneyer working around the turn of the 6th/7th century A.D. He is thought to have also worked in England because there is a *triens in the Cuerdale Find with his name; but as the piece is of curious workmanship, it is perhaps more reasonable to suppose it to be an imitation.

ABBONEL A moneyer's name which appears first in the reign of Aethelstan II of East Anglia (A.D. 880–90), and thereafter at intervals until *c.* 945, variously spelt. There was—most likely— more than one moneyer of this name, related perhaps.

ABBREVIATIONS These, on coins, could fill this book (and have, in fact, filled no less than two standard reference works). In their simplest form, they consist of a single letter (*A above). Contractions are not uncommon (e.g. DNS for *dominus* or SAS for *sanctus*), while *monograms are very common indeed. Interpretation is not always easy; though most of us probably know that DG stands for *Dei gratia* (by the grace of God) on English coins, we might be hard put to it to identify PUS as short for bishop (the last, not first, three letters of the Latin *episcopus*).

ABDERA A town on the southern coast of Thrace (northern

Greece), near the mouth of the river Nestus and opposite the island of Thasos. The coinage struck here from 550–325 B.C. shows as its main type a seated griffin on the obverse. There is a rare *octadrachm of this type (taken over from Teos) struck during the 5th century B.C. Other types during this and the succeeding century alternate the griffin with the head of Apollo on the obverse, and there is a varied series of reverses (discus thrower, dancing girl, Artemis with stag, etc.). From the end of the 5th century we also find magistrates' names on Abdera coins. A very rare tetradrachm of the late 4th century carries the name of Pythagoras and (on the reverse) a bearded portrait; this may well be that of the famous philosopher and mathematician.

ABEELE, PIETER VAN   Dutch medallist active from *c.* 1640–77, chiefly in Amsterdam. He specialised in a kind of hollow *repoussé* type of medallion, the obverse and reverse of which were held together by an encircling ring. Among his best commemorative pieces are portraits of William II of Orange (William III of England), and the Dutch naval heroes De Ruyter and Van Tromp—some with beautifully modelled battle scenes. His signature is sometimes P.V.A., sometimes PA and (more rarely) full name.

ABERDEEN   An occasional Scottish mint, possibly from the time of William the Lion (1165–1214) onwards. It was used regularly between the reigns of Robert III and James III, i.e. 1390–1488, after which no coins were struck here. The majority of coins are pennies, but some *groats and half-groats are also known.

ABERYSTWYTH   A town in Wales, and the first provincial mint to be established by Charles I, and opened in 1638 to exploit silver from the Welsh mines. Its *initial mark was a book, which was the *privy mark of Sir Thomas Bushell, lessee of the Welsh mines. The dies of coins struck here were made in London and it is quite wrong to include them (as is often done) with the English Civil War coinages; the mint was, in fact, closed as soon as hostilities broke out and Bushell moved to join the King at *Shrewsbury.

ABONDIO, ANTONIO   The Vienna Mint Museum preserves many records and some dies of this Italian-born modeller and engraver (1538–91), who spent the greater part of his working life in the service of the Hapsburg Emperors Maximilian II and Rudolph II. His art marks the transitional phase between the Renaissance and the baroque; and though he is notable chiefly for his superb commemorative medals and *Gnadenpfennige, he is known to have executed the master dies of Rudolph II's Thaler coinage. Such Thalers are confined to Hungarian and Bohemian types (also halves and quarters); they are distinguished by a lively representation of the double eagle on the reverse, very different from the more general and stiffish imperial eagle of both earlier and later epochs. Antonio Abondio's son, Alessandro (1580–1663), also served Rudolph II and his successor Matthias, and was active, too, as medallist to the Elector Maximilian I of Bavaria.

ABRAHAM, JACOB (1723–1800)   Prussian coin engraver and medallist active *c.* 1750–94 at the mints of Berlin, Stettin, Königsberg and, finally, a chief engraver and mintmaster, again at Berlin. A new type of Prussian eagle was created by him for the coins of that kingdom in 1761. Among his medals, those for the 500th anniversary of Königsberg and for the victories of Frederick the Great deserve mention. His work is in the style of high classicism, much influenced by *Hedlinger.

ABRAMSON, ABRAHAM (1754–1811) Son of the above, succeeding him in his position as chief engraver and medallist to the Prussian court. After first working in conjunction with his father (several medals being signed by both), he soon began to excel him both in quality and quantity: his active career spanned the years 1771–1810, during which he created some 250 medals and (after his father's death) most of the dies for the Prussian coinage.

ABSCHLAG A German numismatic term used in two quite distinct senses: (1) a later restrike from an original die (also a Russian *novodel) and (2) a special striking of a coin in metal different from that in which it normally circulated. This was often done for presentation purposes (e.g. Thalers in gold).

ABSOLUTION THALER A medallic Thaler struck by Henry IV of France after his reconciliation with Pope Clement VIII in 1595.

ABYSSINIA *Axumite coins.

ACANTHUS A city on the Chalcidian peninsula above Acte, Macedonia. Its coinage dates from *archaic times, always of the same type: a lion savaging a bull. The presence of both animals in this area is attested by Herodotus.

ACCOUNT, MONEY OF Existing in name only, for purposes of reckoning money, no coin of such denomination being actually struck. The guinea is an example of a coin which, though not struck after 1813, remained as a unit of reckoning until recently.

ACHAEAN LEAGUE The most extended—both in time and space—of the monetary alliances of ancient Greece. There were, in fact, two separate ones: the first was relatively brief (370–360 B.C), and comprised only a few cities of Achaia itself; the second league, however, lasted from 280–146 B.C. and also included some forty cities from Arcadia, Argolis, Elis, Messenia and Laconia. All have as the obverse type the head of Zeus, and on the reverse the Achaean monogram with differing cities and magistrates' symbols. The above applies to silver coins only; bronze coins are historically more significant in that the city names and those of the magistrates are often written out in full. They show on the obverse the figure of Zeus, with a sceptre and Nike (goddess of victory), and on the reverse the seated figure of Demeter (corn goddess and sister of Zeus) with a sceptre and wreath.

ACHESON A family of Scottish engravers during the 16th century. James Acheson became mintmaster under James V in 1525 and held the office until 1539, when he refused to strike *bawbees. He was succeeded by his son John, who is best known for the many coins he engraved for Mary Queen of Scots, both at Edinburgh and Paris.

ACHTBRUEDERTHALER A Thaler of Saxe-Weimar, struck from 1605–20, showing eight portrait busts of princes, all of them sons of the Duke Johann Ernst. The more common variety shows four portraits on each side of the coin: the one showing all eight on one side is much rarer.

ACHTEHALBER A term used in Prussia for one-twelfth of a Brandenburg Thaler. An edict of 1722 established its value at 7½ (achtehalb) Groschen. The coin remained current in both East and West Prussia until 1873.

ACHTZEHNGRÖSCHER A coin of Polish origin, introduced towards the end of the 17th century and tariffed at 18 *Groschen, equivalent to one-fifth of the Thaler. The mintmaster Andreas *Tympf was at first responsible for their striking, and the coins took their popular name from him. They took the plce of the previous quarter Thaler and bore the figure 18, but—although of the same size as that earlier coin—held less silver. For the better part of half a century, they were Poland's main circulating currency and thus also became widely known in neighbouring Prussia and Brandenburg, even to the extent of being struck at Königsberg and Stettin mints with local typology. Their silver content continued to fall and finally, with the Seven Years' War (1756-63), became so unacceptable that they ceased to be issued.

ACKEY A shilling-size silver coin struck for the Gold Coast (today's Ghana) in 1796 and 1818 at the *Soho Mint, Birmingham. The name derives from a weight used in the gold dust trade, 16 ackeys being equivalent to 1 ounce of gold. The 1796 issue has as its obverse design the crowned monogram GR, while the 1818 issue shows King George III's portrait facing right. Both show on the reverse the arms of the African Company of Merchants (which administered the territory) with its date of incorporation by Act of Parliament (1750). Halves, quarters and eighths (takoes) were also struck.

ACMONITAL The technical term for stainless steel as tempered for use in coinage. Minor denominations of Italy were struck in acmonital during the period 1939–45; more recent examples are the 50- and 100-lire pieces of the Vatican in 1970.

ACRAGAS A town on the southern coast of Sicily, the Roman Agrigentum. It was one of the first Greek colonies on the island, whose splendid temple ruins still bear witness to its importance. The coinage from 550–406 B.C. (when the town was destroyed by the Carthaginians) is of a splendour matching this importance and rivalled only by that of *Syracuse. All types show the eagle and crab, emblems respectively of Zeus and Poseidon, though in later issues the emblems are subsidiary to the main design.

ACRE A town on the Mediterranean seaboard in what is today Israel, but famous already in the time of Alexander the Great as Ace Phoenices. It was successively an Alexandrian, Seleucid and Roman colonial mint in ancient times. But its most notable activity was during the Crusades, when its types are unique among Christian coinages of the time in (a) being dated, (b) carrying inscriptions in Arabic and (c) showing a cross. This combination is known in both gold and silver, struck under a number of rulers of the kingdom of Jerusalem. By far the rarest and most desirable are the golden *dinars of Louis IX of France (1251).

ACT OF UNION In 1707 the English and Scottish parliaments became one (the crowns were united in 1603). The immediate numismatic effect was to make Scottish denominations equal to English ones; previously they had represented only one-twelfth. Though the intention (certainly on the Scottish side) seems to have been to continue striking coins at Edinburgh, no such coins are known after 1709 and the mint there was finally closed in 1711. Only silver is known, distinguished by E or sometimes E★ below the bust of Queen Anne. The only other concession to Scottish nationalism can be seen in the "Scottish" reverses of certain shillings of George VI and Elizabeth II, i.e., rampant lion device.

ADELAIDE TOKENS Australian gold tokens, to the value of £1 sterling, struck at the Adelaide Assay Office late in 1852, after gold had been discovered in Victoria at Mount Alexander. They were engraved by Joshua Payne, with types as shown here. 24,768 pieces were issued. The first reverse die cracked early, and pieces without the die crack are exceedingly rare.

ADELHEIDSPFENNIGE A particular type of German medieval silver penny, remarkable in that it carries the name of the Emperor Otto's consort (Adelheid) on the reverse. Various reasons have been given for this, the most likely being the great importance which the Emperor attached to his dynastic marriage in A.D. 951 (Adelheid being heiress to the whole of northern Italy). The coins continued to be struck in large quantities for half a century and were widely copied.

ADJUSTMENT MARKS These are sometimes seen on gold and silver coins. The term is employed where there is evidence that a coin was overweight to begin with and has been "adjusted" to its precise weight specification at the mint after striking. Filing marks on early Philadelphia Mint issues are not uncommon, as are scissor marks on earlier, hammer-struck European coins. Whether a "clipper" or a mint official was responsible can only be established by weighing the coin precisely.

ADLI A silver coin of Delhi, introduced *c.* 1324 A.D. under Muhammad III. It weighed 140 grammes but was to pass at the same value as the old *rupee weighing 175 grammes. Not surprisingly, it proved unpopular and had to be withdrawn from circulation within five years. A much later coin of the same name was that of Yussuf Pasha in Tripoli in 1927. This was no more than a gilt *billon piece which that ruler tried to pass off as the equivalent of the Spanish silver dollar. Here, the experiment (or fraud) failed within days, and it was only accepted at 10% of its face value. The name of this coin is sometimes spelt "Adlea".

ADOLFS D'OR A kind of *pistole (value 5 Thaler gold) struck at the mint of Stralsund for Swedish Pomerania under King Adolf Frederik (1751–71), but marked only with the date 1759. There is also a double.

AE The symbol for aes, and thus short for copper or bronze coinage.

AEGINA An island in the Aegean, not far from Athens. It has the distinction of having issued the first purely European coinage (as opposed to issues of Asia Minor). The city emblem was a turtle; and this, without any other symbol or letter, sufficed for almost 150 years (from 600–450 B.C.) to make these "turtles" acceptable as currency throughout the Peloponnese among the seafaring inhabitants who were its principal traders (cf. *owls of Athens, *colts of Corinth).

AENUS A town in Thrace, on the north-eastern shore of the Aegean. The main type of coin throughout the 5th and 4th centuries B.C. showed the helmeted head of Hermes, first in profile, later facing in very fine style.

AES Latin for bronze and—since this formed the first money of Roman times—also money in a wider sense (e.g. *aes militare* = military pay).

AES GRAVE The earliest coinage of central Italy, cast in bronze. First issued by the Republic about 269 B.C. in Rome. The *aes* in its ultimate cast form preceded the introduction of (struck) silver coinage towards the middle of the 3rd century B.C., and continued to overlap with it. In contrast to previous, rougher cast pieces (*aes rude, aes signatum), this was cast in specific denominations (or, rather, weights), from the *as* (1 pound) down as follows: *semis* (½-pound), *triens* or *quatrunx* (4 ounces), *quadrans* or *teruncius* (3 ounces), *sextans* or *biunx* (2 ounces) and the single *uncia*. This Roman pound was standardised at about 273 grammes, and the pieces were distinguished not only by size and weight, but by types: *as* = head of Janus, *semis* = head of

Saturn, *triens* = Minerva or Mars, *quadrans* = Hercules, *sextans* = Mercury, *uncia* = Bellona. A much rarer subdivision is the *quincunx* (5 ounces), and rarer still are the large multiples of *dupondius* (2 asses), *quincussis* (5) and *decussis* (10). Since the pieces are much sought after by collectors, forgeries are common, some of them very able; so any "bargains" should be avoided or at least the aid of experts always sought.

AES RUDE Crudely shaped bronze pieces, without any mark of value and of various weights; the earliest form of Roman money known to us. The shapes are varied (bars, rods, plate-like, etc.) and since they are more often than not found in fragmentary form, no specific weight system has been identified.

AES SIGNATUM The intermediate type between the above two, bearing designs of various types (e.g. bull, shield, eagle). These pieces date from 4th to 3rd century B.C., have been found mainly in central Italy and are even known with the inscription ROMANOM. Greek and Etruscan models are evident in some of the highly varied typology; the weight varies between 1000 and 1850 grammes.

Aes grave, *c.* 269 B.C.

Aes signatum, *c.* 289 B.C.
(slightly reduced)

AFGHANI Monetary unit of Afghanistan. Introduced as a silver coin in 1926, it is today made of nickel-steel alloy.

AFRICAN HEAD CENT One of the cents struck in Connecticut during 1785 under the authority of Congress. It is so called after the curiously negroid shape of the effigy.

AGNEL A medieval French gold coin, so named from the paschal lamb which figures on it; also known as the "mouton d'or". It is believed to have been first introduced by King Louis IX of France in 1266, when it is named in a document; but no coins of the lamb type of that reign have been found. The first known piece dates from 1311, during the reign of Philip IV; and, like his other gold coins, it is notable for being struck in pure 24 carat metal, without the admixture of any alloy. Not until a century later, under Charles VI, was the fineness reduced to 23 carat. The type was extensively copied during the 14th century, notably in Flanders and Savoy. There are also some excessively rare imitations in the Anglo-Gallic series; the "grand mouton" of Edward III and the agnel of Henry V.

Agnus Dei type penny

AGNUS DEI TYPE PENNY An extremely rare penny of Aethelred II (A.D. 978–1016) unique in not showing the King's portrait on the obverse, but instead the Lamb of God. The reverse showing a dove is also unique in the British series. This penny is believed to have been struck in the year 1000, to celebrate the millennium of the Christian era. Although there are no mint documents of the time to prove this, the piece obviously commemorates a very special occasion.

AGONISTIC From the Greek *agon*, a contest; and hence used to describe Greek coins that are related by their design and/or inscription to religious festivals where games were held. The chariot drawn by two, three or four horses (biga, triga, quadriga) was a favourite agonistic design; and often the charioteer is shown being crowned by Nike, goddess of victory. (It is possible that some mints struck coinage only at and for games, when a large influx of visitors was expected.)

AGRA One of the principal mints of the Moghul emperors of India, especially renowned for its coinages of Akbar the Great (1556–1605) and Jahangir (1605–28). Akbar instituted his own "divine" era in 1584, and his coins thereafter carried this as the regnal year, together with the Persian solar month. During Jahangir's reign, round and square *rupees were struck at Agra during alternate months for a number of years. This ruler is also famous (or notorious) for breaking the unwritten Muslim law in issuing a portrait coinage, and for his *zodiacal coins.

AGRICOLA, GEORGIUS Born in 1494 as plain Georg Bauer, he is known by his latinised name as the father of modern metallurgy and mineralogy. His best known work is his *De Re Metallica*; but his works on numismatics are by no means negligible, based as they are on first-hand experience of the relationship between mining and minting in the service of the Elector of Saxony. Three of these (on weights, measures, prices of money and metals, etc.) were published as an "omnibus" volume at Basel in 1550. He died in 1555.

A.H. The common abbreviation used to date the Muhammedan era (Anno Hegirae), which began in A.D. 622 of the Christian era. It is, however, not sufficient merely to add 622 years to a dated Muslim coin in order to arrive at a Western date. The Muslim calendar is lunar, not geared, like ours, directly to the seasons and has about 34 years to our 33. To "translate" Hegira years into Christian years, first divide the Hegira date by 33 and add 622 after deducing the result.

AHLBORN, LEA Chief engraver at the Stockholm Mint, 1854–97. She was the daughter of the previous incumbent of that post, Ludwig Peterssen Lundgren; and in a métier where very few women have achieved distinction, it is fair to say that none has exceeded her in artistic skill and length of service. Under three mintmasters she engraved the coinages of three Swedish monarchs (Oskar I, Karl XV and Oskar II), including two entire new coinages under the acts of 1855 and 1873, besides commemorative pieces and medals. There is no falling-off of skill even in her last years; the 2 kroner 25th-year Jubilee coin of Oskar II (1897) is as fine as any.

AIX-EN-PROVENCE Town in southern France, already known as a mint in Carolingian times under the name of *Aguis urbs*, and documented as one belonging to the Counts of Provence from 1146 A.D. Later, from 1544 to 1786, Aix was a regal mint of various monarchs, with the unusual mintmark "&". A gold coin known as the *Louis d'Aix* was first struck here in 1672, although its type was later adopted by other mints too. The town was also notable for its fine silver, especially during the late 18th century when it had its own guild and hallmark, until well into the 19th century.

AKA A small fractional piece in the earliest gold coinage of Ceylon (late 9th/10th century). On the obverse a standing figure, possibly Lakshmi, holds in her left hand a vase in which is a plant. The reverse has an inscription. (Also *Kahavanu.)

AKCE The first coin of the Ottoman empire, of 1.2 grammes almost pure silver. Introduced as the only denomination in 1328 A.D. under Urkhan, it was roughly equivalent to one-third of the Arabic *dirhem and modelled on the *aspers of Trebizond. Larger denominations of 2, 5 and 10 akces were added during subsequent centuries; for a century and a half, until the introduction of the gold *altun, they remained the Ottoman empire's chief circulating medium. Also known as otmani, this remained the only Turkish silver coin until late in the 17th century, larger payments being made in gold or in European Thalers. Later they became so debased as to be only small change and were finally abolished during the reign of Mahmud II (1835/6). Like all Ottoman coins they carry only script: the name of the sultan, a prayer and (often) the date and place of minting.

AKERMAN, JOHN YONGE English numismatist who in 1836 founded the *Numismatic Journal* which, in 1838, became the *Numismatic Chronicle*, under which title it still exists as the official organ of the Royal Numismatic Society. Akerman was also the author of a number of coin manuals popular and useful in his day but since superseded.

ALAMOS A Mexican mint active from 1864–95.

AL-ANDALUS The Muslim name for Andalucia, Spain. It appears as an inscription on some of the earliest gold dinars and dirhems (A.D. 696–7) struck at Cordoba, to differentiate them from those minted at Kairawan (inscribed Ifrikiya, i.e. African mint).

ALBERTIN A gold coin of the Spanish Netherlands provinces, first struck around 1600 after they had been ceded by Philip II of Spain to the Archduke Albert of Austria and his consort Isabella of Spain. The coin shows their conjoined half-length figures in profile; it was valued at two-thirds of a ducat. There was also a double albertin, showing the two rulers enthroned, and the half with full-length figures standing. The coins were struck at the mints of Antwerp, Maastricht, Tournai and Ypres.

ALBERTUSTHALER German name for the *patagon, after Albert and Isabella, who introduced this type in the southern Netherlands in 1612. Because of the very large quantities in which it was struck, the coin also circulated widely in adjoining countries, and various mints (e.g. Liège, Brandenburg–Prussia and even Denmark) decided to copy it. It became more and more important in Baltic trade, so much so that Peter the Great of Russia based his first silver *roubles (1704–14) on it (not in type, but as regards weight and silver content).

ALBRECHT V (Bavaria 1550–79) Patron of the arts and founder of the Munich "Kunstkammer", one of the most magnificent treasuries of its time. He purchased, among other treasures, the coins and library of Hans Fugger and thus formed the nucleus of what was later to become the Royal Coin Cabinet. The first Bavarian Thalers date from his reign; his own effigy is preserved on a double ducat of 1565.

ALBUS Short for "grossus albus" (white groat); so named after its white appearance due to its relatively high silver content.

Alexander the Great: Silver tetradrachm issued by Lysimachus

Alexandria: Half-drachm of Antoninus Pius, c. A.D. 150, showing on the reverse the Pharos (lighthouse) of Alexandria

The Germans also called it "Weisspfennig", and it enjoyed its widest popularity along the Rhine from Heidelberg right up to the Netherlands during the 14th and 15th centuries. It scarcely continued to merit its name from the early 16th century onwards, when it became debased with much copper.

ALCHEMY For centuries, both scholars and impostors ardently sought the "philosopher's stone" that would turn base metals to silver or gold. The would-be alchemist could find himself in trouble as did Baron Krohnemann, an adventurer who pretended that silver Thalers he minted for the Margrave of Bayreuth were struck from silver he had himself magically made, whereas he had really stolen it from his patron (1678–9). The fraud was discovered and the Baron hanged in 1685.

ALEXANDER THE GREAT Important in the history of coinage because during the course of his conquests he established some twenty mints and thus spread the influence of Greek coinage as far east as India and south to Egypt. The Alexandrian *tetradrachm thus became the widest used currency of the ancient world; its types (together with gold *staters of his father, Philip of Macedon) were widely copied.

ALEXANDRIA (EGYPT) First established by Alexander the Great c. 326 B.C., this city acted successively as a Ptolemaic, Roman and Arab mint in later centuries. The Roman coinage, principally meant for local use, became the most widely used trading currency throughout the Mediterranean, owing to Alexandria's position as a trading centre.

The enormous variety of types and issues permits no easy classification; suffice it to say that this was the Roman "colonial" coinage (i.e. that based on Greek types and script) *par excellence*, from the time of the conquest of Egypt under Augustus and continuing for over four centuries. During the later Roman period, the old *tetradrachm degenerated into a base metal coin barely washed with silver. Of particular interest earlier is the series of 13 large bronzes (*sestertius size) struck under Antoninus Pius (A.D. 138–161), the obverse of each showing the same portrait of the emperor, and on the reverse of each, a different sign of the zodiac (the 13th coin showing them all, surrounding the sun and moon).

For a century or so (c. A.D. 525 until its capture by the Arabs) Alexandria also acted as a Byzantine mint. Very little of the otherwise plentiful Byzantine gold is known from here; and the bronze coinage, though based on the *follis (40 *nummia), was struck only in denominations of 12, 6 and 3 nummia, unique to this city. Unique also is a piece of 33 nummia struck during the reign of Justinian I only and probably of a commemorative nature.

ALEXANDRIA (ON THE ISSUS) The first mint of Alexander the Great, coins of which carry the title of Basileus (King) c. 329 B.C.

ALEXEYEF, FEDOR The first native coin engraver of Russia under Peter the Great (others being "imported" from France and Germany at the same time as machinery for striking coins c. 1700). He is noted as the engraver of the 1704 *rouble, and in 1709 invented a collar for striking coins with an *incuse inscription on the edge, tested and approved by Peter in person. Striking of such coins was, however, delayed until 1718.

ALFONSINO Name given to several coins where the ruler's name was Alfonso. The first was a silver *denier of Alfonso I of Portugal (1325–57), struck to a slightly higher value than the standard coin (9 to the *soldo). The second was called after

Alfonso I of Aragon as King of Naples and Sicily; it was a new type of the *gigliato, replacing the cross with a fleur-de-lis in the angles by the King's own shield of arms. Finally, the gold *ducatone of the rider type of the same monarch was also popularly known as "alfonsino d'oro".

ALLEN & MOORE A firm of Birmingham medallists, especially active and famous around the middle of the 19th century. Joseph Moore, who later traded under his own name, was among the most skilled die-sinkers of his time, and a framed case of his medals is preserved in the Birmingham City Art Gallery. His *model penny and halfpenny (c. 1844) were never adopted; but the portrait punch for his 1860 pattern penny was later used on certain New Zealand tokens.

ALLIANCE COINS Coins, showing a common symbol, of ancient Greek city states banded together in times of trouble. An instance of this was the large group comprising Rhodes, Byzantium, Thebes, Ephesus, Samos, Iasus and Cnidus against the Spartans in 394 B.C.

ALLOY Any combination of two or more metals. Thus bronze, for instance, normally consists of 95% copper, 4% tin and 1% zinc (though these proportions may vary slightly). Both silver and gold are normally alloyed to some extent with copper for coining purposes; gold, when alloyed with silver to more than about 25%, is called *electrum. Today when most coinage is *fiduciary, alloys play an increasingly important part in coin production; the standard now is not fineness of metal but how to make a durable coin as cheaply as possible. Cupro-nickel is the most widely used substitute for silver, but steel and aluminium alloys have also been used. Others include brass, magnesium and palladium. The word alloy is used only when one or two metals have been fused by chemical processes. For examples of coins made of two or more unfused metals, *bi-metallic, plated and plugged coins.

AL MARCO, AL PEZZO These terms refer to the method used to check coinage, whether by the *mark (a weight), or individually, piece by piece. The latter has generally been used for all fine gold coinages, and for the larger silver denominations; from time to time it has, in fact, been specifically decreed under coinage edicts (e.g. *Medina del Campo).

ALOE THALER Despite its name, this is not a coin but a commemorative silver medal. Aloe plants had been introduced into Brunswick-Wolfenbüttel towards the end of the 17th century; their first flowering was celebrated in 1701 under Dukes Rudolf August and Anton Ulrich with medals of two different types.

ALPHA & OMEGA The first and last letters of the Greek alphabet appear as a Christian symbol for "The Beginning and the End" (first Book of Revelations, chapter 1, verse 8) on Roman coins from Constantius II around A.D. 350.

ALTERED COINS Any coins that are changed after leaving the mint. This may entail the addition or removal of some detail, and be official, unofficial or plainly fraudulent. *Countermarks (unless counterfeit) belong to the first category, while the most common examples of fraud are certainly altered dates, e.g. 1928 to 1923 on a George V half-crown, because the latter is much the rarer coin. For an interesting example of the second category (i.e. unofficial alteration without fraudulent intent) *J.O.P.

ALTILIK A Turkish coin of base silver, to the value of 6 *piastres, issued from 1833–9.

Altum, 1481

ALTUN A Turkish gold coin first issued in 1454 by Muhammad II following the capture of Constantinople. It there replaced the Venetian *ducat or *zecchino, hence its popular name of *sequin (which was later extended to embrace Turkish gold coins indiscriminately).

ALTYN A silver coin to the value of 6 *denga or 3 *kopeks. The name was derived from the Tartar word *alti*, meaning six. At first (from 1676 onwards) irregularly shaped, it was struck on a circular flan following the coinage reform of Peter the Great (from 1704 onwards). The survival of the altyn within the decimal system created by Peter is an example of how even the most ardent reformer cannot at once eradicate old patterns of reckoning; the denomination was not dropped until 1718.

ALUMINIUM This metal has been not infrequently used in coinages during the 20th century (alloyed more often than not, as it is rather brittle in its pure state). France, Germany and Romania used it most extensively on the continent of Europe during the 1920s and 30s; and there are some British colonial issues in this metal for both East and West Africa. Its great advantage—lightness—is also its chief drawback; it seems to lack the solid feel of "real" coinage.

AMANI A gold coin of Afghanistan, issued at intervals from 1919 until 1936. At various times during this period, denominations of 5, 2½ and half-amani were also struck; and in 1932 only a piece of 20 afghani, i.e. two-thirds amani (30 afghani = 1 amani). All the coins show the national emblem, a throne room.

AMERICA The continent is too vast to permit its numismatic treatment in any kind of synoptic form. It is best dealt with by examining the histories of individual mints there, and the authorities (and rebels!) for which they struck coinages (see list below). It should, however, be said that there has been a great deal of "two-way traffic" between American and European coinages. If the 2 billion silver *pieces of eight struck in Mexico from the 16th to the 19th centuries provided an almost universal currency during that time (often in *counter-marked form), there were also sporadic attempts by at least some European states to supply their American colonies with currency from the motherland. These topics are dealt with under the headings *Anglo-American and *French-Canadian coinages.

United States mints: Philadelphia, San Francisco, Denver, New Orleans, Charlotte, Dahlonega; also *private gold coinages.

Canada: Ottawa.

Mexico: Mexico City, Alamos, Chihuahua, Culican, Durango, Guadalajara, Guanajuato, Anagangueo, Oaxaca, Potosi, Somberette, Zacatecas.

Other mints of Central and South America: Arequipa, Ayacucho, Bahia, Bogota, Cartagena, Medellin, Mendoza, Minas Geraes, Popayan, Potosi, Rio de Janeiro, Santiago, Santa Fe de Bogota, Santo Domingo.

AMERICAN NUMISMATIC ASSOCIATION Generally abbreviated to ANA. It was founded on 7 October 1891 with just six members and is today the largest and most powerful organisation of its kind, with a membership approaching 30,000. The leading spirit behind it was Dr George Heath of Monroe, Michigan, who had founded a small journal called *The Numismatist* three years earlier (1888). This remains the name of the ANA's monthly magazine today. The success of the ANA is largely due to it steering a "middle-of-the-road" line geared to the tastes of many American collectors. Its annual convention—held in a different American city each year—is at once a social, educational and trade forum, and is usually attended by thousands of delegates, including many from overseas. Recently the ANA has been able to establish well-equipped headquarters in Colorado Springs and is now rapidly expanding its educational activities by way of summer seminars on numismatics. The circulating library (a most useful aid to members) and permanent collections of coins, medals, tokens, paper money, etc., also show rapid growth and are here adequately displayed for the first time. Most important of all, perhaps, is its ''junior'' programme for the encouragement of teenagers to collect coins and study them seriously.

AMERICAN NUMISMATIC SOCIETY   Generally abbreviated to ANS. It was founded in 1858 in New York and is still going strong as one of the most influential (and certainly the richest) of purely scholarly numismatic foundations. Its influence is out of all proportion to its membership (only around 1,000). Annual subscriptions would not begin to pay the salaries of its curatorial staff, let alone finance its magnificent collections, as rich in ancient and oriental as in modern series. Well over 80% of ANS income is derived from various bequests and funds in the name of Archer M. Huntington.

The annual subscription covers many useful services to members, as well as several publications, including the invaluable twice-yearly *Numismatic Literature*, which may list close on 1,000 titles per issue. The *Dictionary Catalogue* of the ANS Library (at over 50,000 volumes, probably the world's most comprehensive) is unrivalled as a reference source, especially in its listings of subject headings derived not only from books but periodical entries. The *Photo Archive*, freely available to members on a loan basis, now comprises negatives (or prints on request) of almost 30,000 numismatic items in ANS collections. Annual *Museum Notes* keep members abreast of important acquisitions in all fields; and the occasional *Numismatic Notes and Monographs* is indispensable to advanced students.

AMPAT   *hat money.

AMPHIPOLIS   Founded by the Athenians in 437 B.C. this town struck an independent city coinage from 424 B.C. until its capture by Philip of Macedon in 358 B.C. This was a silver coinage notable for the fine series of facing-head portraits of Apollo.

Yet more important historically (if not artistically) are the gold *staters of Philip II, coined from supplies of the rich gold mines of nearby Pangaeum. These ''philippi'', as they came to be called, were to become the principal currency of the Black Sea area and thence spread (via Danubian Celts) throughout western Europe.

AMRITSAR   A town in East Punjab, a mint of the Sikhs which struck silver *rupees under Ranjit Singh (1799–1839).

AMULET   A charm worn as protection from evil, to avert sickness, or even to heal. The numismatic connections are twofold: (a) actual coins believed to have these properties, *touchpieces; and (b) medals (often mistaken for coins) not issued as currency but sold for profit, e.g. *ramatanka.

ANCHOR MONEY   Silver coins struck for the British colonies in 1820–22, so called from their reverse showing a crowned anchor. They are unusual in being struck in denominations of half, quarter, eighth and sixteenth of the Spanish dollar, the silver being 891 3/5 fine instead of .925 sterling standard. Royal Mint records show consignments to Ceylon and to the West Indies (whence some found their way to Canada). The coins were engraved by William *Wyon.

ANCIENT COINAGES China and Greece dispute the title to having invented coinage. Both grew out of more primitive forms of money, but their development is so different that there is really no parallel. The basic difference, in that Chinese coins were cast and Greek coins (by and large) struck from engraved *dies, was continued in the Eastern and Western worlds through two millennia.

ANDRIEU, BERTRAND (1759–1822) One of the most celebrated (and certainly the most prolific) among coin engravers of the French revolutionary and Napoleonic eras. His coin and medal dies total around 175, and he was equally skilled in copperplate work, engraving many ornaments for *assignats, tailpieces for Didot's Virgil and the 1,000-franc note of the Bank of France (1817). A letter-heading he engraved for the Conseil d'Etat in 1806 was adapted as the design for the first French postage stamp of 1848. His work spans the years 1789–1822, to within three months of his death.

ANDROCEPHALOUS An adjective from the Greek, signifying a beast or bird with the head of a man. These images are frequent on Greek coins, the sphinx and the bull being perhaps the most prevalent types.

ANDROS The most northerly of the Cyclades islands, which has a coinage going back to the 6th century B.C. Its early obverses show an amphora, alluding to the wine-god Dionysus, whose effigy later takes over as the main type. Following the conquest by the Ptolemies in 308 B.C., down to Roman times, the silver shows Dionysus with his panther, while the bronze shows the head of the wine-god together with some form of the wine vessel.

ANEPIGRAPHIC COINS Coins without inscription of any kind, and which must therefore be assigned to their place and date of origin by evidence of *fabric and *iconography alone. (Also *type muet.)

ANGANGUEO An ephemeral Mexican mint, active only in 1811 during the revolutionary period of Morelos.

ANGE D'OR A gold coin first issued by Phillip VI of France in 1341. It shows St Michael with a sword and shield, standing on a dragon. There were three emissions of this coin in rapid succession, from January 1341 to June 1342, each slightly lighter than the previous one, but all struck in pure 24 carat gold. The coin was later copied by Philip the Bold of Flanders, again lighter and only 23½ carat fine.

Angel

ANGEL An English gold coin, first issued in 1465 and valued at 6s. 8d. The obverse shows St Michael spearing a dragon, the reverse a ship with rays of the sun at the masthead, and a rose and the sun beside the mast. The angel was the only gold coin to be struck by successive English sovereigns without interruption until the reign of Charles I and exists in a large number of varieties, dates and mints of issue and degrees of rarity. It is often found pierced as a *touchpiece, and as such is worth rather less than half of what it would be if not so mutilated.

ANGELET A diminutive of angel, applied to its half. This coin did not have as long a life as its big brother, being discontinued in 1619 during the reign of James I.

ANGELOT An *Anglo-Gallic gold coin, of which the earliest known is assigned to 1427, though documentary references appear already in 1425. It was valued at two-thirds of the gold *salut, but its type bears no relation to the latter. It shows instead a facing angel, half-length only, the lower part hidden by shields with arms of England and France. It was struck at Paris, Rouen, St Lo and Le Mans mints. (Documentary evidence shows that dies were also supplied to the mint at Châlons-sur-Marne, but no coins have been recovered.)

ANGLESEY PENNIES & HALFPENNIES These constitute by far the most extensive series of late 18th-century copper commercial *tokens. The issues of 1787–91 totalled around 250 tons of pence and 50 tons of halfpennies, or almost 12½ million pieces. There are so many minor varieties and edge inscriptions, besides concocted *mules and forgeries, that a complete collection of the series would number more than 400 pieces. A sensible aim (even for a specialist) might be a representative collection of those dated 1787 only; with trial pieces and patterns, these would total around a hundred and no forgeries or concoctions with this date are known. In view of the large number issued, prices are still very reasonable.

All tokens dated 1787 and 1788 were struck at the Parys Mine Company's own mint in Birmingham, other dates at various mints both in Birmingham and London. The Parys Mine Company was one of two companies exploiting Anglesey copper, whose total output exceeded that of all other copper mines in the kingdom combined. The number of minor varieties is doubtless due to the fact that the main type (obverse: Druid's head in wreath; reverse: monogram PMC) remained unchanged throughout, thus calling for a very large number of dies.

ANGLINA The proposed name (as cited in documents) for the rupees of the East India Company at Bombay, 1672. It did not, however, catch on, and was never used on a coin. The earliest coins bear no denomination, merely the words MONETA BOMBAIENSIS; and from 1677 onwards we find the inscription THE RUPEE OF BOMBAIN.

ANGLO-AMERICAN COINS Coins made in England or Ireland for circulation in the American colonies, i.e. not including those struck in the colonies. Also such coins and tokens which, while not specifically designed to circulate overseas, did so for one reason or another. For details *Mott token, Rosa Americana, St Patrick's token, Virginia, voce populi, William Wood.

ANGLO-GALLIC COINAGE The name given to the series struck by English kings from Henry II to Henry VI in their French territories. Though at first these were more in the nature of feudal fiefs (more especially Aquitaine in south-west France), there were long periods during the Hundred Years' War (1337–1453) when English kings laid claim to the throne of France and struck coinage there in all metals at over twenty different mints. Some of the denominations were copies of French types, others were invented by the English overlords specially for their French provinces. For details *agnel, angelot, blanc, chaise, denier, florin, gros, guiennois, hardi, leopard, pavillon, salut.

An odd postscript to the series is found in the reign of Henry VIII, who seized the town of Tournai in 1513, held it until 1518 and there issued some rare groats and half-groats. It should be noted that the town of Calais, though held by England from 1347–1558, never struck money of the above mentioned French types, but was active as an English mint from c. 1361–1440, recoining captured French money into English currency.

ANGLO-HANOVERIAN COINAGE That of the Hanoverian kings from George I to William IV, struck for their European territories: at first the duchies of Brunswick-Luneberg and Brunswick-Wolfenbüttel, later the kingdom of Hanover. Coins were struck at the mints of Brunswick, Clausthal, Hanover and Zellerfeld, besides—on one brief occasion—at London's Tower Mint (1813–15, for payment of Hanoverian troops in the Napoleonic wars). The series, with its dual standards of value (Gutergroschen and Mariengroschen) and no less than three different standards both of silver and gold, is apt to bewilder all but advanced mathematicians; but a useful short guide has recently been published, and a full listing of types (with price-guide) will be found in the 3rd edition of Remick's *British Commonwealth Coins*. The 5-Thaler (1 pistole) gold piece of 1813, bearing the initials T. W. (Thomas Wyon) is the equivalent to the English military guinea and the obvious coin to acquire if one wishes to possess just one of the series.

Anglo-Saxon penny

ANGLO-IRISH COINAGE A term used to distinguish the coinage of Ireland under British rule as opposed to the *Hiberno-Norse coinage earlier and that of the Irish Free State from 1928 onwards. It began with the first invasion of Ireland under Henry II, whose son Prince John was given the overlordship of the province (first coinage *c.* 1185), and ended in 1823, when George IV struck the last pennies and halfpennies specifically for Ireland. All Irish coinage was officially withdrawn in 1826 and English regal coinage served in its place. Though intermittent, the coinage has many features of special interest and issues of great rarity. Among the latter one might pick out those of the pretender Lambert Simnel and the *Inchiquin money of the Civil War period. The average collector is more likely to concern himself with *gun money, *voce populi issues or *bank tokens. Trade *tokens of the 17th century are almost as varied as English ones. Finally, it should be noted that a copper farthing and half-farthing made their first, though ephemeral, appearance in Ireland in 1463, i.e. a century and a half before copper farthing tokens were first introduced in England.

ANGLO-SAXON COINAGE English coinage after the end of Roman occupation and before the Norman Conquest. The period therefore includes copies of Roman types, purely Anglo-Saxon ones and those subject to Viking influences. (Further details will be found under the headings *penny, *sceat and *thrysma.) It also sees the beginnings of ecclesiastical coinages (Archbishopric of York, *c.* A.D. 734, and that of Canterbury *c.* A.D. 765). The silver penny based on that of Charlemagne became the standard unit from the late 8th century onwards and the whole series contains many rare treasures, among which the coins of *Offa take pride of place.

Centaur and lion: the reverses of silver antininiani of Gallienus, *c.* A.D. 260

ANGSTER A silver coin of Switzerland, current from the mid-14th to the mid-19th centuries. It originated in Basel but by 1424 was also being minted in St Gallen, Schaffhausen and Zurich. Originally .964 fine, it now became a coin of base silver (.500 fine). Finally it became a copper coin in Lucerne during the early part of the 19th century, where it survived until 1843.

Elephant: the reverse of a denarius of Julius Caesar

ANIMALS ON COINS Always a favourite theme, both among designers and collectors of coins, and one presenting almost infinite variety. No one could hope to cover it comprehensively at today's prices, and it is essential to specialise by period, by kind (beasts, birds or fish) or even by individual animals.

Another alternative might be "beasts of fable", such as the chimera, griffin, Pegasus or sphinx. A fascinating collection could also be made of at least some of these beasts in the form of *mintmark rather than main type; but this is strictly for the advanced student of numismatics rather than the general collector.

ANNA Indian copper denomination, to the value of one- sixteenth of the *rupee. At first only a money of *account as part of the Moghul currency system, pieces of 2 and 4 annas were introduced late in the 17th century. The single unit became used curiously enough as a coin only once under the East India Company (Patna Post of the Bengal Presidency, 1774), and then not again until 1907 as part of the British imperial series for India. There have been many more frequent strikings of fractions of the anna (down to one-twelfth) and multiples of 2, 4 and 8.

ANNULET From the Latin *annulus*, a ring. It appears—generally in the form of a minute symbol—on a variety of coinages and does not always have the same meaning. At times it has been used as a *mintmark (e.g. York Mint pennies of Edward the Confessor), more often as a *privy mark to distinguish certain issues from others within a single mint and reign (e.g. annulet coinage of Henry VI).

ANNULET COINAGES Coins of Henry V and VI. Introduced first to distinguish certain gold and silver issues, the practice was much extended by Henry VI during the years 1422–7, enabling us by the actual placing of the marks to date issues within a year or so.

ANONYMOUS BYZANTINE BRONZES Coins struck without indication of reign (names or titles) for almost a hundred years, from John I Zimisces (A.D. 969) to Michael VI (A.D. 1057). They can therefore only be attributed to any particular reign on the evidence of stylistic details.

ANTIOCH, SYRIA No less than twelve cities named Antioch are known to have struck money in the ancient world. Of these, however, only the Syrian capital on the Orontes has a long and significant history. It stretches over the same period as *Acre but differs from the latter by its far greater importance in Roman and Byzantine times. Apart from *Alexandria and *Constantinople, it had a greater number of *officinae than any other mint of the Eastern Empire.

After the great earthquake of A.D. 528 the town was rebuilt under the name Theoupolis and the mintmark correspondingly altered. From the known types that have survived, Antioch appears to have been the principal mint to have struck *light-weight solidi between the reigns of Justin II (A.D. 565–78) and Maurice Tiberius (A.D. 582–602): they are twice as numerous as those produced at Constantinople during the same period.

ANTONINIANUS The double *denarius introduced by the Emperor Caracalla late in A.D. 214. It is distinguished from the single denomination in type by the *radiate crown worn by the Emperor (the head of the Empress being set on a crescent on similar coins).

Antoninianus of Trebonius Gallus

ANT'S NOSE MONEY A development of the *cowrie shell form of primitive money, so called because the Chinese characters resemble a face with a big nose. They circulated from around 700 B.C. to the late 3rd century B.C.

APAMEA A town in ancient Phrygia, now west-central Turkey. A mint for the production of *cistophoric coinage was set up there *c.* 180 B.C. and continued into Roman times. The mint is notable for a bronze issue showing a reverse design of a chest or ark floating on the water and inscribed NOE: an allusion both to Noah's Ark and the region where the great flood traditionally occurred.

APTERA A town on the north-east coast of Crete. The first coins were struck there in the early 4th century B.C. and some are distinguished by the signature of the artist Pythodoros on the obverse. On the stater, the types used are a head of Artemis and an armed warrior saluting a sacred tree with his right hand. The warrior is said to have been called Ptolioikos, and was possibly the founder of the city. Coins continued to be struck here until about 65 B.C.

APULIA District in south-east Italy. The principal medium of exchange in this area appears to have been bronze issued in large, heavy cast pieces, although some of the smaller denominations were struck coins, similar to some of the early bronze issues of 3rd-century Rome. Before the 3rd century B.C. (i.e. when the Apulian cities began to strike their own coins), the prolific coinage of *Tarentum in the south served the needs of the district.

AQUILEIA A town in northern Italy, near Trieste, where a mint was established to strike some of the extra coins needed following the monetary reforms of Diocletian, A.D. 295–6. The mint name was carried in various forms, viz. AQ, AQVIL or SMAQ (the first two letters here standing for *sacra moneta*). Coins are known from here until the early 5th century. The town was destroyed by Attila in A.D. 452.

AR The common numismatic abbreviation for *argentum* (*silver).

ARAB-BYZANTINE COINAGE The Islamic militant religious sects, following the flight of Dost Mohammed from Mecca to Medina in A.D. 622, rapidly subdued the civilised nations outside Arabia, and by about A.D. 680 Palestine, Egypt, Syria and Persia had all become, in effect, part of the Islamic Empire. These conquests were at the expense of the Byzantine Empire, and the Arabs were at the outset content to issue coins of Byzantine type, largely in copper, with a few gold but no silver. Among the coins most frequently imitated are the large bronzes (40 nummia) of Justinian II and Sophia, Heraclius and Constans II. The gold solidus of Heraclius as struck at Carthage, showing him with his sons, as well as minor gold denominations, were also copied.

ARAB-SASSANIAN COINAGE In Persia, as in areas which they conquered further west, the Arabs were quite content to take over existing coinages. The main difference from previous types was an additional inscription on the margin of the obverse. Apart from this, types of the last independent Sassanian monarch (Yezdigird III, who was assassinated in A.D. 651) were faithfully copied. Not until nearly fifty years later, under the caliphate of Abd al-Malik, was a new and purely Islamic coinage introduced. Further east, in Bokhara, it did not make its appearance until the rule of Haroun-al-Raschid (786–809).

ARBIEN, MAGNUS GUSTAVUS Danish court medallist active at Copenhagen around the middle of the 18th century, after having first worked with *Hedlinger in Stockholm. Apart from his many medals, he cut dies for the fine species ducats and Thalers at the beginning of Frederick V's reign (1746), in the most beautiful and delicate rococo style.

ARCHAIC A term applied to the earliest style of Greek coinage, from about 650–480 B.C. It does not show the flowing ease of later masters of die-cutting but is characterised by a certain stiffness.

ARCHBISHOPS *ecclesiastical coinages.

Arab-Byzantine coinage: Bronze coin of Abdul Malik, from the mint of Aleppo, *c.* A.D. 705

ARCHITECTURE ON COINS   An indispensable aid to archaeology. Very seldom does the latter show what buildings actually looked like (i.e. what architects call the elevation), evidence being confined to ground-plans and (sometimes) details such as sanitation, mosaic floors, etc. But for a bird's-eye-view of, for instance, the colosseum at Rome in all its glory, coins are still the best evidence. Sometimes they even show us building operations, as on a Thaler of Cologne, showing a crane in position over the half-finished cathedral (*c.* 1700).

AREQUIPA   A mint of Peru from 1836 onwards (mintmark: Areq). Struck a distinctive type of Peruvian silver, with the sun on the obverse and the value on the reverse (cf. *Cuzco, *Lima, *Pasco).

ARGENTINO   A gold coin of the Argentine, first issued in 1881, to the value of 5 *pesos. Roughly equivalent to the English *sovereign, the coin was issued annually until 1889 and then again in 1896.

ARGOR PRIVATE MINT   A mint in Chiasso, Switzerland, that specialises in striking commemorative *proof coinages in gold. It was established in 1951 and has made such coins for Burundi, Rawanda and Zaïre among other countries.

ART IN COINAGE   "One man's meat is another man's poison", in numismatic arts no less than elsewhere. Thus *bracteates were considered crude and barbarous until the 18th century, and *Celtic coins are still referred to, sometimes, as "degenerate" imitations of Greek models. To some of us they look like stylised, abstract art, just as *Byzantine coins may be regarded as ikons in miniature.

By and large, the greatest periods of art are also the greatest in coinage. Thus the splendours of ancient Greece and of the Renaissance are fully mirrored here. So is the Gothic style, especially in the magnificent gold of the 14th century. Rome (like the Renaissance) excelled in realistic portraiture.

These periods have been studied and documented (often with magnificent enlarged photographs) in books (*vide* bibliography at the end of this volume). But the baroque and rococo periods await similar detailed exploration, though there are studies of some individual masters (*Hedlinger, Saint-Urbain, Warin).

Since *Pistrucci, the scene has become somewhat arid: craftsmen rather than artists have dominated it. Among great contemporaries, only Dali and Mathieu have tried their hand at medallic art.

Ashrafi, *c.* 1680

AS   Originally the name of an actual weight (meaning a unit), divided into 12 unciae. The whole of the Roman monetary system was based on it (*aes grave, etc.).

ASHANTI GOLD WEIGHTS   Attractive objects, cast in bronze and in a variety of shapes; mainly dating from the mid-19th century and used on the Gold Coast for the weighing of gold dust. T. F. Garrard's brilliant and scholarly study (see bibliography) classifies no less than 60 different weights; stylistically, there are sub-divisions into early and late periods for both geometric and figurative designs.

ASHMOLEAN MUSEUM   *Heberden coin room.

ASHRAFI   A Persian gold coin current from the 15th to the 18th centuries (when it was superseded by the *toman). It was the gold unit roughly equivalent to the Venetian gold ducat.

ASPER   A base silver (or *billon) coin, widely current in the Middle East (Trebizond, Rhodes, Georgia and Tunis) from the 13th to the 15th centuries. It corresponded to the *denier of medieval Europe.

Asper (trebizond) *c.* 1250

ASSAY From the French *essayer*, to try. In numismatics, the term is used for the (analytical) process employed to check the fineness of *bullion or actual coins. (Also *Pyx.)

ASSIGNAT A form of paper money established during the French Revolution under a decree of 16 April 1790. Cover for these notes was supposed to be given by "national wealth" from expropriated ecclesiastical and aristocratic estates. Though supposedly limited, the first issue was soon followed by a second, and so forth. Collectors distinguish between sixty-one main types to 1795, with literally hundreds of different varieties (signatures, etc.).

ATHENS For controversies around varied early types of this city, *Wappenmünzen. By the middle of the 5th century B.C., Athenian coinage had settled down to the type which makes it perhaps the best known of all ancient coinages, showing on the obverse a helmeted Pallas Athene (goddess of wisdom) and on the reverse her emblem, the owl. The "owls" of Athens, as they came to be known, were one of the great international currencies of the ancient world. The prosperity and civilisation of Athens were based on the silver mines of Laurium, not far south-east of the city, which for over four centuries managed to meet all her needs. Athenians were never, like the Phoenicians, a seafaring nation trading far afield. Trade came to Athens because Athens had the wherewithal to buy and exchange.

The coinage is not in itself as distinguished artistically as we might expect from the centre of the Greek world. There is nothing to compare here with *Syracuse in the west, *Rhodes in the south- east, *Lampsacus in the north-east or even *Tarentum in Italy. It is almost as if Athens did not have to bother. The "owls" continued for centuries to inspire confidence owing to the purity and exactness of their silver content; they have survived (mainly in the form of the ubiquitous Athenian *tetradrachm) in large numbers. Such was the flow of silver from Laurium that fractional coins down to the minute hemitartemorion (one-eighth of the *obol, or one-forty-eighth of the *drachm) were struck in this metal. A regular bronze coinage was not introduced until 350 B.C. and then only because the smaller silver fractions were apt to be lost, even swallowed! Gold was struck only twice. The first and more important issue came with a financial crisis following defeat at sea in 407–406 B.C. Seven golden statues of Nike and other treasures on the Acropolis yielded fourteen *talents of the precious metal, while for lower values (tetradrachms and drachms) silver-plated copper tokens were introduced. A second issue took place under the tyrant Lachares 295–294 B.C.

Athens, tetradrachm, *c.* 500 B.C.

Athens, tetradrachm, 2nd century B.C.

What is known as the "new-style" coinage of Athens during the 2nd and 1st centuries B.C. still presents many unsolved problems. We do know that there is a sequence of 109 annual issues, that even the month in which the coin was struck is registered on it, and that two (later three) different names figure on each coin, making a grand total of 634. But documentary evidence about the exact function of the persons named is lacking; and there are yet other markings which remain unexplained. Some of these control marks may even apply to ingots from which the coins were struck, to ensure that the final number of pieces minted tallied in weight with ingots supplied to the mint. If earlier issues seem artistically uninspired, the "new style" ones are positively unattractive. The owl now looks distinctly dishevelled, and sits cramped on an amphora, amid a clutter of symbols. The month is struck on the amphora itself. Design has gone completely overboard in favour of utility. Even to the most unpractised eye, the coins are at once distinguishable from earlier ones in that they are struck on a far larger *flan.

Both early and "new style" coinages were copied in the Near East and Arabia; but this takes us beyond a general survey into a specialist area.

By way of postscript, one should perhaps mention certain quasi-autonomous bronze coins of Athens struck under Roman imperial rule. Their exact date is uncertain, but they fall somewhere between A.D. 150 and 230. The obverse type is still Athena, but there are reverses where the owl has given way to views of the Acropolis and the theatre of Dionysus, as they were at that time.

ATIA   A copper coin of Goa and Diu (Portuguese India), during the 18th century, c. 1750 onwards. Its value was 12 *reis at Goa and 15 reis at Diu, equivalent to 6 ⅛ Portuguese reis.

ATT   A Siamese copper coin, to the value of one-sixty-fourth part of the *tical.

ATTRIBUTE   We use this word (as a verb) where we are uncertain of the origins of a coin, of any part of its "attributes": place, period, engraver or any other relevant aspect may be unknown.

AU   The common abbreviation for *aurum* (*gold).

AUCTION SALE   A way of buying and selling coins, often fraught with pitfalls for the unwary. It is generally best for the client to entrust commissions to a *dealer, who (if he knows his business) will have a more objective view of what a coin is really worth. It happens not infrequently that auction bids outstrip prices of similar coins in dealers' stock lists. Similarly, a good dealer could well negotiate a private sale more advantageously than the seller might attain in the gamble of the auction rooms. His advice should at any rate be sought. The above assumes a pre-existing relationship of trust between client and dealer.

AUGSBURG   As a centre of the goldsmiths' art, Augsburg has a tradition of fine coinage art from the early Renaissance until the latter part of the 18th century. This is especially so in respect of prolific gold coinages with heads or names of Holy Roman Emperors from Maximilian I to Joseph II. Gold was struck in 1717 to commemorate the Reformation of 1517 and again in 1730, the 200th anniversary of the Augsburg Confession. There are also fine coins of Gustavus Adolphus (1632–5) and of several bishops.

Indirectly, the city has exerted a wide influence on coinage arts and techniques throughout Europe. Many of its more famous engravers (e.g. P. H. *Müller) worked at foreign courts, and Augsburg was the home of the *Fugger family, whose financial tentacles reached all over the Holy Roman Empire. The *screw-press, which the emissaries of King Henry II of France bought from an Augsburg engineer in 1550 to install at the *Moulin des Étuves in Paris, had its origins in Italy (*Cellini); and the Fuggers would have known of it from the time they operated the Papal Mint at Rome (1509–27).

AUGUSTALIS   Gold coin struck by the Hohenstauffen Emperor Frederick II at his mints of Brindisi and Messina in 1231. Its inspiration is entirely antique (not medieval), reminiscent of Roman *aurei and it derives its name from its imperial inscription: FRIDERICUS IMPERATOR ROMANORUM CAESAR AUGUSTUS. A rare (possibly unique) specimen in the Vienna Museum shows the Emperor crowned instead of a wearing a laurel wreath.

Augustalis

Aureus of Pompeii, c. 61 B.C.

Australia: Group of modern Australian coins, from 1935 to 1982. *(Photos courtesy R. Lobel)*

AUREUS (pl. AUREI) The principal gold denomination of ancient Rome from the first century B.C. until it was superseded by the *solidus of Constantine the Great early in the 4th century A.D. Though there had been occasional gold coinages earlier, there were no plentiful issues until the campaigns of Sulla in Asia Minor against Mithridates (*c.* 87 B.C.). This basically military issue (i.e. coins to pay the troops) was copied by Julius Caesar in Gaul; and the regular issue of aurei (to the value of 25 denarii each) began in Rome under Caesar's rule.

AUSBEUTEMÜNZEN A German numismatic term signifying coins struck from metal of a particular mine (or river), the word *Ausbeute* meaning exploitation. They may be of silver or gold, and very often show a representation of the actual mine, or mining operations. Frequent especially in the Saxon and Brunswick-Lüneberg series for mining coins, and the "river ducats" (*Flussgelddukaten) of Bavaria (from Danube, Inn and Isar) from the mid-18th century onwards. The best source for studying such material is the Mining Museum at Bochum in West Germany. It has published a remarkable catalogue with even more remarkable enlargements from mining coins and medals, which show this fascinating industry in great detail.

AUSTRALIA Although discovered by Captain Cook in 1770 and settled (largely by convicts) from 1788, Australia can show no local currency before 1813 (*ring money). From 1822 onwards, English coinage was introduced. The first gold coins are the rare *Adelaide tokens of 1852, the even rarer South Australian gold ingots stamped with weight and fineness (undated, but also 1852), and the exceedingly scarce Port Philip coinage of 1853–4, tariffed (on the reverse) at one-quarter, one-half, 1 and 2 ounces; the obverse showed a sitting kangaroo. Gold was regularly struck at the Sydney Mint from 1855; a mint at Melbourne followed from 1872 and another at Perth from 1899. Early coins at the Sydney Mint (1855–70) are distinguished by two features: first, a reverse showing the word AUSTRALIA across the field in the centre within a wreath, with the words SYDNEY MINT above and ONE SOVEREIGN below; secondly, the alloying metal was mainly silver not copper (6.3% as against 2%), and not until 1870 was the alloy reduced to 0.5% silver. From 1871, all sovereigns became of the standard English type, without denomination and with merely a small initial mintmark (S, M or P, as the case might be). This gold coinage continued at Sydney until 1926, and at Perth and Melbourne as late as 1931.

A silver coinage was not introduced until the last year of Edward VII's reign in 1910 (threepence, sixpence, shilling, florin); bronze coinage followed with the accession of George V in 1911 (halfpenny and penny). These were also the first to bear the legend COMMONWEALTH OF AUSTRALIA. That same Commonwealth decided on a decimal coinage 4 years before the United Kingdom; at the same time (1966), a new mint was established at Canberra. The silver coins remained .925 fine until 1946, and then at .500 fine until they ceased to be struck in 1963/4 when they became cupro-nickel. Among commemorative pieces we should note the florins of 1927 (for the opening of the new Parliament House at Canberra) and 1934–5 (centennial of the city of Melbourne and the state of Victoria. There is also a large and varied series of tokens beginning in 1852.

AUTOMOBILE DOLLAR Struck in 1928 for the Chinese province of Kweichow, this coin still remains one of only two showing a motor-car and is much in demand among collectors of modern world coins. Fifty years later, in 1978, Macau issued a dollar-sized coin to celebrate the 25th anniversary of its Grand Prix. This—to the value of 100 *patacas (silver) or 500 patacas (gold)—shows a racing car.

AUTONOMOUS An autonomous coinage is one struck by a city without external authority. This was the general custom in the ancient Greek world, where about 1,500 city states issued their own coinages; but the great empires (first of Alexander, later of Rome) severely restricted these rights.

In medieval times, autonomous coinages again became more frequent, "free cities" jealously guarding their privileges. Ecclesiastical foundations usually held their right of coinage under imperial patent (within the Holy Roman Empire). It is notable that the early coinage of the Popes of Rome was not truly autonomous, but that the name of the Emperor appears on it as well (9th to the 11th centuries). In England, only the Saxon coinages of the Archbishops of Canterbury and York were truly autonomous; later, their minting rights were exercised only by favour of the King and ceased altogether under Henry VIII (Wolsey as Archbishop of York being the last to strike coins).

AVENCHES In the Canton of Vaud, Switzerland, the town was an important Roman settlement. It is the site of many archaeological discoveries, among them one of the few actual dies of a *Merovingian tremissis.

AVESTA A Swedish mint since 1644. It was opened to exploit metal from the neighbouring "copper mountain" and remained until 1831 the chief place for coining Sweden's copper. Copper blanks were also supplied from here to the specifications of other European mints—e.g. for the first English regal copper coinage under Charles II (1672). Another, less official, aspect of its foreign work occurred when it struck an extensive series of bogus Russian *kopeks for use in Gustav III's war against Russia (1788), dated 1764, 1778 and 1787. These are easily distinguishable from genuine pieces of Catherine the Great, as the Russian crown is replaced by that of Sweden.

AVIGNON A mint of the Counts of Provence until 1348, when it was sold to Pope Clement VI. Papal coins in all metals were struck here at intervals until 1692, from 1503 usually with the name of the papal legate, sometimes with that of the vice-legate too. (Sometimes, again, these are represented only by their arms, not names.) The series is in every respect interesting (albeit complicated), since it includes French as well as Italian types and denominations.

AXE MONEY The axe, whether single- or double-bladed, has always been among man's most prized tools during peacetime, and has also been prized among weapons at least since the Bronze Age. Even from the late Stone (Neolithic) Age, finds (or hoards) of highly polished stone axes have been discovered which suggest that these may have been used as currency, or at least as exchange objects of some value. Homer (in the *Iliad*) tells us that bronze and even gold axes were among the most highly prized battle honours. There may, therefore, be some direct allusion to this in the reverse types of *Tenedos's coinage, that island lying not far from what is believed to be the site of Troy in Asia Minor.

AXUMITE COINS The early coinage of Abyssinia, issued under Axumite kings from about A.D. 300–850. The coinage, which is almost entirely of gold, was based first on the Roman *aureus, later the *solidus. Coins show a crowned bust on the obverse, and a helmeted one on the reverse. Two features make the series significant. First, they are based on Roman models but carry Greek inscriptions. Secondly, following the conversion of Ezanas to Christianity in A.D. 330, legends incorporate crosses after each syllable. This is almost the earliest use of the Christian cross on any official coinage, and certainly the most regular. Though the conversion of Constantine the Great to Christianity had taken place in A.D. 312, the cross appears only intermittently on his and his successors' issues.

AYACUCHO   A mint of Peru active only during 1881–2.

AYR   A mint of Scotland under Alexander II (1249–86) only. Pennies, all rare, were struck here.

B

BABYLON Babylonian *cylinder seals are among the earliest numismatic objects known. As a mint, Babylon dates from the time of *Alexander the Great. At first (i.e. 331–328 B.C.) coins were struck here in the name of the Persian governor Mazaeus, who had surrendered the city to Alexander and was reinstated by him. These are oriental types, with Aramaic script, and show on the obverse the seated figure of Baal. After the death of Mazaeus, we find the silver Alexandrine tetradrachms of standard type (head of Heracles), but with the mintmark M for Metropolis (i.e. capital of the Empire as planned by Alexander). Double *darics of the old Persian type are also found with the mintmark.

BACCHANALIAN COINS A name sometimes bestowed on the gold *mohur of the Moghul Emperor Jahangir (1605–28), showing him holding a cup of wine. This is something quite exceptional in Muslim coinage, as portraiture was frowned upon and bibulousness even more. It may account for the fact that the issue was short-lived, lasting only from *c.* 1611–14.

BAHIA The first mint of Portuguese Brazil, established in 1695 but transferred to *Rio de Janeiro in 1699. When re-established at Bahia in 1714, it carried the mintmark B. Gold coins were struck here for Portugal from 1714–1805, and a special copper issue for Brazil from 1729.

BAIOCCO A coin of the Papal States, to the value of one-hundreth of the *scudo. It was struck at first in base silver, but from the 18th century as a copper denomination (though there is also a multiple of 80 baiocchi in silver, struck by Pope Clement XI in 1712). *Siege pieces exist from the time of Napoleon's invasion of northern Italy (1796–7) for Civita Vecchia, San Severino and Tivoli in values mainly 2½ and 5 baiocchi. It continued as a papal copper coin until 1866 and was struck in large quantities, especially during the early years of the 19th century.

Half-baiocco of Pope Clement XIII, 1759

BAIOCHELLA A small papal *billon coin, first struck under Pius IV (1559–65). It weighed 1 gramme and contained 0.19 gramme of silver. Because it was extensively forged and imitated elsewhere, it ceased to be struck by the Popes after 1592, but continued to circulate for at least another fifty years.

BAJOIRE French term (from *baiser*, to kiss) for *vis-à-vis* portraits on coins or medals. The most famous example is perhaps that of Ferdinand and Isabella on the *excelente of 1497. This was taken up in the early 17th century in the Spanish Netherlands under Albert and Isabella (1598–1621). In the English series, significantly perhaps, this predominantly Spanish type is confined to the joint coinage of Mary Tudor and Philip II of Spain (1554–8). There is also an exceedingly rare portrait ducat of Scotland, with Mary Stuart during her brief marriage to Francis II of France (1558–60).

Bajoire: shilling of Mary and Philip of Spain, 1554

BALANCE HALF-MERK A silver piece to the value of 6s. 8d., introduced in the sixth coinage of James VI of Scotland, 1591. It

Ballooning medal (anon.),
showing the first manned ascent
over Paris, November 1783

takes its name from the reverse design, showing a balance with a sword behind, to symbolise justice (the legend reads HIS DIFFERT REGE TYRANNUS, i.e. "in these things a tyrant differs from a king"). The obverse shows a crowned shield between two thistles. A similar quarter-merk is also known.

BALDWIN & CO. This firm struck gold coins to the value of $5, $10 and $20 in large quantities from 1850–51 in San Francisco, California. The $20 denomination was the first to be struck here. There was some scandal when it was discovered that all the coins were about 5% lacking in intrinsic gold value; and the *Pacific News* on 17 April 1851 reported the somewhat precipitate departure of the manufacturers.

BALLOONING MEDALS A favourite collecting theme, especially among the French who were the pioneers of this branch of aeronautics. Such medals are known from the very first ascent by the Montgolfier brothers in 1783, and have continued right to the present day (first Atlantic crossing, 1979).

BALTIMORE, LORD One of the earliest coinages struck for British settlements in North America is known as Lord Baltimore's Coinage, after the "Lord Proprietor of Maryland", as he was styled (1658). These pieces (silver shilling, sixpence, groat, copper penny) were struck in England. All show the Duke's portrait on the obverse; but the copper penny (which is very rare) has a ducal coronet instead of the family arms on the reverse. There are numerous patterns and die varieties much sought after by collectors of early Americana.

BAMBERG A town in Bavaria, and a bishopric from the early 11th century. Thalers and ducats are known from 1506 onwards, the gold coinage being particularly plentiful (and even today less expensive than most) during the second half of the 18th century. There are some specially fine *sede vacante pieces, and the "contribution Thalers" struck in 1795 from church and private silver. Perhaps the most interesting piece historically is the ducat of 1600, showing the founders of the bishopric (King Henry II and his wife Kunigunde) holding a model of the cathedral.

BAMBOO MONEY Small bamboo sticks, ranging in length from about 4 to 20 centimetres, inscribed with coloured inks and impressed with burnt-in stamps (mainly of banks), are known in China from the 18th century until about the end of the 19th. They are known in values of 100 upward to several 1,000 *cash, and are often holed towards the top so that they could be strung and hung up together. The written symbols (value, etc.) are protected by a transparent lacquer.

BANCO A term found over and over again in numismatics, but with varying meanings. In its origins, "banco" money is an Italian concept found as long ago as the early 16th century (*Casa di San Giorgio). The great imports of metals from the New World and consequent fluctuations in their value caused the banks to conceive of an "ideal" currency by which to reckon their accounts, irrespective of day-to-day variations. The longest and most sophisticated use of banco currency was that of the Hamburg Bank, extending from 1690 to 1873. During this period, all transactions were reckoned in "banco" Thalers and "banco" marks, which were, however, never struck. The bank insisted on deposits in fine silver bars, and the customers' accounts stood at whatever was the current rate for silver, converted into "banco" Thalers at 9¼ to the mark (weight) fine. This, being fair to all, worked well.

A more unscrupulous use of banco currency was to strike an actual coin—a Thaler, for instance—to a lower standard of weight or fineness than that current at the time of striking. This was really only a shift by which the bank (or the state, if it was a state bank) would make a handsome profit—not necessarily at the customer's expense—if it was really credit-worthy and these coins were accepted in day-to-day transactions at their face value. But they rarely were. Issues of Brandenburg in 1695–6 and Prussia in 1766 both proved unsuccessful (over 100,000 of the latter remaining unissued because they were unacceptable to the public, finally being melted down in 1790).

The first really successful issue of coins marked "banco" was the *skilling one of 1835 in Sweden (in denominations of 2, 1, two-thirds, one-third and one-sixth skilling). It is significant that these were in copper and thus a *token coinage anyway. In such small denominations people felt they were running small risks: there were, after all, 48 skillings to 1 riksdaler.

Finally, the word "banco" appears, as might be expected, on very many banknotes. Here it may either be used in the generic sense above, or may refer to the name of the bank actually issuing the notes (e.g. Stockholms Banco in the 1660s).

BANCOZETTEL DIVISIONARY COINS Coins with the description of *Bancozetteltheilungsmünze* were issued in 1807 in denominations of 15 and 30 *Kreutzer at Vienna, Carlsburg, Kremnitz, Nagybanya and Schmöllnitz mints (Austria). This was because of wide divergence of value between the Austrian paper money (*Bancozettel*) and normal currency. They are still relatively common, except for a rare die error in date, 1087.

BANK COMMEMORATIVE COINS Banking and coins being closely linked, it is natural that banks—especially national ones—are occasionally celebrated on coins, for anniversaries, etc. The theme is perhaps of special interest to those who collect paper currency of such banks (where available). But such thematic material as there is would seem to be of fairly recent origin: the earliest traced in 20th-century catalogues is the £50 gold piece, struck for the 10th anniversary of the Bank of Israel in 1964. The silver 50-schilling to commemorate the 150th anniversary of Austria's National Bank in 1966 comes next, a handful of others (e.g. Egypt, Mongolia, Netherlands, Antilles) all date from the 1970s, while the 10th anniversary of the Caribbean Development Bank was celebrated in 1980 by a number of West Indian islands including Barbados. Other financial institutions are only very occasionally to be noted—e.g. the 200th anniversary of the Vienna Stock Exchange in 1971.

BANKNOTE A piece of paper money which bears the imprint of a bank, and (usually) states that the bank will exchange it for a given sum in coin. Such a promise used to imply gold or silver; it no longer does.

The study and collection of banknotes is quite as fascinating as that of coinage. Although the history of banknotes is relatively short (dating only from the 1660s) an enormous number of banks have issued notes: in England alone 720 private and country banks with note issues totalling £30 million are recorded in the year 1810. Since paper is a much more ephemeral material than metal, and since in any case the notes often turned out not to be worth the paper they were printed on, it follows that far fewer notes than coins will have survived. The most extensive collection of banknotes in England is that of the Institute of Bankers, which also maintains the best reference library on the subject, while in the U.S.A., the collection of the American Numismatic Society, New York, vies with that of the Smithsonian Institute, Washington, for first place.

Bank of England dollar

Three-shilling bank token

One could obviously compile an encyclopedia the length of this one on banknotes alone. Resisting the temptation, and concentrating on the interests of coin collectors, the present writer would merely refer the interested reader to pp.81–5 of Albert Pick's *Papiergeld*, where there is a comprehensive listing of notes that have coins as part of their design. Such coins are not necessarily contemporary. Thus a Greek 10 milliard drachm note of 1944 shows a *decadrachm of ancient Syracuse. A "parallel" collection of this kind seems worthwhile; another would be of notes and coins of the same denomination issued (as sometimes happens) at the same time. In the British series the guinea with its fractions and multiples is perhaps worthy of special study. It continued as a note until 1833, i.e. twenty years longer than as a coin.

BANK OF ENGLAND DOLLAR A coin with the inscription FIVE SHILLINGS—DOLLAR and the name BANK OF ENGLAND was struck for currency use only once (1804), though earlier proofs are known. This, and some later *bank tokens in lower denominations, is also one of the few examples (prior to 1920) of English silver coinage struck to a standard of less than .925 fine, its actual silver value being only about 4s. 9d., since the coins were overstruck on Spanish dollars (pieces-of-eight), which were only about .900 fine silver. Previously, i.e. from 1797 onwards, such pieces had been countermarked with a small stamp of the head of George III to validate them as currency in England. Both kinds are today prized collectors' items.

BANK (of England) TOKENS Bank tokens to the value of 3 shillings and 1s. 6d. were issued from 1811–16. They are not uncommon, but there are some very rare proofs in gold and platinum. Patterns for a 9-pence token were also prepared (1812), but this issue never materialised.

The denominations were never repeated in the English series: cf. *Bank of England dollar. Though comparable to the dollar, they are distinct from it in *not* carrying the name of the bank, merely the designation "bank token". Their silver content was lower than their face value.

BANK OF IRELAND Founded in 1782, the Bank of Ireland first issued notes a year later in denominations ranging from £10 to £500 (12,700 notes in all, totalling £882,500). This first issue was printed in England; but from 1784 the Bank had its own printer (William Wilson) and engraver (Edward Fitzgerald), and then issued notes in guinea as well as pound denominations. All these were in Irish currency, which at that time implied 13 Irish pence to a British shilling.

During the silver scarcity of the early years of the 19th century, the Bank was authorised to issue silver tokens (cf. *Bank of England tokens). The series began in 1804 with a token to the value of 6 shillings (with a portrait of George III as the obverse and a figure of Hibernia as the reverse). This was followed by tokens of similar design for 5 and 10 pence in 1805 and pieces of 30 pence in 1808. All these were struck, like their English counterparts, at Birmingham's *Soho Mint.

BANK OF IRELAND TOKENS Various silver pieces struck for the Bank of Ireland from 1804–13. The largest and earliest (1804 only) were overstruck Spanish dollars to the value of 6 shillings. Other denominations were 30 pence (1808 only), 10 pence (1805 and 1812) and 5 pence (1805). All were struck at the *Soho Mint in Birmingham.

BANU The name of the *cent in the decimal currency of Romania, established on the footing of the *Latin Monetary Union in 1867 (100 bani = 1 *leu). Bronze coins of 1, 2, 5, 10 and

50 bani dated 1867 and 1869 were struck at the *Heaton Mint, Birmingham, for the Bank of Romania.

BARBADOS John *Milton.

BARBAROUS RADIATES Gaulish and British copies of the Roman *antoninianus. They come, however, in various shapes and sizes; the term is therefore generic and does not apply to any particular denomination.

BARBER DIME *dime.

BARBER HEAD COINS Any coins or *patterns designed by Charles E. Barber of the United States Mint, especially the Liberty head *dimes, quarters and half-dollars issued from 1892 to 1916.

BARBER QUARTER *quarter.

BARBUDA A *billon coin of Ferdinand I of Portugal (1367–83). The King is shown in profile, helmeted and crowned with the vizor up.

BARCELONA A town in Spain, and a mint since Roman times, when *siliquae of victory type were struck here under Maximus (A.D. 411). It became more important in *Visigothic times and was finally united with the kingdom of Aragon under Alfonso II (1163–96). Early silver coins copied Carolingian *deniers, and gold copied the Moorish *maravedis, sometimes with Arabic legends.

Barbuda

The later history of the mint is no less interesting. From 1614 it struck types based on the double *excelente of Ferdinand and Isabella; in 1641 it joined in the revolt against Philip IV and struck pieces with the inscription PRINCIPATUS CATALONIE. From 1642–52, the town enjoyed (?) the protection of France; and there are emissions of both Louis XIII and Louis XIV, besides siege pieces of 1652, before it again fell to Spanish armies under Don Juan of Austria. There are more emergency issues dating from 1812–14 during the Napoleonic wars.

BAR CENT An experimental or pattern piece of the USA, with a monogram on the obverse and 13 horizontal bars (symbolising the then United States) on the reverse. There are records to show that it first circulated in New York towards the end of 1785. Its design may be based on that of an army button, and it was possibly struck by Thomas *Wyon in Birmingham as an alternative design to the *Nova Constellatio coppers of 1783–6.

BARHINA A gold coin, in the form of a rectangular bar, issued as emergency money in the Portuguese colony of Mozambique in 1835. It was current for 400 Portuguese *reis, but was stamped M—2½, the M standing for matical, a local gold weight. A half of this denomination was also issued; but as, through an oversight, it held proportionately more pure gold, it quickly disappeared from circulation to be melted down and is consequently much rarer.

BAR MONEY The stamping of gold and silver bars for currency purposes dates from ancient Roman times and continues to this day (*bullion). Its most extensive use was probably in the so-called "coinless period" of medieval Russia (12th to early 14th centuries), when silver ingots shaped either hexagonally (Kiev) or as bars (Novgorod) were the main circulating monetary medium. For details *grivna.

BARONIAL COINS (English) Feudal coinages are, on the whole, much more numerous than regal ones in medieval times, especially in French and German territories. For England, the reverse is true: apart from a few *ecclesiastical mints, coinage was the jealously guarded prerogative of the sovereign. The sole exception to this rule is to be found in the period of 1138–47, when England was torn between the adherents of Stephen and Matilda and some dozen identified barons struck coins on their own account. There may well be more, as many crude types remain to be identified.

BARRE, JEAN-JACQUES (1793-1855) French engraver who from 1842–55 was chief engraver at the Paris Mint. He had distinguished himself as early as 1834 in cutting the coinage for Louis-Philippe and was also responsible for the coinage of Louis Napoleon (1848). He was also a prolific medallist, and a notable engraver of banknotes (Banks of France, Lyon, Rouen and Toulouse, 1841–3).

BARTON'S METAL Copper plated with gold. Its use in coinage is confined to certain *patterns of 1825 in the English series.

BASEL A town in northern Switzerland, bordering on both France and Germany. Coins are known from Merovingian times. The first gold pieces date from the early 15th century; and from the 17th century onwards there is a magnificent series of city views on multiple ducats. Apart from the independent city coinage there are also pieces of the bishopric and canton. The most famous artist to work here was probably Urs *Graf, better known as one of the great copperplate engravers of the German Renaissance.

The currency history of Basel is complicated in the extreme. Sharing its border with Germany as well as many trading links with south-western German towns such as Freiburg, Colmar and Breisach, it joined the *Rappenmünzbund in 1403 but—although not part of the German empire—was forced by a threat of a silver blockade to submit to the Augsburg Mint Convention of 1559. As regards coins of the bishopric, the jurisdiction of this extended into neighbouring cantons of Switzerland and even into parts of what is now France; and coins were tariffed in livres tournois, Basel livres and even écus bons or Bienne Thalers according to the areas in which they were to circulate. Basel therefore mirrors in miniature the extraordinary currency confusion of *Switzerland in general prior to 1849.

BASE METAL A somewhat loose term comprising any metal that is not precious or "noble". Until the 18th century, this would have meant everything except gold and silver (and possibly their *alloy, *electrum). Then the discovery of *platinum in South America added a third precious metal. Though rarer and dearer than the others, it has proved intractable and unattractive in coinage.

BAT *tical.

BATH METAL A whitish brass, with an admixture of much more zinc than copper. For its use in coinage, *rosa Americana.

BATZ (pl. BATZEN) A Swiss denomination, first introduced at Berne during the 15th century to the value of 4 *Kreuzer. It was later copied by other Swiss cantons and also parts of southern Germany. Batzen remained current in certain cantons even after the reorganisation of the Swiss monetary system in 1848, at the value of 10 to 1 franc.

BAWBEE A *billon coin of Scotland, current for 6 pence, introduced in 1539 as part of the 3rd coinage of James V. It was not struck after 1558, but revived as a copper denomination under Charles II, and was last struck under William II (William III of England) in 1697.

Batz: Zurich, 1519

BAZARUCO A base metal coin (sometimes of copper but more often of pewter) widely used in the Indian possessions of Portugal (Goa, Diu, etc.). It was first introduced early in the 16th century, to the value of 2 *reis. Multiples of up to 20 are known and the coin survived well into the 19th century as local small change. No early ones seem to have survived, since the composition of the metal tended to softness and easy oxidisation.

BECHOT, MARC (1520–57) "Graveur général", the first to hold this title, following the French coinage reforms under Henry II in 1547. He was responsible for all dies sent to provincial mints (then exclusively cut by him or under his supervision in Paris). A very fine engraver, whose best piece is probably the *Henri d'or à la Gallia.

BECHTLER FAMILY This family operated a private mint in Rutherford County, North Carolina, from 1830–52—a longer period than that of any other firm coining territorial gold. Theirs is the distinction of striking the first $1 gold piece in the USA in 1832 (there being no government series until 1849). The series has many other features of interest: e.g. the striking of pieces with inscriptions CAROLINA and GEORGIA (according to where the metal came from); and pieces inscribed with both weight and carat standard (20, 21 and 22 carat pieces being known). This is not to say that "short value" was given. The Bechtlers were skilled and honest metallurgists, and where the gold contained alloys or other foreign matter, coins were made heavier to give full value in all denominations which they struck ($1, $2 and $5).

BECKER, CARL WILHELM One of the most skilful forgers of all time, who between 1815–25 cut over 600 dies, mainly of Greek and Roman coins but including also some Carolingian, medieval and modern. When he was finally caught, his dies and machinery were seized and are today part of the Berlin collection. A minute analysis of all these forgeries was made by Sir George Hill in his *Becker the Counterfeiter* (Spink & Sons Ltd., 1955 ed.). Becker never made the mistake of casting his forgeries, but engraved all his own dies, and often overstruck worn ancient coins with his new designs. This ensured that the weight and metallic composition of his pieces were correct; the only clues are therefore stylistic ones, and all but the most practised eyes may be deceived by them. Even today they sometimes turn up in sales, catalogued as genuine specimens.

BECKER, PHILIP CHRISTOPHER (1674–1742) One of the best German coin and medal engravers of the Baroque era, though perhaps even more famous for his gems. He worked a great deal at the court of Vienna (where the mint preserves some of his dies to this day); also for Peter the Great of Russia, for whom he cut both seals and coins (at St Petersburg Mint, from 1718).

BELLI, VALERIO (1468–1546) Renaissance engraver of gems, coins and medals, active both at Vicenza (where he was born and died) and at the mint of Rome. He was chief medallist to Pope Clement VII before 1527 and worked also for Pope Paul III and Cardinal Farnese. He claimed to have engraved some 150 coin dies and among his medals is a fine self-portrait.

BELL MONEY The term has been given to two entirely different currencies. First, it is applied to a primitive copper currency of China in the shape of a bell. Second (and more important) are the pieces struck during the French Revolution from metal made of bronze from melted-down church bells. The period of June 1791 to 1792 saw no less than seven governmental decrees relating to the manufacture and distribution of coins from "métal de cloche", as it was called. Many experimental trial pieces were submitted during these and following years (right up to 1798), the most famous of which is a series of patterns submitted by a Lyon firm (*Mathieu, Mercié & Mouterde). Medals were also struck; and there is one (exceedingly rare, only three or four specimens struck) actually commemorating the famous bell from which the metal was taken. This was Rouen's "Georges d'Amboise" so named after the bishop who had given it to the town in 1501.

BENEDICTION TYPE PENNY   A coin struck only during the reign of Aethelred II (979–1016), showing on the reverse the *Hand of Providence with two fingers extended in blessing.

BENEVENTUM   *Italy.

BERGERAC   A town in the Dordogne valley, south-western France, and the seat of an *Anglo-Gallic mint from 1347. Coinage rights were granted by Edward III to Henry Earl of Lancaster, who had captured the town (1344) and who made use of his rights there by striking *gros and demi-gros of both *tournois and *leopard varieties until his death in 1361. Pieces until 1352 bear the title COMES (Count), later ones, after Henry had been raised to the dukedom in 1352, the title DUX.

BERGERON, ETIENNE   Mintmaster at *Troyes, 1550, and at *Paris from 1553. The coining machinery which Bergeron installed at Troyes was identical to that which had been brought from Augsburg to Paris (*Moulin des Étuves) and there is evidence to suggest that Troyes struck pieces some months earlier than Paris.

Bergeron seems to have been particularly gifted mechanically; the pieces at Troyes are exceptionally well struck and output in Paris, which had been more or less experimental until his arrival there, increased dramatically once he took over. Indeed, it was his success with the new methods which aroused the jealousy of traditional moneyers, who placed every possible administrative obstacle in his way and ultimately drove him out. In 1557 we hear of him on a mission to Nancy in the service of Charles III of Lorraine (almost certainly in connection with the installation of coining machinery there) and from 1561–72 he was in charge of the mint at Pau in the kingdom of Navarre—a "moulin" once more. His mark at Troyes and Pau is an E surmounted by a crescent, while in Paris he adopted EB in monogram form. The latter is also found on the *teston morveux of Orléans, 1562–3.

BERMUDA   *Somer Islands.

BERNE   The name of a Swiss canton and its principal city, today the capital of Switzerland. Its coinage can be traced back uninterruptedly to 1224, during which time it has struck everything from thin, *uniface *bracteates to heavy gold (the latter beginning in 1492). Since 1850 it has been the seat of the Swiss Federal Mint, alone authorised to strike coins for Switzerland. A very fine collection is maintained at the Bernisches Historisches Museum. Also *batz, dicken, Mörikofer, plappart.

Berne: Gold duplone, 1819

Berne is also notable for having issued the first Swiss banknotes: those of its Deposito-Cassa in 1826.

BERWICK   A town on the border of England and Scotland, whose occasional use as a mint by both English and Scottish rulers during medieval times reflects the changing fortunes of the border wars. The last coins known from here are *groats and their halves struck under James III of Scotland (1460–88).

BEZANT   The medieval name for the Byzantine gold *nomisma, which was the principal gold coin of Europe until the 13th century. It was copied by the Crusader kings of Cyprus

(Lusignan dynasty, from 1268). Loosely, the term is also applied to certain mixed types (Saracenic bezants) of the kingdom of Jerusalem during the 12th century, which carry Arabic inscriptions proclaiming the Christian faith.

BEZANT BLANC   Term applied to certain of the Cypriot issues (see bezant), characterised by *scyphate fabric and a large admixture of silver.

BICHE   French adulteration of *pice, and struck during the reign of Louis XV at the Mahé Mint on the south-west coast of India. These coins—which were also struck in halves and quarters of the denomination—were roughly shaped and show on the obverse five fleurs-de-lis, and on the reverse the date (struck between 1730 and 1767).

BILINGUAL (and multilingual) COINS   There are many coins carrying inscriptions in two or more languages. In ancient times, we find Indo-Bactrian and Greek, Greek and Latin, Greek and Persian, Greek and Hebrew. With the rise of the Arab Empire in early medieval times, there are Arabian-Latin inscriptions on coinages of both Spain and Sicily. In the Dutch East Indies colonial series, there are coins inscribed in Dutch, Arabic and Malay.

BILLON   A mixture of copper, pewter, lead and a little silver—in other words, a base metal. Most extensively used in the 3rd century A.D. by the Roman emperors, it has also been frequently used for low denominations in medieval and modern coinages.

BI-METALLIC COINS   Coins made of two obviously different metals, separate and not fused (for which latter *alloy). There have been many trials for these at one time and another (e.g. *model penny); but the only type adopted for circulation, at any rate in the English series, is the tin farthing of 1684–5 with a central copper plug and inscribed edge. *Clad coins are a different category.

BIMETALLISM   A currency term, denoting that a country adheres to two standards at once, generally gold and silver. It has never really worked, since wide fluctuations in the relative values of the two metals has meant constant revaluations.

BIOGRAPHICAL DICTIONARY OF MEDALLISTS   Compiled by Leonard *Forrer from 1900–30, this remains the most comprehensive work on the subject, containing biographies and details of the work of more than 10,000 medallists, seal, coin and gem engravers from ancient to modern times. Designers and manufacturers are also listed; and under each biographical entry, productions are carefully divided into currency, patterns and proofs, tokens, medals and jetons. As in any work of this kind by one man, there are points of detail which need revising in the light of more recent research; but it remains a monumental and indispensable source of reference.

BIRMINGHAM   One of the world's most important minting centres, though never itself a mint in the sense of being the seat of a coinage in its own right (the nearest places being Tamworth and Coventry). Birmingham's pre-eminence—the word is not too strong—in minting operations grew directly out of its skill in other manufactures (*buttons). References will be found under Allen & Moore, Matthew Boulton, J. R. Gaunt, J. G. Hancock, Ralph Heaton, P. Kempson, King's Norton Mint, W. Lutwyche, Marrian & Gausby, Pinches (family), Soho Mint, Taylor & Challen, Wyon (family).

BIT   At first used as a rather obvious slang term for *cut money, the word was later used to apply throughout the West

Indies as a money of *account, varying (according to time and place) from 7½ to 9 pence. Its basis was the Spanish *real. The *dollar varied in value from 10 to 11 bits. When silver coins to the value of 10 and 15 cents were struck for the West Indies from 1797–1823, they were locally known as "short" and "long" bits respectively.

BLACK DOGS A term of disapproval applied to a number of base coins with very little silver content and much lead or pewter. First apparently used in the reign of Queen Anne (especially for bad shillings); later of the *Cayenne sous when they came to circulate in the West Indies.

BLACK MONEY A term found in use already during the early 13th century, for very base silver with a dark tinge. The French term for these coins was "denier noir", and a lot of them found their way to England during the time of the Plantagenet kings. An ordinance of 1351 commands that "all manner of black money which has been commonly current in the King's name should be utterly excluded".

BLACKSMITH HALF-CROWN A Civil War issue of Kilkenny, Ireland, undated, but struck probably during 1642 by supporters of King Charles I who called themselves "The Confederacy". It is a crude copy of the Tower Mint half-crown, showing the King on horseback.

BLANC A French word meaning white; and hence, by association, a generic term for a number of coins which (at any rate when first issued!) were notable for the purity of "whiteness" of their silver (contrast *black money). Of these, the most important were the blanc à la couronne, blanc aux écus, denier blanc à la fleur-de-lis, grand blanc, gros blanc, petit blanc. No less than three different blancs were created by Charles VII of France: blanc aux rondeaux, blanc dentillé and blanc des gens d'armes. Compare also *albus, hvid and witte. When used of a gold coin, the term implied that it was largely adultered with silver (*bezant blanc).

BLANK The numismatic term for the properly prepared piece of metal on which a coin is struck. Often, but by no means always, such preparation is undertaken by the mint which is to strike the coins. It can, however, be equally well done by an outside contractor. Thus England's first regular copper coinage under Charles II (1672) was struck on blanks supplied from Sweden (*Avesta); and the *Heaton Mint, Birmingham, in its day, supplied millions of blanks to mints in various foreign countries, apart from the Royal Mint.

By "properly prepared" we mean that the pieces of metal for the coins-to-be are of the correct diameter, weight, metallic composition and smoothness required. The various processes involved call, perhaps, for knowledge and skills greater than the actual striking, which is today largely automated.

BLONDEAU, PIERRE A French engineer employed at the Tower Mint, first under the Commonwealth and later to supervise the *milled coinage of Charles II. Blondeau not only reintroduced the *screw-press to England (for previous uses here *Meystrell, Briot), but also brought with him his secret invention for marking the edge of coins. This he first employed on some patterns of 1651, then on patterns of the Protectorate (1656, 1658), and finally on the regular coinage of Charles II (crowns and 5-guinea pieces only, from 1663), with the inscription *DECUS ET TUTAMEN.

There is no evidence that Blondeau was himself a designer or engraver; the words PETRUS BLONDEAUS INVENTOR FECIT should be taken to refer to the mechanical processes only.

BODLE A Scottish denomination, to the value of 2 pence, struck only from 1677–87. It was also known as the half-*plack or turner.

BOGOTÁ Capital of Colombia, South America, and an important mint since 1652. The early mintmark NR stands for Nueva Reina, i.e. the new kingdom (of Spain), as it formed part of the Spanish Peruvian possessions. In more recent times, the mintmark has been B, Ba or even Bogotá spelt out in full. During the first century of its operations, only silver was struck; gold values from 1 to 8 *escudos date from 1765–1820. The mint continues to this day to strike much of the coinage of the independent Republic of Colombia.

BOLIVAR Monetary unit of Venezuela since 1871, named after the country's liberator, Simon Bolivar. Multiples of 5 to 100 were struck in gold in 1875; but the 5-bolivar piece was also the principal silver coin, struck to the same standard as the French 5 francs.

BOLIVIANO The monetary unit of Bolivia since 1863 in the decimal coinage then introduced (100 copper *centavos = 1 silver boliviano). It was struck as a crown-size piece from 1864–87.

BOLOGNA Town in northern Italy, with a distinguished and varied history as a mint. Beginning as an autonomous city republic, it passed later under the rule of the Pepoli, Visconti and Bentivoglio families successively, all of whom have left coinages as witnesses to their rule. There are pieces of Charles V of Spain (last coronation of a Holy Roman Emperor by the Pope, 1530), of the Cispadine Republic 1797, of Napoleon, and of the Duchy of Emilia in the mid-19th century. But by far the most important series is that as a papal mint producing the most extensive and varied coinage outside Rome from the 14th to the 19th centuries.

BOLOGNINO A special Bolognese type of the *denaro, first struck towards the end of the 12th century. It was extensively copied by other Italian towns.

BOMBAY A mint of the East India Company (Bombay Presidency) since 1671. It struck coins of both local and European type until 1834. In 1835 the mint began to strike coins of a unified style for the East India Company; in 1858 it was, with the company's other assets, transferred to the Crown, and has struck coins for successive British monarchs since (mintmark = B, or a dot). There was an issue of sovereigns, in 1918 only, with the mintmark I below the St George reverse. The same mintmark is to be found on certain pennies and halfpennies struck for Australia in 1942 and 1943 (though these are also found without any mintmark). The mint is still active for the present Republic of India, the mintmark now again being a dot, sometimes set within a small diamond.

BONK A popular name for rectangular copper coins of Java as struck under Dutch rule from 1796 onwards. Denominations from the half-*stuiver to 8 stuivers are indiscriminately referred to as bonks in various contemporary records.

BONNET PIECE Gold coin of James V of Scotland, to the value of 1 ducat, so called after the type of the obverse, showing the King wearing a broad, flat cap. Struck in 1539 from gold found at Crawford Muir, this exceedingly rare coin is also the first in the Scottish series to bear a date.

BONNET TYPE The second type among the pennies of William the Conqueror (1066–87), so named after the very broad

Bonk

Bonnet piece (slightly enlarged)

jewelled and tasselled crown which the King is shown wearing (cf. *canopy type).

BONZAGNA, GIAN FEDERIGO Italian medallist of the second half of the 17th century, who worked at the mint of Parma. He cut a great number of dies for the Dukes Pierluigi and Ottavio Farnese, and made medals for no fewer than five popes from Paul II to Gregory XIII, including a "celebration" of the St Bartholomew massacre.

BONZAGNA, GIAN GIACOMO Elder brother of *Gian Federigo, and like him employed for most of his working life at the Parma Mint. He was made engraver for life in 1546, worked chiefly for Pope Paul III, and cut not only coins and medals but also seals for papal bulls.

BOOTH, WILLIAM A celebrated forger who set up a clandestine die-sinking and engraving establishment at Perry Bar, Staffordshire, in the early years of the 19th century. He had the extraordinary nerve—misplaced, as it turned out—to issue his own penny token in 1811, thus advertising his presence which might otherwise have remained undetected. He counterfeited both coins and banknotes with equal skill, specialising in Bank of England issues (£10, £5 and £1 notes; 5 shillings, 3 shillings, and 1s. 6d. Bank Tokens). He was caught, sentenced and hanged in 1816.

BORDEAUX One of the most important French mints, active for at least 1,000 years until 1878, and now so again: just as the Royal Mint has transferred its main operations to Llantrisant in Wales, so the French state mint has recently moved from Paris to Bordeaux. It was also an important seat of *Anglo-Gallic coinage from the late 12th century onwards, especially active under Edward III in the name of the Black Prince. He struck there no less than five different gold denominations: *leopard, guiennois, chaise, pavillon and hardi. From 1539, when Francis I reformed the French mints, its distinguishing letter has been K; and following the defeat of Napoleon II and the establishment of the Third Republic in 1871, it remained the only French mint in operation outside Paris.

Borotinki

BOROTINKI Polish shillings in copper, struck between 1659 and 1663 by the million, and so called after the mint warden Titus Livius Borotini. Imposed as legal tender, they led to driving all gold and silver out of circulation (and most of it out of the country) for the better part of a century. The obverse showed the bust of King John Casimir (1648–68) facing right, the reverse a galloping horseman.

BORREL, ALFRED More famous for his many medals, this artist none the less deserves mention for certain coinages he executed at the turn of the century, notably for Martinique (1897), Crete (1900–1), Bulgaria (1901) and Morocco. The nickel 1-franc token for Martinique especially is a masterpiece of *fin de siècle* design.

BOSPORUS Not to be confused with the narrow strait joining the Black Sea and Sea of Marmora, in ancient times this was an independent kingdom, straddling the strait of Kertch along the shores of the northern Black Sea (present-day Crimea). A few early coins of Phangoria, its capital, show resemblances to the much more famous ones of *Panticapaeum. The main interest here lies from the 2nd to the 5th centuries A.D., when Bosporus struck the only gold coinage apart from that of imperial Rome, which recognised it as an ally rather than treating it as a colony. Obverses always show the bust of the ruling king, and on the reverses, that of the Roman emperor. The series degenerated into *electrum and finished up as little better than *billon.

BOSWELL, JAMES (1740–95)   The diarist tells us that he was "something of a virtuoso" (the 18th-century term for a lover of arts and antiques), and that he was in the habit of collecting a specimen of the coinage of every place he visited. Unfortunately, he tells us little else, except in connection with Corsica, where his comments on the coinage of Paoli are illuminating. He visited the mint at Murato and "got specimens of their different kinds of money in silver and copper, and was told that they hoped in a year or two to strike some gold coins". This is the only known reference to such a projected gold coinage of Corsica, which never materialised owing to Paoli's downfall. No less interesting are Boswell's comments on the earlier Corsican coinage of self-styled "Emperor" Theodore in 1736. "There was," he tells us, "such a curiosity over all Europe to have King Theodore's coins, that his silver pieces were sold at four zecchins each; and when the genuine ones were exhausted, imitations of them were made at Naples, and like the imitations of antiques, were bought up at a high price, and carefully preserved in the cabinets of the virtuosi." Collectors, it seems, do not change through the centuries.

Botdrager (Holland, William V), late 14th century

BOTDRAGER   A type of double *groot current in Holland, Gelderland and Utrecht during the second half of the 14th century, showing on the obverse a lion with a helmet in the shape of a pot (the literal translation of botdrager being "pot carrier").

BOULOGNE   A mint under Carausius (A.D. 286–93), who controlled the northern coast of Gaul as well as Britain at that time, having broken with Rome. There is no mintmark, which distinguishes these issues from those under Carausius at London (L) and Colchester (C). Boulogne was later (10th century onwards) a feudal mint under independent counts.

BOULTON, MATTHEW (1728–1809)   Birmingham manufacturer and perhaps the most celebrated private individual to be concerned with coinage and minting machinery. From 1786 onwards, he concentrated the greater part of his time and energies on building up the *Soho Mint, and apart from coins and medals produced there also sold his new machinery to Russia, Denmark and Spain. As an entrepreneur of genius he employed many of the finest artists of his time (*Droz, Küchler).

Matthew Boulton

BOUQUET SOU   A Canadian token of 1837 or thereabout, struck in large quantities for a great variety of users (though the originator was probably the Bank of Montreal). Around a hundred die varieties have been noted, differentiated by such minutiae as the number of leaves on the wreath (reverse type), permuted with the number of shamrocks, roses, thistles and ears of wheat in the "bouquet" of the obverse. The non-specialist collector will be concerned, however, with only three main types. The first is that bearing the words "Bank of Montreal" and the mis-spelling "un sous" (most probably by Birmingham die-sinkers). The second reads simply "Token Montreal" and has "un sou" correctly spelt. The third is known as the "star and cap" variety or the Rebellion Token. This was made for the Banque de Peuple and bears a star and a *liberty cap (half hidden to the left and right of the wreath) as symbols of independence. It is believed that the bank's accountant sympathised with the 1837 Canadian rebels and ordered these additions to be made.

BOVET, AUGUSTE   *Borg family.

BOVY FAMILY   A celebrated family of engravers and medallists of Geneva, Switzerland. They were in charge of the mint

Silver bracteates of St Gallen (*c.* 1200), Mulhausen (*c.* 1200), Erfurt (*c.* 1150) and Fulda (*c.* 1265). It can be seen that two somewhat different techniques were used in making these: one on a small flan with very high relief; the other on a broad and flat flan. The former are almost like buttons, the latter rather medallic and, in their intricacy of detail, miniature masterpieces of Gothic art

there from 1825 until it closed in 1848. Antoine Bovy (1795–1877) engraved almost the entire coinage from 1838 onwards, and later worked for the Swiss Federal Mint at Berne. It should, however, be particularly noted that the initials A.B. on 25, 10, 5 and 1-centime pieces of 1847 are not his (as might be supposed) but belong to Auguste Bovet, a far less renowned engraver. Bovy's coin dies are unsigned, with the exception of the 10- and 5-franc pieces of 1848, where the signature reads ANT. BOVY.

BOWRING, SIR JOHN   English civil servant and colonial administrator, who was one of the prime advocates of a decimal coinage for Great Britain in the mid-19th century. During his term of office at Hong Kong he had been impressed by the speed with which the Chinese managed their decimal calculations, aided only by a simple abacus. Bowring's unceasing lobbying was largely responsible for the adoption of the silver *florin as an experimental measure in 1848.

BOX MEDAL, BOX THALER   A favourite collector's item, known already from the 16th century but much more common in the 17th and especially so in the 18th. A medal (or coin) was split sectionally; the two halves were then hollowed out and a delicate screw thread added, so that the two halves now formed a shallow box. This was the box medal (or box Thaler) in its purest form: difficult to make, and difficult to open, too, except by firm and even pressure between the palms of two hands. They were a favourite means of smuggling messages, for in a good example the join would be practically imperceptible. Sometimes they enclosed a miniature, which might even be hand-coloured, though more often engraved. Later and more elaborate box medals were, in fact, fairly obvious small circular boxes, inset on both sides with medallic designs. Here, a favourite enclosure was a whole series of related miniatures: small, circular paper medallions (e.g. battles of Frederick the Great, of the Duke of Wellington, etc.).

Early box medals made of genuine Thalers and with original enclosures are now very rare and sought-after. Only a dated message or portrait miniature, of the same period as the coin itself, may be deemed more or less authentic.

BRACTEATE   A thin, uniface piece of metal (from Latin *bractea*) which, when stamped with a design, does not merely absorb it on the surface but reproduces it on the other side in reverse pattern. Such thin pieces are known from ancient Greek times: they have been found in tombs impressed with coin designs (such "shadow" coins being a gift to accompany the departed to the world of shadows). There is also very fine Viking jewellery of bracteate fabric; and though, again, this is not "coin" in the strict sense, it probably passed as currency among Scandinavian tribes before the 9th century A.D.

Bracteates came into their own as coinage from the 12th to the 14th centuries and as such appear to be a Germanic invention. They spread from Thuringia south as far as Bohemia and Switzerland, and east as far as Poland, but by and large remained a local phenomenon, the greater part of them being struck within the confines of what we know as Germany today. They were known in their own day as "Hohlpfennige" (hollow pennies) and circulated side by side with other pennies of orthodox fabric. Their fragility suggests that they had a purely local and temporary purpose—perhaps for payment of taxes—though documentary evidence is scant.

The finest bracteates belong to the century before the reintroduction of gold as a major currency medium (i.e. about 1130–1230) and represent early Gothic art in miniature in its finest form. Whereas other pennies of the time were crudely struck and purely utilitarian (we need only look at the *Tealby coinage of Henry II, for example), bracteates are decorative, commemorative pieces of great pictorial interest. The larger surface for a given weight of silver encouraged superlative artists quite literally to ''spread'' themselves, with sometimes astonishingly beautiful results. Themes are both religious and secular.

BRAMANTE, DONATO (1444–1514) Celebrated architect of the Italian Renaissance, said to have invented the *screw-press, and to have used it first for striking papal bulls. There is an undated medal of Bramante by *Caradosso, who (according to Vasari) struck it on Bramante's own press. It has, however, come down to us in cast form only.

BRANDT, HENRI FRANCOIS (1789–1845) Born in Switzerland, this engraver studied first in Paris (under *Droz) and later in Rome. From 1817 until his death he was chief engraver of coins and medals at the Prussian royal mint in Berlin, and is probably the most skilful artist ever to have worked there. Besides a great number of coins, medals, seals and decorations of Prussia, he also cut dies for certain Hanoverian coins from 1840–45, and for the principalities of Anhalt and Saxony.

BRASHER DOUBLOON A gold coin struck in 1787 in New York by Ephraim Brasher, goldsmith. Only six are known, of which four are in public collections. This is probably the most sought-after coin in the whole of the USA series; and its price, were one of the two specimens still remaining in private hands ever to come on the market, is anyone's guess.

The coin's weight and value were roughly equivalent to that of the Spanish *doubloon ($16). It showed on its obverse the sun rising behind a mountain, on its reverse the American eagle with the punch-mark EB on the eagle's breast or to the left of it. There is an even rarer half-doubloon, of which only a unique specimen is known today.

BRASS The only extensive use of this metal in coinage before the 20th century was by the Chinese: though their coins are generally said to be cast in bronze, they are more frequently of brass (i.e. containing 30% zinc).

BRASS FARTHING There was never any such coin, and the precise numismatic meaning of the expression ''not worth a brass farthing'' must remain open to conjecture. We find it first used by Erasmus with regard to the profitability of his Chair of Greek at Cambridge, 1506–9. Since there were no farthings, brass or other, in circulation at that time, he may well have been referring to the Nuremberg *jetons, of which a great number had found their way into English monasteries by that time, and which the uninitiated or illiterate might well mistake for coinage of some kind.

BREECHES MONEY A popular and slightly derogatory (perhaps Cavalier?) term applied to coins of the Commonwealth (1649–60), the two joined shields showing some resemblance to a pair of breeches.

Breeches money

BREITER THALER *broad Thaler.

BRENET, NICHOLAS GUY ANTOINE (1773–1846) French coin engraver and medallist, whose main activity falls in the Napoleonic era. He was responsible for more than fifty of the official medals executed at the Paris Medal Mint under the supervision of *Denon, and also cut the dies for Napoleon's head as adopted for the coinage from 1804 onwards (*laureate head from 1807), with the legend NAPOLEON EMPEREUR. He lived long enough to celebrate in a medal the return of Napoleon's remains from St Helena (1840).

BRETON, PIERRE NAPOLEON (1858–1917) Canadian dealer, collector and numismatist who published in 1894 a general catalogue of Canadian coins, tokens and paper money on which all subsequent and more detailed studies are based. His listings of Canadian trade tokens were particularly thorough.

BREZIN, MICHEL (1755–1828) French coining engineer, who worked at the Paris Mint and *c.* 1792 made a number of patterns demonstrating his method of striking coins in a collar, with edge-marking device.

BRICK TEA A currency widely used in China and Tibet for about 900 years, until the middle of the 19th century. The tea was compressed into blocks (mixed generally with some wood shavings to make it more durable), and the standard unit, weighing approximately 2½ pounds, was valued at 1 tael. Bricks were indented (not unlike bars of chocolate today) to make it easy to break them up for small change. The value and the name of the issuing bank were impressed on each segment.

BRILLEN-DUKAT An exceedingly rare ducat in the Danish series (with equally rare half), struck in 1647 under Christian IV. The coin is interesting for a variety of reasons, quite apart from the prominent pair of spectacles which give it its name. It was struck from a small amount of gold extracted from Norwegian silver ore by the King himself (with the aid of his mintmaster Christian Herbach) at Rosenborg castle. And its *legend may be read in two different ways. VIDE MIRA:DOMI: may be freely translated as "see what wonders may happen at home"; but if we regard the stops as abbreviation signs, the legend would run VIDE MIRABILIA DOMINI, i.e. "see the wonders of the Lord".

BRILLENTHALER This variety of Thaler was struck by Duke Julius of Brunswick-Lüneberg from 1586–9 at his Goslar and Wolfenbüttel mints. The spectacles (Brillen) can be seen hanging from the arm of the "Wild Man", together with a skull and an hour-glass.

BRIOT, NICHOLAS (1580–1646) The most famous of a family of engravers, active in France from *c.* 1606–25 and in England thereafter. He was a tireless advocate of mechanical striking processes; but his enthusiasm outstripped his mechanical skill, for it cannot really be claimed that the much-vaunted "improvements" with which he tried to impress the French mint authorities (by means of both patterns and controversial pamphlets) show any advance on what had been done at the *Moulin des Étuves as early as the 1550s or by *Meystrell at the Tower Mint in the 1560s.

After endless battles at the Paris Mint, he found a sympathetic patron in Charles I (probably inspired by his French wife, Henrietta Maria) and was at first employed purely as a medallist. Here he is important for introducing to England the technique of edge-inscription invented by Aubin *Olivier in 1551, a technique which Briot used on Charles I's Scottish coronation medal. It is surprising, but none the less a fact, that no edge-inscribed patterns for English or Scottish coinage by Briot exist, though he used the technique on all his French patterns.

Whatever one's views on Briot as a mechanician, he stands in the front rank as an engraver and produced work of unsurpassed delicacy for both the English and Scottish coinage. He proved a faithful servant to Charles I, active not only at the London and Edinburgh mints but also (during the Civil War) at York and probably Oxford. Part of his difficulties with the Paris Mint authorities was certainly due to his fondness for taking French leave: Forrer (*Biographical Dictionary of Medallists) records him as being active for the Duke of Lorraine and the Duchess of Montpensier, among others, at a good half-dozen mints.

To collect Briot in depth today would be an expensive hobby. All his patterns are dear, the French ones prohibitively so. Even the Tower Mint regular issues are by no means cheap. "Best Buys" are undoubtedly the York and Edinburgh mint issues. All his medals are desirable, with the "Dominion of the Sea" one probably holding pride of place. His Scottish *unite is particularly fine. But it would perhaps be true to say that he was always slightly hampered by the exigencies of practical coin design, and that his best work is in the field of *patterns, medals, jetons and even coin weights.

BRIOT CROWN   Named after the French engraver (see entry above) who designed it for the coinage he struck with his own machinery for Charles I, 1631–2. It is a particularly fine piece showing the King on horseback (reverse: crowned shield). There are several rare and expensive *patterns for the same issue.

BRIQUET   *vuurijzer.

BRISTOL   An English mint since Anglo-Saxon times, from Aethelred II onwards, and a Norman and Plantagenet mint until Edward I. It also operated for short periods under Edward IV, Henry VIII, Edward VI and during the Civil War (1643–5); and it was one of the mints for the great recoinage under William III, 1696–7.

BRISTOL TOWN TOKENS   Although the great token periods fell in the 17th and the 18th centuries (as described under heading *token), Bristol could boast of a farthing one during Queen Elizabeth I's reign. England's second city, as it then was, felt the shortage of small change more keenly than most; and since the unofficial tradesmen's tokens were often forged or simply disowned, in 1577 the Corporation asked to be allowed to stamp its own guaranteed issue. The Privy Council gave its permission quickly and, although the pieces are undated, contemporary documents show that £15-worth were issued in January 1578. By 1583 there were well over 100,000 of these tokens in circulation. They are almost square in shape, but with a circular device on both sides: obverse = tower and ship; reverse = C.B. This is the first such purely local coinage, not to be confused with regal coinages struck at many medieval town mints, or with ecclesiastical ones such as York and Durham.

BRITAIN, ANCIENT   The earliest coinage which can be attributed to Britain is the *tin money, imitated from types used on coins struck at *Marseilles. On the obverse is shown a representation of Apollo and on the reverse is a charging bull. Following the first Belgic invasion of Britain in about 75 B.C., coins based on those types shown on the gold stater of Philip of Macedon became current in the south. The second Belgic invasion (after Caesar's reconnaissance in 55 B.C.) brought the Atrebates and Regni tribes from Gaul, who also issued imitation staters and a quarter-stater. The first inscribed coins are those of Commius, the Atrebatic chief. Later coins, by Eppilus and Verica, are of silver and based on contemporary Roman denarii.

North-west of London the Catuvellauni tribe struck further

Britain, Ancient: Gold stater of Cunobelin (Colchester, A.D. 10–40). This king served as a model for Shakespeare's Cymbeline

variants of the Macedonian stater. Inscribed coins of this tribe bear the names of Tasciovanus and his son Cunobelin (Shakespeare's Cymbeline) among others. The bronze coinage of Cunobelin also shows a strong Roman influence. In Kent the Trinovantes produced imitation staters, a number of which bear the name of Addedomarus.

In the Fen country the Iceni coined both gold staters and silver coins, some inscribed. The Brigantes in Yorkshire issued gold staters in about A.D. 50, with silver coins bearing chieftains' names later the same century.

Further west, there is evidence of only two tribes. In what is today partly Dorset and partly Somerset, the Durotriges made some exceedingly crude imitation staters and a series of cast bronze coins; while late in the 1st century B.C. the Dobuni (Oxfordshire and Gloucestershire as far as the Severn valley) struck both gold and silver.

Places of coinage are largely indeterminate. The only mints that can be definitely assigned are Calleva Atrebatum (the Silchester of more recent times), under Eppilus; Camulodunum (the modern Colchester), from Tasciovanus onwards; and Verulamium (St Albans), again from the time of Tasciovanus. It is, incidentally, on a coin of Calleva under Eppilus that we first find the word REX on a British coin.

BRITAIN CROWN A gold coin to the value of 5 shillings introduced by James I in 1604. The name derives from the inscription, the first to refer to the joining of the kingdoms of England and Scotland: HENRICUS ROSAS REGNA JACOBUS (Henry unites the roses, James the kingdoms). There is an allusion here, too, to the *Crown of the Double Rose of Henry VIII. The value of the coin was raised to 5s. 6d. in 1611.

BRITANNIA (on coins) The figure of Britannia, seated with spear and shield, is familiar to everyone from recent copper coinage and was, by popular demand, retained in the new British decimal coinage on the 50p piece. The origin of the type goes back to Roman days when two emperors, Hadrian (A.D. 117–38) and Antoninus Pius (A.D. 138–61) chose to commemorate their British dominions on coins. Their type closely resembles the modern one, first introduced on farthings and halfpennies of Charles II. This was said to be modelled on Charles's favourite mistress, Frances Stewart (later Duchess of Richmond) but the evidence—based largely on Pepys's reference to a medal said to represent that lady—is inconclusive.

BRITANNIA GROAT A coin introduced during the reign of William IV in 1836. There had been no 4-pence piece in the English coinage since the days of Charles I (except in the *Maundy Money); and its reintroduction now was on the initiative of Joseph Hume, who argued its need in Parliament as omnibuses and hansom cabs began to proliferate in London's streets. The coin, which owes its name to the reverse type, was unpopular with cabbies because of its small size: they promptly nicknamed it "Joey". None the less, it proved useful, for it continued to be struck almost annually until 1855. A final striking occurred in 1888, with the jubilee head of Queen Victoria on the obverse; but this was for colonial use only, £2,000 nominal value being struck for the government of British Guiana.

BRITISH COLUMBIA *New Westminster Mint.

BRITISH MUSEUM One of the great collections of the world is housed here, behind a discreet mahogany door labelled Department of Coins and Medals. You must ring a bell for admittance,

Britannia on coins:

Sestertius of Hadrian

Dupondius of Antoninus Pius

and you will then find yourself in an ante-room, where you will be asked to sign the visitors' book with your name, address and precise nature of your enquiry. The Coin Room itself is behind strong steel grille doors. A member of the staff likely to be able to help you will appear and usher you into the inner sanctum, where you will be comfortably installed on the visitors' side of the huge horseshoe-shaped table that still effectively isolates you from any coin cabinet. That, however, is the limit of the formalities and precautions (at least visible), and anything you may wish to study will now be brought to you. Nor do the facilities end here; you may consult any book or periodical in the library, make drawings, ask for photographs to be taken or even obtain plaster casts (the department keeps a "bank" of those commonly required). Finally the staff will always be glad to advise you where else to pursue your researches if the department's holdings are unexpectedly weak in your particular field of interest.

It should be emphasized that this is not a "money museum" in the wider sense: primitive currencies form no part of the collections and only recently (1979) has a collection of paper money been commenced. Nor is it a place for the casual visitor; however, displays of coins are featured in the galleries of the relevant departments, and in the "2000 Years of British Coins and Medals" gallery. Pieces may be left for authentication, but not for valuation, for which a reputable dealer or auctioneer should be approached.

The basis of this, perhaps the greatest of the world's great collections, was laid by bequests by Sir Robert Cotton in 1710 and Sir Hans Sloane in 1753. The catalogue of Greek coins alone, published from 1873 onwards and still incomplete, will run to over thirty volumes.

BRITISH TRADE DOLLAR   A coin specifically created for trade in the Far East, where silver dollars (Spanish, American, Mexican, etc.) have always been the favourite form of currency. The coin was struck at intervals from 1895 to 1935 at Bombay, Calcutta and London mints. Though the main type did not change throughout this period, there are more than thirty varieties of mint- and date-marks (or fifty-two if we include various proofs, some struck in gold).

There is a Chinese copy of this coin, almost identical save for lower silver content and the inscription FOR JEWELLERY instead of ONE DOLLAR. Doubtless it enjoyed popularity for this purpose.

BRITISH WEST AFRICA   *ackey, one-tenth of a penny, two shillings.

BROAD   A 20-shilling gold piece, engraved by Thomas *Simon for Cromwell in 1656. It is generally classified as a *pattern rather than currency.

BROAD THALER   Commemorative Thalers were often struck on a broader *flan than normal, to make the most of design possibilities. Such coins should not be confused with *multiple Thalers, for they were of the same weight as normal pieces (being, of course, thinner as well as bigger).

BROCKAGE   The technical term used to describe accidental overstriking of one coin by another. It does not generally occur with individually hammer-struck coins, only in a coining machine if one coin fails to eject before the next one is struck. In a more general sense, the term has been used in the past for any misstruck coin: there is even a reference to "brockage" in the coining of Elizabethan sixpences, suggesting an etymology derived from "broken".

BRONZE Given man's long tradition of working in bronze for arms, implements and ornaments, it is not surprising that bronze was also among man's first monetary media (though perhaps not coins, strictly speaking). If we accept China's claim that coinage originated earlier there than in the West, then bronze is certainly the world's most ancient coinage metal, stretching in an unbroken sequence over 3,000 years. In the West, the Romans had a bronze coinage for almost 300 years before they turned to silver (*aes rude, aes grave and aes signatum): while even today the alloy of aluminium-bronze is one of the most used for small change.

Bronze coins should never be cleaned, their value (especially in the Roman series) depending to a large extent on their patina. This is an incrustation resulting from oxidisation, and may be caused by soil, moisture, changes of atmosphere, etc. The tinge given to the coin thereby is often greenish, but the finest patina scintillates with a variety of colours.

A very rare bronze, perhaps the most beautiful of all, is found in certain coins of the Chinese Emperor Hui-Tsung (1101–26). He was a collector of early bronze vessels, and as he would only admit flawless pieces to his collection, he ordered the destruction of others, the metal of which was then used to cast his coins. Such pieces show what looks almost like an enamelled surface, with tints of green, blue and even cinnamon red.

BRUCHER, ANTOINE This artist was appointed engraver at the *Moulin des Étuves, Paris, in 1558 and held the post until his death ten years later. He is responsible for some fine medals and jetons (especially of Charles IX of France). It is less well known (but incontrovertible from documents in the French national archives) that he cut dies for the coinage of 1561 of Mary Queen of Scots in her first widowhood. One can only regret that these dies were taken back by *Acheson to Edinburgh instead of being struck (as were certain Scottish patterns of 1553) on the new and sophisticated Paris machinery.

BRUCHSAL, ALEXANDER Flemish engraver at the Tower Mint during the reign of Henry VII from 1494. He is responsible for the introduction of Renaissance-type portraiture on English coinage from 1504 onwards (*testoon). The realism of this portrait of the King is in marked contrast to previous purely conventional representations of kingship and remains unexcelled in delicacy of craftsmanship.

BRUNSWICK Capital of the dukedom of the same name. Its importance as a mint dates from the time of Henry the Lion in the 12th century, who struck many fine *bracteates here. Among these there is one of special English interest: that celebrating Henry's marriage with the "Empress" Matilda. The mint continued in operation until 1859 and produced many pieces in the *Anglo-Hanoverian series, including the only known pieces of the later King George IV with his title as Prince Regent (GEORGIUS D.G. PRINC.REGENS) while acting as regent to Duke Karl during the latter's minority (TVTOR.NOM.CAROLI.DVIS).

BU A Japanese coin (or rather, unit of coinage, ichibu meaning 1 bu), the quarter of a *ryo and the quadruple of the *shu. First introduced in 1599, it was a small rectangular disc, first of base gold, later of silver. In one form or another it continued in circulation until the introduction of Japan's modern coinage during the early 1870s.

BUDÉ, GUILLAUME (1467–1540) The greatest French scholar of the Renaissance, who as "maître de la librairie" under Francis I helped to lay the foundations of what is today the

Japanese bu, *c.* 1837

Bibliothèque Nationale and was one of the guiding spirits of the Collège de France. As a numismatist, he was outstanding in his time. His analysis of Greek and Roman coinages, under the general title *De Asse et Partibus Ejus*, went through no less than seventeen editions from 1514 to 1550, and was also translated into Italian and Portuguese.

BUER, ABEL Die-sinker of New Haven, Connecticut, during the late 18th century. His principal known productions are the *African head and *Fugio cents.

BUFFALO NICKEL The Buffalo or Indian Head Nickel designed by James E. Fraser features the profile of an Indian head on the obverse and the likeness of the American bison Black Diamond from the New York Zoological Gardens on the reverse. Through the years many Indians have claimed to have been one of the three models he used in forming the obverse design. They were, in fact, chiefs John Tree, Iron Tail and Two Moons.

The coin was struck regularly from 1913–38, most of these years at Denver and San Francisco mints as well as Philadelphia. The run includes one of the three rare overdates occurring in 20th century US coinage (1918D over 17). It also includes a D over S mintmark variety (1938), and one of the most popular mint error coins, the three-legged buffalo of 1937, from the Denver Mint. This error was created when the die was over-polished in the area of the buffalo's front right leg, making it disappear in the striking.

BUGATTO, ZANETTO Milanese sculptor, who around 1470 modelled for Duke Galeazzo Maria Sforza what was probably the most magnificent series of gold medallions ever commissioned. None survives, but we know that they were executed, for there is a record of the Genoa Mint showing that one of them was melted down there in 1505. Its gold content was approximately 36 kilograms, the equivalent of 10,288 ducats. Ten such medallions were ordered by the Duke, each showing his own bust on the obverse and that of his consort, Bona of Savoy, on the reverse.

BUGSLAWER A popular name for large silver coins of Bogeslaus X (1471–1523), Duke of Stettin and Pomerania. This is obviously a corruption of the Duke's name, which these particular coins bore, as distinct from others inscribed merely DUX POMERANIAE.

BULL AND HORSEMAN COINS A common coinage of the Rajput dynasties of Hindustan and central India, first introduced by the Hindu kings of Kabul and Ohind around the middle of the 9th century A.D. The obverse type shows a recumbent bull and the reverse a mounted horseman. This coinage quickly became debased in metal and degenerate in style, but none the less outlasted the dynasty and was still being copied in the time of the Muslim Sultan Muhammad-ibn-Sam towards the end of the 12th century. (*Delhiwala.)

BULLET MONEY This globular—or perhaps better described as skull-shaped—coinage was the principal coinage of Siam from *c.* 1350 until 1861 (when Western-type coinage machinery was installed at Bangkok). Even after that date it continued to circulate widely, not being finally demonetised until 1904.

The bullet money, as it is commonly called, has a slight indentation on the top, in which are generally to be found two stamps: one signifying the mint, the other a government symbol. But small denominations may do with only one stamp occasionally, and large ones have been known with as many as six, often *countermarks of banking houses. The coinage is known in both gold and silver, with some overlapping of denominations (*tical).

Basically, all these coins are weights, made of cast silver bars cut into pieces of the required length, then bent back on themselves under heat to form the almost globular shape.

An attempt to classify the various issues from medieval times to 1782 (beginnings of the Mongkut dynasty) was made by Le May (*The Coinage of Siam*) as long ago as 1932: he identified and sought to attribute 45 main bat markings and another 15 seen on smaller units, in rough chronological order. But much of this remains conjecture, whereas the markings from 1782 are fully documented.

BULLION   Uncoined metal, usually gold or silver, in the shape of bars, plates, ingots or other regular forms. It is still the preferred currency on which governments rely for their "reserves", and in which large international monetary settlements are made.

BULLION PIECES   Coins, or coin-like objects, in gold or silver, that state the fineness and weight of metal content rather than any particular denomination. They are most common at times and in places where a regular mint is lacking, e.g. siege and other emergency money. They have, however, also been struck in our own time by certain government mints after gold and silver have been officially demonetised. Thus Mexico, when it reissued the 50-peso gold piece of 1921–31 in 1943, omitted the denomination, stating merely gold weight and fineness; and the same country in 1949 brought out an "onza" of pure silver. Other examples are the *tolas issued by various Indian banks, and gold pieces struck for Saudi Arabia by the Philadelphia Mint in 1945–7, to the weight and fineness of 1 and 4 English sovereigns. Today's best known bullion piece is the South African Krugerrand, which contains precisely 1 troy ounce of fine gold and is marked accordingly.

BUNGTOWN COPPER   A popular name for bad imitations of English halfpennies, which circulated in large quantities, throughout the north-eastern states of American colonies (especially Pennsylvania) during the latter part of the 18th century.

BUN PENNY   The second type of Queen Victoria's "young head" pennies and the first in bronze (the earlier type having been struck in copper). It was issued during most years from 1860–94, and the popular name is self-explanatory from the Queen's hairstyle.

Bun penny

BURGOS   A mint of Castile and Leon since the reign of Alfonso VII (1126–57). It adopted the *mintmark B at the beginning of the *legend, and retained this after becoming one of the seven regal mints of Spain under Ferdinand and Isabella from 1497 onwards.

BURG TYPE PENNY   A rare Anglo-Saxon penny of the reign of Edward the Elder (A.D. 899–924), showing a gateway or tower.

BUSHELL, THOMAS   Owner of silver mines in North Wales, who in 1637 obtained permission from Charles I to operate a mint at Aberystwyth. Bushell's personal *privy mark was an open book, which we find after 1642 on Shrewsbury coinage and from 1643 at Oxford. He was a faithful royalist, who closed the Welsh mint soon after the outbreak of the Civil War and helped the King financially. The Welsh plumes seen on Aberystwyth, Shrewsbury and Oxford coins alike refer to the source of the silver from which they were struck.

BUTTERFLY THALER   Struck by Augustus III of Poland in 1733 to commemorate the death of his father Augustus II. The butterfly seen on the reverse is more in the shape of a moth, with three overlapping sets of wings to symbolise birth, life and death.

BUTTONS The links between coin-making and button manu-facture go back (at any rate in England) to the end of the 17th century, when Isaac Newton successfully quashed a petition by Gerard Bovey, button-maker, for the return of certain "engines" impounded by the mint. Bovey had imported them from Nuremberg in 1695 and claimed they could not possibly be used for any other purpose than the making of buttons; Newton (who was at that time warden of the mint) held that the presses could be used for coinage.

Gold solidus of Anastasius, A.D. 491–518

He was doubless right. *Boulton in Birmingham, *Mathieu in Lyon, *Roche in Dublin are but a few of the names that spring to mind of button-makers who turned to coinage. Some were more successful than others; but it is arguable that those most successful in button-making also made the best coins. Nor is this surprising, for the skill and elaboration that went into the design and cutting of 18th-century button dies must have made the cut-ting of coin dies look relatively simple.

BYZANTINE COINAGE Christian symbolism on coinage begins with Constantine the Great after A.D. 312 (*christogram); and since the same ruler also introduced the *solidus and switch-ed the centre of power from Rome to his new capital of Con-stantinople (founded A.D. 330) we may well see the beginnings of Byzantine coinage here. But many more changes were to take place before we may talk of a distinctive Byzantine type, which is characterised by a formalism quite different from Greek and Roman realism. The characteristic facing type was not firmly established before Justinian I (A.D. 527–65), who also intro-duced a dating system (based on his regnal year) in A.D. 538. Prior to this, Anastasius had in A.D. 498 introduced a new bronze coinage (*nummium); this, and the gold, made up the principal currency for almost 1,000 years. Other landmarks are the introduction of the *hexagram under Heraclius (A.D. 610–41) and the appearance of Christ's portrait under Justinian II (A.D. 685–95). The first attempt at Christian iconography on coinage was shortlived (iconoclasm took over for a century and a half), and it is not until the latter half of the 9th century that the picture of Christ, and later the Virgin, appears more frequent-ly. The end of the 10th century witnesses the beginning both of a long series of *anonymous bronzes and the new gold *nomisma. Later history is one of growing debasement both of metal and style. Thus one of the last Byzantine coins of all is a dreadfully crude one of that very emperor John VIII Palaeologus who was so superbly modelled by *Pisanello in 1438: a meeting of East and West, of a dying and a new art.

Bronze 40 nummia of Justinian I, c. A.D. 538

Enormous strides have been made in the study of Byzantine coins over the past twenty years. Perspicacious collectors would do well to turn to these "ikons in miniature" before they catch up in popularity and price with Greek and Roman series. Gold is, in fact, doing so rapidly. The much undervalued bronze is perhaps worthy of special attention, and there are fascinating sidelines such as *coin weights, which in the Byzantine series are particularly varied and decorative. Copies of Byzantine types, in Italy, Arabia, Russia and other countries, are a study and collec-ting field in their own right.

Messrs Seaby of London have recently published *Byzantine Coins and their Values*, a priced collectors' guide listing 2,260 types. This is the first such detailed catalogue to appear in any country or language for the non-specialist, and takes account of

Silver hexagram of Heraclius, A.D. 610–41

Gold solidus of Justinian II (1st reign, A.D. 685-717)—the first coin to show an effigy of Christ

all the specialist research referred to above. The useful introduction has chapters on denominations, mints, types, inscriptions, etc. The author, David R. Sear, has done a superb job of classification and condensation, and his remarks on "Collecting Byzantine Coins" (pp. 12–13) are especially valuable. With this fine tool to hand, interest in the series will doubtless accelerate. Also *Alexandria, Antioch, Carthage, Cherson, Constantinople, Cyprus, Cyzicus, Ravenna, Rome and Syracuse for productions of individual mints.

BYZANTINE DENOMINATIONS   *follis, hexagram, semissis, solidus, tremissis.

BYZANTINE MINTS   *Byzantine coinage.

Silver miliaresion of Leo IV, A.D. 775-80

Gold nomisma (scyphate fabric—see text) of Isaac II, 1185-95

Byzantine coins: Just a few coins from this immense series, dating from the 5th to the 12th centuries

C

CADIÈRE A silver coin of Dauphiné during the reigns of Charles V and VI only. It is similar in type to the *carlin or *gigliato but lacks the lilies in the field on the reverse and is of a higher weight and value. The same name was later given to a very rare gold coin of Anne of Britanny, which is the first coin in any of the French series to bear a date (1498). The etymology of the word is obscure (also *delphinal types).

CALAIS An English mint on the soil of France, from 1363–1412 and again from 1424–8, then sporadically only until about 1440. Both gold and silver were struck here. The gold coins are particularly plentiful, the *noble being distinguished by a large C in the centre of the reverse and a flag at the stern of the ship on the obverse.

CALCUTTA A mint under the East India Company (Bengal) from 1765, when the seat of government was shifted here from Madras. It remains a mint of the Republic of India to this day and has, on occasions, struck coinages for other parts of Britain's past empire (e.g. Australia). The early coinage has the peculiarity of ''frozen'' dates and bearing the mintmark of Murshidabad; only the records of the East India Company make clear how much was struck where, and when.

CAMELIO, VITTORE GAMBELLO (1460–1539) Renaissance medallist and coin engraver, who worked at the Venice Mint and the Papal Mint at Rome. He is important for being among the first to cut dies on steel, and was as famous for his contemporary medallic portraits (including the painters Gentile and Giovanni Bellini) as for his imitations of the antique.

CAMPAIGN MEDALS These collectors' objects uneasily straddle the fence between numismatics and militaria, and as such can receive only summary treatment here. The chief difference between the collector of coins and/or commemorative medals on the one hand and campaign medals on the other is that the latter is really much more concerned with the person (or persons) to whom the award was made than with the object itself. Thus—to take but one example—a Trafalgar medal in itself is valuable, but a *display* of Trafalgar medals including one for a member of every ship's crew that took part in the battle is every campaign medal collector's dream. Naturally, too, medals awarded to members of Nelson's flagship *Victory* will command a premium. And the Victoria Cross, as the highest and rarest award of all, is always dear, even if the recipient has no other claim to fame.

CAMPAIGN MONEY *emergency money.

CAMPEN *Kampen.

CANADA For early history, *French-Canadian coinage. From 1763, the British did little, if anything, to alleviate the chronic shortage of Canadian circulating currencies; very largely it was trappers who supplied a medium for exchange into food and other necessities of life via beaver pelts. Not until 1832 were

Canada:

Canoe Dollar, 1937. *(Photo courtesy R. Lobel)*

Canadian Constitution Dollar, 1982. *(Photo courtesy R. Lobel)*

halfpenny tokens (with the head of George IV and the inscription PROVINCE OF UPPER CANADA) issued for Ontario. From 1670, the country had been largely administered (in so far as that was necessary) by the Hudson's Bay Company, whose non-metallic currencies are a study on their own. A concern calling itself the Canadian Banking Company issued a 5-shilling note in 1792, but nothing seems to be known about it. From 1837 onwards, there were bilingual (French and English) tokens issued by the Bank of *Montreal, and of Quebec (also *bouquet sou); various tokens are also known to have been issued in New Brunswick (which had a special reverse type—a sailing ship) and Nova Scotia, and penny and halfpenny tokens exist for the combined provinces of Upper and Lower Canada. A decimal coinage was introduced by 1858 (5, 10, 25 and 50 cents in silver) with the head of Queen Victoria and the word CANADA under the bust; official cents and half-cents followed in 1861. With the foundation of the Dominion of Canada in 1867, the various provincial issues ceased and were replaced by silver denominations to the values of 5, 10, 25 and 50 cents; the 1-cent piece was of bronze. No dollar was struck until 1935 (*Canoe Dollar); but 5- and 10-dollar gold pieces were struck at the *Ottawa Mint during 1912–14, while gold sovereigns of the English type (apart from the mint letter C) were also coined there from 1908–19. Although the silver dollar appeared late, there have been many types since 1935, and gold has again been extensively struck since 1967 (the "Maple Leaf" coins at .999 fine being the purest gold coins available anywhere, as good as bullion bars). The modern series has many commemoratives, including one of the few showing an old steam engine (1981, celebrating the 100th anniversary of the Canadian Pacific Railway). Also *Newfoundland Mint, Prince Edward Island.

CANADIAN TRADE DOLLARS A new and varied field of coin collecting, of special interest to enthusiasts in North America. These dollars are local issues only, but none the less legal tender within their prescribed boundaries and time limits (which may range from one week to one year). Around 500 different types are known from over 170 municipalities since 1960, when the first such piece was issued to celebrate the Golden Jubilee of Prince Rupert (British Columbia) in 1960. About a dozen mints throughout Canada have been responsible for their striking, among them the Royal Canadian Mint in *Ottawa and the *Sherritt Private Mint in Fort Saskatchewan, Alberta. There have also been, but much more occasionally, 25-cent and 50-cent pieces, and notes of values from 25 cents to $3. Most coins are in nickel but proofs in silver or even gold are known for some issues. To rank as a coin and not just a medal, the piece should carry the inscription "Dollar", "Souvenir Dollar" or "Good for One Dollar" and (usually) the expiry date, although this is missing on some early issues which nevertheless rank as currency. The first general catalogue was published by Charlton Press of Toronto in 1980; it has a useful checklist of issuing authorities but is often inadequate in details of mints, mintage figures, etc. (except for the Sherritt Private Mint). European collectors are most likely to want those which reflect their own interests, e.g. mining Thalers: the Klondike dollar of 1968, showing a miner panning for gold, and a similar Dawson, Yukon Territory piece of 1973.

CANDAREEN A unit in the Chinese decimal system, being the 10th part of the *mace and the 100th part of the *tael. The Chinese dollar is inscribed 7 mace 2 candareen.

CANOE DOLLAR   The Canadian silver dollar, as first struck for the 25th anniversary of George V's reign. It takes its name from the reverse design which—with minor variations—continued to be struck until 1952. (See illustration on page 58.)

CANOPY TYPE PENNY   The third type of penny among those struck for William the Conqueror. The facing head shows him wearing what can perhaps be best described as a kind of miniature shrine.

CARADOSSO, CRISTOFANO (c. 1452–1527)   Perhaps the most important goldsmith of his age, Caradosso's active career spanned the years 1474–1525. He worked at the mints of Milan, Mantua and Rome. His Milanese period includes the engraving of most of the finest coins of the Sforza family, and of those of Louis XII when the French monarch occupied the city. He founded the Guild of Roman Goldsmiths in 1509, and it was while at Rome that he made what was probably the first medal to be struck on the screw-press: a portrait of its inventor, the architect Bramante.

CARAMBOLE   Name given to an *écu struck under Louis XIV for Flanders during 1685–6, only at the Lille Mint.

CARAT   A way of expressing the fineness of gold (24 carat being pure gold, 18 carat 75%, etc.). Not being a very accurate measure, it has been largely superseded in today's numismatic reference works, which generally quote gold content as a proportion of "1,000 fine". Thus the English sovereign of 22 carat gold is more accurately expressed as .916 fine.

The carat was also a small silver coin struck in Cyprus and Rhodes under the Lusignan dynasty from the late 13th century onwards. It was current in the Near East for one-eighth of the *asper, and equally accepted in western parts of the Mediterranean as one-sixteenth of the *gigliato.

CARLIN   Denominations in both gold and silver, which took their name (under an ordinance of 1278) from Charles I of Anjou. They were struck at Naples, Brindisi and Messina for the Kingdom of the Two Sicilies. The gold coin (carlin d'or) is also known as the *salute, from its type (showing the Virgin Mary and the Angel of the Annunciation). Struck in pure gold, without alloy of any kind (in which it resembled French gold coins of the same period), it was only made during the reigns of Charles I and Charles II, i.e. until 1305.

Gold carlin of Charles of Anjou, struck in Sicily, c. 1280

The silver coin (carlin d'argent) was modelled on the French *gros tournois, but saw several metamorphoses from the time of Charles II onwards (*gigliato, alfonsino, coronato). In one form or another this silver coin survived in southern Italy until the time of Francis II of Bourbon (1859) and became widely popular in other parts of the Mediterranean (Malta, Provence, Bologna, etc.).

CARLISLE   A border town that was frequently raided by the Scots and struck coins for David I (1124–53) and his son Henry, Earl of Northumberland (d. 1152). Silver *sterlings or pennies only are known. During the English Civil War, *siege pieces were struck at Carlisle from October 1644 to June 1645; these are octagonal in shape and to the value of 3 shillings and 1 shilling.

CAROLIN   Two gold coins and two silver coins in the Swedish series have been given this name. The gold appeared under Charles IX in the early 17th century (value 16 *Marks) and under Charles XV during 1868–72 (value 10 French francs). The silver was struck under Charles XI from 1664 (value 2 Marks) and again, during 1718 only, the last year of Charles XII's reign. Of this, there are also multiples of 2 and 4 caroliner.

CAROLOUS (or KAROLUS) *dizain.

CAROLUS D'OR Introduced by Charles V for the Spanish Netherlands in 1515, this is one of the gold coins which gave the *florin type a bad name. Its gold content was less than two-thirds its full weight.

CAROLUS GULDEN A silver denomination introduced by Charles V for the Netherlands in 1543. It was a crown-size piece to the value of 20 *patards, i.e. the equivalent of the *carolus d'or.

CARPENTRAS The town of Carpentras, in the South of France (not far from *Avignon), was a mint of the Popes during the first half of the 14th century—more precisely, until the town of Avignon itself was purchased in 1348 by Pope Clement VI. It was the principal town of the Comtat Venaissin, acquired by the Popes as early as 1274.

CARSON CITY *United States mints.

CARTHAGE The great Phoenician colony in North Africa struck coinage based on Greek types and was later active as both a Roman and a Byzantine mint. The splendid early coins are much influenced by those of Sicily, which Carthage invaded in 410 B.C. Predominant types are the horse and the lion, often with a palm-tree as reverses, with the head of Persephone on the obverse. As a Byzantine mint, Carthage continued to be active until it fell to the Arabs during the reign of Justinian II in A.D. 706.

Carthage: Silver tetradrachm, 4th century B.C.

From the time of Heraclius (A.D. 610–41), the gold *solidus struck here was of a thick, dumpy *fabric, though the coin remained of full weight and gold content value. In fact, it was no different from the *semissis and *tremissis in diameter, but distinguished only by weight and thickness from the fractional denominations. The reason for this peculiar "globular" fabric remains obscure. Gold coinage struck here during the reign of Constans II (A.D 641–68) is specially extensive, with no less than seventeen main types of solidi known.

CARTHAGO NOVA Mint established in southern Spain after its conquest by Hamilcar in 237 B.C. Certain of its coins are believed to show the portrait first of Hamilcar, later of Hannibal, and finally (after its capture by the Romans in 209 B.C.) of the Roman general Scipio Africanus.

CARTWHEEL Name given to the heavy copper 2-penny piece, featuring a raised edge with *incuse inscription, struck by Matthew Boulton at his *Soho Mint in 1797. The name has been adopted in recent years for the quarterly periodical of the Birmingham Numismatic Society.

CASA DI SAN GIORGIO One of the earliest public banks, founded in 1408 in Genoa by a number of wealthy citizens, all substantial creditors of the state and determined to see that the state's financial affairs were run so as to safeguard their interests. This private supervision of public coffers (as it was initially) had, in later centuries, some quite remarkable consequences, among which deposit and giro systems and the invention of *banco money were fairly orthodox. More spectacular and unusual was the bank's readiness to forego normal interest rates and accept instead the right of taxing Genoese territories—or even accepting such territories by way of collateral security for long periods. Thus Corsica, Cyprus and parts of the Crimea were at various times virtually colonies of the Casa di San Giorgio, which ruled over them in every sense, not just financially. The bank's power and influence lasted until well into the 18th century.

CASALE Capital of the marquisate of Monteferrato in Italy, this town was ruled successively by the Paleologus and Gonzaga families from the 14th to the 17th centuries, with a very brief interregnum by Charles V (1533–6). There is much splendid gold and silver, and siege pieces of 1628–30.

CASH A word signifying ready money as opposed to credit, derived from French *caisse*, a box holding money. It is also the most common denomination of Chinese currency (the 1,000th part of the *tael), characterised by a hole in the centre for easy stringing and carrying. Such strings of cash are shown on early Chinese paper money. As a type remaining unchanged (except for inscriptions, mintmarks, etc.) for 2,000 years, Chinese cash is unique among the world's currencies.

CAVALLI, GIAN MARIA (d. after 1508) Coin engraver at Mantua from 1481, until called to the mint at Hall in Tyrol by the Emperor Maximilian I in 1506. The pieces he made there (e.g. of Maximilian and Bianca) were all of commemorative medallic character.

CAVALLO One of the Western world's first regular copper coinages, introduced by Ferdinand of Aragon in 1472 for the kingdom of Naples and Sicily. It takes its name from the reverse type, a horse. Multiples of 2, 3, 4, 6 and 9 cavalli are known—not surprisingly, for the unit was equivalent to only 1/200th of a ducat.

CAVALLOTTO A silver coin to the value of one *grosso, first issued by Louis XII of France in the town of Asti during its French occupation (1498–1513). The reverse shows St Secundus of Asti on horseback, carrying a church. There are a number of varieties (horse to right or left, trotting or galloping), all attractive and (like most of the Franco-Italian series) sought-after and expensive.

CAVINO, GIOVANNI (1500–70) Celebrated die engraver of Padua, who together with the scholar A. Bassiano "invented" a whole series of Roman coins and medallions. These are not really *counterfeits but should rather be classed as *fantasy coins, in the sense of free interpretations of ancient originals, and Renaissance works of art in their own right. Indeed, one comes across more counterfeit "paduans" than real ones! Many of Cavino's dies are today preserved in the Cabinet des Médailles at the Bibliothèque Nationale in Paris.

CAYENNE SOUS Struck for the colony of French Guiana in 1781 and 1782, these were *billon pieces to the value of 2 and 3 sous. There are also some earlier pieces, struck during the reign of Louis XV with a simple crowned C, for general circulation throughout the French colonies. British settlers in the West Indies would have none of these coins, referring to them as *"black dogs". For small change, they preferred to cut up the Spanish dollar (of fine silver) into as many as eight pieces (*cut money).

CEITIL Europe's first copper coinage in modern times, introduced under John I of Portugal in 1415. Its name is taken from the town of Ceuta captured that year. The coin's value was one-sixth of the *real and it was struck in a variety of types until 1560.

CELLINI, BENVENUTO (1500–71) Perhaps the most celebrated goldsmith and jeweller of the Renaissance, though few of his works in this genre are today authenticated (except the salt-cellar he made for Francis II of France, now in the Vienna Kunstmuseum). We are, however, well informed about his activities as a medallist and die-engraver, both through his rumbustious *Autobiography* and his *Treatise on Goldsmithing*. In the latter, he has several chapters describing the making of medals:

Cash of 1735, with the mint name in two languages (Chinese and Manchu) on the reverse

Double sou struck for Louis XVI, 1789

Ceitil (Manuel I of Portugal, 1495–1521)

casting, striking by hand with the hammer and—most important—by the newly invented screw-press. In the former, he mentions his activities as engraver of coins and medals to Popes Clement VII and Paul III, besides Alessandro de Medici at Florence. We may thus assign and identify most of his pieces, though all are unsigned.

CELTIC COINS The appreciation of Celtic coins still lags behind that of most others. Only slowly are numismatists realising that these objects cannot be dismissed as "barbaric" imitations of Greek or Roman models nor be judged by modern aesthetic standards. The closest parallel is perhaps that with Hindu sculpture, where the inspiration is also basically religious or mystical.

Unfortunately, written records of Celtic culture are so scarce that the symbolism of their coins is still largely a matter of guesswork. An inspired attempt has recently been made by L. Lengyel in his *Le Secret des Celtes*. Although not really meant for coin collectors it is indispensable for its many fine photographs.

Celtic coins: Bronze coin of Cunobelin (Colchester, A.D. 10–40)

CENT The cent is the 100th part of the *dollar wherever it is current. Countries using dollar currencies have included Canada, British Guiana, British Honduras and Danish West Indies, Cuba, Fiji, Hawaii, Hong Kong and China. It is also the 100th part of certain other decimal currencies not expressed in dollars. In Ceylon, Mauritius and the Seychelles 100 cents = 1 rupee, and in the Netherlands and Dutch East Indies they are equivalent to 1 florin or gulden.

There is a cent dated 1791 for Sierra Leone, anticipating both French and American decimal currencies by two years. But the date may well be fictitious and celebrate the foundation of the Sierre Leone Company rather than the first issue of coinage, which—it has been argued—probably took place only some years later.

The most famous cent is, of course, that of the USA, introduced in 1793. There are a great number of varieties, but the main categories are that of the large cent (1793–1857) and the small cent (1857 to date). Varieties of the earlier type remain faithful to the overall design of the Liberty head; but there are three distinct main obverses of the later, small cent. First, from 1856–8 only, came the flying eagle; then the Indian head until 1909; and finally the Lincoln head which is still current.

CENT (USA) *flying eagle cent, Indian head cent, large cent, Lincoln cent.

CENTAVO The 100th part of the *peso, which appears in many decimal currencies of Central and South America.

CENTESIMO The 100th part of a decimal unit: in Italy of the *lire, in Uruguay of the *peso.

CENTIME The 100th part of the French *franc, as introduced by the revolutionary government by decree of 7 April 1795. Some 100 million of the first copper cents were struck during the three years from 1796–9; but from the consulate of Napoleon onwards (early 1800) the quarter-franc in silver became the smallest denomination struck. The copper centime, however, continued to be legal tender until May 1852, when a new bronze centime was ordered to be struck with the effigy of Napoleon III. A republican type was again introduced in 1872, and a revised type in 1898, which remained current until 1920. the denomination then once again disappeared until reintroduced in 1962 as part of de Gaulle's "new franc" currency. It was now struck in stainless steel and is still current.

CENTIMO The 100th part of various Latin-American denominations, issued as a copper coin in Venezuela, Dominica and Costa Rica among others.

CESATI, ALESSANDRO One of the greatest of Renaissance engravers of coins, medals, seals and gems. He was known as "Il grechetto" by reason of his Cypriot parentage. The exact dates of his birth and death are not known, but his documented activity—chiefly at Rome—stretches from c. 1538–64. He worked at the mint there from 1540–61, then for a short time at Parma, after which he returned to Cyprus. Vasari called him "the first medallist of his age" and records that Michelangelo exclaimed of one of his medals of Pope Paul III "art cannot advance beyond this".

CHAISE D'OR A French gold coin, first introduced by Philip IV in 1303. It takes its name from the figure of the King seated on a throne. It was struck only for three years, but revived later under Philip VI and extensively copied in Flanders during the 14th and 15th centuries.

CHALKOS The Greek word for copper or bronze (there being, as in the Latin *aes, no distinction). Later, from the time of the Peloponnesian War onwards, the word was used to describe a copper denomination valued at one-eighth of the *obol or one-forty-eighth of the *drachm. The period of its widest diffusion was following the reign of Alexander the Great.

CHÂLONS-SUR-MARNE A mint of the French province of Champagne from the time of Charles le Chauve onwards. It was active for, among others, the Bishop of Verdun, and was a regal mint for Henry IV during the time of the Ligue (1489–93), with the mintmark CH in monogram form. From this time dates an interesting medal which shows on the reverse the interior of a mint as it was then—most probably the Châlons Mint itself.

CHARLOTTE *United States mints.

CHASE MANHATTAN MONEY MUSEUM *collections.

CHAUDOIR, BARON STANISLAS DE (1791–1858) Russian numismatist who published from 1836–7 a three-volume work in French on Russian coins and foreign coins that circulated in Russia. Though in parts superseded by more recent scholarship, it remains a good general historical survey, particularly valuable for its extensive bibliography of earlier sources.

CHERSON An occasional Byzantine mint (crude bronze coins only), the most northerly of all, situated near present-day Sebastopol in the Crimea, on the Black Sea. Coins were intermittently struck here from the 6th to the 10th centuries A.D.

CHERVONETZ A general term for foreign gold coins used in Russia, and more particularly for the Dutch ducats which began to circulate there extensively during the 18th century. These proved so popular that the Leningrad state mint began to copy them in large quantities during the period from 1835 onwards. It is estimated that 29 million of these pieces were struck, used largely for military and foreign payments. A gold denomination of this name to the value of 10 *roubles was issued by the Soviet Union in 1923 only.

CHIHUAHUA A Spanish royalist mint during the Mexican War of Independence, 1812–22. Coins struck here were confined to the 8 reales. The earliest issues (1810–13) were in fact cast; when struck from dies during 1814–22, these were often overstrikings on the early cast pieces, though pieces of original fabric are also known. All pieces are countermarked with the letter T and a crowned pomegranate—usually on either side of a royal bust on the obverse, but sometimes on the reverse, between pillars. Chihuahua later became a regular mint of the Republic of

Mexico, with the mintmark CH or Ca, and remained active until 1895.

CHILPANCHINGO   A mint of the Mexican revolutionaries, 1811–13. Their leader, Morelos, called the first constituent assembly here, which in principle still recognised the sovereignty of Fernando VII, though it declared the territory of Nueva España independent. Some fairly crude coins were cast and struck with the legend beginning VICE FERD VII and in the name of the Suprema Junta de América. Later coins were struck for the Congresso Nacional. Both 2 and 1 silver reales are known; larger denominations consisted of worn 8 reales with counterstamps of the smaller types.

CHINA   With a history as old as that of Greece, the Chinese monetary system has, none the less, made little impact on the West—with one exception: paper money. For the rest, Chinese coinage was, for almost two millennia, cast rather than struck. Initially, it developed slowly out of implements which themselves were used as a means of exchange: spades and knives. The later ''knife coins'' are small and look more like keys; finally, only the circular top with a square hole remained and the familiar bronze *cash was born. The expert can, of course, distinguish thousands of different varieties through the centuries, but basically, cash remained, with fairly infrequent multiples, China's main currency until the latter half of the 19th century, when the first machinery for Western-type struck coinage was installed at the Kwantung Mint. (Some earlier issues had been struck for Shanghai in London and Hong Kong.) From this point onwards, Chinese coins are exhaustively documented in Western monographs and catalogues. With no less than 40 provincial mints, Japanese occupation money, communist civil war issues and a multitude of other intricacies, the last 100 years probably offer as many opportunities to the collector as the previous 2,000. Rarities and curiosities (like the *automobile dollar) abound; many of these—especially silver trade dollars—have been extensively forged. The scholar will still seek out earlier issues in preference; there are medieval pieces made of *bronze and with superb calligraphy that nothing later can rival.

Documentary references to paper money go back to the 7th century A.D., but regular issues were not made until the 12th, and these were described by Marco Polo. The earliest that have survived, however, date from the latter part of the 14th century (Ming dynasty) and are of a rough mulberry bark paper, to the value of 1,000 cash. A small hoard of these was discovered in the base of an overturned Buddha statue during the attack on the Peking Summer Palace, in 1860. They are thus a key piece in any paper money collection.

CHINA DUCATS   While coins minted from African gold are relatively frequent (*guinea, guinea ducat), only once did a European country boast of a coin struck from Chinese gold. This was Denmark in 1746, with ducats from gold brought back by the Danish East India Company and carrying the inscription EX AURO SINICO. Two types are known: one with crowned arms on the reverse, the other showing a sailing vessel which Friedberg (*Gold Coins of the World*) describes as an ''ancient galley with banner'', but which is more likely a Chinese junk with sail half furled.

CHO-GIN   An elliptical silver currency bar, cast in Japan during the period 1695–1722.

CHOP MARKS   From Hindustani *chop* (stamp or seal); hence a small countermark placed on coins in the Far East by private traders, mainly on the many circulating trade dollars, Mexican pesos, etc., to guarantee their silver content. Generally they are in the form of minute Chinese lettering, although well-known larger trading-houses might use their own symbols which would be known to customers (e.g. a rosette). As the coins passed from house to house, more marks would be added, and there are "chopped dollars" that carry so many that the original design of the coin has almost disappeared. The value of such coins is, of course, very much decreased when the original itself was a rare piece, while in the case of common issues, the value may be enhanced by one or more rare markings, or even by the picturesqueness of many.

CHRISTIAN D'OR   A Danish *pistole, struck at irregular intervals between 1771 and 1870 by Christian VII, VIII, and IX at the Altona and Copenhagen mints.

CHRISTOGRAM   The monogram of Christ, consisting of a conjoined P and X. It appears on many Roman and Byzantine coins from the early 4th century A.D. onwards, after the conversion of Constantine the Great to Christianity. There are also rare uses of it on medieval coins.

Emblem on bronze coin of Magnentius

CHUCKRAM   An Indian denomination which appears to have been current only in the native state of Travancore. The single unit was struck in copper, the double in silver. 4 chuckrams were equal to 1 gold *fanam. This old Hindu monetary system, dating from the 18th century, was continued until 1945.

CHUR   Town in Switzerland, which struck both city and episcopal coinages from the 16th century onwards. The city emblem (which is featured prominently) is the ibex, a mountain goat. In earlier times, Chur had occasionally served as a mint for Carolingian and later German emperors.

CIGOI, LUIGI (1811–75)   A notable forger active in Udine, Italy, especially of later Roman imperial coins. He worked both with original dies engraved by himself and with genuine old pieces which he "improved".

CINCUENTINO   The largest Spanish silver coin to the value of 50 *reales. The coin has a diameter of 73 millimetres and different specimens have weighed between 166 and 172 grammes. It was probably struck for presentation rather than currency purposes and is known only during the 17th century, under Philip III, Philip IV and Charles II.

CISTOPHORUS   A special type of silver coin, to the value of 3 drachms, struck in Asia Minor and particularly the kingdom of Pergamum during the 2nd and 1st centuries B.C. It is named after the *cista* or mystic basket of Bacchus from which a serpent is seen crawling. Sixteen towns are known to have struck these coins; the city name is usually abbreviated, and the city emblem shown as a subsidiary feature of the design, with additional features such as magistrates' marks. The coins continued into the period of Roman occupation, when they were equal to 3 denarii and the Roman governor's symbol replaced that of the Greek magistrate.

CIVIL WAR TOKENS   Emergency tokens, similar in purpose to the English series of tradesmen's tokens issued during the 17th and 18th centuries, but issued during the period of the American Civil War, 1861–5. They are usually in the 1 cent denomination and are known in a variety of metals (copper, brass, white metal and even silver). It is estimated that some 50 million were issued, and around 10,000 different varieties have been recorded.

CLAD COINS   Coins which have an outer "shell" of a different substance from the "kernel". In official and legal

Clazomenae, tetradrachm, 5th century B.C.

coinages, this is largely a 20th-century development and is the natural result of trying to produce what is in any case only *token money as economically as possible. In former times, to give copper coins an outer layer of silver, or to gild silver coins, was, of course, a favourite device of forgers.

CLARK GRUBER & CO. *Colorado gold.

CLAZOMENAE The coinage here, one of the principal Ionian cities, began in the 5th century B.C. with *electrum *staters showing, as a main type, the fore-part of a winged boar. Its chief glory lies in the 4th century types with the almost facing type of Apollo's head (obverse) and swan (reverse). These coins are known in both gold and silver.

CLEMENTI A papal silver coin to the value of 15 *baiocchi, first struck under Clement VII, from whom it took its name.

CLUB FRANÇAIS DE LA MÉDAILLE This Club is administered by the Paris Mint—more precisely, by a department of it called the *Monnaie des Médailles. Its object is to foster public appreciation of coins and medals (a) by encouraging regular purchases and (b) by issuing a quarterly bulletin that deals with all aspects of numismatic art and technique. The minimum requirement is a promise to purchase at least four of the Club's productions per annum; the bulletin then comes free of charge. And "bulletin" is surely too modest a title for a richly illustrated magazine (usually from 150–200 pages) on art paper, superbly laid out and printed by the Imprimerie Nationale. This not only gives details of all the Paris Mint's productions but ranges widely over the whole field of numismatics, ancient and modern, particularly in its relationships to other arts (e.g. sculpture, copperplate engraving, etc.). The Club's address is 11 Quai de Conti, Paris 6.

Oskar Kokoschka
(W. Schiffer)

COB MONEY Coins struck on roughly-cut *flans, irregularly shaped, and often too small to contain all of the types and legends on the die. Such money was prevalent throughout the Spanish-American mints until well into the 18th century, when the *screw-press and protective edges were first introduced there (1732).

COIN The most common, though by no means only, form of currency (for others *banknote, primitive money, token). In origin, the coin is a weight (something we are still reminded of in the name of a *pound, for example). But whereas monetary transactions in gold and silver go back to ancient Babylonian times, i.e. to at least 2000 B.C., it was not until the 7th century B.C. that someone had the bright idea to stamp a piece of metal with some kind of device to guarantee its weight and value. It is almost certain that this was first adopted privately, among merchants, to obviate the need for weighing each piece of metal (at that time no more than a rough, ovoid lump) separately.

Very soon, the state took over responsibility for this and has tried to maintain a monopoly of coinage ever since. The devices we find on coins are therefore generally official: of a magistrate, a king, an ecclesiastical ruler, a president, etc. Republics have sometimes favoured symbolic devices representing liberty (*Liberty head, liberty cap); but republics have been no less insistent than rulers by divine right on guarding coinage as a governmental prerogative.

A fundamental revolution in the function and nature of coinage began only during the present century. Until just over fifty years ago, it was generally accepted that a coin was worth its weight in gold (or silver). Suspicion attached to most coins not of these two precious metals, as it did to banknotes. Nowadays coins are struck in these metals very rarely, and then only for *commemorative purposes, sold at a high premium over face value, and not used as currency. Some countries even forbid the private citizen to hold gold and/or silver coins.

COIN WEIGHTS A coin weight is a weight which exactly reproduces the weight of a particular denomination (guinea, sovereign, or what have you). Unlike the coin which it is used to check, it is generally made of base metal. It may reproduce the design of the particular coin which it represents; it may be inscribed with its precise weight; or it may state the value of a foreign coin in native currency at a particular time. All this was basically to help money-changers, for whom sets of weights were manufactured. Weightmakers had their own guilds and high standards of accuracy were enforced.

Several hundreds of such weights are known from medieval times to the end of the 18th century in the European series alone. But this is only part of the story. Perhaps the most remarkable coin weights of all are the glass ones of Islam, dating from the late 8th century A.D. These Arab weights, sometimes mistaken for coins, are accurate to within 3 milligrams—a degree of precision not even dreamt of by European mint authorities and balancemakers until a thousand years later.

Two very different coin weights: the top one is English, 18th century, but showing the value of a Portuguese moidore; the lower one is an Arab glass weight of the 8th century

Going back still further, we have late Roman and Byzantine "exagia", of which there is a particularly fine collection in the Geneva Museum. The Byzantine pieces, often inlaid with silver, are collectors' art objects in their own right.

COLCHESTER One of the earliest mints in England. It was a mint for the Celtic king, Cunobelin. Later it was active also under the usurping Emperors Carausius and Allectus during the 3rd century A.D. (with mintmark C) and as a Saxon and Norman mint from Aethelred to Henry II. There are also rare *siege pieces of 1648 (10 shillings gold only).

COLLECTIONS On the face of it, collections may be basically divided into public and private; but there is much more to it than that. Many public collections began as princely or private ones. Thus what is today the Munich Coin Cabinet began as the "art and antiquity" treasury of Duke Albrecht V of Bavaria; the foundations of the Cabinet des Médailles at the Bibliothèque Nationale in Paris were laid by King Henri II of France; and the *British Museum collection saw its origins in munificent bequests by Sir Robert Cotton and Sir Hans Sloane. Public collections continue to benefit from private gifts or loans, or by purchases of private collections *in toto*. A recent example of the former is the Philip Grierson collection of medieval coins, now in the care of the *Fitzwilliam Museum, Cambridge; of the latter, the C. Wilson Peck collection of Soho Mint issues, acquired for £10,000 by Birmingham City Art Gallery and Museum.

One must unfortunately add that many so-called public collections remain largely private in so far as the general public is concerned. The treasures which they contain are to be seen by appointment only, for purposes of what their curators deem to be serious study, after establishing the prospective visitor's *bona fides*. At the other extreme there are certain museums which are noteworthy for the extent and variety of their displays. Very often, they belong to financial institutions (e.g. Chase Manhattan Money Museum, New York; Svenska Handelsbanken, Stockholm). The Karlsruhe Landesmuseum extends its display not only to coins, medals and banknotes but to related fields such as philatelic design, minting machinery, etc.

The visitor to any foreign country would be well advised to study guides to local museums, generally obtainable from tourist offices. Quite small places sometimes house unexpected treasures (e.g. Gariel collection of Burgundian coins at Auxerre, and Musée Joseph Puig at Perpignan for coins of Languedoc).

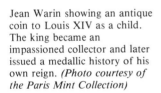

Jean Warin showing an antique coin to Louis XIV as a child. The king became an impassioned collector and later issued a medallic history of his own reign. *(Photo courtesy of the Paris Mint Collection)*

Private collections as such tend to remain private, since organised crime on the one hand and the rapacity of the taxman on the other discourage display except to close friends.

COLOGNE The numismatic history of this famous city on the River Rhine goes back to the reign of the Roman Emperor Gallienus (A.D. 253–68), more precisely the usurpation by Postumus (A.D. 258) of territories which embraced the Gallic and Germanic provinces as well as England. He struck coins in all metals (gold, silver and bronze) at his Cologne mint, and also at *Trier. Later there are sporadic Merovingian and Frankish coinages, and more permanent ones after Charlemagne had elevated the town to the seat of an archbishopric. With the foundation of the Holy Roman Empire in A.D. 919 we see the beginnings of a regular city coinage for the German kings and emperors; from 1474 coins were struck at Cologne as a free city under a grant by the emperor Frederick III. Archepiscopal mints subsidiary to that of the city itself were established in at least six other towns of the Rhineland; in addition, from A.D. 1386, the archbishop became one of the Prince Electors of the empire and struck coins in this as well as his ecclesiastical capacity. Thalers were struck from 1547 to 1777, among which those showing the 'Three Kings from the Orient' are the most sought-after types. The French invasions of the late 18th century led to the final closing of the Cologne mint in 1797. (*Deutz.)

COLORADO GOLD Gold was discovered in Colorado at the end of the 1850s; and though there was no gold rush similar to that which took place in California ten years earlier, there were none the less three companies which took advantage of the possibilities. The most important of these was the banking firm of Clark Gruber & Co., which established itself at Denver in 1860. Difficulties at that time were considerable: dies and presses had to be ordered from Boston and sent by ox wagon, all the time subject to Indian attacks. The project proved worthwhile, however, and Clark Gruber struck 1860–61 pieces to the value of $2.50, $5, $10 and $20. Of these, the majority followed the prevailing pattern of the Liberty head (obverse) and eagle (reverse). There were, however, a small number of pieces ($10 and $20) struck in 1860 only with the obverse legend PIKES PEAK GOLD, showing Colorado's highest mountain and the word DENVER below. These have always attracted collectors and are today very rare and expensive, the $20 piece especially so.

The words PIKES PEAK GOLD occur also on some even rarer pieces of John Parsons & Co. ($2.50 and $5), both undated but probably also struck in 1860–61. Little is known about this company, but on a $20 gold ingot dated 1860 (once again exceedingly rare) they call themselves "Assayers", and from local newspaper items of the times it would seem that they operated near the Taryall mines in the South Park area of Colorado. They may well have been involved in mining operations directly, for their obverse type shows a quartz stamp mill.

A little more is known about a third firm, J. J. Conway & Co., which operated at Georgia Gulch, another rich gold-mining area. The *Rocky Mountain News* of 21 March 1861 commented on the excellence of their machinery and productions and called them "jewellers and bankers". Their pieces ($2.50, $5 and $10) were purely descriptive and functional, not pictorial, carrying on the obverse the bare words J. J. CONWAY & CO. BANKERS and on the reverse the legend PIKES PEAK above large numerals of denomination, repeated in small lettering below. All are exceedingly rare.

COLTS OF CORINTH   Together with the "owls" of Athens and "turtles" of Aegina, this is one of the most famous among the international currencies of the ancient world. The popularity of the Pegasus (winged horse) type was such that it was not only struck by Corinth over three centuries but also copied by many other Greek city states.

The early coins (mid-6th century B.C.) show merely a rough incuse square on the reverse, the punch-marks of which took on a swastika form a little later. From around 500 B.C. a thicker and smaller *fabric was used, and within the incuse square there appears (on *staters and *drachm) the helmeted head of Athena (like Pegasus, part of the Bellerophon myth). This early reverse type was soon followed on the larger coins by the head of Aphrodite, Corinth's principal deity, while smaller coins (*diobol and hemiobol) show marks of value only. From the beginning of the "fine style" period (c. 400 B.C. onwards), there is a marked change in the Pegasus design: the wings are no longer closed but open, and this continues throughout the 4th and 3rd centuries B.C. (even under the Macedonian occupation of Corinth), until the city joined the *Achaean League in 243 B.C. and henceforth struck coins of its common type. The weight of the Corinthian stater (8.4 grammes) made it particularly useful as a trade coin on both sides of the Ionian Sea; it was copied by more than twenty widely dispersed mints.

Corinth "colt" of fine style, 4th century B.C.

COLUMBIAN HALF-DOLLAR   This was the first *commemorative piece struck officially by the USA. It was issued in 1892 in connection with the world Columbian Exposition in Chicago, celebrating the 400th anniversary of the discovery of America by Christopher Columbus.

COMMEMORATIVE COINAGES   Coinages to celebrate special occasions are nearly as old as coinage itself. In early Greek days, coinage was not the main but only a subsidiary form of currency, and *agonistic coinages were the rule rather than the exception. Later, when coinages were more widespread and this was no longer the case, we still find plenty of commemorative pieces (e.g. *decadrachms of *Syracuse). Roman and Byzantine pieces of this kind are much rarer and generally take the form of *medallions (i.e. large pieces not struck to a particular coin weight or multiple thereof). The *franc à cheval is a notable medieval piece; but the great periods of commemorative coinage are the Renaissance and the Baroque. Birth and death, war and peace, marriage and pestilence and many other themes promoted special coinages. The Popes celebrated (and perhaps partly financed) the progress of building St Peter's, Rome, in a whole series of *scudi; and the Protestant churches did not lag behind in celebrating the centenary of the Reformation. The trend—always favoured and supported by collectors—continues to this day with such coins as the Eisenhower Dollar and crowns celebrating the Silver Jubilee of Queen Elizabeth II.

COMMEMORATIVE COINS (USA)   The commemorative series of the USA comprises both gold and silver pieces, of which the silver half-dollars are by far the most extensive, totalling 48. Die, date and mint varieties bring these up to a grand total of 142. In addition, there are nine gold dollars in five issues (six distinctively different pieces), two quarter-eagles, and the famous 1915 Panama-Pacific $50 gold piece struck in both round and octagonal form. The only silver pieces which are not half-dollars are the Isabella Quarter of 1893, struck in commemoration of the Chicago Columbian Exposition, and the Lafayette Dollar of 1900. This last is important as being the first authorised US coin to bear the portrait of an American president (Washington, whose bust appears on the obverse conjoined with that of General Lafayette, while the reverse shows the statue of Lafayette on horseback, as erected in Paris as a gift of the American people). Other pieces that deserve mention for their numismatic rather than commemorative interest are the 1915 Panama-Pacific Exposition silver half-dollar (the first commemorative piece to bear the motto IN GOD WE TRUST as on regular coinage), and the 1933D Denver Mint reissue of the Oregon Trail Memorial (the first commemorative piece issued by that mint, though established as long ago as 1906).

The series, which will be found detailed in full in any of the standard USA catalogues (Yeoman, Krause), is still very collectable pricewise—surprisingly so, indeed, in view of the small mintage figures for some issues and their artistic and historical value, which in many instances surpasses that of the regular coinage. The first issue of the Missouri Centennial, for example, was struck in only 5,000 specimens; that of the Alabama Centennial in 6,006 specimens; and the splendid Grant Memorial piece of 1922 (first issue again, with a star in the obverse field) shows an even lower mintage figure—only 4,256 pieces. Yet none of these is dear by today's standards, while the original issue of the Daniel Boone Bicentennial (1934), admittedly struck in an edition of 10,000, is almost ridiculously cheap. It should be noted that in this issue, as in some others, there are restrikes of later dates, and by different mints, some of which command substantially higher prices than the originals—yet another indication of collectors' vagaries.

CONCAVE COINS   *Regenbogenschüsselchen, scyphate.

CONDITION   The condition of coins and medals is of the utmost importance to collector and dealer alike in assessing their value. Generally speaking, there are three grades only which the serious collector will wish to possess: very fine (abbreviated VF in catalogue descriptions), extremely fine (EF) and *fleur de coin* (FDC), implying that the coin is just as struck from the die. There are many lower grades; and there have also been attempts to make intermediate grades—without much success. Such grading merely tends to confuse: if a coin is less than extremely fine, it is surely better termed very fine than "almost extremely fine".

On the face of it, it might seem that the rarer the coin the lower the grade in which it might prove acceptable. But this does not necessarily follow. There are many rare coins which have always been rare, i.e. were struck in small quantities and probably used for presentation purposes only. In the nature of things, such pieces would be safely put away somewhere and would not, in the ordinary sense, circulate at all. The same applies to the larger gold denominations of most countries and periods, ideal for hoarding or tucking away under the proverbial mattress.

Smaller silver and above all copper or bronze coins, however, that no one at the time they were issued would pay much attention to, are much more likely to have passed from hand to hand over the years or centuries. If they are found still in very fine condition it is by chance rather than design; and such chances should be seized whenever they present themselves.

There are yet other considerations in deciding what degree of preservation may be acceptable (or what price may be demanded and paid) for any particular piece. It may be known, for instance, that though an issue was plentiful, much of it was melted down soon after. So the rule of the thumb by which an EF piece is worth twice the price of a VF one and half that of an FDC specimen is a very rough and ready yardstick only. The ratio may stand more in the proportion of 10:1 or even more where common coins easily found in worn condition are, in fact, exceedingly rare as superb specimens.

CONDOR   A gold coin to the value of 10 pesos, current in Chile and Ecuador. It was first introduced in 1851.

CONFEDERATE HALF DOLLAR   In 1861, Confederate rebels seized the US branch mint in *New Orleans and—on a hand-press—struck an experimental piece, the only "official" pattern for a coinage of their own. Its obverse was similar to current US-type half dollars, but the reverse carried the inscription CONFEDERATE STATES OF AMERICA: HALF DOL. around a wreath, within which was a liberty cap over a shield with seven stars and seven perpendicular bars. This coin (or, rather, pattern) remained unknown until 1879, when Dr F. B. Taylor, a former mint engraver who had kept the dies, decided to sell them. 500 pieces were subsequently struck from the original dies; even these are today exceedingly rare. (Of the original, only four were struck, according to records.)

CONSTANTINOPLE   The city founded by and named after Constantine the Great became in A.D. 330 the principal mint of the eastern Roman Empire and remained so until the final fall of the Byzantine Empire in 1453. The output was enormous: at one stage, the mint had no less than eleven *officinae. From the time of Anastasius (A.D. 491–518) it had a virtual monopoly among the thirteen Byzantine mints of coining money in gold and silver. The mintmark CON is standard from the middle of the 5th century; previously, it had been at various times C, CP, CONS, CONSP and CONOB. Mintmarks disappear almost altogether in the Byzantine series from the time of Constantine V (A.D. 741–75) onwards, and it becomes almost impossible to assign particular coins to particular mints.

CONTORNIATES   Medallic pieces of the late Roman Empire, always of bronze, about the size of a *sestertius, with a groove running along the edges of both sides. They come with a wide variety of designs, often of games or circus scenes, and may have served as some kind of admission ticket.

Contorniate, late 4th century

CONTRACT COINAGE   Any coinage produced by being farmed out under contract, instead of being struck by full-time paid officials of a government. Such coinages are much more usual than is generally believed. Mints were often privately operated in medieval times on a "leasing" basis (often, too hereditary).

But the great period of contract coinage begins only with the Industrial Revolution and Matthew Boulton with his *Soho Mint. It reaches its climax during the second half of the 19th century, when the *Heaton Mint produced coinages for governments all over the world. Nor is the contemporary scene without interest in this respect. In 1966 the Royal Mint won a Queen's Award to Industry for Export Achievements, having struck during that year (apart from UK coinages) 774 million coins in 109 denominations for thirty-five Commonwealth and foreign countries.

Sub-contracts for parts of coinages are not unknown, or for specific items such as *blanks.

CONVENTIONSTHALER   Coins struck according to the monetary convention of 1753 between Austria and Bavaria, to a uniform standard of .900 fine. They generally carry the legend

AD NORMAM CONVENTIONIS, or the indication of value X *eine feine Mark* (10 of them being equal to the Cologne Mark weight). The most famous and widespread of such Thalers after 1780 was the ubiquitous *Maria Theresa Thaler.

CONWAY, J. & J. *Colorado gold.

COPENHAGEN A Danish mint since 1512, and Denmark's principal, almost only, place of coinage from about a century later. The royal collection of coins and medals, now housed in the National Museum, is one of the finest in Europe.

COPERNICUS, NICOLAS (1473–1543) It is too little known that the great astronomer wrote, during the early years of the 16th century, a treatise on the theory of coinage which had far-reaching effects on monetary reforms in Poland, and directly inspired the fine new coinage in gold and silver of King Sigismund I (1528).

COPPER This metal has been used for coinage from ancient times to the present day, either in its pure form or as an alloy (*bronze, brass). Its chief source in the Greek and Roman worlds was Cyprus, in more modern times Sweden, and during the past century or so, the Urals, Caucasus and North America. The term "coppers" has passed into the language for "small change" in general, despite the fact that the coins were made of bronze since 1860.

CORINTH *colts.

CORONA *Korona.

CORONA DANICA So called after the reverse inscription, this Danish crown introduced in 1618 showed on the obverse the full-length figure of the King standing. It was struck to a lower standard than the *speciesdaler—a fact the public soon grew wise to.

CORONAT *Kwartnik.

CORONATION MEDAL First struck in the English series for Edward VI in 1547. Commemorative medals are not subject to the same stringent rules and regulations which apply to coinage, and collectors must distinguish carefully between official issues (generally struck in small quantities at the Royal Mint) and those made by private entrepreneurs.

CORONATO First applied to a *billon coin of Sancho IV of Castile (1284–95), the name was later given to a *grosso of Ferdinand I of Naples (1458–94) which pictured his coronation at Barletta.

CORSICA This Mediterranean island was first colonised by the Phoenicians and has since had a chequered history of occupation—the longest, perhaps, being that of Genoa from the 15th to the 18th centuries. Occasional finds of various coinages from all foreign occupants are recorded, but there was no mint on the island (nor any special "colonial" coinage struck for it) until the 18th century, when in 1736 the adventurer and self-styled "emperor" Theodore was welcomed by the inhabitants in 1736 as liberator from the Genoese yoke. He established a mint at Corte, which struck a few pieces that rapidly became collectors' items owing to the briefness of his "reign". The second and only other period of indigenous Corsican coinage took place while Paoli ruled the island from 1755 to 1768; he added a mint at the small village of Murato besides that at the then capital, Corte, and struck coins in both silver and bronze, all with the device showing a Moor's head. There are references to both coinages in *Boswell's account of Corsica.

CORTE *Corsica.

COUNTERFEITS These are of two main types. The first is generally contemporary with the coin in question, and is made to

Corona danica, Christian III, 1619

Coronato (1st issue, end of the 13th century)

cheat the issuing authority and general public. The second is of later manufacture, to cheat collectors of rare pieces.

The first is generally fairly easy to recognise: modern methods of analysis can quickly spot any tampering with the metallic content of a coin. The second presents many more problems, especially as regards ancient coinages when methods of striking were primitive and each coin is in any case (when struck by hand and not by machine) slightly different from every other.

Since collectors' or rarity values of some coins in the Greek and Roman series may—if in excellent condition—be fifty or even a hundred times the actual silver content value, it will pay the forger to use the silver from genuine but worn specimens of the same series to create something new yet deceptively old. Where conditions of hand craftsmanship continue, as they do in the Middle East, chemical or physical analyses cannot help if the raw materials are absolutely genuine. Only the most practised eye will be able to judge the minute stylistic differences between an ancient master-cutter of dies and a modern master-copier.

If the luminaries of the art world were for years deceived into accepting Van Meegerens as Vermeers, and still quarrel whether this or that Rembrandt is genuine or a copy, coin experts may be forgiven for occasionally going astray. The late L. S. Forrer, a dealer of more than fifty years' experience, told this writer that he might on occasion reject a coin as a "wrong 'un" for no better reason than that it felt wrong, without being able to point to any one feature to justify his opinion; and he confessed that this sixth sense might as easily fail him on another occasion.

The following categories have been much (and well) copied: Greek decadrachms, Roman aes grave, rare medieval and Renaissance gold, the rarer silver bracteates and Thalers, siege pieces, cut and countermarked coins. Lately, there has been a spate of forgeries of commoner pieces in the Greek and Roman series, for as more and more collectors have turned to these they cease to be "common"—yet are not so much in demand as the very great rarities, which will be minutely scrutinised as a matter of course (probably by a whole consortium of experts) before being offered for sale. So one cannot too often repeat the golden rule: buy from a professional coin dealer whose judgment you can trust, avoid antique shops and market stalls unless you like (and can afford) a gamble.

(Also *altered coins, fantasy coins, novodels, restrikes, Becker, Cavino.)

COUNTERMARK A mark, generally stamped, placed on a coin (or part of a coin: *cut money), for a variety of purposes. It may be to "legitimise" it as legal tender in some other currency or locality; it may be to increase or decrease its value; or it may even be to render it obsolete and illegal. Countermarks are found on coins of all periods from the ancient Greek to the present day and the collecting of them is a special study with more pitfalls than most. In so far as either the coin, or the countermark, or both may be forged, extreme caution is advisable. The Caribbean series is by far the best documented.

COWRIE Among the multitude of primitive currencies of the world the cowrie shell has a special place, for it was accepted as a denomination through large parts of Asia and Africa for many centuries. Thus in the Moghul Empire it was valued at 1/160th of the *anna or 1/2,560th of the *rupee. In Siam, during the 18th century, 6,400 cowries were worth 1 *tical. In 19th-century Angola, 2,000 cowries made up 1 *macuta; and in Uganda the official rate of exchange until 1897 was 50 cowries to 1 penny. In the French Sudan, cowries were not demonetised until 1907, and were accepted by the administration for payment of fines, taxes, etc.

CRACOW   A Polish mint of importance from the reign of Casimir the Great (1333–70) onwards, who introduced here the *Groschen of Bohemian type. There is a brief city coinage of 1835, and the mint may have been used for unofficial patterns of the non-Emperor Napoleon II in 1829.

CROCKARDS   Also   called   pollards   in   contemporary documents, these were spurious imitations of English pennies struck by feudal lords across the Channel and enjoying (despite their base metal) considerable circulation in England during the 13th century. An act of 1299 legitimised them as halfpennies, but only for a year; and as the silver content was, in fact, rather more than a halfpennyworth, holders were encouraged to bring them to the mint for melting down. They were forbidden altogether by another act of 1310.

CROOKSTON DOLLAR   Name given to the crown-size piece of Mary Queen of Scots, issued during the period of her marriage to Henry Darnley. More precisely, this is the second issue of the fourth period of her reign, the denomination being the *ryal of 1565–7. There was a legend that she and Darnley had courted under a famous old yew-tree at Crookston Castle; be that as it may, the tree shown on the coin is obviously a palm.

CROSAZZO   A large silver coin of Genoa, first issued in 1666. It enjoyed wide popularity for well over a century in all the principal cities of Europe, as its silver content (.985) was higher than that of any other denomination then current.

CROSSRAGUEL ABBEY   *St Andrews.

CROWN   The first English coin to be called by this name was the Crown of the Rose, valued at 4s. 6d. This was a gold coin (modelled on the French *écu de la couronne), introduced during the reign of Henry VIII in 1526. It is exceedingly rare, for it was superseded only three and a half months later by the Crown of the Double Rose (value 5 shillings). This is as common as the other is rare, and still one of the most collectable of English gold coins. It is also interesting for the varieties in which it may be found. These may carry the initials H - K, H - A, H - I, for Henry and three of his six wives (Katherine of Aragon, Anne Boleyn and Jane Seymour).

The gold crown was supplemented in 1551, under Edward VI, by a large silver piece, again to the value of 5 shillings. Silver crowns have since been struck by almost every English monarch until Queen Victoria's reign, as currency. Since Edward VII, they have been struck as *commemorative pieces only, mainly in coronation sets but for certain other special occasions only. The only exception to this was the Churchill Crown in 1965; but this too soon disappeared from circulation (despite the enormous quantities struck) to become a collectors' item at a premium.

There are many covetable pieces in the long series of silver crowns, which include many fine *patterns. Among these, Simon's *Petition Crown must take pride of place.

Collectors of crowns will generally concentrate on the *milled series from the reign of Charles II onwards. So it is perhaps worth mentioning that gold and silver crowns were struck side by side until 1662; and a parallel collection of such issues from 1551 onwards might prove more rewarding than the more orthodox approach.

Cruzado of Alfonso V
(1438–81)

Cuartillo

CROWN GOLD This standard (22 carat) was applied by Henry VIII for the first time in *crowns (see above entry) , and has been used exclusively for all English gold coins since the reign of Charles I.

CRUX-TYPE PENNY This penny was struck in the reign of Aethelred II only (A.D. 979–1016) and is so called after the four letters C R V X which can clearly be seen in the four angles of the cross.

CRUZADO A gold coin of Portugal, first introduced by Alfonso V in 1457. It is interesting in being the first modern European coin to be struck from African gold, as the result of Portuguese explorations around the West African coast. It was current for 400 *reis, and was in 1643 superseded by a silver cruzado (the cruzado de prata) to the same value but of Thaler size.

A rare type of the earlier coin is the gold cruzado calvario. It was struck only under John II during the years 1555–6, with a reverse showing an elongated, Calvary-type cross.

CUARTILLO A copper coin produced in Birmingham for Colombia in 1831.

CUARTO The silver quarter-*real as introduced in the coinage system of Ferdinand and Isabella of Spain by the edict of *Medina del Campo, 1497. The name was also given much later to the half-*peso of the Republic of Bolivia as introduced in 1830. This coin had a very bad name owing to its low silver content and was struck at La Paz though it bears the Potosi mintmark. Also *quarto.

CURRENCY From the Latin *currentia* (a stream), hence anything that flows. Today, money in the widest sense, anything acceptable as cash; coins, banknotes, even travellers' cheques. The credit card is the latest departure. In primitive times—and in some primitive societies even today—almost everything has passed for currency, from cattle to beads. In fact, our adjective ''pecuniary'' (of money) is derived from the Latin for cattle. Also *aes signatum.

CUT MONEY This makeshift has been adopted at various times and places when there has been a shortage of fractional currency, i.e. small change. At its simplest, it is a coin cut in half, in three pieces, in four or even in eight; at its most elaborate, a coin pierced off-centre with an irregular pattern (serrated, octagonal or even heart-shaped), with both the cut out ''plug'' and the remainder of the coin ''legitimised'' by a *countermark.

The most extensive series by far is that of the Caribbean, where the Spanish dollar (8 *reales, hence the popular ''pieces of eight'') was subject to many permutations of mutilation. The value of such pieces depends not so much on the condition of the original coin, which is very often worn, but on the clarity (and genuineness!) of countermarks. The series is perhaps more full of pitfalls than any other for the unwary collector, and a detailed study of specialist literature is advised before embarking on it.

CUZCO An ephemeral mint of Spanish America, known to have operated (from certain rare issues that survive) from 1698–9 and again during 1824. From 1698 we know the gold 2 *escudos, from 1824 the gold 8 escudos and the 8, 2 and 1 reales in silver (if the 4 reales was also struck, none seems to exist now).

CYLINDER SEALS *seal.

CYPRUS The legendary island of Aphrodite also supplied a great deal of the ancient world's need of copper. But quite apart from this, Cyprus has had an unusually varied numismatic history. In the ancient series alone, there are coins with Cypriot, Greek and Phoenician inscriptions; later, the island became subject first to the Ptolemies of Egypt, then to Rome. For a short time, under Heraclius (A.D. 610–41), coins were struck there for the Byzantine Empire; and from medieval times onwards we find Cyprus under such different rulers as the Lusignan dynasty, Venice and the Turks. When Great Britain took over the island for administrative purposes in 1878, she took over also the Turkish monetary system which had been in force for 300 years, with the *piastre as the monetary unit.

CYZICUS   This town produced what is perhaps the most varied among the Greek city coinages of ancient times, from around 600–350 B.C. Over 220 different types of heads, figures, animal forms, etc., are known. There are many interesting features, as yet partly unexplained, to be noted in this coinage. Thus Cyzicus was among the few towns to retain an *electrum coinage throughout the period; its city emblem (a tuna-fish) was a subordinate and not predominant feature of the overall design; and it introduced realistic portraiture of city worthies (as opposed to deities) long before this became a habit elsewhere.

These features are the more remarkable because Cyzicus, by virtue of its position on the Sea of Marmora, was one of the principal trading points between the Aegean and Black Seas. Hoards prove that the coinage found equal acceptance widely throughout both areas. And yet it offends against all the canons of other *international coinages of the ancient world, characterised as these are by bold and little-changing types over long periods (*colts, darics, owls, turtles).

Perhaps Cyzicus is the exception that proves the rule; it made a change from the general uniformity, so people everywhere liked these colourful coins. Whatever the reason, the collector whose tastes run to variety today cannot do better than concentrate, among ancient coinages at any rate, on the electrum staters of Cyzicus. This single mint presents almost a microcosm of the Greek world: gods and goddesses, nymphs and satyrs, games and warriors, beasts and birds—all are found here.

As a Roman mint, Cyzicus was active from the reign of the Emperor Gallienus (after A.D. 260) to that of Leo I (closed before A.D. 474), and as a mint of the Byzantine Empire from A.D. 518–629. During both these periods, bronze only was struck there.

D

DAALDER Dutch for *Thaler. A larger silver coin equivalent to the German one was first introduced into Brabant (which is now partly Holland, partly Belgium) as patterns or presentation pieces in the reign of Charles V; as currency from the reign of Philip II onwards. There were also many independent city issues (e.g. *Deventer); but it was not until the Earl of Leicester took over the administration of the United Provinces that crown-size pieces were struck in any quantity. (Also *Leijcesterdaalder, Leeuwendaalder.)

DADLER, SEBASTIAN (1586–1657) A celebrated medallist, born in Strasbourg and active in a number of German cities. From 1625 onwards he was court medallist at Dresden, where he died. His work is in the most elaborate baroque style and of enormous technical skill.

DAHLONEGA *United States mints.

DALA Bastardisation of the word dollar, and the native word for the Hawaiian silver coin struck for King Kalakaua in 1883. Only 500,000 of these pieces were struck, at the San Francisco Mint: and of these only about 10% remained in circulation, the rest being withdrawn and melted down. Because of the attractive design (by Charles Barber, chief engraver of the US mint at Philadelphia) many of the dalas were mounted as jewellery and are therefore difficult to obtain in fine condition.

DALER The Scandinavian word for *Thaler. Such crown-size pieces, modelled on the German pattern, were first regularly issued in 1534 in Sweden (under Gustaf Vasa) and in 1537 in Denmark (under Christian III), though there had been some earlier patterns. The Swedish pieces are particularly magnificent, and no less than three main types are known of the first year of issue. (*Husum daler.)

DAM A copper coin of Delhi introduced by the Sultan Sher Shah (1540–45). Fractions down to the sixteenth were issued, and it has been suggested that the expression "not worth a damn" may be derived from this.

DANDYPRAT An obscure, small English coin, apparently first struck by Henry VII in 1492 to the face value of twopence but of debased silver, for payments to troops in France. The precise type remains as mysterious as its name and etymology: the word is found later in the 16th century but used in the sense of "dwarf" or "insignificant fellow", but which is the original and which the derivative meaning remains uncertain. It appears to have fluctuated in value during the 16th century: T. Hills in his *Arithmeticke* of 1600 writes, "3 halfe-pence maketh 1 dandiprate." Attempts have also been made to identify it with "spurred" pennies referred to in certain documents dated 1499 and 1505. Much scholarly ink has been spilt over this trifle to little avail.

DANEGELD This is not a coin, but a form of tax levied by English monarchs to buy off the Danish invaders in the latter part of the 10th century. By association, English pennies of the time, as found in vast quantities in Denmark, are therefore sometimes called Danegeld.

DANFRIE, PHILIPPE French metalworker of great skill, active during the second half of the 16th century. Danfrie's activities spanned many fields, ranging from typography (he cut several alphabets of what are known as "civilité" types) to the making of elaborate surveying instruments. As a coin and medal engraver he headed the Paris Mint from 1582–1604, and was also responsible for coins of Béarn and Navarre.

DANIEL-DUPUIS, JEAN-BAPTISTE A talented medallist working at Paris during the latter half of the 19th century, very much in the "art nouveau" style. Besides many cast medals and plaquettes, he also designed the 1896 cent of French Indo-China and the 10-centime piece of 1898 for the French Republic.

DARIC A gold coin of the ancient Persian Empire, first struck under (and named after) Darius the Great, 521–486 B.C. It weighed 8.40 grammes, contained 3% silver alloy, and became the most widely diffused gold coin of the ancient world, accepted throughout the Mediterranean and Black Sea areas and east as far as India. Enormous quantities were struck under both Darius and Xerxes: Herodotus tells how the Lydian Pythius took a treasure of 3,993,000 with him on the campaign of Xerxes—which the King brought up to a round figure of 4 million! Types are similar to those of the silver *siglos (20 sigloi = 1 daric).

Double darics, though also of similar type, belong to a much later period and are generally assigned to various generals and satraps appointed by Alexander the Great after his defeat of the Persians. They are distinguished by Greek letters, monograms and other symbols—probably mintmarks—in the field.

DASSIER FAMILY This family dominated the mint of Geneva for the better part of a hundred years. Domaine Dassier was chief engraver there from 1677–1720, and was succeeded by his son Jean, who held the post until his death in 1763. His son Antoine, in turn, succeeded him (until 1780). Another of Jean Dassier's sons, Jacque-Antoine, worked at Paris, Rome, Turin and London (from 1740). During the latter period as assistant engraver at the Royal Mint, he also made a number of medals of specifically numismatic interest, among them portraits of Martin *Folkes and Sir Hans *Sloane. His father Jean had previously made a series of kings and queens of England to the time of George II.

DATES Quite apart from various different calendars in addition to that of our Christian era, there are other ways of expressing dates on coinage. The most common is that of a regnal year of a monarch, i.e. counted from his date of accession. It is worth remembering that even this can have pitfalls: thus in Britain, for example, Charles II counted the beginning of his reign not from 1660, as shown in our history books, but from the date of his father's execution in 1649 (the Commonwealth being, as it were, "wiped out" for this purpose of reckoning).

Sometimes dates are expressed in abbreviated form, as on the *portcullis coinage of Elizabeth I, where only 0 (for 1600) and 1 (for 1601) are shown. On the other hand, the *gun money of James II shows the month as well as the year, and coins giving a full date are not unknown, particularly if they commemorate a special event.

Danfrie, Philippe: Medal for the French Artillery, 1601 (actual diameter: 50mm)

Gold daric of Xerxes of Persia, and silver and gold staters of Croesus of
Lydia, 5th century B.C.

Gold medallion with a portrait of Alexander the Great, 336-323 B.C., from
the Aboukir hoard

Facing page:

Above: Roman gold aurei with portraits of Marc Antony and his son Antonius, and (*above*) a legionary gold aureus with the eagle and standards honouring the First Cohort of Praetorians, issued just prior to the battle of Actium in 31 B.C.

Below: Byzantine gold 36-solidus piece of Justinian I, A.D. 527-65, struck in 534 to celebrate the conquest of North Africa by Count Belisarius. A unique piece, it was the largest surviving gold coin from the ancient world, but it was stolen from the Paris Cabinet in 1831 and is no longer in existence; the illustration is from an electrotype

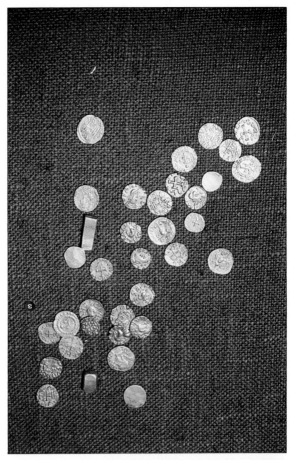

Right: Group of thirty-seven gold Merovingian coins, three blanks and two ingots found in the purse in the Sutton Hoo ship burial at Woodbridge, Suffolk, in 1939. The hoard dates from *c*. A.D. 625 and each coin is from a different mint. It has been suggested that the total number of pieces, forty-one, represents payment for the ghostly crew of the ship

Below: Obverse and reverse dies for a hammered shilling struck from the actual obverse die

Above: Gold triple unite of Charles I, 1625-49, struck at Oxford in 1644. On the reverse is the royalist declaration in four lines

Left: Hoard of Stuart silver coins found at Chilton Foliat, Wiltshire, in 1966, contained in a Westwald mug. Declared treasure trove, it consisted of a Charles I half-crown, sixteen Charles II crowns and forty-four half-crowns, their face value totalling £9 12s. 6d. (£9.62½). The coins had been buried *c.* 1680

European coinages are rarely dated before 1500 but become more frequently so after the middle of the 16th century. The first English coin to carry a date is a silver shilling of Edward VI, showing the Roman numerals MDXLVIII; the first Arabic numerals appear on his silver crown of 1551.

Finally, there is the question of "frozen" or other false dates. Millions of sovereigns struck from 1926–49 at the Royal Mint carry the date 1925, as but one example among many.

DAUPHIN, LE PETIT   This was a *billon coin for Dauphiné, showing a crowned dolphin (*delphinal types).

DAVID D'ANGERS, PIERRE-JEAN (1788–1856)   French sculptor and medallist who modelled during his long working life from 1814 onwards almost every contemporary celebrity. David specialised in large, uniface medallions; and those cast in his lifetime, by himself or under his supervision, are often true masterpieces. Victor Hugo, who was one of his sitters, compared him with Michelangelo; and while this is certainly exaggerated praise, some of his portraits (e.g. that of Madame Récamier) have a delicacy not surpassed since. These medallions are still occasionally to be found at a fraction of what one would pay for a drawing or even print of the same period.

David d'Angers: Portrait medallion of the French painter Delacroix (reduced)

DAVIDSGULDEN   A special type of gold *Gulden, struck in Holland only under Bishop David of Burgundy at *Utrecht (1456–96), with the obverse type showing King David as a harpist.

DEALER   At the top end of the scale, a man who is likely to be as knowledgeable about coins as any museum curator (and more knowledgeable than some). He will most likely be a member of the International Association of Professional Numismatists (numbering around a hundred of the top dealers throughout the world), and he will guarantee unconditionally the authenticity of every piece he sells. The trust and friendship of such a person are well worth cultivating. Like any such relationship, this demands a certain amount of faith—and faithfulness. A good dealer will reward this twenty times over. He will learn your habits and requirements, and the depth of your pocket. He will have surprises in store for you, or reserve pieces he knows you are looking for, even though he also knows you cannot afford to pay for them at once. It is therefore indefensible, if not positively offensive, to refuse a piece because you have seen it 10% cheaper elsewhere. A good dealer is never a cheapjack: he knows the value of his goods and of his services and is entitled to a fair profit on both. By all means grub in market stalls and bazaars if you wish; there is joy in that chase too, and in finding some rare treasure which only your eye recognises as such. But do not boast too much of your triumphs to your dealer, or he may end by viewing you as a rival rather than a client.

DEBASEMENT   The temptation to make money out of coins is not confined to collectors and dealers; few governments have been able to resist it, from the time of the Roman Empire to our own day. But whereas previously there has always been an outcry, and sooner or later a coinage of high standard was restored, we are now (it seems) permanently resigned to accepting our "silver" in the form of cupro-nickel. Plastic tokens will doubtless soon follow: what, after all, are credit cards? Such coins as are still occasionally issued in gold or silver must be "bought" at several times their face value, and are, in truth, medallic commemorative pieces, not currency. And even here debasement stares us in the face all too clearly: with rare exceptions these pieces have no artistic merit. The bait, such as it is, lies solely in the "limited edition" appeal, which may tempt speculators but never numismatists.

DECADRACHM The 10-drachm piece of ancient Greece, struck only occasionally and in the main probably for commemorative purposes rather than general currency use. Decadrachms are known of *Athens, *Carthage and *Egypt, and of the two Sicilian towns *Acragas and *Syracuse—these latter among the finest and most sought-after of ancient coins.

DECIMAL COINAGE As old as coinage itself, at any rate in China. In the Western world only the Etruscans used it in ancient times. Among modern states, Russia was the first to introduce it under Peter the Great; but it was not until the American and French Revolutions that it came to establish itself more widely. Napoleon's conquests were instrumental in spreading it through most of western Europe, though often (as had been the case with Russia) earlier monetary systems continued side by side with it for a while. The *Latin Monetary Union of 1865 was another big step forward. By the end of the Great War, most of the world had adopted a decimal coinage; but it was to take another fifty years before the United Kingdom and the Irish Republic followed suit.

Economists continue to argue whether, indeed, the system is as practical as its advocates claim. It is certainly true that for small amounts people tend to think in halves, thirds and quarters rather than tenths; and it is significant that the "quarter' (25 cents) remains a denomination in the dollar currency of the USA to this day.

DÉCIME Name given to the 10-cent piece in the French decimal system, 1793, and also adopted at Geneva in 1794. For a precursor three hundred years earlier *dizain.

DECIMO Equivalent to 10 *centavos in the decimal system as adopted by South American countries during the 19th century.

DECLARATION TYPE Those coins of Charles I issued during the Civil War period (chiefly at Oxford), both in gold and silver, which carry on the reverse the abbreviated form of the official royalist declaration: *Religio Protestantium, Leges Angliae, Libertas Parliamenti.* They usually show on the obverse the half-figure of King Charles I holding a sword and an olive branch.

DECUS ET TUTAMEN Latin for "an ornament and a safeguard", that being the double purpose served by *edge- inscriptions. The words have been used on the edges of English silver crown pieces since 1662 and on gold 5-guinea pieces from 1668. John *Evelyn, as he tells us in his *A Discourse of Medals,* claims the credit for suggesting the motto. Its most recent use is on the British £1 coin, issued in 1983.

DEKA A fractional gold coin of Ceylon during the 9th and 10th centuries A.D.

DELHI A mint of the Muhammadan sultans of Delhi from the 13th to the 16th centuries. For the most interesting pieces struck here, *gani.

DELHIWALA A degenerate type of the *bull and horseman coins, as struck by the Sultan of Delhi during the late 12th century A.D., in billon or copper. The figures (or figure) are hardly distinguishable: generally there is only one (on the obverse), and an inscription on the reverse. The coinage continued, with much rarer issues, through the reigns of the second and third sultans until 1210 A.D.

DELPHI Only very small fractional pieces were struck at this, perhaps one of the most famous places of the ancient world. There is one exception: the year 346 B.C., when the Amphictyonic Council met here at the end of the Phocian war, and coins as large as the silver *stater were struck. This was very much in the nature of a commemorative issue, with the head of Demeter on the obverse and the figure of Apollo (whose famous oracle was situated here) as the reverse type.

DELPHINAL TYPES Types that were struck especially for—and generally by a mint in—the French province of Dauphiné. They are distinguished by the dolphin, which may appear as the main part of the coin's design, boldly (e.g. petit *dauphin) or may be more or less concealed either on the obverse or the reverse (*cadière).

The type originated when the independent duchy of Dauphiné was ceded to Philip VI of France in 1349 on condition that the heir to the French throne should henceforth be known as the Dauphin. Money of delphinal type was struck from the time of the future King Charles V, with the title Dauphin de Viennois. The last coinage of this type is one of 1702 under Louis XIV at the Grenoble Mint.

Silver and billon coins for Dauphiné are relatively common, but gold is rare (no gold being known after 1641).

DEMARATEION A particular variety of the *decadrachm of *Syracuse. It was struck around 480 B.C. to celebrate the victory of Gelon over the Carthaginians at Himera. It is said that Gelon's wife Demarete interceded with him for the beaten foes, and in gratitude for his clemency the Carthaginians gave her a silver treasure, some of it later being made into these coins.

DEMY The half piece of the Scottish gold crown (*lion), introduced by Robert III in his first coinage of 1393. It is similar to the larger piece except for lacking the figure of St Andrew in the cross on the reverse. The issue of these pieces continued under James I and II of Scotland.

DENARIUS The principal silver coin of the Roman Republic and—to a lesser extent—of the Roman Empire. The first denarius dates from around 211 B.C., and was tariffed at 10 asses with a weight of 4.5 grammes. It showed on the obverse the head of Roma, and the numeral X. The reverse showed Castor and Pollux (the Dioscuri, legendary helpers of Rome at the battle of Regillus). Also on the reverse was the inscription ROMA. These early denarii fall into five main groups, distinguished by different helmet types, various mint or control symbols and—most important of all—a reduction in weight over some fifty years (until 155 B.C.) to 4 grammes.

The "reduced" denarius continued for about 200 years, the most important change (123 B.C.) being a retariffing at 16 asses. This change is clearly shown on the coins, for a short time by the numeral XVI, then the sign $\times$. Meanwhile, the Dioscuri had also given way to other reverse types, which were to multiply even more during the later Republic, the period of the Social Wars and the time of Pompey and Julius Caesar. Certain moneyers (e.g. the Piso Frugi family) show a cast series of "sequence marks", suggesting that every die in the very large issues of the time was subject to some kind of control.

When Augustus introduced the gold *aureus, this was to the value of 25 denarii. Not until the time of Nero was there any substantial change in the value of the denarius, then retariffed at 96 to the pound. After this, it declined in silver content and value, becoming more and more debased under successive emperors.

DENARO The Italian *denier. It is derived directly from the Roman penny or *denarius, reintroduced into the western European monetary system by Charlemagne and struck at the mints

Roman republican denarius—of Piso Frugi, 89 B.C.

of Lucca, Milan, Pavia, Rome, Venice and Verona. Grimoald III (A.D. 778–806) introduced it into the monetary system of Beneventum in southern Italy; his coins carry the monogram of Charlemagne. Later, the denaro was adopted by the city of Venice, which struck no less than twenty-four varieties of it over 200 years.

DENGA The principal and in many provinces only coin of Russia during the late medieval period (c. 1360–1490). It is the Eastern equivalent of the silver penny but varied enormously in weight and fineness of standard. Attribution is in many cases still uncertain, though many major types have now been assigned to the principalities of Moscow, Suzdal, Nizhny-Novgorod, Ryazan and Tver. An attribution to specific mints will probably never be possible, as the coinage was often farmed out to silversmiths who might either make the coins in their own workshops or come to the prince's court when necessary.

But, if difficult, the coinage is certainly rewarding for its amazing wealth of designs, ranging from the mythological to scenes of everyday life (including, on some coins of Tver, rare representations of moneyers at work). As an archaeological treasure-house, this coinage is no less rich than that of Greece or Rome, yet remains relatively unexplored by students outside Russia (cf. *puls, denning).

Denga of Vassiliev V (1425–62)

DENIER The silver penny in the Carolingian currency system, based on the old Roman *denarius (12 deniers = 1 solidus, 20 solidi = 1 libra; hence the abbreviation l.s.d. for pounds, shillings and pence). 240 deniers were struck from 1 pound of pure silver, at least theoretically. The denier, like other denominations before and since, suffered debasement: one-third copper was mixed with it by the beginning of the 12th century. (For England, *penny.)

DENNING A Danish copy of the Russia *denga, struck for trade with the eastern provinces of Finnmark under King Christian IV. Like their Russian prototypes, these coins were struck on an irregular, more or less oval-shaped *flan; the obverse shows the ruler on horseback, the reverse has a Russian language inscription of the Danish king's titles. Though undated, the coins are known from documents to have been struck in 1619 at Copenhagen, under mintmaster Johan Post. Similar coins, but to the value of 4, 2 and 1 Lübeck *shillings and with German legends, were also struck at the Glückstadt Mint in 1622, and by certain princes of Schleswig-Holstein and the Archbishop of Bremen around the same period.

DENOMINATION Name given to any particular coin to denote its value. Such value is not necessarily stated on the piece itself: English gold coins, for instance, have traditionally never told their users how much they are worth.

DENON, BARON DOMINIQUE VIVANT (1747–1825) Though never more than an indifferent artist himself, the Baron Denon is perhaps the key figure in the development of what is known as the "Empire style" under Napoleon. Denon was already over fifty when he accompanied Napoleon to Egypt, and his publication of the archaeological discoveries made there would be enough to secure his fame, marking as it does the beginnings of modern Egyptology. He then became successively director of the Paris Mint, of the Sèvres porcelain works and Gobelin tapestry manufactory and finally (as controller-general of French museums) exercised complete dictatorial control over almost every artistic endeavour. "Official" art could go no further than this; and though at least half a dozen eminent engravers

Denon medal by Galle

(*Andrieu, Brenet, Droz, Dupré, Duvivier, Gatteaux) exercised their skills in producing Napoleonic coinage and the medallic history of the reign, it was Denon who devised and sketched the design for every piece. Similar glorification of the Emperor may be traced in every aspect of the ornamental and useful arts. Denon was himself a voracious collector, and when his art treasures came to be sold after his death, the sale catalogue of them filled three stout volumes.

DENVER *United States mints.

DEUTZ A mint of the archbishops of *Cologne during the 16th century. Cologne's first *Thaler was struck here in 1547.

DEVENTER An important mint of the bishops of Utrecht from the 10th to the 16th centuries; also that of an *autonomous city coinage and an imperial mint. There is an interesting combined "three cities" coinage struck here from 1534–88, together with the towns of *Kampen and Zwolle. Such coins show the three city shields: an eagle for Deventer, a city gate for Kampen and a cross for Zwolle.

DEVICE A coin's "signature", as it were. The word is used to describe any kind of design which is not a portrait. Heraldic designs are favourites, but animals, birds, flowers, etc., are common, as also are *monograms.

DHARANA The local name for crude, punch-marched coins of India, dating from the pre-Christian era, though probably rather later than the earliest Greek coins. Their weight is irregular, their outline only vaguely circular or rectangular. In Ceylon they were called purana.

DIADEMED A bust or head which is shown wearing a crown or other symbol of authority (cf. *laureate, radiate).

DICKEN The word literally means thick. It is used solely to describe certain Swiss silver coins, modelled on the Italian *testone but of greater thickness and weight. They were current for one-third of the gold *florin and were struck for about 130 years in a number of Swiss towns (the first being Berne in 1492).

DIDRACHM A 2-drachm piece of ancient Greece; except in certain instances, not nearly as common as the 4-drachm (*tetradrachm). Perhaps its most interesting manifestation is its survival in Italy as the first silver denomination of ancient Rome, in the *Romano-Campanian coinage.

DIE A piece of metal (most commonly steel, though iron was used by the ancients and brass has been used in modern times) engraved with an *incuse design, from which coins in *relief are stamped. The process may be reversed or partly reversed: i.e. any part of the die which is raised from its flat surface instead of being gouged out, will appear in intaglio on the finished coin (inscriptions on the raised rims of Boulton's *cartwheel 2-penny pieces being a case in point).

The making of dies is directly related to the engraving of gems; and it is no exaggeration to say that the finest gem engravers also cut dies for the finest coins. It is thus no accident that we find the most beautiful examples of coinage in the greatest period of Greek art and during the Renaissance. Where dies are at two or three removes from the creator of the original design, their final quality is bound to suffer (*reducing machine).

DIE-NUMBERED COINS In 1863 the Royal Mint experimentally introduced the habit of numbering dies of certain (but by no means all) denominations and continued this until 1880 in certain cases. The series bristles with unsolved problems, which the Royal Mint reports from 1870 onwards do nothing to elucidate.

Dicken: Zurich type of 1519, the reverse showing the city arms

'Romano' didrachm, c. 250 B.C.

Thus the number of dies used (as reported) is always very much higher than the highest number on any known coin of a particular year; and the purpose of the experiment remains obscure.

DIFFÉRENTS   A French term, meaning signs which differentiate one coin issue from another. Each mintmaster, warden, engraver (and sometimes even designer) would have his own "signature" as it were, and a coin may bear as many as three different initials, monograms or other signs: mint official, engraver and place of coinage.

All the above might be (and often were) published in proclamátions: whereas a special class of différents known as "points secrets" never were. They were deliberately inconspicuous dots, placed *under* certain letters of a coin's *legend to identify the mint. Sporadically used in France since Louis XI, but only by a few mints, the system was elaborated under Charles VI (1389–1422) to embrace all twenty French regal mints. It was abolished when Francis I established his system of mint letters in 1540.

DIME (USA)   The 10-cent piece of USA coinage, introduced in 1796 and still current today. The early history of the coin is similar to that of the *half-dime (i.e. varieties as under draped bust, heraldic eagle, liberty cap, Liberty seated). Quite specific differences, however, begin with the introduction of the Barber Dime in 1892. The Liberty head faces right instead of (as on half-dime) left, and is surrounded by the words UNITED STATES OF AMERICA and not by stars. It should be noted also that the reverse inscription always reads ONE DIME (never 10 cents), whereas the half-dime or nickel always bears the denomination 5 CENTS from the introduction of the *shield nickel onwards. From 1913–45, A. A. Weinman's winged head of Mercury (facing left) is featured on the obverse, with fasces on the reverse: and the Roosevelt Dime (bust also facing left) was introduced in 1946. This is still in circulation, though the silver standard which had been current for over ninety years was replaced by a cupro-nickel clad copper coin in 1965.

DINAR   An Arab gold coin, first struck in Syria under Abd-al-Malik in A.D. 696. Early issues copied the gold solidi of the Byzantine Emperor Heraclius; but within a year or two the coin became standardised according to the rigid Muslim rule which allowed inscriptions only, without any kind of human or figurative representation. Mints are not shown before A.D. 815, when Fustad and Baghdad are named (Damascus being the most likely place of coinage prior to this).

The dinar remained the principal gold coin of the Muslim world throughout the Ottoman Empire and was extensively copied, not least by the Crusaders who even adopted on their issues (to ensure their acceptance) the name of Mohammad! These pieces were commonly known as "sarrazinos", and even an excommunication edict of Pope Innocent IV did not succeed in rooting out what he called the "abominable practice".

In modern times, dinar has been the name given to a silver coin of Serbia, from 1904–15; and it has been the monetary unit of Yugoslavia since 1921.

DINERO   The Spanish denier or silver penny. To be precise, it was of silver only during the reign of Ferdinand III (1230–52) who introduced it. When reissued by Alfonso X in 1258 it contained rather less than 33% of pure silver and was promptly dubbed "negro" or "prieto" (dark brown).

Much more recently, dinero has been the name given to the

Dinar: Coin of Caliph Haroun-al-Raschid, Baghdad Mint, A.D. 801

Dirhem: Early type, from Umaiad caliphate, mint of Damascus, A.D. 698-9

Dobla de la banda of John II, 1406–54, Castile and Leon

10-centavo piece of Peruvian currency, struck after 1857 as a silver coin.

DINHEIRO The Portuguese equivalent to the *denier, but never struck in silver, always in *billon. It was current from c. 1155 until two centuries later; its half was struck under Ferdinand I (1367–83).

DIOBOL A Greek silver coin, one-third of the drachm. It was the standard payment to Attic citizens for attending the games and other public functions. Also *triobol.

DIRHEM The standard silver coin of the Arab world, similar to the *dinar in its restriction of type and copied, like it, by the Crusaders. It spread with Arab conquests throughout northern Africa and into Spain. The Turks struck a dirhem in copper during the 12th and 13th centuries. Finally, it is the currency unit of modern Morocco, struck as a silver coin in 1960, and since 1965 in nickel.

DIZAIN An early French experiment at decimalisation, the dizain (to the value of 10 *deniers) was introduced by Charles VIII in 1488 and survived through the reign of Louis XII into that of Francis I until 1539. The coins are referred to in official documents as Karolus, Ludovicus and Franciscus. These names are taken from the respective types, which had on the obverse large crowned initials K, L and F. Some very rare half-dizains or 5-denier pieces are also known. The coin was very much the "odd man out" between the *douzain and *sixain (12 and 6 deniers respectively), and for this reason did not survive Francis I's coinage reforms of 1540.

DOBLA Literally double, and as such loosely applied to a number of gold coins: e.g. the double gold ducat struck by Charles V for Naples and Sicily, the double *scudo (16 silver *lire) of Genoa in the 16th century, etc. As a denomination in its own right, the dobla exists in various forms as part of the Spanish coinage from the 14th century onwards. The coin was introduced under Alfonso XI (1313–50) as the dobla castellana: a gold piece to the value of 40 *maravedis and named after its obverse type (a castle with three turrets). This type was continued under Peter I (1350–69), who supplemented it with a portrait type (the first in the Spanish medieval series). Henry II (1369–79) added a rider type copied from the French *franc à cheval; and, finally, the dobla de la banda under John II (1406–54) shows a shield diagonally crossed by a wide ribbon or sash (that of the Ordre de la Banda, first instituted by Alfonso XI). Superb multiples, some as high as 20 dobla, were struck by some of the above monarchs as presentation pieces and are among the most magnificent of medieval gold coins.

DOBLON A gold pattern piece of Uruguay, struck only in 1870.

DOBLONE Multiple (rather than double) gold pieces of the Italian Renaissance and the Baroque. The term has been applied to (among others) gold coins of 4 *scudi struck in Bologna and at the Vatican, and to a gold coin of 8 scudi struck at Modena. There is also a pattern piece in bronze of Pope Clement XI (1700–21) bearing the legend DOBLONE DOPPIO D'ITALIA.

DOBRA A Portuguese gold coin which first copied the French *écu d'or (under Peter I, 1357–67) and then the *franc à pied (under Ferdinand I, 1367–83). It was reintroduced in more modern times by John V (1706–50) as a portrait coin.

D.O.C. The initials of the Danish East India Company. They appear in monogram form on certain silver and copper coins for Tranquebar on the Coromandel coast.

DODECADRACHM The largest of all Greek coins, to the value of 12 drachms. It was struck in Carthage, from 237 B.C. onwards, after Carthaginian victories in Spain brought much silver from there.

DODKIN Mentioned in Stow's *Survey of London*, 1598, as the official name for a foreign coin of inferior metal (see also *obols and *galley halfpence). Those tendering it were liable to prosecution under acts of Henry IV and V.

DOHOZARI A minute gold coin of Persia, to the value of one-fifth of the *toman. Its weight was just over half a gramme, and it was struck only from 1896–1907.

DOIT A very small Dutch copper coin, to the value of 2 *Pfennige, current from the latter part of the 16th to the early 19th century. The lack of small change in late Elizabethan England (and the Earl of Leicester's presence in Holland as governor-general of the Dutch Provinces) caused this coin to have a wide circulation in England, and to become proverbial for trifling sums (e.g. Shakespeare: " . . . a doit to relieve a lame beggar" in *The Tempest*.)

Doit, Dutch East Indies, 1746

DOLLAR The word is, of course, a bastardisation of the German *Thaler, and as such was applied to certain pieces in the Scottish coinage long before it was adopted by the Americans. Thus the 30-shilling piece of 1567–71 under James VI was also known as the Sword Dollar, and the double *merk of 1578 as the Thistle Dollar. A denomination officially known as the dollar was also struck for Scotland under Charles II, with fractions of half, quarter, eighth and sixteenth.

The dollar as a currency unit has been adopted by many countries all over the world, including members of the Commonwealth like Australia and New Zealand and former British dependencies like the Bahamas and West Indies.

DOLLAR (USA) (1) *Silver*. The silver dollar provided the base from which all other coins in the USA currency system, as established by the act of 2 April 1792, were calculated, with gold coins provided for on a ratio of 15 to 1 from this standard. The first type of silver dollar shows the Liberty head facing right, with flowing hair, and was issued in 1794–5 only. The next type, showing the draped bust, continued until 1798. Both these show a small eagle within the wreath on the reverse. The year 1798 saw the introduction of what is known as the heraldic eagle type: a much larger and more stylised bird, carrying the US shield and in its beak a banner with the legend E PLURIBUS UNUM. This, together with the draped bust obverse, was continued until 1803, with nigh-on fifty die varieties. There are also certain spurious dollars, struck later for collectors, with the date 1804; and collectors still pay, for reasons best known to themselves, exorbitant prices for these.

The striking of silver dollars was then interrupted for a period of over thirty years, not being taken up again until 1840. The new type, known as the Liberty seated dollar, has an obverse closely modelled on the *Gobrecht patterns of 1836–9, but with a quite different reverse eagle design and the designation ONE DOL. This type continued, with only minor mint and die varieties, until 1873. The *Trade Dollar, which was introduced in that same year, falls outside the regular USA series, which was not resumed until 1878 with the Morgan Dollar. Very many varieties of this huge issue were struck until 1904 and again, after an interval of seventeen years, during 1921. There are many scarce dates, since over 270 million are known to have been melted down for export of bullion and recoinage.

The year 1921 also saw the introduction of the new Peace Dollar, so called after the word PEACE inscribed on the rocky crag on which the eagle (reverse) is perched. The *radiate Liberty head facing left (obverse) is a fine design by Anthony de Francisci. This was to be the last regular issue silver dollar struck in the USA: the Eisenhower Dollar introduced in 1971 is cupro-nickel clad copper, though a limited number of collectors *proofs have been struck in .400 silver.

(2) *Gold*. The issue of a gold unit was not authorised in the original US coinage law of 1792, although a legal tender ratio of 15 to 1 was specified therein. It was not to materialise until 1849, under an act dated 3 March, largely at the instigation of the influential gold lobby spawned by the general opposition to bank money and by the California gold rush. During its forty-one-year life, the issue was to be offered in three basic types (Liberty head, small Indian head, large Indian head), all of which were designed by James B. Longacre. The gold standard throughout was .900 fine, with the first type being thicker but 2 millimetres smaller in diameter than the others. All show on the reverse the inscription 1 DOLLAR and the date within a wreath. No coins from branch mints are known after 1861; of the mint varieties, that of 1861D (Dahlonega Mint) is by far the rarest—though one should add that there are mint records showing that a total of four pieces were struck at Charlotte, North Carolina, none of which is known to exist today.

For larger USA gold denominations, *double eagle, eagle, half-eagle, quarter-eagle, three dollars, stella.

Half-doppia of Charles Emanuel III of Savoy, 1756

DONG Currency of Annam (Indo-China) since the 10th century; a cast coin derived from Chinese *cash, with a central square hole. It was at first made of bronze, but from about the 14th century, of pewter. Most of those still found today date from the 19th century and are of a copper/pewter/zinc alloy. Later in the 19th century there were larger bronzes to the value of 60 dong, equal to 1 tien (equivalent once again to a Chinese currency unit, the *tael).

The obverse inscription, "thong bun", means simply current coin, and the dong is today the currency unit of Vietnam. During the French occupation of Indo-China, the dong was frequently known as a sapèque—a corruption of the Malaysian words *sa* (one) and *paku* (necklace), since the coins were most frequently strung and carried in this manner.

DOPPIA Literally, Italian for double; and in this sense it has been used for coins of many Italian states—e.g. Bologna, Genoa, Livorno, Milan, Naples, Parma, Rome, Turin, Tuscany and Venice. Usually a multiple gold piece, the doppia was occasionally the basic gold unit, as in the coinage of Sardinia from 1730, in which multiples up to 5 doppia and divisions to a quarter are known.

DORRIEN AND MAGENS SHILLING One of the very rarest shillings in the English series, suppressed by Order in Council on the very day they were struck in 1798. The banking firm of Dorrien and Magens had sent a quantity of bullion to be coined at the Tower Hill Mint—as, indeed, anyone was entitled to under the law as it then stood. But the government took umbrage at what it considered to be an infringement of the royal prerogative and was able to enforce the melting-down of almost the entire issue on the nice legal pretext that no royal proclamation had sanctioned it. The dies were copied fairly well from those of the

Shilling of George III, 1798

common shilling of 1787, and it may well be that there are still a few pieces in circulation which have escaped detection so far.

DOUBLE A copper coin of Guernsey, introduced in 1830, to the value of half a farthing. There are multiples of 2, 4 and 8 doubles; and from 1861 the coins were struck in bronze.

The word double has also been used by itself as an abbreviation for such denominations as the *double tournois in France and the double groat of Ireland under Edward IV.

DOUBLE EAGLE ($20 USA) The largest regular issue US coin, the $20 gold piece was born as a direct result of the economic realities following the discovery and exploitation of California gold. Its standard is exactly double that of the *eagle, at 516 grains .900 fine, and it was authorised by an act of 3 March 1849.

Like the other Coronet designs, this one is the work of Longacre, with the motto again being added in 1866. The denomination at first figured as TWENTY D. on the coin's reverse, but was spelt out in full as TWENTY DOLLARS from 1877 onwards. The only issue of particular note in the series is the 1861 and 1861S with a distinctly different reverse, distinguished by its tall, slim lettering, executed by A.C. Paquet, but quickly withdrawn from production.

Guernsey: 8 doubles, 1914

The *Saint-Gaudens double eagle introduced in 1907 is perhaps America's most beautiful coin and one of the few truly great 20th century coin designs. The early high relief strikes are magnificent; but even as issued for general circulation in a striking of over 4 million during 1908, the piece is a highly desirable collectors' item. The earliest issues show numerous varieties (arabic or Roman numerals, plain or lettered edge, with or without motto IN GOD WE TRUST), the acquisition of which is today academic for all but millionaires. The same applies to the 1927D issue which, though 180,000 are recorded as having been struck, was almost entirely melted down and to all intents and purposes cannot be found. As against this, the 1913S issue, with only 34,000 specimens recorded as struck, still offers remarkable value at a catalogue price hardly double that quoted for the most common issues running into several million.

DOUBLE LORRAIN A special variety of the *double tournois struck for Lorraine during the reign of Louis XIII, from 1633–42 only, at the mint of Stenay.

DOUBLE TOURNOIS A small copper coin of France, struck from 1577 onwards. Those struck at Paris are much neater than others, for they were struck by machinery even while the *Moulin there was not used for gold and silver coinage.

DOUBLOON From the Spanish *dobla. The word has been loosely used in English since Shakespeare's day for Spanish-Mexican gold pieces which flooded Europe from the 16th to the 18th century; more especially the double *escudo piece.

Gold doubloon of Ferdinand VIII, 1812

DOUZAIN As the name implies, a coin adding up to twelve units; in this case the multiple of the French denier tournois, and the equivalent of the English shilling. It was introduced under Francis I during the first half of the 16th century.

DRACHM The monetary unit of both ancient and modern Greece. Of its multiples (in ancient times), the *tetradrachm (4 drachm) is most common; but 2, 5, 6, 8, 10 and 12-drachm pieces were also struck at various places and various times (though never all at one time or place as part of a single monetary system).

As a monetary unit of modern Greece (adopted in 1833) the drachm is divided on the decimal system into 100 lepta (*lepton).

DREILING Issued in Hamburg and Lübeck from the beginning of the 15th century as a *billon piece to the value of 3 Pfennige. The coins are remarkable for *not* carrying the figure 3; instead, from about 1570, they showed the number of them which went to make up 1 Reichsthaler (at first 128, from 1609–1710, 192).

From the end of the 18th century onwards, the Dreiling was struck in copper by most of the north German states. Some special issues of note include that for Altona of 1787 and a revolutionary issue of Kiel in 1850.

DRESDEN   The principal mint of the kingdom of Saxony from the 17th century onwards. It continued to be active as a mint of the German state throughout the Weimar and Hitler regimes, and after 1945 as a mint of East Germany.

DRIELANDER   Popular name for a coin of Brabant, also issued in Holland and Hainault. It had the value of a double gros and was first struck under John IV of Brabant (1415–27), showing two shields leaning towards each other.

DROZ, JEAN-PIERRE (1746–1823)   Perhaps the most skilful and certainly the most famous engraver and medallist of his day. Born in La-Chaux-de-Fonds in Switzerland, Droz studied in Paris and first won acclaim with his very fine pattern piece known as the Écu de Calonne (after the French finance minister of the time). This was struck, with edge-inscription, in a six-segmented collar of Droz's own invention, at the Paris Mint. Matthew *Boulton was among those who admired both the coin and the new machinery. Droz was invited to Birmingham, but the association proved an unhappy one for both parties: though Droz produced superb patterns, he was unable to satisfy Boulton's requirements for the multiplication of dies for mass production purposes. Only the Bermuda penny of 1793, Droz's last work at Soho, was struck in any quantity.

He returned to France, and in 1799 was appointed Keeper of Coins and Medals at the Paris Mint—a post which he held throughout the Napoleonic era. Meanwhile he was much in demand by other governments as a ''consultant'' and struck patterns for Spain, the United States and his native canton of Neuchâtel among others. In French coinage, the head of Napoleon as engraved by him appears both on the 20- and 40-franc gold pieces from 1804–14, and he was also responsible for the fine pattern 5-francs of the ''Hundred Days'' in 1815. Among his medallic work, the coronation medals for Napoleon in 1804 and several medals and jetons for the Banque de France are perhaps the most noteworthy.

DUA   *hat money.

DUBLIN   Principal city and mint of Ireland. The earliest pieces were struck here almost 1,000 years ago as part of the *Hiberno-Norse coinage, and Dublin became and remained a sporadic place of coinage under many English sovereigns from the 12th to the end of the 17th century. Later pieces were struck for Ireland in London or Birmingham, with the unofficial *voce populi series in 1760 as the sole exception. There is also an extensive series of trade *tokens from 1653–79 and at the end of the 18th century.

DUBOSQ & CO.   Theodore Dubosq was a Philadelphia jeweller who established himself in San Francisco in 1849, where he struck $5 and $10 pieces, all dated 1850. They copy the prevalent Philadelphia Mint Liberty head/eagle type and are all exceedingly rare today.

DUCAT   A gold coin, weighing 3.5 grammes precisely and of almost 100% purity (.986–.989 fine). The Republic of Venice, which first introduced it in 1284, struck it with only minor vari-

Droz, Jean-Oierre: Medal celebrating the coronation of Napoleon I by Pope Pius VII at Notre-Dame cathedral, Paris 1804

ations continuously through six centuries; and the ducat became the standard gold coin throughout Europe.

This is not to say that other rulers copied the style slavishly; far from it. Literally hundreds of central European rulers adopted the weight standard without adopting the type, especially after 1566 when it had received official imperial sanction. Attempts to list such types are made by Johann Tobias Koehler in 1759–60 and again by J. C. Von Soothe in his *Dukatenkabinett* of 1784. Neither of these is anything like complete: nor are the listings in Friedberg's *Gold Coins of the World*. Thus, for example, the single reign of Leopold I of Austria (1657–1705) can show over 180 ducats from fourteen different mints: and Christian V of Denmark struck around a hundred of no less than twenty-three different types at the Copenhagen Mint alone during his much shorter reign (1670–99). These figures do not include multiple ducats or fractions, only the unit.

In German and Austrian principalities, bishoprics, etc. alone, more than 250 coin-issuing authorities struck the ducat, some for short periods only, others for centuries (the archbishops of Salzburg, for example, from 1500–1782, both round and square). (See also *ducatus di camera, Flussgolddukaten, guinea ducats, mining coins.)

DUCATONE A large silver coin of Italy, first struck in Milan by Charles V in 1551, from 1566 in Savoy and 1570 in Venice. It was the silver equivalent of the gold *scudo (value 5 lire, 12 soldi).

DUCATOON A large Dutch silver coin, struck in the Netherlands from the end of the 16th to the end of the 18th century. It was also known, from its type, as the ''silver rider''; its official name derives from the fact that its silver value was—theoretically at least—equal to that of the gold *ducat.

DUCATUS DI CAMERA As a money of *account, introduced by the Popes for internal reckonings of the Curia during the 14th century. Calixtus III (1455–8) introduced it as a gold coin in its own right, with the distinctive type of St Peter in a ship. As such it was struck by most of the Renaissance Popes for over a century, until Pius V (1566–72).

DUMBARTON A Scottish mint active only for a short period during the reign of Robert III (1390–1406). It appears to have struck *groats only.

DUMP Name given to the centre, cut-out part of the New South Wales *ring (or ''holey'') dollar, counterstamped to the value of 15 pence.

DUNBAR A Scottish mint under William the Lion (1165–1214) and Alexander III (1249–86). It struck silver pennies only. The town is further notable as being the only Scottish one known to have struck a *token during the 17th century, dated 1668 and with the name of its issuer, Geo. Coombes.

DUNDEE An occasional Scottish mint, with its only certain activity during the reign of Robert II (1371–90), when *groats, half-groats, pennies and halfpennies were struck here. During the late 18th century, Dundee was the only Scottish town to strike silver as well as copper *tokens, four varieties of a silver shilling being known.

DUPLONE A gold coin struck in various cantons of Switzerland (e.g. Berne, Solothurn) between 1787–1829, to the value of 16 francs. It was also adopted by the Helvetian Republic in 1800. Multiples up to 12 duplones are known in the Berne series (the largest struck from Thaler dies).

Facing page: Group of ducats

Cologne, Archbishop Salentin, 1575

Hesse-Cassel, William IV, 1636

Hungary, Matthias II, 1614

Berne, 1697

Poland, Sigismund III, 1630

Denmark, Frederick IV, 1700

Sweden, Gustav II Adolf, 1632

Regensburg, Joseph II (1764–92, coin undated)

DUPONDIUS   A weight of 2 pounds, and hence a Roman coin valued at 2 asses. In the early Italian series, one of the cast bronze coins emanating from southern Italy rather than Rome herself; under Augustus it was struck in brass (orichalcum).

DUPRÉ, AUGUSTIN (1748–1833)   French engraver active before, during and after the French Revolution. His fame was great even beyond the borders of France. At the request of Benjamin Franklin, he engraved the *Libertas Americana* medal in 1782, a type later adopted with minor modifications for the first United States coins.

Dupondius (reverse) of Domitian, A.D. 88

Dupré, Augustin: Portrait medal of John Paul Jones, Admiral of the American Revolution, 1779 (actual diameter: 54mm)

DUPRÉ, GUILLAUME (1574–1647)   By common consent, the greatest of French medallists of the late Renaissance. Like his early Italian predecessors of the 15th century, he worked exclusively in the technique of casting: he was a modeller, not engraver. None the less, in his official capacity as "controller of the king's effigy", he exercised considerable influence on the coinage; and Nicholas *Briot's coins at the Paris Mint from 1607 onwards are certainly engraved after his designs.

DURAND, ANTHONY   19th century English numismatist who lived in Switzerland and published in 1865 at Geneva his *Médailles et Jetons de Numismates*. This still remains the most comprehensive listing of medals representing men and women famous in the history of numismatics—either as scholars (from Petrarch onwards) or collectors (e.g. Queen Christina).

DURANGO   Still the capital of the province of the same name, the town of Durango began striking coins in 1811 with the arms of the province instead of a royal bust (crude striking of silver 8 reales). A rough version of an imperial bust (Fernando VII) followed in 1812, and copper of one-eighth reales was also struck until 1824, when the royalists finally surrendered to insurgent forces. The mint remained one of the Mexican Republic's until 1895. The mintmark was D and gold was also struck here.

DÜRER, ALBRECHT (1471–1528)   The greatest of German artists has a small but none the less significant niche in any numismatic gallery. While only three medals can be definitely attributed to him, they influenced (in Forrer's words) "the whole galaxy of Nuremberg artists who brought German Renaissance Medallic Art to a level, in certain respects, with the best school of Italian 15th and 16th century Medallists". There is also the certainty that he influenced the coinage through his friendship with his great patron, the Emperor Maximilian I.

Dupré, Guillaume: Portrait medal of the Duc de Sully (actual diameter: 44mm)

Durham house: Silver Shilling
of Edward VI

DURHAM Both a regal and espiscopal mint through four centuries. There are occasional issues under William I and II, regular ones from Henry I onwards. The episcopal coinage begins under Edward I and continues until Henry VIII (it is perhaps worth noting that from 1523–9 Cardinal Wolsey enjoyed the See of Durham as well as the Archbishopric of York and struck pennies here).

DURHAM HOUSE Palace of the bishops of Durham in London, long destroyed but formerly situated between the Strand and Adelphi. It was used as a temporary mint of Edward VI only from 1548–9. There are two types of exceedingly rare half-sovereigns and four types of shillings. The striking of groats was also authorised in the mint decree, but none has so far been found.

DURO Another name for the *peso, the Spanish-American piece of 8 *reales. The coin was originally known as the peso duro ("hard' money or weight); thus both forms of the name are a contraction of the whole. As a name on an actual coin, the word duro occurs only once: the 1808 siege piece of Gerona, struck under Ferdinand VI of Spain during the Napoleonic wars.

DUURSTEDE One of the earliest mints of the Netherlands, dating from *Merovingian times, when gold *tremisses were struck there. It later became important as a Carolingian mint.

DUVIVIER (FATHER AND SON) The elder Duvivier, Jean, was born in 1687 and died in 1761; his son Benjamin, born in 1728, lived to the age of 91. Between them, their careers span the reigns of Louis XV and XVI, the French Revolution and the Napoleonic era. Both were exceedingly prolific: Jean engraved over 400 dies, among them no less than seventeen different heads of Louis XV; and his son became the favourite medallist of Louis XVI.

EAGLE ($10 USA)   The highest denomination coin authorised by the original US coinage act. The coin was struck initially from 1795–1804, with the Liberty head (wearing a liberty cap) facing right, the initial "informal" eagle reverse being changed to the heraldic type in 1797. Minting of these large gold pieces then ceased altogether for a period of thirty-four years, there being no equivalent to the turban head types of half- and quarter-eagles. The Coronet Eagle, introduced in 1838 and designed by Christian Gobrecht, was, however, to prove the model for the smaller pieces which followed in 1839 and 1840 for $5 and $2.50 respectively. Like them, it survived with few changes until 1907 (the motto IN GOD WE TRUST was added in 1866 above the eagle reverse).

An Indian head type was introduced in 1907, designed like the *double-eagle, by Augustus Saint-Gaudens, America's leading sculptor. The initial issues did not carry the motto IN GOD WE TRUST, because President Theodore Roosevelt personally objected to its use on coins, but it was restored through congressional pressure in 1908. This coin, unlike the other US gold denominations of the time, does not have a reeded edge but raised stars: 46 from 1907–11, and 48 from 1912 onwards, after Arizona and New Mexico had become states of the Union.

ECCLESIASTICAL COINAGES   A huge field, quite apart from *papal coinage. There are some series (e.g. archbishops of Salzburg) which are quite as extensive and splendid as those of any secular ruler, and have been the subject of detailed specialised catalogues. For English readers, it may be particularly interesting to note that coinages of the archbishops of Canterbury and York antedate those of the Popes. Admittedly, they did not then extend over as lengthy a period and were abolished at the time of the Reformation. On the European continent, there were literally hundreds of prelates who exercised coinage rights (which, incidentally, were often a grant on privilege from the Holy Roman Empire; seldom, except in the case of papal legates at Avignon, from the Pope). Bishoprics, abbeys and even nunneries all struck money. Gold was by no means uncommon (except in England, where it remained the sole prerogative of the Crown). Apart from the Salzburg series, which rivalled in magnificence that of the Popes themselves, Liège, *Utrecht, *Cologne and *Trier all have fine gold series stretching through centuries. (*Fulda, Quedlinburg, Salzburg.)

ECKHEL, JOSEPH HILARIUS (1737–98)   Austrian abbot, director of the Habsburg Imperial Coin Cabinet in Vienna, whose eight volumes entitled *Doctrina Nummorum Veterum* (1792–8) laid the foundations for all subsequent studies of Greek and Roman numismatics. Only Eckhel's geographical arrangement seems arbitrary: he begins in Spain and works eastward, from the historian's point of view the wrong way round, since coinage began in Asia Minor. For the rest (study of metals, weight systems, mint organisation, etc.) others have continued to build on his essential groundwork of scientific principles.

ÉCU French for a shield, and hence applied to a large number of coins bearing this device.

ÉCU D'ARGENT (or écu blanc) Another and less common name for the *Louis d'argent.

ÉCU D'OR First struck under Philip VI of France, this remained the principal gold coin until displaced by the *Louis d'or of Louis XIII. There were many varieties, distinguishing different types in different reigns: e.g. écu au soleil (with sun), au porc-épic (with porcupine), à la salamandre (with salamander), à la couronne (crowned).

EDGE-INSCRIBED COINS The technique of edge-inscription dates from the mid-16th century and is generally ascribed to Aubin Olivier at the Paris Mint, c. 1555. The purpose was, of course, to prevent "clipping" of coins; but early machinery was not suitable for mass producing such pieces, and the process is confined to *patterns or *piéforts until the latter part of the 17th century. It was another Frenchman, *Blondeau, who invented a new process in the 1650s, which was adopted by the Royal Mint for crowns and 5-guinea pieces in 1663. The French waited another twenty years before introducing it on their crown-size pieces in regular issues. Edge lettering could be either raised or recessed, the latter being the more satisfactory process, as small protuberances on coin edges are particularly vulnerable to knocks or wear. Instead of inscriptions, decorative patterns were often used (*engrailed).

It is odd that Nicholas *Briot, who knew the process well from his Paris Mint days, never appears to have tried it on patterns for English coinage: the only example of his usage of the technique there is on the gold Scottish coronation medal of Charles I. One might mention one other numismatic oddity, eleven centuries earlier, on a Byzantine coin weight of the Emperor Justinian I (A.D. 527–65), now in the Geneva Museum. This bronze piece bears on its edge an engraved inscription which is believed to refer to John Capadocius, prefect of the Praetorian Guard from A.D. 531 and an important official in the Emperor's financial administration.

EDINBURGH MINT The principal place of Scottish coinage from David I (1153–65) to Mary (1542–67), and the only mint after that. It continued in operation after the union of the two kingdoms under James VI (James I of England) until the reign of Queen Anne.

EGYPT Advanced though the ancient Egyptians were in the arts and sciences, they had no coinage of their own until after the time of Alexander the Great. The Ptolemaic dynasty issued, from the mint of Alexandria, many splendid pieces, among which those with the veiled head of Queen Arsinoe deserve pride of place. Historically, the name of Cleopatra (actually the seventh of that name to bear the title) will be most familiar; those coins where her portrait is shown together with that of Mark Antony are rare and much sought after.

The story of Egypt after the fall of the Roman Empire is extremely confused. There were periods of Byzantine and even Ethiopian occupation, but by the 7th century Islam established some kind of rule over the country, and the centre of power moved by the 11th century from Alexandria to Cairo. Various

Octadrachm of Queen Arsinoe, c. 270 B.C.

caliphates succeeded each other, unitl Egypt became a province of the Ottoman Empire during the 16th century, and a vice-royalty was established in the 19th century. The unchanging Ottoman type of ruler's *tughra and reverse inscription continued even when Great Britain took over Egypt as a protectorate in 1882 (as a convenient way of protecting her own interests in the Suez Canal area). With the establishment of the semi-independent Kingdom of Egypt under Fuad I (1922–36) we also get the first portrait coinage of modern times; a break with tradition continued under King Farouk (1936–52), though since then only once again seen, by way of a commemorative piece on the death of President Nasser. Since the birth of the Republic (1953), Egypt has taken a special pride in its coinage, with a wide variety of commemorative issues, often based on ancient Egyptian iconography but also as often showing scenes and buildings of the present, e.g. Aswam Dam, National Bank etc. The monetary unit remains the *piastre, with 100 to the Egyptian £.

Modern commemorative half-pound for 1956 Suez War (Hegira date shown on coin)

E.I.C.   Short for East India Company. The initials are to be found on some guineas and half-guineas between 1729 and 1739 (also a 5-guinea piece of 1729 only), signifying that they were struck from gold imported by the Company.

EIRAKU SEN   Japanese cast bronze coins of traditional Chinese *cash type (i.e. round with a square centre hole). They were in fact made in China for export to Japan, c. 1570–1640.

ELECTRUM   As a natural alloy of gold and silver, electrum was found in large quantities in the sand of the river Pactolus, Asia Minor, and was the first metal used for coinage in the Western world. In this natural state, the percentage of gold stood around 73% and silver at 27%; but it tended, of course, to vary. None the less, electrum coinage continued to flourish in Asia Minor even after Croesus had established pure gold and silver coinages at a ratio of 13½:1. These later electrum coinages were, however, alloyed artificially to a more precise standard, which gave the much more easily calculable ratio of 10:1 of electrum as against silver.

Argument has continued to rage about what is or is not electrum, since pure gold almost always contains some slight admixture of silver anyway. The upper limit is now generally held to be 80% gold (i.e. we call it gold when it is more than .800 fine), the lower limit at 35%. Celts and Merovingians were later to debase gold coinages with admixtures of both silver and copper to such an extent that the word electrum is only applied to these for want of something more accurate. The most important electrum coinage in the Christian era is that of Byzantium, from the middle of the 11th century onwards.

Electrum: Stater of Croesus, c. 550 B.C.

ELEPHANT (AND CASTLE)   *guinea.

ELEPHANT CASH   *kasu.

ELEPHANT TOKENS   Curious pieces, the origin and purpose of which are still obscure. There are three major types, all showing as the obverse design a large elephant. The three different reverses bear the legends GOD PRESERVE LONDON, GOD PRESERVE NEW ENGLAND, and GOD PRESERVE CAROLINA AND THE LORDS PROPRIETORS (the last word sometimes mis-spelt PROPRIETERSS). The first piece is undated, the others are dated 1694. It has been suggested that they may have been initially struck around 1672 for the use of the African Company (*guinea), the inscription harking back to the Great Plague; but the later use of the elephant in conjunction with American inscriptions suggests comic (or satirical?) rather than serious intent.

ELIS As guardian and organiser of the Olympic Games, and in proximity to the temple of Zeus at Olympia, the city of Elis struck a remarkable series of silver coins from the 5th to the 3rd centuries B.C. The main type of the earlier coins is the eagle carrying a serpent or tortoise, with a thunderbolt on the reverse. Later types show the heads of Zeus or Hera, less frequently the nymph Olympia, with an eagle or thunderbolt reverse.

EMERGENCY MONEY A generic term for all kinds of currency issued and accepted as such—generally within a limited geographical area—when regular coinage is in short supply. There are various categories, such as: *campaign money,* struck in the field by a general to pay his troops; *siege pieces,* struck by citizens or the commander of a beleaguered town; *insurrectionists' coinage,* struck by a revolutionary to pay his followers; **tokens,* issued by many towns, banks or private traders when the central government could not meet the demand for small change.

No comprehensive listing exists, though there are specialised catalogues in most of the above categories. The last of them includes huge quantities of paper money (and even postage stamps used as currency). Some idea of the range may be gathered by noting that in Germany, in 1923 alone, some 8,000 localities issued around 65,000 different notes (i.e. an average of eight denominations each). Coinage, so-called, during the years 1916–22 ranged from iron and tin to porcelain and even pressed coal and amounted to about 7,000 different varieties in 1,500 places. In France, all currency up to the value of 2 francs was left to local chambers of commerce for the whole of the period 1914–23: taking into account also local issues by the German army of occupation, there are more than 10,000 coins and notes. Russia and Poland offer similar examples, though not on quite such a large scale. (Also *obsidional coins.)

ENCASED POSTAGE STAMPS *postal currencies.

ENGENHOSO A gold coin of Portugal, the first of that country to be struck by machinery, and also the first to be dated (1562). The name implies the manner of its striking (i.e. engineered); Jao de Goncalves is the inventor responsible, and there is no evidence to connect him with earlier French experiments.

ENGRAILLED Technical term for a certain pattern of edge-marking of coins, formed by a ring of dots or curved lines.

ENRIQUE A Spanish gold coin, first struck under Enrique IV of Spain (1454–74) and named after him. It is basically a copy of the French *chaise d'or, showing the King seated on a throne. Multiples of up to 50 enriques were struck as presentation pieces.

ENZOLA, GIANFRANCESCO Medallist of Parma, active during the last quarter of the 15th century. Apart from his medals, he is known to have engraved coins under Ercole d'Este for Ferrara, where he was master of the mint *c.* 1472.

EPHESUS An early mint of Ionia in Asia Minor. It is famous for the first known coin (an electrum stater) bearing an inscription, which reads ''I am the badge of Phanes''. This is believed to refer to a merchant (rather than a ruler) as guarantor of the piece. Main types of the Ephesus coinage were the bee and the stag; the latter occurs, in the 3rd century B.C., with a particularly lovely head of Artemis as the obverse type.

ERFURT Town in Thuringia, where *bracteates were struck for its archbishopric from the 12th to the 15th centuries and local city coinage from the mid-14th century onwards.

ERONDELLE, JEAN   A French engraver, and one of the earliest to be employed (1552) at the Paris *Moulin des Étuves. He did not stay there long, finding it more profitable to sell the secret of mechanical coinage to the King of Navarre, whose service he entered in 1554 to introduce the same processes at the mint of *Pau.

ESCALIN   A silver coin of the Netherlands, current during the early part of the 17th century, roughly equivalent to the English shilling.

ESCUDO   Spanish for shield, and the name used for a variety of types (both gold and silver) bearing this device. The first gold coin to be so-called was the one that took the place of the *excelente in 1537. This remained the principle Spanish gold denomination until 1833 and it also became the chief gold coin of Spanish America (Argentina, Bolivia, Chile, Colombia, Costa Rica, Ecuador, Mexico, Peru). The Portuguese introduced a gold coin of the same name in 1722, and continued to strike this with multiples up to 4 escudos until 1835. It survives as the monetary unit of modern Portugal and its former colony of Angola, but is now struck in bronze or other base metals—though multiples have occasionally been struck in silver.

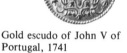

Gold escudo of John V of Portugal, 1741

ESPADIN   A *billon coin of Portugal, introduced by King Alfonso V in 1460, to commemorate the Order of the Sword (Espada) a year earlier. The same name was later given to the half- *justo, because of its similarity in type.

ESPHERA   A gold coin struck in Goa (Portuguese India) from 1509–15, so called after the world's sphere which is shown on the reverse. Only the half is known, and the coin is undated.

ESSEQUIBO   A territory in what was later to become British Guiana, where during the late 18th century much *countermarked and *cut money originated and circulated, distinguished by the letters E & D (the latter for the adjacent territory of Demerara). Since the Dutch were predominant in this part of the world, a later coinage was struck in *stiver denominations.

ESTERLIN   *sterling.

ETRURIA   In their coinage, from the 5th century B.C. onwards, the Etruscans followed Greek models of technique and style, but were notably different in being the first in the Western world to adopt a decimal system. Both gold and silver bear marks of value from 100 down to 1. On the gold, a lion's head is the most common type, on the silver a gorgon.

EUAINETOS   The most celebrated of all ancient coin engravers, active at three different Sicilian mints (Syracuse, Catana, Camarina) on coins on which his signature appears. The *decadrachms of Syracuse are perhaps the finest examples of numismatic art ever produced; and Evaenetos has with justice been called the Phidias among engravers. Though his art is most evident in the large, commemorative silver pieces, the smaller gold is perhaps even more remarkable for its delicacy of execution within a very confined space. The period of his finest work falls around 400 B.C.

EVELYN, JOHN (1620–1706)   English diarist, and much more of a scholar than Pepys: he became Secretary of the Royal Society and twice declined its presidency. His *Numismata—A Discourse of Medals Ancient and Modern* (1697) is the first illustrated work in English on the subject. Like many cultivated amateurs of his time he took the word "medals" to embrace also coins and the two are mixed indiscriminately in his book, though in rough chronological order. (Also *decus et tutamen.) His *Diary* has references to the stay of Peter the Great in London and that monarch's interest in coinage and the mint.

EXCELENTE Spanish gold coin struck under Ferdinand and Isabella from 1497 and continuing unchanged through part of Charles V's reign until 1537. Multiples of 2, 4, 10 and 20 were also struck. The coining edict allows even for a piece of 50, but none has been found.

The type, of two facing busts (also called *bajoire), was extensively copied in the Spanish Netherlands, and also under Philip and Mary of England.

Gold single excelente of Ferdinand and Elizabeth

EXERGUE That part of the coin which, if separated by a line, formed a small segment at its base. It is by no means an obligatory feature of coin design but often used (especially on the reverse) to contain such features as *mintmarks, engraver's initials and—most frequently—the coin's date of issue.

EXETER An English mint since Saxon times, and in the Norman series active until the reign of Edward II. Later, Exeter struck coins during the Civil War (1643–6) and again during the period of the great recoinage of 1696–7.

F

FABRIC The fabric of a coin is everything that goes to make it up, except stylistic factors: the sum, in other words, of raw materials and technical processes. Though its evidence alone can never be quite conclusive, it weighs heavily (together with *iconography) in deciding the origins of a coin, and whether it be genuine or *counterfeit.

FALCONER, JOHN The son-in-law of Nicolas *Briot, and joint master with him at the Edinburgh Mint from 1636 onwards. It is doubtful whether he was himself an engraver, all the Edinburgh coins of the time showing the typical Briot style. "Falconer's issues", as they are known, are distinguished by an F, and were made during Briot's frequent absences while serving King Charles I at various other mints during the Civil War.

FALS A copper coin of the Umaiad and Abbasid caliphates (late 7th century A.D. onwards), struck generally with the names of mints in various parts of the Islamic Empire, and often also with the names of provincial governors. The word itself is an obvious corruption of *follis (Roman imperial and Byzantine bronzes). The name survived into the 19th century for the copper coins of Persia, which were issued autonomously from a large number of provincial mints, with profuse animal types. There appears to be no common value or weight standard in this varied and attractive series, which remains inexpensive to collect.

Anonymous fals of Persia, 1718

FALTZ, RAIMUND (1658–1703) An important coin and medal engraver, who worked principally for Frederick III of Brandenburg. Born in Stockholm, he was trained in Paris and on his return to Sweden was briefly active for the Pomeranian Mint under Charles I until called to Berlin in 1688.

FALUCE A coin current in Ceylon under both Dutch and British rule; its value was one-quarter of a *fanam.

FAMAGUSTA A town in Cyprus, which issued a variety of *emergency coins when besieged by the Turks in 1570.

FANAM A small Indian gold denomination, first issued by the Tamil states of southern India during the 9th century A.D., and in Ceylon from the 14th century. There are many different types.

Much later, during the 16th century, the name was given to a silver coin; and this denomination was adopted by the English in their coinage for southern India at a value of one-eighth of the *rupee. Similar coins were struck by the French for Pondicherry and the Danes for the possessions in Tranqubar.

Fanam: Silver type of Madras, 18th century

FANTASY COINS As opposed to forgeries, which try and copy existing coins as closely as possible, fantasy coins are simply "invented". This poses no problems in modern times (i.e. from the Renaissance onwards) when we have issues fully documented by published edicts, often accompanied by engravings. In the case of medieval and ancient coins, the situation is very much more tricky. If a hitherto unknown piece of apparently genuine *fabric is unearthed, who is to say with certainty whether it was put in the earth two years ago or two thousand? Bogus archaeological "digs" are not unknown, especially in the Lebanon; and whereas glass and pottery can be shown to be new and not old by the latest scientific methods, however clever the faker—purely from minute analysis of their physical and chemical composition—the same is not true of metal. In any case, the metal may well *be* old, merely overstruck with a new design (which again was not uncommon in ancient times). Only the most practised eye will unveil the "fantasy" of a superlative faker here.

FARTHING   Silver farthings were first struck during the reign of Edward I. Before that, the only coin current had been the silver penny, and it was not uncommon to cut these into four to meet small transactions. The word farthing in fact means fourthling, i.e. one quarter.

Copper farthing tokens first appeared under James I (*Harrington farthings). A regular issue of copper farthings did not begin until 1672, under Charles II, and then continued without intermission until 1699 (William III). Issues thereafter were sporadic like all copper coinage until 1821, when regular issues were reintroduced under George IV. The final chapter is that of the bronze farthing (from 1860), which continued until the denomination ceased to be struck in 1956. Farthings remained legal tender until 1961.

FEN   Decimal unit of the Republic of China since 1955, struck in aluminium in denominations of 1, 2 and 5 fen (100 fen = 1 yuan). Previously, the fen had been a bronze coin of the then Communist revolutionaries in Manchukuo during 1933–4.

FENNIGOW   Polish for *Pfennig (penny).

FERDING   For origin of name, *farthing. The ferding was a silver coin of Sweden, first struck for the Bishop of Dorpat in 1528. After the conquest of Estland by Erik XIV, it was struck also as part of the regal coinage at Reval and Riga mints. Ferdings are known to have circulated in adjacent parts of Russia.

FERRARA   Italian city state, which in 1452 issued the first Renaissance portrait coin, a ducat of Borso d'Este, the dies cut by Antonio Marescotti. As this is an exceedingly rare coin, Milan under Francesco Sforza is often given credit for this "first"; and it should be emphasized that the Ferrara piece is the earlier by ten years. Ferrara continued to strike coinage of exceptional artistic quality for the next eighty years under successive dukes. The most famous piece is the *testone of Ercole I d'Este, engraved by Gianantonio da *Foligno. This shows on the reverse the celebrated clay model, long destroyed, by Leonardo da Vinci of a horse and rider, originally meant as an equestrian monument to Francesco Sforza.

FEZ   An African mint of the Morabite dynasty of Morocco, which struck mainly gold *dinars from the 11th century onwards.

FIDUCIARY CURRENCIES   Fiduciary—from Latin *fides* (faith)—is the adjective applied to all currencies that are taken, as it were, "on trust". Hence all *tokens and *paper money come under this definition; also a great deal of *emergency money. Modern coinage has been more or less fiduciary since gold ceased to pass as currency after the First World War; and the last vestiges of even a silver-based currency were swept away during the past twenty years, completely so by 1968 when the Swiss 5-franc silver piece was replaced by one of cupro-nickel.

FIELD   That part of a coin not covered by the portrait, inscription, etc. Such blank areas may be quite extensive and the collector—especially of modern coins and *proofs—will always examine the field carefully for scratches or other defects.

FILIBERTO   A gold coin of Savoy, introduced by and named after Emmanuel Philibert (1533–80). It was first struck in 1561 to a value of 9 lire; and the reverse design and legend (an elephant among a flock of sheep, captioned "infestus infestis") must rank among the most unusual ever.

FILIPPO   A silver crown-size piece first struck in 1598 under Phillip II of Spain for Milan, and intermittently under other rulers until 1776.

FIND   A find is distinguished from a *hoard in that it generally consists of a single or very few coins, accidentally lost rather than deliberately concealed. Remarkable finds can still occur in hedgerows or on fields. A superb example was the gold medallion of Constantius II turned up by a plough in southern Germany during the early 1930s and today in the Karlsruhe Museum.

FITZWILLIAM MUSEUM   The Cambridge University coin collection was founded by the bequest of 1589 by Andrew Perne, Master of Peterhouse, of his cabinet of coins and seals. In 1856 the miscellaneous accumulations of coins belonging to the University were transferred from the Library to the Fitzwilliam. In 1864 the Greek coins and gems in the collection of Lt. Col. W. M. Leake were purchased under the terms of his will, to form the nucleus of the extensive Greek coin collection. By gift and bequest, between 1906 and 1912, the Greek coins in the J. R. McClean collection were added. The collection has been further improved by such gifts of choice materials as that of A. W. Young, 1936, and the Rev. H. St J. Hart in 1963. Meanwhile, the Museum has bought judiciously during the present century, so that today the Greek coins rank amongst the finest in public collections.

The Roman coin collection is a fully representative series of this vast range of issues. The collection has been accumulated from many gifts and purchases, of which the outstanding group is the imperial gold portrait pieces which formed a part of the A. W. Young gift in 1936. The Byzantine collection comprises mainly the C. D. Sherborn gift, 1939, and the C. W. Bunn collection presented in 1950. It is particularly valuable for the long series of documentary bronze coins which it contains.

The largest part of the Museum's collection outside the ancient series is that of Great Britain, from Celtic times to the present. The collection is representative in character, especially after the sumptuous additions to the late medieval and modern series made by the J. S. Henderson bequest, 1933, and the A. W. Young gift, 1936. The Museum has only a small collection of medieval and modern European coinage, but Professor Philip Grierson has placed on deposit his own superb series of European medieval issues.

The only important group of oriental coins is that of continental India. These include superb pieces of the Mughal Empire, and an important specialist collection of Assamese coins bequeathed by A. W. Botham in 1963.

There are also representative collections of English and foreign medals. The English series is particularly fine, again mainly due to the generosity of A. W. Young, 1936. Of the foreign medals, only the Italian and French series are extensive. The small collection of seal matrices includes the only identifiable portion of Perne's bequest of 1589.

The collection of engraved gems and cameos was founded by

the purchase of the Leake cabinet. Substantial additions came from the bequest of F. McClean, 1904, and S. G. Perceval, 1922. A small but beautiful group of Italian Renaissance gems was included in the Shannon bequest, 1937. (Details by courtesy of Graham Pollard, Keeper of Coins and Medals.)

FIVE-CENT PIECE   *buffalo nickel, half-dime, Jefferson nickel, Liberty head nickel, shield nickel.

FLAN   The blank piece of metal used for striking a coin, fully prepared and checked as to correct weight and diameter, though coins of the same denominations are sometimes struck on a larger than normal flan, to distinguish separate issues, for commemorative purposes or other special mint controls.

Final adjustments to the flan were sometimes made after striking, especially in the days before machinery was used and all coins were struck by hand, or rather by hammer. Since the metal might spread unevenly under the impact of the hammer, trimming after striking might be not only necessary but even desirable to ensure a really beautiful, circular coin. So the flan would be made deliberately overweight, and the excess trimmed off with scissors and/ or file later. Generally speaking, such care would only be given to high value gold or silver commemorative pieces, where weight control was in any case exercised on the *al pezzo basis.

FLEUR DE COIN   Generally abbreviated to FDC, this French term means literally "flower of the die" (*not* coin), and implies a coin in condition as struck, with the "bloom" of freshness still on it, and without the trace of any scratch or even of handling. It should never, strictly speaking, be used of hammered coinage at all, and much more sparingly than it is in describing recently struck money.

FLINDRICH   A 4-*Groschen piece of Oldenburg, Westphalia, struck during the second half of the 15th century.

FLORENCE   Apart from a few Carolingian *deniers, probably struck around A.D. 768, the numismatic history of Florence begins towards the end of the 12th century and finishes in 1861. The first part of that history, until the end of the independent republic, will be found treated under the word *florin. The second period is that of the Tuscan grand dukes, from Alexander in 1531 to Leopold II. While following in the main other denominations current in Italy during that period, Florence again introduced, in 1719, a gold coin distinctive to itself: the *ruspone. (Also *Cellini.)

FLORETTE   A variety of the French *gros, struck by Charles VI of France from 1417–20, and by Charles VII, first as Dauphin during 1422, and again as King from 1426–9. The type (of a crown surmounting three lilies) was also somewhat crudely copied by Henry V in a coin so debased as to be more *billon than silver, and by the Duke of Burgundy during the years when France was divided into three (i.e. 1417–22). No less than thirty main varieties are known during that period, plus eight in the later (also much debased) emission under Charles VII from 1426 onwards.

FLORIN   Both a gold and silver coin, of the same type and size, issued simultaneously in Florence (1252), with the former ten times the value of the latter. The gold florin was to establish itself (together with the Venetian *sequin or *ducat) as one of the great European currencies, with one notable difference. Whereas ducats kept almost entirely to the high Venetian standard (.986 fine) whenever and wherever they were adopted throughout

Florin: Original type of 1252; this one is a gold coin

Europe, the florin type was almost everywhere debased (though never by the Florentines themselves). No rational explanation can be found for this diversity of fate.

The English, after a brief flirtation in 1344 under Edward III, forgot all about the florin for 500 years, when it was revived as a silver coin (first issued in 1849) in a half-hearted attempt at a decimal currency, to the value of one-tenth of a sovereign. The words "one florin—one-tenth of a pound" did in fact figure on all florins until 1887 as a reverse inscription, when they were replaced by "two shillings—one florin"—a poor substitute, one may feel. But poorer still the dropping of the word "florin" altogether from 1937 onwards, and poorest of all the dismal and bleak "10 new pence" of today. It would have been an appropriate moment to revive the splendid old name, continental in origin anyway, when the British were at long last moving into line with European decimal currencies.

To end this complaint on a slightly happier note: what I would call the "genuine" florin (i.e. boasting of its decimal connections, however tenuous, until 1887) may be collected in nearly seventy major varieties, besides a most interesting series of patterns (27, plus 3 reverse *mules), engraved by William *Wyon in 1848. For those who like to dig deeper, no fewer than twenty of the varieties dated from 1864–78 are known with *die numbers; and since the Royal Mint Report for 1873 indicates 281 obverse dies used for that year alone, opportunities for collectors of minutiae are many and intriguing.

Florin of Victoria, 1901

FLUSSGELDDUKATEN   The sand of river beds is often gold-bearing; and ducats struck from gold thus extracted are known by the above name (i.e. river gold ducats) if they carry mention of the fact in the legend and/or picture. They are confined to the German series from the 17th to the 19th centuries, the rivers being the Danube, Edder, Inn, Isar, Rhine and Schwarza.

FLYING EAGLE CENT   The short-lived flying eagle cent (so named after its obverse design) was conceived as the replacement for the large cent, offering the public a more convenient, clearer and more durable coin than the old coppers. It was made of an alloy of 88% copper and 12% nickel, its 72 grain weight being less than half that of its predecessor, and 12 grains less even than that of the half-cent (one reason, no doubt, for the withdrawal of the latter that same year, 1857). A thousand proofs, today very rare, were struck in 1856, and just over 40 million coins for circulation during 1857–8, the latter year with die varieties in the lettering.

FOLIGNO   A town in central Italy, and a papal mint at various times from the middle of the 15th century. Gold was struck there for a short time under Paul II and Leo X only; and it provides an interesting link with the first printer to be established in the town, who set up his press in the mintmaster's house (*printing and numismatics).

FOLIGNO, GIANANTONIO DA   Engraver who worked at the Ferarra Mint from 1505–22 and was responsible for many of the fine *testones struck under Alfonso I d'Este.

FOLKES, MARTIN   An 18th century English antiquary and numismatist, whose *Tables of English Silver and Gold Coins* (published by the Society of Antiquaries in 1763) was the first attempt to make a comprehensive illustrated catalogue of English coinage from the Norman Conquest to Folkes's own day. Folkes had earlier (1745) published briefer lists on his own account; and though even the latter work is now long superseded, it is still

Folkes: medal by J. A. Dassier

Bronze follis of Diocletian,
A.D. 284-305, from the mint
of Antioch

much sought-after by collectors for its antiquarian interest and
the quality of its engravings.

FOLLARO   A copper coin of southern Italy, struck under
Byzantine influence (*follis), from the 7th century.

FOLLIS   A bronze coin slightly washed with silver, first
introduced as part of the coinage reforms of the Roman Emperor
Diocletian (A.D. 295–8). Its exact relationship to the silver and
gold coinage is not known: the suggestion that it was a double
*denarius is only guesswork. What is known for certain is that the
word's original meaning was money bag; and that it was later
(from Anastasius, A.D. 498, onwards) applied to the largest of
the bronze coins instituted under the currency reforms of that
Emperor, valued at 40 *nummia (with the actual mark of value
M shown on the coin). From A.D. 539 onwards, the follis was
dated, beginning with a XII as the 12th regnal year of Justinian I.

Byzantine influence being what it was throughout the Mediterranean and Middle East, it is not surprising that we find the follis
appearing in Italy as the *follaro and among Arab states as the
*fals, both from the late 7th century onwards.

FORINT   Hungarian for *florin. It is often found abbreviated
as Frnt on Austrian silver coins struck for Hungary. It remains
a unit in the Hungarian monetary system today, and commemorative silver multiples have been struck at intervals since 1946.

FORRER, LEONARD (1870–1954)   British numismatist of Swiss
birth, who spent his entire adult working life in the service of the
London firm of Spink & Son Ltd. There he not only founded and
edited the *Numismatic Circular* (a mixture of dealers' catalogue
and learned magazine), but in a period of over thirty years compiled his monumental *Biographical Dictionary of Medallists.*
His catalogue of the Weber collection of Greek coins and his
Notes sur les Signatures de Graveurs sur les Monnaies Grècques
are other notable works.

FORRER, LEONARD STEYNING (1898–1968)   Son of the
above and, like his father, a coin dealer all his life: first with
Spink, then independent, finally with Schulman of Amsterdam.
His *The Art of Collecting Coins* (1954) is perhaps the best general
introduction to the subject: learned yet stimulating, with an excellent glossary and bibliography.

FORRER, ROBERT (1868–1947)   Swiss antiquary and numismatist, whose *Keltische Numismatik der Rhein- und Donaulande*
remains the standard work on eastern Celtic coinages, though
published as long ago as 1908. He also compiled one of the very
best general archaeological encyclopedias.

FOULIS, THOMAS   Scottish die-sinker, active at the Edinburgh
Mint towards the end of the 16th century. He engraved, among
other coins of James VI, the 40-shilling piece of 1582 and the
Thistle Noble of 1588.

FRACTIONAL CURRENCY   A term applied to small United
States banknotes of under $1 value (3c.–50c.).

FRANC (French)   The history of the French franc is a long one.
It began as a medieval gold coin under John the Good in 1360
with a type known as *franc à cheval,* showing a knight in full
armour galloping away on his horse. It is, in fact, said to have
been struck as ransom money for the King, then a prisoner of the
English; and the name as well as the type may well symbolise the
King's return to freedom (the literal meaning of "franc" being
"free").

John's successor, Charles V, struck a new type known as the
franc à pied (i.e. on foot), with the King shown standing beneath

Gold franc à pied of Louis de
Mâle, Flanders, 1346–84, a
copy of a popular French type

a Gothic canopy and holding the sword of justice. At the end of that reign (1380) both types were discontinued and significantly not taken up again except under Charles VII as a defiant gesture when most of his kingdom was under English rule (1423). After this, the coin disappears altogether as a French gold denomination, though the galloping horseman brandishing a sword appears in many variations among coinages of other countries (Flanders, Spain, etc.).

A silver franc was first introduced under Henry III in 1577, replacing the *teston which had until then been the principal silver portrait coin. It was a considerably heavier and larger coin than the former, roughly equivalent to half a German *Reichsthaler. Its weight was again increased under Henry IV at the beginning of the 17th century; but it was struck in small quantities only and was finally superseded by the *louis d'argent in 1641.

The third French franc, again of silver, dates from the time of the French Revolution and was introduced as the principal silver denomination of the new decimal system in 1795. As a crown-size piece, the 5-franc multiple enjoys much the same favour among French collectors as do English silver crowns here or silver dollars in the USA. It was minted in enormous quantities under Napoleon (both as Consul and Emperor, 1801–15), and enjoys the distinction of having been struck at a wider range of his eighteen mints over the whole period of years than any other denomination; 191 major date and mint varieties have been listed, which minor varieties and patterns would easily double. (By way of comparison, we may note that the entire series of British crowns from George III to Victoria [1818–1900] including all patterns, etc., totals only around 150 pieces). Recorded mintages range from the staggering 31,049,880 of the Paris Mint in 1811 down to 449 at Nantes in 1807. The 5-franc piece is also the only coin to have been struck by the Commune de Paris during the troubles of 1871, bearing a trident as the sign of the mintmaster Camelinat. The later history of the coin is less interesting, though it is worth noting that 5-franc pieces continued to be struck in silver (.835 fine) until 1968, before their final ignominious decline to cupro-nickel.

Denominations of 20 and 40 francs were struck in gold under Napoleon I. During the Second Empire, the series was to range from 100 francs down to 5 (the latter being struck for some years concurrently with the silver piece), and a 50-franc piece took the place of the former 40-franc one. 10 and 20-franc gold pieces continued to be struck under the Third Republic until 1914. A new 10-franc piece in cupro-nickel, showing a "stylised" map of France and designed by the famous painter Georges Matthieu, was introduced in 1974.

FRANC À CHEVAL   *above.

FRANC À PIED   Franc.

FRANC (Swiss)   The first grafting of a franc on to the Swiss currency occurred in 1799, following the invasion of Switzerland by French revolutionary armies and the establishment of the Helvetic Republic. The resulting monetary system was a curious hotchpotch, decimalised in its lower denominations, but including such multiples as 40 *Batzen (i.e. 4 francs) in silver, and gold 16 and 32 francs. Not until 1850 did the new Swiss Confederation unify the currency exactly on the French model, with 5-franc pieces in silver and 10 and 20 francs in gold.

FRANCESCONE   The silver *scudo as introduced into Tuscany by Francesco I (1574–87). The name was probably applied to all Tuscan scudi thereafter.

The original French silver franc, 1583, as introduced under Henri III in 1577

FRANKFURT-AM-MAIN The most important city of Franconia, and a mint since *bracteates were struck there for Emperor Frederick I (1152–90). As a free city, Frankfurt struck its own autonomous coinage from 1346, and the first gold florins were struck soon after, during the reign of Charles IV (1347–78). From the mid-16th century, splendid commemorative pieces begin to appear both in gold and silver, for Frankfurt was not only an imperial city but the seat of imperial coronations from 1562 onwards. The city's historical museum has a very fine coin collection, with a virtually complete representation of Frankfurt's own issues; an illustrated guide is available.

FRANKLIN, BENJAMIN (1706–90) The great American statesman, who was trained as a printer in England (*Franklin Press Token), had influence not only on US coinage (*Fugio cent) but also on other aspects of numismatics. At the early age of 23, he published a pamphlet on paper money and was active as a banknote printer for most of his life. While he was ambassador to France during the American War of Independence, he commissioned from the Paris Mint several fine medals commemorating events and personalities. He figures, too, on many struck in France at the same time, including an especially fine portrait medallion modelled by *Nini, which is known in terracotta as well as metal.

FRANKLIN MINT Started towards the end of 1963 as a private venture in Philadelphia, the Franklin Mint has grown to be the most successful purveyor of commemorative medallions of its kind. It now operates not only in the USA but in ten foreign countries, claims to have an active list of over one million buyers and sales approaching $200 million per annum. Among the firms it has taken over is the English one of John *Pinches; and it is today one of the few American public corporations with a quotation on the London Stock Exchange.

The firm's policy has always been to offer medals in series rather than singly; it is also a leader in the highly popular field of pictorial silver ingots, guaranteeing the price of the "run" of a series (which may extend by monthly subscription over two or even three years) irrespective of any rises in metal value. Many of its issues (which also include silver plates, bronze sculptures and, most recently, items in porcelain and finely-bound books) have shown a good investment value, with high appreciation over the initial offer price. New issues are generally announced some three months or so before a specified closing date for potential subscribers; while this undoubtedly helps the mint assess precise demand and foward metal buying commitment, the purchaser cannot know in advance the size of the so-called "limited" edition. Though this may put off some, it obviously encourages others, as the mint's continued success shows.

Since 1971, the mint has been successful also in obtaining a certain number of *contract coinages for *proof issues from various foreign government agencies. This testifies to its generally high standards of production. It has established a museum of medallic arts at Franklin Center, just outside Philadelphia and adjoining its plant, which is among the most advanced in the world.

FRANKLIN PRESS TOKEN An English token, dated 1794, which still remains something of a mystery. Of halfpenny size, it shows a printing-press on the obverse, with the inscription "payable at the Franklin Press, London". Benjamin Franklin worked at Watts Printing Works in London during his stay from 1724–6, and the press he used is later said to have been named after him. However, when Watts died in 1763, all trace of it was lost and there is no record of it in 1794. The token is most probably a concoction by *Lutwyche, who also shipped *Washington Tokens to the USA purely as a speculative venture—i.e. not as coinage but for sale as medalets, cashing in on famous names.

FREDERIK D'OR Danish gold coin, first struck in 1827 by Frederick VI (1808–39). Several types are known, and the double was also struck. The denomination was abbreviated to FR. D'OR on the final type (shown above Danish arms supported by two wild men with clubs); this was simply changed to CHR. D'OR for the reign of Christian VIII (1839–48), with subsequent appropriate changes for Frederick VII (1848–63) and Christian IX (from 1863–70, when the coin was superseded by the new decimal Krone coinage). The coin weighed 6.642 grammes and was .903 fine.

FRENCH-CANADIAN COINAGE The earliest French coinage was authorised to be struck in Paris during 1670. They were silver pieces to the value of 15 and 5 *sols and a copper *double. The copper piece is the only one to bear a specific reference to its American destination; all bear the mintmark A. Mention of Canada is also made in the edict of 1717, which authorised copper pieces to the value of 12 and 6 *deniers, though these were also to be current in the Caribbean and Louisiana. These coins were struck at Perpignan with the mintmark Q.

All these coins are exceedingly rare, the 1670 double probably unique. No French mint was ever established on Canadian soil; the scarcity of imported coin was only alleviated by local issues of *playing-card money. Issues of this can be dated (from documents) as early as 1685, though none has survived prior to 1714. Though not strictly coinage (i.e. not struck as currency), the *jetons of Louis XV deserve mention. There is a series of ten celebrating various aspects of French-Canadian colonisation, beautifully engraved by *Duvivier and struck in silver.

FRENCH REVOLUTIONARY CALENDARS The collector may well feel perplexed when he comes across two French coins, both bearing the date 1793, yet one with the additional inscription "an 5", the other "an 2". He will be even more puzzled if it is pointed out to him that of two coins both marked "an 4", one was struck in 1792 and the other in 1795 . . . !

The table that follows will, it is hoped, clear up some of the confusion. It will be seen that no less than three different calendars were dreamt up at various times, to run from various different dates; and in the happy muddle that characterised the times, it did not by any means follow that one calendar was dropped as a new one was adopted.

An accurate chronological listing of all French revolutionary coin issues is, in fact, only possible by following official coinage decrees as published consecutively in *Le Moniteur* (the government gazette). At any rate, this applies until 22 September 1797, when we enter upon "an 6" and no more confusion is possible between the divergent dates as shown in columns 1 and 3 of the table.

Synoptic Table

Year	Era of Liberty	Era of Equality or of the Republic 1st formula	Era of the French or of the Republic 2nd formula
1789	an 1		
1790	an 2		
1791	an 3		
1792	an 4	an 1: from 22 September to 31 December	an 1: from 22 September
1793	an 5	an 2: from 1 January to the decree of 5 October	an 2: from 22 September
1794			an 3: from 22 September
1795			an 4: from 23 September
1796			an 5: from 22 September
1805			an 14: from 23 September to 31 December
1806	Return to Gregorian Calendar		

FRIBOURG Town (and canton) of Switzerland, with its own coinage from the 15th century. During the 19th century, no less than three banks issued paper money here, all of which is today very rare.

FRIEDRICH D'OR Struck by Frederick II (the Great) of Prussia throughout his long reign (1740–86) in a number of types, which finally stabilised in 1764. Lower-grade gold was used by some of the Silesian mints during the Seven Years' War, but by and large the coin remained steady at the exact equivalent of the French *louis d'or (6.70 grammes, .916 fine). The varieties of busts, from young, armoured, middle-aged to old, and reverses showing various forms of eagle with trophies, besides mint and die (mint engravers) varieties, make this long series a fascinating one to study, although not a cheap one to collect. Halves were frequently struck, but doubles less so, the last in 1776.

In one way or another, the coin continued to be struck until 1853. It became also known as the *pistole: the equivalent of several other gold coins to the value of 5 Thalers, common in German states before the unification of the Empire in 1870.

FRIESE, TILEMANN   Mayor of Göttingen (Germany) who in 1588 published under the title *Münz-Spiegel* (Coin Mirror) one of the first popular numismatic treatises. Earlier such works (e.g. *Agricola, Budé) had generally been written for other scholars, in Latin, and dealt with classical coinages only. Friese, on the other hand, compiled a general survey for readers in his native tongue, and was as much concerned with contemporary as with ancient coins, and with such subjects as rates of exchange between Germany and other countries.

FUANG   One-eighth of the *bat or *tical in the European-style coinage of Siam as introduced under King Mongkut (1851–68). The machinery on which these pieces were struck was one of the first foreign installations carried out by *Taylor and Challen of Birmingham.

FUETER, CHRISTIAN (1752–1844)   Mintmaster at Berne, Switzerland, from 1792–1837 and engraver of most of the coins there during that period. He was trained by his more famous compatriot Mörikofer and modelled himself both on his master and the even more famous *Hedlinger. Coins of Appenzell and Lucerne are also attributed to him.

FUGGER   The great *Augsburg merchant banking house struck both gold and silver coins after its head had been ennobled as a Count of the Holy Roman Empire late in the 16th century. More interesting, though less known perhaps, is its association with the Papacy as licencee of the Roman Mint from 1508. The patent, originally granted by Julius II, was intermittently restored by Leo X and Clement VII. Coins struck under the Fugger mintmastership are distinguished by a small trident, which may appear on the obverse or the reverse of the piece. One of their finest productions is the double ducat of Leo X with the Three Wise Men on horseback as the reverse type. Since payments in the Fugger ledgers are recorded to *Caradosso—at that time chief engraver to the Roman Mint, who is known to have experimented with mechanical means of striking—Augsburg's later technical preeminence in northern Europe is probably due to this close association with Rome.

FUGIO CENT   The first coin to be issued under United States authority (as opposed to coinage of individual states), struck by order of Congress during 1787. The thirteen linked circles represent the totality of states making up the Union at that time, while the word "Fugio" and the meridian sun shown on the obverse refer to the passing of time. The legends "We are one" and 'Mind your business" are generally attributed to Benjamin *Franklin, and the pieces are therefore also known as Franklin Cents. Dies for the coins were engraved by Abel Buel of New Haven, where the pieces were also struck. A number of varieties—some very rare—are known; and restrikes were made from old dies rediscovered in 1858.

FULDA   An abbey in Franconia, Germany, which from the early 12th century struck large and beautifully executed *bracteates. They generally represent the abbot, either alone or with the patron saint Boniface.

FULLERTON, COLONEL (1754–1808)   The author of some *fantasy pieces (half-crowns, shillings, 6-penny pieces, half-pennies and farthings), engraved by John *Milton to his design and struck at the Royal Mint by special permission of the Prince of Wales. The pieces bore the Prince's bust on the obverse (as Senschal of Scotland) and on the reverse the arms of England. They never circulated but are much sought-after for their beauty and rarity as *patterns. Fullerton also caused to be struck two other pieces which come under the category of penny tokens: one with the helmeted head of Wallace, the other with a profile bust of Adam Smith—both exceedingly rare.

FUN   A copper denomination of Korea, issued only in 1894 together with a 5-fun multiple.

FUNDUK ALTUN   An Ottoman coin introduced under Ahmet III (1703–30), replacing the *altun. It differed from the earlier coin in omitting all religious formulae, retaining only the Sultan's *tughra.

FYRK   A Swedish denomination, to the value of one-quarter *øre. It was struck in both silver (intermittently from 1522–1601) and copper (1624–60).

G

GADHYA PAISA Small coins of dumpy *fabric, which circulated in Gujarat (India) in the 6th century A.D. They are usually of base silver, and Indian influences in stylistic patterns have not yet entirely driven out Sassanian ones.

GAETA A town near Naples; the seat of an *autonomous coinage during the 11th and 12th centuries, and then of the Norman dukes of Apulia from the late 12th to the 14th centuries. More recently (1848–9), coins were struck here for Pope Pius IX while in exile from Rome during the revolutionary troubles of those years.

GALEOTTI, PIETRO PAOLO (1520–84) Coin and medal engraver, active chiefly at Florence where he cut the majority of the dies for the Grand Duke Cosimo I from about 1550 onwards. A scudo of 1573 is particularly fine; and Vasari also mentions a series of twelve medals representing Cosimo's achievements and improvements to the cities of Florence and Pisa. The artist was a pupil of Benvenuto *Cellini.

GALLE A mint of Ceylon under Dutch rule, where copper *stuivers and their doubles were struck from 1783–95.

GALLE, ANDRÉ (1761–1844) French coin and medal engraver who served his apprenticeship in the button establishment of Le Cour at Lyon, of which he later became sole proprietor. His pattern coin with the head of Mirabeau was the first—and perhaps finest—of the trial pieces in *bell metal submitted to the French assembly by the "artistes réunis" of Lyon. Among his medals, one of Matthew *Boulton will be of particular interest to English collectors. Galle was also a fine copper-plate engraver, and in 1819 cut the plate for the 500-franc note of the Banque de France.

GALLEY HALFPENCE A popular name for inferior foreign currencies struck in base metal, which Italian and other merchants tried to exchange at Galley Quay on the Thames during the 14th century (also *dodkin).

GANI One of the earliest attempts at a *token currency. It was made under Sultan Muhammed-ibn-Tughlaq of Delhi from 1329–32. He issued pieces in brass and copper marked "sealed as a tankah of fifty ganis". Though everyone had heard of and knew the *tankah both as a gold and silver coin, the experiment was not a success, despite the Sultan's explicit guarantee (which was in fact kept) that all tokens would be redeemed.

GARIEL, ERNEST (1826–84) The most perspicacious collector of French medieval coins in the second half of the 19th century. Aided by a cement fortune which enabled him to retire early from business, he devoted the rest of his life to building up two quite distinct collections. The first, regal coinage of the Carolingian dynasty in France, was meticulously catalogued by him in three volumes (Strasbourg 1883–4). The second, Burgundian coins from Merovingian times to the 15th century, is today in the

Gadhya paisa of Gujarat, 6th century B.C.

museum of Auxerre, to which he donated it and which has catalogued it (1908).

GARTER COINS AND MEDALS   The Order of the Garter has been conferred on numerous foreign rulers through the centuries; some of them have celebrated the event by reproducing it on commemorative coins or medals. An early example is a medal of 1593 of Duke Frederick of Württemberg, by François Briot; there are coins of the Electors of Saxony in the 18th century; it also appears on a two-thirds Thaler of William IV in his role of King of Hanover (1832).

GATTEAUX, FATHER & SON   Nicolas Marie Gatteaux was born in 1751 and began his career at the Paris Medal Mint in 1773, a year before the death of Louis XV (a medal of whom is among his first works). In the subsequent years until 1802 he engraved no less than 288 others, besides coinage patterns, *assignats, revenue stamps and lottery tickets. His son Jacques Edouard (b. 1788) was active from 1807–55 and was quite as prolific as his father, though as a medallist only.

GAUL, FRANTZ (1802–74)   19th-century Austrian coin engraver and medallist, who rose to be head of the Imperial Academy of Engraving at Vienna. He is responsible for all Austrian coins issued from 1848–57, and a number of pieces in the Austro-Hungarian series, the double Gulden of 1873 celebrating the 25th anniversary of Franz Joseph I's reign being probably his last work.

GAUNT & SON, J. R.   Button and badge makers of Birmingham and London. The firm also undertook one contract coinage, of a brass shilling for British West Africa, which is very rare today (only 1,600 struck, with the mintmark G).

GAYRARD, RAYMOND (1777–1858)   Prolific French sculptor and medallist. His work for the coinage is confined to patterns submitted in 1848 for the Second Republic.

GAZETTA   A Venetian copper coin of the 17th and 18th centuries, struck for possessions of Venice in the eastern Mediterranean. One (of 1658) bears the name of Candia (the modern Chania), then the capital city of Crete; and there are later types for the Ionian islands.

GEBEL, MATTHES (d. 1574)   Active in Nuremberg from around 1525 to 1555, Gebel marks an important turning point in the history of the German Renaissance medal. Of the more than 300 portraits he made—mostly cast in silver—the vast majority are of middle-class citizens. The diameter of his medals is smaller than was previously common, between 40 and 45 millimetres. At the end of Gebel's working life, the transition from the medal as a decorative item for princes or patricians to a household object is complete. From here, it was but a short step to the series production methods of Valentin *Maler. This is not to say that Gebel's art lacked finesse: he had an astonishing talent for characterisation on the small module which he chose, and he has left us, among other fine portraits, a moving one of *Dürer (on his death in 1528).

Gebel used soap-stone to carve his models. Only a very few of his medals are signed MG, and these all date from 1543 or later.

GEBHART, ULRICH   *Gemisch.

GELA   One of the most important towns of ancient Sicily, with a varied coinage from *c.* 500 to 400 B.C. The dominant type is the forepart of a man-headed bull, representing the local river-god.

GEMISCH, STEPHAN   First mintmaster at *Joachimsthal, and responsible for the larger silver pieces struck there (*Thaler). The dies were engraved by Ulrich Gebhart.

GENEVA An important mint from Merovingian times onwards, Episcopal issues are known here from the 11th century and gold from the 16th. The output (until 1848) is too large to be detailed even in outline (a two-volume catalogue has been published); but perhaps emergency coins bearing the inscription "Monnaie pour les soldats de Genève" during the struggle with Savoy deserve mention. The French *decime was adopted during the revolution of 1793–4. For most of its coinage the city adopted the inscription POST TENEBRAS LUX. (*Genevoise.)

GENEVA MUSEUM *coin weights.

GENEVOISE Popular nomenclature for the *écu d'argent of 10 *decimes, introduced in Geneva's decimal system during 1794, but abolished already in 1795. It substituted the words "République Genevoise" for the earlier "Genève République", and "Après les ténèbres la lumière" for "Post tenebras lux".

GENGEMBRE, PHILIPPE Clever mechanician who at the end of the 18th century invented a number of useful improvements at the Paris Mint. One was concerned with countermarking, another with cutting the *flan and stamping the coin in one operation, a third with the edge-stamping of coins. Under Napoleon (who commissioned a pattern *para for Egypt in 1799), Gengembre rose to become inspector-general of the coinage.

GENNARO, MARIA ANTONIO Neapolitan engraver and medallist, active during the first half of the 18th century at a number of mints. Besides working on the coinage for Naples and Sicily around 1702, he was employed by Charles VI at Vienna from 1713, and his signature is also found on pieces for Poland, Saxony and Salzburg. He died in 1744.

GENOA The numismatic history of this city has been curiously neglected, at least in the English language, in comparison with Florence and Venice; yet it is possibly richer and certainly more varied than either of the others. Quite apart from the coinage of the independent Republic, there are no less than six different periods of French and Milanese occupations from 1396–1512; there are certain bank issues of the *Casa di San Giorgio; there is its role as a mint under Napoleon (first from the Ligurian Republic, later as an imperial mint for France herself); and, finally, from 1815–60, as part of the kingdom of Sardinia. (Also *Bugatto, genovino.)

Genovino, late 13th century

GENOVINO The standard gold coin of *Genoa, authorised by a decree of 1149, though in fact not struck until towards the end of the following century, and thus anticipated by both the *florin and the *ducat as Europe's first regular gold coinage of the Middle Ages. Like that of the other coins, its type was to remain constant for centuries (obverse: castle gate; reverse: cross), with some floreate elaborations when the Doges were named, from Simon Boccanegra (1339) onwards. There are some exceedingly rare issues under French occupation (Charles VI, Charles VII and Louis XII) and under John Galeazzo Sforza of Milan.

GEORGE D'OR The *pistole or 5-Thaler gold piece as struck by the Hanoverian dynasty intermittently from 1758–1857. An interesting issue for the English collector is that engraved by Thomas *Wyon and struck at the Royal Mint from 1813–14 for the payment of troops in the Napoleonic wars.

GEORGE NOBLE English gold coin introduced by Henry VIII in 1526 to the value of 6s. 8d. It was a short-lived issue (until 1533 only) and is very rare (the half-noble is probably unique). The

George noble of Henry VIII

name is taken from the coin's reverse type, showing St George slaying the dragon.

GEORGIA *Tiflis.

GERSH A unit in the currency system of Ethiopia under the Emperor Menelik II (1889–1913). It was valued at one-tenth of the *talari and struck in silver. Multiples of 2, 4 and 8 gersh were also struck.

GESSNER, HANS JAKOB (1677–1737) Mintmaster and coin engraver of Zurich during the early 18th century. Besides many coins at the Zurich Mint from 1706–37 he engraved many fine medals, among which a protrait of Zwingli (made in 1719 on the 200th anniversary of the Reformation) is particularly noteworthy. He is known to have worked also at the mint of Berne.

GESSNER, SALOMON (1730–88) Famous chiefly as a painter and poet, this Zurich artist (not related to Hans Jakob) has a very rare and beautiful Thaler of 1773 named after him, as he sketched its original design. Only a few specimens were struck before the dies cracked.

GHENT Town in what is today Belgium; a mint from the time of Charlemagne and later for the counts of Flanders. Its main interest for the English collector lies in the extensive series of imitation *rose-nobles struck here during 1581–2.

GHURUSH A large silver denomination, introduced in 1687 into the Ottoman coinage under Suleiman II. The name is derived from the German *Groschen, but the coin is more of *Thaler size, though not as heavy. Like the Spanish *peso, such coins were most commonly dubbed *piastre in western European parlance.

GIBRALTAR A British possession since 1704, "The Rock" has only since 1842 had a small coinage in the *quart(o) denomination. From 1802–20, there is a variety of *tokens (also in quarts).

GIGLIATO A silver coin introduced in 1304 by Charles II of Anjou. The obverse type shows a ruler seated on his throne; the reverse (from which the coin takes its name) shows lilies in the angles of a floreate cross. The coin was struck in huge quantities by Charles's successors and extensively copied (for example, by the Popes at Avignon during the period of the "Babylonian captivity"). So it became one of the most widely accepted throughout the Mediterranean area—and even as far east as the western shores of Asia Minor (Ephesus, Magnesia, Palatia).

GIGOT A copper coin of Brabant, issued at Antwerp and Bruges for Francis of Anjou after the Dutch provinces had broken away from Philip II of Spain (1581). The Flemish name for these coins was negenmanneke.

GIL, GERONIMO ANTONIO Engraver at the Mexico Mint during the last quarter of the 18th century; as renowned for his many coins as for his fine series of *proclamation medals.

GILT Gold plated. The coin may be either silver (in which case the piece is known as silver-gilt or by the French term *vermeille)*, or base metal.

A great many of *Boulton's trial pieces and medals were gilt, but this gilding was always done to perfection in preparing and polishing the blanks before the pieces were struck. Collectors should beware of anything looking at all rough, which almost certainly means an attempt at later "improvement".

Cast medals of the Renaissance and the Baroque eras were also often gilt—in this case invariably after casting. Delicate details of the original bronze are more likely to be spoilt than enhanced by the process; and no work of art conceived in one medium will look its best in another. Personal taste may to some extent be a touchstone here; to the purist, a fine bronze medal that has been later gilded is rather like a Daumier lithograph that has been "hand-coloured".

GIULIO The *grosso largo of the Popes during and subsequent to the Renaissance. The coin was named after Pope Julius II who was the first (from 1503 onwards) to feature his portrait extensively on this piece.

GIUSTINA A silver coin of Venice to the value of 8 *lire, introduced under Nicholas da Ponte (1578–85). The coin takes its name from the reverse type, showing St Justina.

GLASGOW An uncertain Scottish mint, possibly active during the reigns of Robert II and/or Robert III (1371–1406). The evidence for its existence is indirect: no actual coins are known, but there is a contemporary forgery in base metal with a legend reading VILLA DE GLASGOU. There are also reports of the existence of a genuine *groat of a similar type in the 18th and 19th centuries.

GLASS WEIGHTS *coin weights.

GNADENPFENNIG Literally translated, this means "penny of grace". It was, in fact, a special type of medal, more often than not oval in shape and in a setting of precious stones, awarded as a mark of favour by kings and emperors in the late 16th and early 17th centuries. The Habsburg dynasty is especially rich in medallic memorials of this kind, which were often beautifully enamelled.

Schau=Pfening, welchen Pabst Sixtus IV
Herrn Burgermeist: Roust A:1474 verehrt

Gnadenpfennig: Also occasionally called Schaupfennig. This one was presented by Pope Sixtus IV to the Mayor of Zurich in 1474

GOA This Portuguese mint on the eastern coast of India is important as being the very first of the modern world to strike a local colonial coinage of specific type. It is further notable for being the only such mint to strike gold coinages during the 16th century. This is in marked contrast to the practice of colonial Spain which, although it operated no less than four mints in the Americas before the 17th century (*Mexico City, Santo Domingo, Lima and Potosi), confined strikings there to crude, roughly-

Godless florin, 1849

shaped versions of Spanish silver reales, copper maravedis, etc. No overseas Spanish mint was authorised to strike gold before 1620. *Esphera, Pardao, Santa Fé de Bogotá, Xeraphim.

GOBRECHT, CHRISTIAN (1785–1844)   Chief engraver at the Philadelphia Mint from 1840–44. While still an assistant engraver, he cut some beautiful patterns for a new silver *dollar (finally issued from 1840 onwards). Gobrecht had earlier been an engraver of banknotes in Philadelphia.

GODLESS FLORIN   The first English silver *florin of 1849 omitted the words "Dei gratia" in the legend. It was accordingly given the above name by the public, and much agitation ensued to restore the missing words. The type was replaced only two years later by the *gothic florin.

GOFFIN, DANIEL   French engraver of Sedan, during the early years of the 17th century. He cut dies for, among others, Sedan, Raucourt La-Tour-à-Glaire and Château-Regnault. From around 1615 to 1630, probably only *Briot excelled him in workmanship among French engravers. A less reputable part of his career began towards the end of the 1620s, when he engraved imitations of German, Italian and Spanish coins at a mint of La Vanette.

GOLD   The most precious of metals. Before the discovery of platinum, gold has been used for coinage almost from the beginnings. Apart from its beauty, its great advantage is that it does not tarnish or corrode. Its one disadvantage as a coinage metal is softness, and it is generally used with a hardening *alloy (most often copper) in coinage.

It would be foolish even to begin to list the desirable gold coins of the world. Greek and Roman gold are today beyond the reach of the average collector; and even fine and rare specimens of so recent a coin as the guinea are relatively expensive. The 20-franc piece of Napoleon I and the English* sovereign from Victoria onwards are probably the best hunting-grounds for someone hoping to build up a representative collection. The former offers a choice of no less than eighteen mints; the latter has intriguing possibilities of collecting die numbers from 1864–74. Other reasonably priced opportunities still exist in the Byzantine and certain oriental series, while the *tola coinages of modern Indian banking houses have not yet been comprehensively catalogued and will be a spur to those who like to combine collecting with original research.

GOLD COAST   *ackey.

GOLD IN THE UNITED STATES   The first report of a gold find by Thomas Jefferson in 1782 (a lump of ore by the Rappahannock River in Virginia) did not, apparently, cause any kind of "gold rush". The largest gold coin authorised by the Mint Act, 10 years later, was the *eagle of $10; its double did not follow until 1849, and was the direct result of enormous discoveries in California, from 1848 onwards. (There had been smaller discoveries meanwhile in North and South Carolina, and in Georgia.) There were to be bigger ones still in Colorado, Nevada and South Dakota in due course; and although today the US lags behind Canada in actual gold production, it still maintains the largest gold reserves in the world at Fort Knox.

Enormous quantities of gold coins were struck until the Wall Street crash of 1929; then, within 4 years, not only did all such strikings cease but American citizens were prohibited by law from holding all except "numismatic" gold coins,—i.e. those of some rarity value. Meltings of gold coins surrendered during the period 1933–50 have been estimated at $1,600 billion, leaving extant no more than $260,725,000 in face value. By far the greatest number of meltings (83%) were among the $20 *double eagles; this is known to be 38% of all such coins struck, and explains the relatively high premium it commands above bullion value as a collector's coin.

The restrictions on holding gold continued with only minor variations until 1974; it was officially "freed" on 1 September of that year, and the Franklin Mint celebrated the event by striking a Panamanian 100-Balboa piece on 31 December that could be purchased much above face value by collectors. Meanwhile, the US has continued to avoid any striking of "official" issues; but this will change with the 1984 Los Angeles Olympics, for which a $10 gold commemorative is to be struck, but limited to 2 million and only available to collectors as part of the set which also in-cludes silver pieces. Designs at the moment of writing are yet to be finalised, but "patterns" by way of artists' drawings are here shown.

1984 gold 10-dollar coin
(courtesy of the U.S. Mint)

GOLTZIUS, HEINRICH (1558–1617) Dutch painter and line engraver. He made a fine portrait medallion of the Earl of Leicester as governor-general of the Netherlands.

GOLTZIUS, HUBERTUS (1526–87) A leading numismatist of his time, who published a whole series of volumes on ancient numismatics from *c.* 1557 to 1579. He himself sketched and engraved the illustrations for these works, to compile which he visited (as he tells us) and examined nearly one thousand col-lections in Italy, France, Holland and Germany.

GOOD SAMARITAN SHILLING A spurious American piece. Formerly thought to be a pattern for the *pinetree shilling of Massachusetts, it has now been proved to be a 19th century forgery.

GORCUM A town in Holland and occasionally the seat of a mint, both official and unofficial. The latter activity—during the second half of the 16th century—is numismatically the more interesting. During the 1580s, Gorcum struck imitations of the English *rose-noble, and also gold and silver coins for Don Antonio, who disputed the throne of Portugal with Philip II of Spain from 1580 to 1590. These coins, struck between 1584 and 1589, are excessively rare; but certain dies have been preserved in the town's archives to this day.

GORTYNA A mint of ancient Crete, which celebrates in its coinage the legend of Europa and the bull. A new twist is given to the legend by the Gortynians, for it is evident on certain varieties of the coins that Jupiter, not content with carrying her off in the shape of a bull, afterwards pursues her up a tree in the disguise of an eagle.

Gortyna: stater, late 4th century B.C.

GORY OBAN The half-*oban: a Japanese gold piece issued only in 1837.

GOSLAR Like *Joachimsthal, this town in the Harz mountains owes its importance as a mint to the proximity of silver mines—in this instance within the nearby Rammelsberg, where rich deposits were discovered in A.D. 968. Coins were struck here for around 200 years—all silver pennies—the principal types being the *Adelheidspfennige, later facing busts of St Simon and St Jude and (under Henry V, 1106–25) the first "rider on horses" type to be known in the German coinage. Finally, a unique type showing a stag was struck in *bracteate fabric during the years 1166–8 during Goslar's uprising against Henry the Lion (probably as an emblem of the Lords of Dassel, who supported the revolt).

GOTHA One of the most important mints of Saxony for more than three centuries. It struck coinage both for the kingdom of

Gothic crown of Victoria, 1847

Saxony and the duchy of Saxe-Gotha, reaching its highest renown (and rate of production) under Christian *Wermuth during the first quarter of the 18th century. It did not finally close until 1838. The town, today in the German Democratic Republic, has a very fine collection, both of ancient Greek and Roman coinages and of Saxonian coins and medals.

GOTHIC CROWN   Issued in 1847 and 1853 as a *proof only. The coin is named after the typographical design of its *legend, which recalls the gothic letter of the first typefaces before the invention of a Roman type. It was not at the time put into circulation because of the conscious attempt—which was to last forty years—to oust the crown and half-crown in favour of the *florin. Today it is one of the most sought-after pieces by English collectors.

GOTHIC FLORIN   This type (for an explanation of whose name *gothic crown) replaced the *Godless florin in 1851 and was struck continuously (except during 1861 and 1882) until 1887. There are forty-four major varieties excluding *proofs and an interesting series of die-numbered coins from 1864–78. (At the moment of writing, 355 different die-date varieties have been recorded.)

GOUIN, SALOMON   Dutch sculptor and engraver, who was the first among the many foreign workers recruited by Peter the Great (c. 1700) for his great coinage reform. Gouin engraved the very first half-*rouble to be struck by machinery in Moscow, during 1701; and he continued to be, together with *Haupt, one of the principal artists concerned with coins and medals under Peter the Great until 1713.

GOURDE   A silver coin of Haiti, first introduced under Henri Christophe (1812–20). It was the equivalent of the French 5-franc piece.

GRAF, URS   One of the most celebrated engravers of the German Renaissance (c. 1485–1537). Trained originally as a goldsmith, Graf spent a great deal of his life as a mercenary soldier and was something of a freebooter, with several spells in prison. He is known to have been employed at the mint of *Basel between 1516–32 and most probably engraved the gold Gulden and *Dicken with the fine portraits of the Madonna and Child of that period.

GRAMO   Spanish for the gramme weight; found as a denomination only on the 1-gramo and 5-gramos pieces of a private gold coinage issued by Julius Popper on Tierra del Fuego in 1889.

GRANADA   The town in Spain which was subject longest to Moorish influence, still seen today in the magnificent Alhambra. Gold and silver coins of exclusively Moorish style and fabric were struck here until 1492, when the Muslims were finally overthrown by Ferdinand and Isabella. Under the edict of *Medina del Campo (1497), Granada became one of the seven regal mints of Spain, distinguished by the initial letter G.

GRAND BLANC   The largest silver piece of the *Anglo-Gallic series, introduced by Henry VI.

GRANO   This was first of all a southern Italian weight, to the norm of 1/600th of an uncia, introduced by the Emperor Frederick II in 1222. Later (c. 1460) it became the smallest copper denomination in the coinage of Ferdinand II of Naples and Sicily; and from the 16th to the 19th centuries it was also the smallest copper coin of Malta, until replaced by the third-farthing under British rule.

GRANT MEMORIAL COINS   Struck by the United States Mint in 1922 to celebrate the centenary of the birth of President

Grant, both as a gold dollar and silver half-dollar. There is a variety with a star above Grant's name, which is very much rarer on the silver piece.

GREEK COINAGE   The term is generally applied to all coinages of the Mediterranean and Black Sea regions, including what is today North Africa, from the 7th to the 1st centuries B.C. Only excluded from this definition are coinages that originated at Rome (or its provinces) from the 3rd century B.C.

The origins of Greek coinage are to be found not in Greece proper, but in Asia Minor *c.* 650 B.C. Rough oblong pieces were struck probably at *Sardes, in *electrum. The first regular gold and silver issues followed—again in Asia Minor—about fifty years later. *Ephesus (still in Asia Minor) gave the ancient Greek world its first coin with an inscription.

The island of *Aegina and the city of *Athens soon after adopted a coinage system of their own; and the invention then spread with considerable rapidity until it embraced more than 1,500 different localities. Greek coinage was essentially a local, city coinage, with some notable exceptions (*Athens, Corinth, Cyzicus). The Empire of Persia confined itself to one main type (both in gold and silver). It should also be remembered that coinage was by no means universal, even among powerful trading nations: the Phoenicians, in particular, were late starters.

Artistically and technically, Greek coinage derives from engraving gem-stones as seals—an art going back at least another millennium. It is to the skill of these artists that Greek coinage owes its unsurpassed splendour. Many of the coins are miniature jewels in gold or silver; and in some instances the same signatures have been found on coins as on engraved gem-stones. As opposed to modern coins, Greek ones are much more "dumpy" or ovoid, with the design standing out in high relief. Again, there are exceptions, and certain coins even show the obverse design mirrored as an *incuse one on the reverse.

The immense diversity of Greek coin types reflects Greek religion and mythology in all their manifold guises. Realistic portraiture of living human beings is of the greatest rarity before the 4th century B.C. (*Cyzicus) and does not become common until the 2nd. Plants and animals, like gods and goddesses, abound; views of cities or even of temples are infrequent.

Greek Coinage: Tetradrachm of Seleukos I, 3rd century B.C.

GREEK IMPERIAL COINAGE   A misnomer for what is really Roman *provincial* coinage, during imperial times, in parts of the former Greek empire dating from the expansionary period of Alexander the Great and including most of Asia Minor, as well as stretching north into Bactria and south into Egypt. The word 'Greek' is justified here only in so far as inscriptions continued to be struck in that language and script, and that the reverses continued to show local types; the obverse always bore the Roman emperor's effigy. There is a vast variety, chiefly in bronze, by literally hundreds of cities and towns, among which *Alexandria was for three centuries to remain the most important.

GREGORIAN CALENDAR   A reform of the calendar, which in medieval days had fallen into what can only be called disarray, was mooted as early as the 1470s, when Pope Sixtus IV called the astronomer Regiomontanus from Nuremberg to Rome; but nothing came of this, as Regiomontanus was murdered within months of his arrival. It was left to Pope Gregory XII, aided by the astronomer Clavius, to standardise the Christian (or rather Roman Catholic) calendar more or less as we know it today, in a papal bull dated 2 March 1582. In this, the beginning of the year was moved from 25 March to 1 January.

None the less, the accurate dating of any coin must remain conjectural through large parts of Europe. The Protestant countries followed suit only hesitantly and at various times during the next two centuries (England in 1752), and not until 1776 did a decree of the Holy Roman Emperor shift the beginning of the year from 7 June to 1 January in part of his dominions. More confusion was caused soon after in France by the institution of the *French Revolutionary Calendar.

Certain countries delayed the introduction of the Gregorian Calendar very much longer. Egypt introduced it in 1875, China in 1912, Russia in 1918, Greece in 1923 and Turkey not until 1927.

GRENADA This island in the Caribbean formed at first (until 1763) part of the French colonial empire: together with Guadeloupe, Martinique and St Lucia it was a group known as Isles du Vent (Windward Isles). Special denominations of 12 and 6 *sols were struck for this group under Louis XV in 1730. Under British rule it had no currency of its own, only Spanish dollars more often than not in the form of *cut money and distinguished by the letter G in *incuse impression.

GRIFFON A type rather than a denomination. There are coins of the Netherlands from the early 15th century onwards showing one or more fabulous beasts of this name (which is also a not infrequent type in ancient Greek coinages).

Griffon: Gold state of Abdera (reverse), 4th century B.C.

GRIPENHIELM DUCAT A very rare Swedish gold coin, struck in 1695 and named after Baron Nils Gripenhielm, governor of the province of Dalecarlia. Gold had been discovered in the silver ore mined at Öst Silvberg and was used for these pieces (of which only about a hundred were struck). These coins show on their obverse the bust of King Karl XI of Sweden, and on the reverse the inscription EX AURO SVEC. REPERTO IN DALIA & ÖST: SILV.BERGH A 1695, with Gripenhielm's name beneath in tiny script.

GRIPSHOLM A recently discovered mint, south-west of Stockholm. It is now known that it was hastily set up by Karl Duke of Södermanland in 1598 to strike *daler in *Klippe form needed to pay troops in the war against Sigismund of Poland.

GRIVNA This Russian word covers a multitude of different meanings and uses. Beginning as a unit of weight in early medieval times, grivna were then successively money of *account from the 11th century, gold currency bars from the 12th, and similar silver bars from the 13th century. Finally, the grivna was a base silver coin to the value of 10 *kopeks.

GROAT An English silver piece to the value of 4 pennies. It began to be struck, sporadically and in small quantities only, under Edward I, but did not come into its own until the reign of Edward III. At least forty main varieties are listed from 1351 onwards, and there are some twenty under Edward IV. The type remained that of a facing head until the new and very beautiful profile design under Henry VII (Alexander *Bruchsal). Nothing as distinguished was to appear again: the coin did not escape the general debasement under Henry VIII and was abandoned under Edward VI. (Also *Britannia groat.)

Groat of Edward III (1351-77)

GROAT, SCOTTISH A 4-penny piece, and also its half, was introduced into the Scottish coinage in 1357 under David II. The coin was not (like its English equivalent) of a new design, but really only a larger copy of the existing penny. In 1526, under James V, the Scottish groat was revalued at 18 pence. Finally, Mary Queen of Scots introduced a 12-penny groat of *billon in 1558.

GRONINGEN A province of the northernmost part of Holland, with its principal town of the same name. This has been a mint of importance from at least the mid-15th century (with dated silver coinage going back to 1455). There are also siege and other necessity pieces of no less than four different dates: 1577, 1591, 1597 and 1672.

GROOT The silver *gros of the Netherlands, imitated from the gros tournois of France and first struck under John II of Brabant (1294–1312).

GROS Introduced by Louis IX of France in 1266, this silver coin was worth 12 *deniers and reflected (together with gold coins reintroduced) a new expansion of trade in Europe. The type was also known as the gros tournois (from the town of Tours, where it was first struck); and its design, spreading as it did to the very edge of the coin, was deliberately devised to make clipping more difficult.

GROSCHEN Derived from the French *gros, the Groschen became the principal silver coin of the Holy Roman Empire. But whereas the gros tournois was renowned for its purity of metal and fine design, the Turnosgroschen, Turnose or Groschen (as it was finally called) became a byword for debasement, both of style and silver content. The name survives to this day as a popular one for the now copper or nickel pieces of 10 Pfennige.

GROS HEAUMÉ A silver coin issued by Charles VI of France in 1420. The shield of the kingdom is surmounted by a helmet. The type was copied by the Bishop of Liège in the 1430s, but with a very different reverse.

GROSSO An Italian word meaning simply large or broad, and used to describe the first Italian coin to be struck to a value higher than the denaro or silver penny. The value has varied from the original Venetian piece of 1202 (4 denari): the dukes of Milan, for instance, struck grossi of 8 and 5 *soldi.

GROSSO LARGO A silver *grosso on a larger than usual *flan. It was introduced in the papal coinage during the 13th century (*giulio).

GROSSONE The principal silver coin of the popes at Rome from the 14th century onwards. It showed the pontiff seated on the obverse, with the crossed keys of St Peter as reverse type. It continued to be struck until the late 18th century, and the type of seated ruler facing was adopted (with local arms for the reverse) by many Italian states.

GUADALAJARA A royalist mint during the Mexican War of Independence, 1812–23. Coins were struck here during the captivity of Ferdinand VII: 8 and 4 escudos in gold and silver 8 reales. The mint remained in operation for the Republic of Mexico until 1895, with the mintmark Ga.

GUADELOUPE A French island in the Caribbean. For early coinage history *Grenada. In the late 19th century distinctive types were struck for Guadeloupe alone in values of 1 franc and 50 centimes.

GUANAJUATO A royalist mint during the Mexican War of Independence. It operated for a short period from December 1812 to May 1813, when it produced a small issue of silver 8 reales. When it reopened in 1821, it struck silver 8 and 2 reales in the name of Ferdinand VII. It became a mint of the Republic of Mexico in 1822, but continued for some time to strike coinage of imperial type before new dies were made available. With mintmark G, or G with small o within the letter, it remained operative until 1900.

Gros tournois of Louis IX of France

Grossone of Gregory XI, 1371–78

Guineas:

Charles II 5-guinea piece (1668)

GUATEMALA A mint of Spanish America established only *c.* 1728, although application was made by the governor in 1714. Both gold and silver were struck here until 1822. The early mint-mark was a G, changed to NG after the city had been largely destroyed by an earthquake in 1773 and rebuilt twenty-seven miles to the north (Nueva Guatemala). The earliest, roughly-cut silver is known as macata.

GUERCHE A silver coin of the Emperor Menelik II of Ethiopia (1889–1913), issued only in 1897. It was valued at one-sixteenth of the *talari.

GUERNSEY *double.

GUESSIN A mint of Aquitaine under Edward I between 1286–92. Both *deniers and *obols were struck here, with types of a lion or a leopard with a cross, and the mintmark G.

GUIANA (BRITISH) *Britannia groat. Earlier coinages were struck from 1809 in the name of Essequibo and Demerara and expressed in values of Dutch *guilders and *stivers.

GUIENNOIS A gold coin in the *Anglo-Gallic series, first struck under Edward III from 1360 onwards, at the mints of Bordeaux, Limoges, Poitiers and La Rochelle.

GUILDER The Dutch *gulden, as it was called in England from the date of its first appearance around 1600. For its use as a denomination within British territories, *Guiana (British).

GUINEA A gold coin, first issued in 1663 under Charles II of England to the value of 20 shillings, but rising (because of the general debasement of silver) to as high as 30 shillings in 1695. Its value was fixed at 21½ shillings after the great recoinage of 1696, and it was not finally stablised at 21 shillings until 1717, on which basis it has continued almost to this day as money of *account (though the last gold coin was actually struck in 1813).

The word "guinea" itself arose in popular usage, because the coins were struck from African gold—at least when marked with the elephant or (later) elephant and castle, symbols of the African Company. In mint indentures the word does not occur until 1717.

A full collection of guineas from 1663–1813 would number over 200 pieces, not counting *patterns or *proofs, and would today be beyond the means of most collectors. Even a type collection is not easy to assemble, a fine 1663 "elephant" now costing well over £1,000 ($1,500).

A gold coin to the value of 1 guinea was issued by Saudi Arabia in 1959. The obverse shows a palm and two crossed sabres, while the reverse has a large figure 1 and the word guinea in Arabic.

Arguably, therefore, the guinea is today best collected not as a coin but as a banknote, in which form its history stretches from 1758 (first issue by the Royal Bank of Scotland) to 1833. This is a field which still awaits its cataloguer and offers many aspects of particular interest. There is, for instance, the guinea note of the Royal Bank of Scotland dated 1777, which is the first example of a British note printed in three colours; and there is the whole intriguing story of revenue stamps, leading to such oddities as a note for 9½ guineas (i.e. £9. 19s. 6d.), purely to avoid the increase in stamp duties occurring at £10. Finally, the half- and third-guineas issued regularly from 1797–1812 (during which period few whole guineas were struck) could form a "parallel" collection of gold coins and fractional banknotes of the same denominations.

GUINEA DUCATS Gold coins struck by Brandenburg and Denmark from gold of their African possessions. The Brandenburg series is confined to the years 1682–96 and to one type only,

James II Guinea (1687)

George III guinea (1804)

showing on the reverse instead of the usual ruler's arms a three-masted sailing ship. The Danish series is much more varied and extensive, beginning in 1657 and ending only in 1747. Besides a most splendid elephant (very different from his minute and discreet counterpart on the British *guinea), there are various views of Fort Christiansborg, the Danish stronghold on the Guinea coast, sometimes showing also the harbour (with or without ships). For another interesting Danish coin, *China ducat.

GUJARAT *Gadhiya paisa.

GULDEN (GOLD) The "Goldgulden" of German cities and states were struck from the early 15th century onwards. They were roughly of the size of a *ducat, but did not keep to the strict and very high standard of that coin, either in weight or pure gold content. Very rare 25-Gulden in gold, dated 1923 and 1930, exist from the free city of Danzig.

GULDEN (SILVER) Originally, this was an abbreviation for *Guldengroschen, but in the 17th century the Gulden became a different coin, to the value of two-thirds of the *Thaler. The Netherlands gulden is a different coin again, being struck to a value of 28 *stiver from 1601. The Swedish gulden, or gyllen, was struck first as a coronation piece by Gustav I Vasa in 1518, and then again from 1522 to 1535, and is obviously modelled on the German *Guldengroschen of the time. The Gulden was the monetary unit of the free city of Danzig from 1920, struck first in silver and later in nickel.

GULDENGROSCHEN The first large silver coin of modern Europe, struck in 1486 at the mint of Hall in the Tyrol. It was the precursor of the *Thaler, and was also known as the Guldiner. Its silver value was equivalent to the gold value of the coin above.

GUN MONEY Money of necessity, struck by James II for Ireland, 1689–90. It derives its name from the fact that it was made mainly from the metal of old cannon which had been melted down. A particular feature of this issue is that it is dated month by month. Since England had then not yet adopted the *Gregorian calendar, it should be remembered that the New Year began on 25 March. Consequently January 1689 follows December 1689, and a coin marked March 1690 may have been issued during the same month as one dated March 1689.

Nearly 250 die varieties have been listed of this series, and certain very rare patterns in gold are also known.

GYLLEN *Gulden (silver).

Gun money: Sixpence of July 1689

HAGENAUER, FRIEDRICH   A prolific medallist of the German Renaissance, Hagenauer is perhaps also the most itinerant; we find him in Munich from 1525–6, in Augsburg from 1527–32, and later in Baden, Swabia, Strasbourg (where he was born) and Cologne. His models were cut in wood and often cast in silver rather than bronze, for he worked on a relatively small scale and favoured much detail. In his Augsburg period alone, he modelled over a hundred citizens there. His signature appears as a monogram of the letters FH on most of his medals, which are further characterised by mainly plain, linear inscriptions on the reverse. The dates of his birth and death are not known, but his last signed work is from Cologne and dated 1547.

HALALA   The smallest unit of the Yemen coinage, first struck in 1923 as a bronze and later a copper coin.

HALBSKOTER   A type of *Groschen struck only under Winrich de Kniprode, Grand Master of the Teutonic Order, in 1370, though there are patterns or trial pieces also of the Grand Master Michael in 1416. The type is copied from that of the *gigliato.

HALERU   Slavonic for *Heller, and the smallest unit of the Czech coinage since 1923 (100 haleru being equal to one *koruna). The denomination has at various times (and in various metals) been struck in multiples of 2, 3, 5, 10, 20, 25 and 50.

HALF-CENT   First issued as part of the United States coinage in 1793. Although it survived as a regular issue for sixty-five years, the half-cent was never a popular issue with the public. In total face value less than $40,000 of half-cents were issued from 1793–1857, when it was discontinued in accordance with an act dated 21 February. In most years 100,000 or less examples were issued, and for about twenty years, from 1830–49, none was actually struck for circulation, excepting 1832–5, while the coinage was suspended completely from 1812–24. In only two years (1804 and 1809) did the production exceed one million examples ($5,000).

With approximately 85% of the production concentrated in no less than 6 years (1804–9 inclusive) many half-cent dates and varieties are extremely scarce. However, just as it was never a popular coin of issue, neither has it ever gained popularity in the collecting fraternity. It therefore offers one of the few remaining opportunities to obtain a scarce coin at a reasonable price. The main types are as follows:

Liberty cap (head facing right), struck only in 1793
Liberty cap (facing left), 1795–7
Draped bust, 1800–8
Turban head, 1809–36 (with intervals as mentioned above)
Braided hair, 1840–49 in *proof only, also available
  as a restrike
  1849–57, regular though smallish issues except 1852, again
  proof only

HALF-DIME   This was the silver predecessor of today's *nickel. The basic history of the series throughout its eighty years' mintage closely parallels that of other US fractional silver coinages of the period (i.e. 1794–1873), except for the fact that its coinage was suspended from 1806–28.

Originally authorised, like the nation's other silver coins, as a .8924 fine issue, it was altered to .900 fine under the law of January 1837 which similarly influenced the other denominations.

Issues of 1794–5 show the "flowing hair" type bust facing right, replaced by a draped bust (also right) from 1796–7. There are thirteen, fifteen or sixteen stars around the bust according to the date. An heraldic eagle (i.e. holding a shield) replaces the rather splendid and savage bird shown on the reverse of earlier issues from 1800–5. When the coin, after a break abovementioned, was reintroduced in 1829, it showed a liberty cap bust, this time facing left, and an altered heraldic eagle reverse. The last and lengthiest issue is that known as the Liberty seated type introduced in 1837, with now a plain HALF DIME reverse surrounded by a wreath. The most notable varieties during its thirty-seven years of issue concern the stars around the rim, a figure with and without drapery and arrows facing outward from either side of the date in certain coins of 1853 and all issues of 1854–5. (These signify a weight reduction brought about by an act of February 1853).

HALF-DOLLAR (USA)   The half-dollar was an important product of the US Mint during its early years, primarily because during a period of more than thirty years, beginning in 1805, it was the only coin which was available for large transactions. Apart from sporadic issues of $2.50 and $5 gold pieces during the period, no other large silver or gold coins were produced from 1804–38.

The liberty cap design first engraved by John Reich was introduced on the half-dollar in 1807. Owing to the huge number struck from 1807–39, and since this was still an era when dies were hand-engraved, there are numerous die varieties for most dates, totalling over 600 for the whole period. Important changes took place in the closing years of this type. First, in 1836, the coin was converted from a lettered-edge type to one with reeded edges. At the same time, the denomination on the reverse was changed from "50 C" to "50 CENTS". In 1837, the weight of the coin was reduced from 208 to 206.25 grains, and the fineness raised from .8924 to .900. In 1838 the designation of value on the reverse was again changed from "50 CENTS" to "HALF DOL". This year also saw the first striking of half-dollars at the New Orleans Mint.

Liberty seated and Barber half-dollars are to all intents and purposes identical to the *quarter of the same type. A new type, called the Walking Liberty Half, was designed, like the new *dime introduced in the same year, by A. A. Weinman in 1916 and was current until 1947. There are few varieties except mintmarks, which appear (for branch mints only, as usual) on the obverse until 1917, thereafter on the reverse.

The Franklin half-dollar (obverse: head of Franklin facing right: reverse: Liberty Bell) was introduced in 1948; its designer was the then chief US Mint engraver John R. Sinnock. The series was ended prematurely when Congress ordered a new half-dollar to honour President Kennedy, assassinated in November 1963. There have already been three quite distinct issues of the Kennedy half-dollar: in .900 fine silver during 1964, .400 clad silver 1965–70, and cupro-nickel clad copper beginning 1971. There is also a 1970 Denver Mint limited collectors' issue. Gilroy Roberts designed the obverse and Frank Gasparro the reverse (eagle).

HALF-EAGLE (USA) The history of this denomination closely parallels that of the *quarter-eagle, with the legal specifications always double those of the lesser value. But strikings of the turban head design were more regular (though in small issues) during the period 1807–34, with many more varieties, overstruck dates, etc., than in the smaller piece. The first date for the Coronet type falls one year earlier here, i.e. 1839 (though this date does not include New Orleans among the branch mints). In 1866 the motto IN GOD WE TRUST was added above the head of the eagle on the reverse. Apart from this, the issue continued unadventurously until superseded in 1908 by Bela L. Pratt's Indian head design, in all respects identical to the $2.50 piece issued at the same time and with a similar history, except for a longer interval of no strikings between 1916 and 1929.

HALF-GROAT This denomination was introduced during the coinage reform of Edward II in 1351, the same year in which regular issues of the *groat itself began.

HALFPENNY The first halfpennies were issued during the time of Alfred the Great (A.D. 871–99), under Alfred as King of Wessex and also as part of the Viking coinage of East Anglia and the mint of York. But such issues were both small and infrequent. Until the time of Edward I, it was more common just to cut pennies in half, four parts or sometimes even three (the third of a penny being mentioned in some Saxon documents). It was in 1280 that Edward I introduced the halfpenny as a regular issue (together with the *farthing). It was struck as a silver coin until the time of the Commonwealth.

Copper halfpennies were first struck under Charles II in 1672. They were followed by some of tin under James II and William and Mary. Copper was reinstated under William III from 1695–1701. Queen Anne struck no halfpennies and their issues were infrequent under the first three Georges. For a period of almost a quarter of a century under George III, from 1776 to 1798 inclusive, no halfpennies at all were struck, leading to the widespread use of *tokens during that time. Not until Queen Victoria's reign did the halfpenny really come into its own. In 1860, the metal was changed from copper to bronze, and so it remained until the last halfpennies were struck in 1967.

HALIFAX CURRENCY Halifax, Nova Scotia, valued the Spanish *piastre at 5 shillings throughout the 18th century, as opposed to the official rate of 4s. 6d.

HALL A mint in the Tyrol, of particular importance from the late 15th century onwards. It was here that the Archduke Sigismund began to reform the coinage during the 1470s, leading ultimately to the first Thaler-size pieces struck in 1486 (*Guldengroschen). As an imperial mint of the Habsburg dynasty, Hall continued in operation until 1804. Its final use was as a mint of the patriot Andreas Hofer during the uprising against Bavaria in 1809.

HALLER *Heller.

HALLIDAY, THOMAS Birmingham die engraver and manufacturer of tokens and medals, active from c. 1810–42. He was responsible for a great many of the tokens produced from 1810–19, but perhaps his chief claim to fame is that the great William *Wyon learnt his craft at his establishment.

HAMBURG One of the principal cities of Germany, with a correspondingly important coinage through five centuries. Its crowning glory are the great 10-ducat pieces (Portugalöser). In the 13th century, Hamburg was together with *Lübeck the principal town of the Hanseatic League, and their joint coinage passed as currency throughout northern Europe. The "Free and Hanseatic City" continued to strike its distinctive coinage (showing a three-turreted gate) in gold until 1913 and in silver right up to the outbreak of the First World War a year later.

HAMERANI (FAMILY) A celebrated family of coin engravers and medallists, who worked for successive popes for almost two centuries (c. 1620–1807). Eight of them through five generations are known to us, among them two women, Anna and Beatrice. Of them all, perhaps Giovanni Hamerani (1649–1705) was the most skilful and prolific, working for no less than five popes and also for Queen Christina of Sweden during her residence in Rome.

HAMMERED COINAGE All coinage struck by hand (or rather with a hammer) before the introduction of machinery. In the English series, however, the term is used specifically to describe coinage before 1662 when machinery was finally established, even though there were sporadic *milled issues during the century before them.

HANCOCK, JOHN GREGORY Jr Infant prodigy among die engravers, who made about half-a-dozen medals at the age of eight and nine, c. 1800. He was born at Birmingham on 24 June 1791 and learnt the craft from his father, himself a noted medallist and maker of *tokens. Little John's entire output seems to have been concentrated into the space of about six months, and the artistic and technical progress from the first to the last of his productions is truly remarkable.

HAND OF PROVIDENCE TYPE PENNY A type of penny found only during the reigns of Edward the Elder (A.D. 899–924) and Aethelred II (A.D. 978–1016). The former is rare; the latter exists in varieties showing on the obverse the King either with or without a sceptre. The hand on the reverse appears sometimes between the letters *alpha and omega. (Also *Benediction type penny.)

HANNIBAL, EHRENREICH (1678–1741) German coin and medal engraver born in Stockholm, who from 1705 worked for the House of Hanover at Brunswick. He became mintmaster at Clausthal in 1713 and engraved, among many other pieces of English interest, coronation medals of George I and II, and a medal commemorating George II's visit to the Harz mines in 1729.

HANOVER For the kingdom, and pieces of English interest, *Anglo-Hanoverian coinage. The city was active as a mint from 1331 and remained so until 1878 (during the last few years as a mint of the Prussian kingdom, with mintmark B).

HARDHEAD A *billon denomination to the value of three-halfpence, introduced in 1555 under Mary Queen of Scots.

HARDI Gold (hardi d'or) and silver (hardi d'argent) coins, both introduced in the *Anglo-Gallic series by Edward the Black Prince in 1368. The types, though different in details of both the obverse and the reverse, are obviously derived from the French *masse d'or of Philippe III Le Hardi (1270–85)—hence the name. The hardi d'or was struck also under Richard II and Henry IV; while the silver coin was later imitated by the French kings Louis XI, Charles VIII and Louis XII at a number of French mints, and finally by Francis I at Turin.

HARD TIME TOKENS These tokens were issued during the period 1834–44 and fall into two main groups. The first are really

Hardi: Gold type of Edward the Black Prince, c. 1368

Hard time tokens: A typical satirical piece of 1837

political *medalets of a satirical nature, on President Jackson's struggle with the United States Bank. The second group consists of real tradesmen's tokens, used instead of the large cents—of the same size and metal—which were then in short supply.

HARRINGTON FARTHINGS   Tokens struck under a patent of James I dated 19 May 1613 and granted to John, Lord Harington of Exton. The series is exhaustively analysed by *Peck and still presents unsolved problems. An interesting technical point is that these tokens not infrequently turn up in strips—a proof that they were not individually struck but mass-produced on a kind of rolling-mill.

HARZ SILVER MINES   *Goslar.

HASSE, JOHN   English merchant, who visited Russia for the Muscovy Company in 1554 and gave us the first account of Russian coins, weights and measures to be printed in English. This was published in Hakluyt's *Voyages* (1589 edition) and has since been separately reprinted.

HAT MONEY   Coinage of Pahang (Malay peninsula) struck in tin during the early part of the 19th century. The name is taken from its peculiar shape. The denominations are stamped on the hat's "brim" and there are three of them: the ampat (or 4 cents) approximately 3 inches wide, the dua (its half) and the satu (its quarter, or 1 cent).

Hatpiece of James VI of Scotland, c. 1591

HATPIECE   A very rare gold piece of James VI of Scotland, issued in 1591 (6th coinage) to the value of 80 shillings. It shows the bust of the King wearing a tall hat, with a thistle behind. The reverse is perhaps even more remarkable, with a lion carrying a sceptre, above which is a cloud in its turn surmounted by the word Jehovah in Hebrew script.

HAUPT, G.   One of the Germans imported into Russia by Peter the Great in his efforts to produce a coinage the equal of any in Europe. He signed himself variously H, G.H. or HAUPT F (short for *fecit,* i.e. made), and these signatures appear on various coins and medals issued during the years 1706–10.

HAWAII   An island in the Pacific which has been part of the United States since 1900, and has used US coinage since then. As an independent kingdom (1791–1894), it struck coins only twice, in 1847 and 1881–3. The first was confined to copper cents, the second was a silver coinage ranging from 5 cents to $1.

HEATON MINT   Situated in Birmingham, and today known as The Mint (Birmingham) Ltd., this is perhaps the most famous of the private mints that have from time to time struck *contract coinages for governments throughout the world. Certainly, it was unrivalled during the second half of the 19th century. A record book remains showing no less than 408 separate contracts from 1851–1901, many of these for several denominations. An incomplete list is given in *Forrer; a catalogue raisonné remains to be made. The mintmark H appears on many but by no means all issues.

HEAUMÉ D'ARGENT   *gros heaumé.

HEAUMÉ D'OR   Flemish gold coin, the largest of those issued by Louis de Mâle, struck from 1367–8 at Ghent. The type is named after the enormous helmet supported by two lions, and should not be confused with the *lion heaumé.

HEBERDEN COIN ROOM   The name given (since it was established in 1922) to the coin collection of the Ashmolean Museum in Oxford. Coins at Oxford had previously been housed at the Bodleian Library and in various colleges. Charles Buller Heberden, who had been Principal of Brasenose College from

1899, left a sum of £1,000 to the University in 1919, to be used as the then Vice-Chancellor saw fit. It is therefore as much to the credit of the holder of that office, L. R. Farnell, as to Heberden himself, that the coin room housing all the Oxford collections and bearing Heberden's name came into being. The combined collections today rank among the biggest and most important of the British Isles (for others, *British Museum, Fitzwilliam Museum).

HEBREW INSCRIPTIONS   One would, of course, expect to find these on coins of both ancient and modern Israel. There are, however, other noteworthy examples, for which refer to entries under *hatpiece and *Ulfeldter. There are also certain *bracteates of Misico III of Poland (end of the 12th century), some giving his name and title in Hebrew, others just the name in its Polish form but written in Hebrew characters.

HECTE   A Greek coin to the value of one-sixth of the *stater. There are extensive and attractive series of these miniature jewels in both gold and electrum of *Cyzicus and *Mytilene (island of Lesbos).

HEDEBY   The earliest known Danish mint, where coining began c. A.D. 825. The first pieces are copies of Carolingian *denier types, but attractive pictorial coins of typically Norse or Viking inspiration (Scandinavian house, Viking ship, two cocks) soon made their appearance. There are also more abstract designs of a mask and coiled snake, which owe nothing to any numismatic prototype.

HEDLINGER, JOHANN KARL (1691–1771)   Coin engraver and medallist of Swiss origin and one of the most sought-after artists of his day. He worked first at Lucerne, then at the Paris Medal Mint and by 1718 was appointed chief engraver at the Stockholm Mint. The greatest part of his working life was spent in the service of the Swedish court, though he took occasional leave of absence to work for the rulers of Poland, Russia and Prussia. He retired to his native town of Schwyz in 1746 after resigning from the Stockholm Mint, devoting himself after that date almost entirely to special commissions of medals and seals for various persons and occasions. Among these is a fine medal of George II of 1760. Hedlinger was showered with honours during his lifetime, and a beautifully engraved work showing most of his creations was published at Basel in 1776, within five years of his death. Then followed two centuries of neglect; but in 1978 appeared a magisterial "catalogue raisonné" by Peter Felder, giving details of every known piece in public and private collections, besides wax models, working drawings, portraits of Hedlinger, etc.

HEISS, ALOIS (1820–93)   Leading Spanish numismatist of the 19th century, whose three-volume general catalogue published in Madrid from 1865–9 remains a standard reference work for Spanish coinage from the Arab invasion onwards. He followed this in 1870 with a book on ancient Spanish coinages (i.e. Greek, Roman and Celtic).

HELLER   A type of silver penny which originated at Schwäbisch-Hall (Würtemberg) and became one of the most widely diffused in southern Germany, Austria and Switzerland. Though mainly current during the medieval period, it survived as a copper piece in the coinage of modern Austria and as a bronze piece of German East Africa until the First World War.

HEMIDRACHM   The half-drachm of ancient Greece, more commonly known as the *triobol.

HEMIHECTE   The half of the *hecte.

HEMIOBOL   The half-obol (one-twelfth of the *drachm). Not very frequent, it is found mainly in the coinages of ancient Athens and Corinth.

HEMITARTEMORION   One-eighth of the *obol, this tiny silver denomination is known only in the Athenian coinage.

HENRI D'OR   A French gold coin, first struck by Henri II in 1549. It was also the first regular gold portrait coin of the French Renaissance, previous portraits having been confined to silver *testons.

HENRI D'OR À LA GALLIA   Following shortly after the henri d'or, in 1552, this was the first gold coin to be struck by machinery. It is notable for the classical grace of the seated figure of Gaul on the reverse. A *piéfort of its double was the first coin to be struck with a raised edge-inscription (dated 1555).

HERMITAGE COLLECTION   The Hermitage in Leningrad occupies in Russia much the same position as does the British Museum in England—with the National Gallery thrown in for good measure. The full extent of treasures in the coin and medal collection is not known, as no general catalogue exists; but it certainly ranks with London, Paris and Vienna as one of the world's very greatest.

HEXAGRAM   A Byzantine silver coin, introduced by the Emperor Heraclius (A.D. 610–41) and struck for the next hundred years or so. Its name is derived from its weight, that of 6 scripulae (in effect, 6.6 grammes approx.).

HIBERNO-NORSE COINAGE   The earliest coinage of Ireland, by Viking invaders, dating from the end of the 10th century. At first purely imitations of Anglo-Saxon pennies, the coins later developed a distinctive character of their own. About a hundred different main types have been listed. The series came to an end with some very rare *bracteates of the early 12th century.

HILDESHEIM   A town in Westphalia, not far from Hanover, which struck coins as a bishopric from the 11th century onwards and as a free city from the late 15th century. There are some fine *bracteates of Bishop Adelhog (1170–90), and one of the finest German Renaissance portrait coins, a 5-ducat piece of the Emperor Charles V, was struck when he confirmed the city as an imperial mint in 1528.

HILLIARD, NICHOLAS (1547–1619)   Though remembered today principally as the finest English miniaturist, Hilliard was in fact also both goldsmith and jeweller to Elizabeth I and James I. His name first appears in Royal Mint records during 1584, when he was commissioned, together with Derek Anthony, to make the second great seal of the realm for the Queen (which remained in use until her death in 1603). At least two medals have been definitely attributed to him by Dr Roy Strong (*Portraits of Queen Elizabeth I,* 1963). In 1617, James I granted him a new patent which gave him a virtual monopoly of royal portraiture; in it he is called specifically "embosser of medals in gold". Whether Hilliard lived to exercise these rights is uncertain, for he was then seventy and died two years later. We do know that he sold licences to Simon de *Passe and his brother, whose work show strong traces of Hilliard's influence.

HIMERA   One of the principal towns and mints of ancient Sicily. Early types show a cock (6th century B.C.), later ones (5th century B.C.) the nymph Himera sacrificing at an altar.

HIRSCH PRIVATE MINT   The full name of this concern was Hirsch Messing and Kupferwerke (brass and copper works). It was only very occasionally active as a mint and struck the cupro-nickel coinage for Uruguay (from 1 to 5 *centesimi) in 1901.

HOARD The "bag of coins under the mattress" is far older than mattresses. People have hoarded and hidden coins since they were first made. When such hoards are discovered today they often give us valuable clues as to coinage: its circulation and its age. This is particularly true when hoards are discovered together with other archaeological artefacts: each may help to cast light on the other. No hoard should be dispersed until its composition has been carefully analysed within the context of its discovery by qualified scholars. (Also *treasure trove find.)

HOCHSTETTER, JOACHIM Little is known of this artist (who seems to have been of German origin) except that he entered on a contract to strike groats for James V of Scotland in 1527. They are distinguished by superior workmanship, and by the long pointed nose of the King's profile.

HOG MONEY Coins of Bermuda (or the Somer Islands, as then called), struck between 1616 and 1624. Being the very first in the *Anglo-American colonial series, they are of equal interest to collectors on both sides of the Atlantic. Known denominations are the shilling, sixpence, threepence and twopence piece. All the coins are of copper or brass, lightly silvered and crudely struck.

Hog money: the VI above the hog shows the value, i.e. sixpence

The type is named after the wild pigs which roamed the island (the obverse design). The reverse shows a ship—most probably that which took the first English settlers there.

HOLEY DOLLARS *ring money.

HONG KONG A British colony since 1841, this island city had a mint of its own from 1866–8 (as a branch of London's Royal Mint), where silver denominations of the dollar, half-dollar, 20, 10 and 5 cents were struck.

HUMBERT, AUGUSTUS A watch-case maker from New York, he was sent to San Francisco in 1851 to act as United States Assayer before the establishment of an official government mint there. His appointment gave the firm of Moffat & Co. (who were active from 1849–52) an edge over the other issuers of private Californian gold. The Moffat/Humbert partnership was marked by a variety of splendid octagonal $50 pieces, distinguished by fine guilloche markings on the reverse, and generally to .887 fine, with this indication of (887 THOUS.) and Humbert's and/or Moffat's name, together with the US eagle, on the obverse.

At the request of local bankers and businessmen, smaller (round) denominations were struck at $10 and $20 pieces in 1852.

HUNG TSUNG Chinese scholar (1120–74) who has left us what is probably the earliest extant work on numismatics, dating from the beginnings of Chinese coinage to the middle of the 10th century. It contains descriptions and plates not only of Chinese currency and medals, but also of certain foreign pieces, usurpers' coins, forgeries, etc.

HUSUM DALER Struck at the mint of Husum in Denmark in 1522, this was the first realistic Renaissance portrait coin to appear in any Scandinavian country. It dates from the year prior to the then Duke Frederick of Holstein assuming the title of King Frederick I of Denmark (1523–33). The plaited cap and fringe beard are characteristic of Scandinavian male fashion of the time, and the somewhat bad-tempered expression on the King's face shows that the artist was not inclined to flatter. The reverse bears the Duke's coat of arms with a crowned helmet above.

HVID   A Danish silver coin to the value of 4 Pfennige. Its origins may be traced back to the late 14th century, but it attained importance only about a hundred years later. The obverse usually shows the King's crowned monogram or initial letter; the reverse bears some resemblance to the English *long-cross penny.

HWAN   A Korean silver coin, the first to be struck in Western style (1888).

HYBRID COINS   *mules.

I

ICHIBU-GIN   A rectangular coin of Japan (value 1 bu), struck in 1837, 1859 and 1868.

ICONOGRAPHY   From Greek *eikon*, an image; in modern parlance, the study of it as regards art and style. There are literally hundreds of coins where only an appreciation of stylistic differences (or similarities) will enable us to "place" them, both in time and geographically. This is especially true of ancient coinage. Greek gems, seals, vase paintings and sculptures all play a role in assigning a coin to this or that period or place. By collating *finds and *hoards of coins with other archaeological evidence we are likely to get much nearer the truth; and many long-held views have had to be revised during the past half century, hand in hand with the advance of archaeology as an exact science.

IFRIKIYA   *Al-andalus.

ILAHI ERA   The divine era of Akbar the Great (1556–1605), dating from 1584 as a regnal date shown on his coinage, together with the Persian solar month.

ILYIN, A. A.   Russian numismatist and the first Soviet curator of the *Hermitage collection. He was part-editor of the great Mikhailovitch Collection Catalogue, and co-author with I. I. Tolstoi of *Russian Coins from 1725–1801*. Spasskij tells us how Ilyin used to list coins from his private collection in the medieval section of the Hermitage catalogues, if missing there, with the remark "donor unknown".

IMADI   Major unit of Yemen currency as introduced in 1923, superseded by the *riyal in 1942.

IMHOOF-BLUMER, FRIEDRICH (1838–1920)   Eminent Swiss collector and numismatist, who inaugurated the study of die-link sequences and helped to lay the foundations of all modern research into the chronology of ancient Greek coinages. His own magnificent collection of Greek coins is today in the museum of his native town of Winterthur.

IMPERIAL   Name given to the Russian 10-rouble gold piece, as first struck under the Empress Elizabeth I in 1755. As an inscription on actual coins, however, it is only found on those struck from 1895–7 (with poliimperial on the 5-rouble pieces of the same time).

INCHIQUIN MONEY   Silver necessity money of Ireland, issued during 1642 under the auspices of Lord Inchiquin, Vice-President of Munster. There are denominations of crown, half-crown, shilling, 9 pence, 6 pence and groat. All pieces are cut in irregular shapes and stamped with a circular mark of weight, not value. See also *Ormonde money.

INCUSE   Another word for intaglio, i.e. the opposite of *relief. The design is impressed into the surface of the metal instead of being raised from it. There are some incuse coins of ancient

Inchiquin money (slightly reduced): "dw" shows the weight of the silver, i.e. 19 pennyweight

Greece. In more modern times, a mixture of incuse and relief design was a favourite device of *Boulton as an additional safeguard against forgery (*cartwheel penny). When the edges of coins are marked, the incuse method is to be preferred, for individual letters standing out on the thin edge of a coin are subject to quick wear.

INDIA   The earliest Indian coins are hardly less old than those of ancient Greece or China. The currencies of this vast subcontinent do not lend themselves to any general categorisation. Languages and *iconography are as strange to Western eyes as they are varied (to those with the scholarship to perceive the subtle differences). Even fairly recent issues, dating from the establishment of the East India Company in the late 17th century, still present unsolved problems. One-fifth of Remick's catalogue of British Commonwealth coins since 1649 is taken up by Indian coins; and the indefatigable Major Fred Pridmore has already spent longer on examining this series than on the whole of the rest of the Empire put together.

Despite—or perhaps because of—this complexity, Indian coinages (and, indeed, paper money) offer great chances to the enterprising collector. Even at today's price of gold, for instance, it is still possible to put together a representative collection of the diminutive *fanams of different native states, where much research concerning types (let alone varieties) remains to be done. If more money is available, Gupta period gold coins cost but a fraction of Roman ones and are no less rewarding artistically; or you can collect silver coins of the great Moghul emperor Akbar, struck by his mint month by month (round and square alternately). The opportunities are endless.

INDIAN HEAD CENT   After just two years the flying eagle design on the small cent, which James B. Longacre had copied from the *Gobrecht pattern dollars of 1836–9, was replaced by his Indian head design. Two major changes were made during the life of this type, the first being in 1860 when the laurel wreath reverse was replaced by an oak wreath and shield device; the second in 1864 when the metal composition in the cent was changed to bronze and the weight reduced to 48 grains (an act of 22 April 1864). This was to halt the practice of hoarding which had set in as a result of the Civil War and also led to many *token issues.

INGOT   Any rough bar, usually rectangular in shape and of silver or gold, stamped with the weight and fineness of the metal. The most common occurrence of ingots was in mining areas, far from any official mints, where they were cast as money by weight instead of being struck as coins. They date back to Roman times and are also common as siege pieces. Today, ingots are still cast (but much more carefully) for the use of banks and governments. Small silver ingots are also sold by coin dealers, usually at .999 fine. Banks abroad, and since late 1978 also in the UK, sell small gold bars or ingots, again at .999 fine, across the counter, in weights as little as 5 grammes and up to 1 kilogramme.

INITIAL MARK   This is not necessarily an initial (though it well may be) but is the technical numismatic term for any kind of symbol standing at the beginning of the *legend to identify place and/or date of issue. The English coinage alone has well over a hundred different initial marks from the reign of Edward II to Charles II. There are no less than twenty-one varieties of the cross, which predominates in the early period. Other symbols (e.g. rose, pall, sun, crown) do not appear with any frequency until the reign of Edward IV (from 1461). (Also *mintmark.)

INSURRECTIONISTS' COINAGES   *emergency money.

INTERNATIONAL COINAGE   All coinage is international in so far as it finds acceptance in countries other than that which issued it. Such was the case as long ago as the days of ancient Greece with the "owls" of *Athens and the "colts" of *Corinth among others. During the past century or so, however, there have been definite and conscious attempts—at any rate in Europe—to create supranational coinages by way of inscribing them with denominations of more than one country. In the wake of the Latin Monetary Union (1865), Britain and France joined in experiments which got as far as the *pattern stage. Patterns struck at the Royal Mint include one of 1867 inscribed "One franc—Ten pence" and one of 1868 inscribed "Double Florin—Five Francs—International". Similarly, the French mint in Paris had 25-franc pieces additionally inscribed in terms of 10 florins and 5 dollars.

More recently, since the Second World War, there have been such attempts as Esperanto and United Nations pattern crowns; these, however, are more in the nature of medallic mementoes since neither of the organisations responsible enjoys sovereign status. More serious was the decision of the EEC (European Economic Community) to create a common European currency by 1980. This has so far failed to materialise. (Also *bilingual coins.)

INVERNESS   A Scottish mint first opened by Alexander III to help strike his extensive series of *long-cross pennies, c. 1250. Apart from this, Inverness appears to have been operative again only under James I (1406–37), when some pennies and half-pennies were struck here.

IRELAND   Ireland's coinage history is as varied and extensive as any; but good, up-to-date guides to it were lacking until Seaby and Spink published their priced catalogues from *Hiberno-Norse issues to the present day during the early 1970s. Even now, there is no general history of the series later than John Lindsay's *A View of the Coinage of Ireland*, which appeared as long ago as 1839.

Irish penny, George III, 1805

Yet Ireland has struck—or had struck for it—every kind of money, official and unofficial, over a period of ten centuries. Indeed, Ireland offers a rich hunting-ground for those whose interest lies in primitive currencies dating even prior to the Viking invasion: there is ring money in gold, silver and brass. As Lindsay tells us (basing his comments on the detailed researches of Sir William Betham) " . . . not only did these rings pass as money in Ireland, but they are all graduated according to Troy weight, and are all different multiples of the Half Pennyweight; he has also proved that the gold ornaments, supposed to have been fibulae, etc., and which have so much exercised the ingenuity of the Learned, are also graduated in like manner, and must follow the same rule of appropriation."

There is, in fact, so much that specialisation is almost inevitable. The *Hiberno-Norse series, or the silver pennies of English rulers during medieval times, each afford a life-time's study. So would the copper of English rulers from Henry VI to Elizabeth: surely a gap to be filled by anyone who specialises in English copper coins, yet a series which begins, in Ireland, over a century and a half earlier (1460). Then again there is the Civil War period, at least as intricate and fascinating as in England (*blacksmith half-crown, Inchiquin money, Kilkenny money,

Irish penny, 1952

Ormonde money), and the *gun money struck under James II 1689–90; there are *Wood's halfpence and the *voce populi tokens of the 18th century. Tokens, indeed, offer a particularly rich field from the 17th century onwards and include some struck by *Boulton for the *Bank of Ireland.

The coinage of the Irish Free State since 1928 is too recent to call for much comment except, perhaps, as regards its origins. What other country has had the imagination to appoint a committee under the chairmanship of its greatest poet (W. B. *Yeats) to supervise a selection of designs? Among those invited to submit patterns were Carl Milles of Sweden, Pablo Morbiducci of Italy and the great Yugoslav sculptor Metrovic; but it was Percy Metcalfe of England who won the competition. (*Anglo-Irish coinage, Bank of Ireland.)

ISAR   *Flussgolddukaten.

ISLAMIC COINAGE   From modest beginnings by way of copying Byzantine types at the end of the 7th century A.D. (with a single mint, probably at Damascus), Islamic coinage soon took on its own distinctive character and spread to more than a hundred mints with the conquests of Islam, ranging from western Spain to India, during the Moghul Empire. With very rare exceptions (e.g. *zodiacal coins), it shunned all pictorial representations. For all who do not read Arabic script it remains a closed book, devoid even of decorative devices, except that sometimes the inscriptions occur within an inner square or circle. From the 16th century onwards, a kind of flourish is seen in the *tughra of Ottoman coinage. It remains to be noted that Islamic minting standards were of the highest, and that the gold and silver content of *dinar and *dirhem respectively was probably subject to smaller variations than the *tolerances permitted by western European and medieval coinages.

ISTRUS   A Greek mint in Moesia, on the shores of the Black Sea not far from the mouth of the River Danube. The reverse type of the coinage struck here from the 4th century B.C. is similar to others of the region (sea-eagle on a dolphin), but the obverse is unique. It shows two young facing male heads, one upside down, which are said to symbolise the rising and setting sun—in itself an allusion to the importance of Istrus as a trading entrepôt between East and West.

ITALY   The ancient numismatic history of Italy is, at first, that of individual cities colonised by the Greeks (e.g. *Tarentum) and of *Etruria. Thereafter, it becomes part of *Roman coinage, later still of *Byzantine and *Ostrogothic coinages. The duchy of Beneventum in southern Italy struck a gold coinage of Byzantine type from the 6th to 8th centuries A.D.

Owing to the multiplicity of city states—and the domination of some of them by French, Spanish and even German rulers—a summary of numismatic history of this country is as impossible as that of Greece. *Florence, Genoa and Venice rate separate entries, as do *papal coinages. The modern kingdom, dating from 1861, adopted the decimal system. A period of particular numismatic interest is that from 1797–1814, under Napoleon and various members of his family acting as satraps, when old and new monetary systems existed side by side.

IVANOFF, TIMOTHY (1729–1802)   One of the greatest of Russian coin engravers and medallists, active from 1758–1800, and responsible for most of the coinages of Catherine the Great at the mint of St Petersburg.

J

JAITIL   A divisionary coin of the sultans of Delhi during the 14th century (50 jaitils = 1 *tankah).

JAMNITZER, WENZEL (1508–85)   One the greatest German goldsmiths and engravers of the 16th century, equally noted for his skill in etching, enamelling, embossing and carving. He is known to have worked as a die-cutter at the Nuremberg Mint from 1542–59, though no particular coins can be assigned to him with certainty.

JEDBURGH   A Scottish mint only under Malcolm IV (1153–65), from which reign some exceedingly rare pennies are known.

JEFFERSON NICKEL   The design of this issue (Jefferson's bust facing left on the obverse, with a view of his country villa at Monticello as the reverse) resulted from a public competition, won by Felix Schlag against some 390 artists for a $1,000 cash award. Although Schlag's obverse design was largely retained, a completely new reverse was prepared by the mint's engraving staff. The design went unsigned for nearly thirty years, until a small FS was added below the bust in 1966, in tribute to the last private artist to conceive a regular issue US coin design.

During the war years, the nickel composition of this piece was abandoned in favour of a copper-silver-manganese alloy containing 35% silver. By the 1960s, the bullion value of these coins exceeded their face value. To distinguish these issues from the nickel version, large mintmarks were placed above the dome of Monticello on the reverse, including a P for Philadelphia, the only time in which the US mother mint has been so distinguished on her domestic issues (1942, 1943, 1944 and 1945 only). New master dies, sharpening the features of the obverse portrait, were engraved for the 1971 issues. The coin has been regularly struck at Denver and San Francisco Mints as well as Philadelphia. Catalogue prices do not seem to reflect in any way the much smaller mintage figures as compared with the *Lincoln Cent, for example, and must surely rise, especially for the historically unique P mintmark issues of 1942–5.

JESSE, WILHELM (b. 1887)   Noted German numismatist, who apart from his own many articles on medieval coinages compiled a most valuable source-book of medieval German monetary and coinage decrees.

JETON (OR JETTON)   From French *jeter* (to throw). A fascinating branch of numismatics, too little explored in England though the subject of specialised studies and collections abroad. The jeton began life as a reckoning or casting-counter, used by merchants and bankers for quick calculations. Most probably (as its name suggests) invented in France, it spread rapidly throughout the Continent and found in Nuremberg one of its principal places of manufacture. Jetons are often as artistically

Group of jetons from an 18th-century manual

designed and engraved as coins and medals. (Also Hans *Krauwinckel.)

But it was in France that jetons retained their use and popularity longest. They are, in fact, made by the Paris Medal Mint to this day. Jetons in silver and even gold became an accepted form of gratuity or bonus in departments of state. They were handed to the recipients in beautifully embroidered purses, especially at the New Year. For many years, the *Mercure de France* published the New Year jetons in its January issue. In 1683 alone, officers of the Trésor Royal under Louis XIV received 800 golden and 26,000 silver jetons. If relatively few survive today it is because this "private currency" was then hardly valued for its artistic quality but promptly turned into plate or cash.

In England, not surprisingly, the jeton found its finest artistic flowering during the reign of Charles I, under the influence of his French queen, Henrietta Maria. Whole series of jetons engraved by *Briot are known; also cylindrical boxes in which they were kept, probably for use as gaming counters at court.

JOACHIMSTHAL   A mint of the counts of Schlick, where large *Guldengroschen were first struck in 1519. It was the vast output of the Joachimsthal mines and mint which caused these coins to be called at first Joachimsthaler, later simply abbreviated to *Thaler.

JOAO   A Portuguese gold coin, first struck under King Joao V in 1722, to the value of 6,400 *reis. It is remarkable for being the very first portrait coin to be struck in the Portuguese regal coinages—and surely the last such portrait coin to be introduced in Europe. It continued to be struck through seven successive reigns until 1835, enjoying wide popularity because it was consistently up to declared standard in weight (14.3 grammes) and fineness (.916 fine). For its career as a trade coin in the West Indies, see under *Joe.

JOBERT, LOUIS (1637–1719)   A Jesuit priest and one of the early "popularisers" of coins and medals. His *La Science des Médailles*, first published in Paris in 1692, went through German, Dutch and Italian editions and was again reprinted in Paris as late as 1739 with revisions.

JOE   English name for the Portuguese *Joao, which circulated widely in the West Indies during the 18th century. Because of its popularity, it was counterfeited towards the end of the century both in Birmingham and North America with coins of inferior fineness; and countermarks were used by both British and French West Indian authorities to distinguish the good from the bad. It is possible that the word "Joe" is derived from Joseph rather than from Joao; for the coins of Joseph I (1750–77) are more often found countermarked than earlier issues of Joao V (1722–50).

JOEY   *Britannia groat; also slang for the later 3-pence piece.

J.O.P.   The initials of Joseph Oliva Patenaude, a jeweller of Nelson, British Columbia. They are to be found on certain Canadian silver dollars from 1935–49. Patenaude, who died in 1956, had a curious theory about the wide circulation of silver coinage, and by stamping them with his initials hoped to keep track of them and prove his theory. He bought 1,000 of the first (1935) issue and lesser quantities of each year from 1936–49. Though he committed an illegal act he was never prosecuted, as his motives were not dishonest, only harmlessly eccentric.

J.S.O.   These initials appear on certain $5 and $10 Californian gold pieces and are those of J. S. Ormsby. He is known to have operated a private mint in Sacramento around 1849–50. Though the coins are undated, the thirty-one stars surrounding the 10 DOLLS inscription on the reverse of the larger piece would seem to indicate that this was struck in 1850, for California became the thirty-first state of the Union in that year.

JUBILEE COINS AND MEDALS   The practice of celebrating silver and golden jubilees of monarchs is—in the English coinage at any rate—a fairly recent one. The first such special issue was for the golden jubilee of Queen Victoria in 1887. In the papal series, however, the celebration of Holy Year (every twenty-five years) has been numismatically commemorated since 1450, when Pope Nicholas V issued a medal bearing the reverse inscription ANNO JULBILEI ALMA ROMA (this being, incidentally, also the first dated papal piece). Thereafter, from 1475 onwards, magnificent gold pieces (often to the value of 3 ducats or more) and smaller silver pieces of special commemorative type have been regularly struck. Sometimes mints other than Rome were also employed, as for Gregory XIII in 1575 (Ancona, Bologna and Macerata). Perhaps the most varied and interesting issue in this series is that celebrating the Holy Year of 1700, for it happened to coincide with the death of one pope (Innocent XII) and the election of another (Clement XI). Both popes are therefore represented on special coins and medals issued for the occasion, the earliest being dated 1699.

JUGATE   Conjoined or placed side by side. Portrait coins often show "jugate busts", i.e. two portraits "staggered" so that one is slightly behind the other. Compare also *bajoire.

JULIUSLÖSER   Large medallic *Thalers, issued by Duke Julius of Brunswick (1574–88) in denominations from 2½ to 16. They show his bust on the obverse and his arms surrounded by zodiacal and planetary devices on the reverse. The coins are believed to have been a form of compulsory savings: the German word *lösen* means to redeem, and the coins were not everyday currency but to be redeemed only in time of emergency. The number which each citizen was obliged to hold depended, of course, on his wealth and income.

JUSTO   A gold coin of John II of Portugal, introduced in 1485 and valued at 2 *cruzados. It is named after its inscription, JUSTUS ET PALMA FLOREBIT, and was struck in 22 carat gold. Its half was the *espadin.

K

Kahavanu of Ceylon, 10th century

KA Greek coin engraver's signature which appears—sometimes also in the more abbreviated form of just K—on coins of Heracleia, Metapontum, Tarentum and Thurium of the most exquisite design and style (*c*. 345–334 B.C.).

KABUL Capital of Afghanistan since that country became an independent kingdom in 1747, and since then also the principal mint of the country.

KAHAVANU Gold coin of Ceylon from around the end of the 9th century depicting on the obverse Vishnu standing and on the reverse seated figures. Smaller pieces of similar type are the deka and aka. Since none of these coins carries regnal titles or other names, they are difficult to date precisely.

KAIKI SHOHO The first gold coin of Japan (A.D. 760) of which only a single specimen is known (in the imperial collection).

KA'KIM An early currency of Siam (9th century A.D.) of conical shape and pierced. It remained in use, at any rate in the northern part of the country, until late in the 18th century. Possibly a development of ring money, the bars were mainly stamped to the value of 1, 2 and 4 *ticals; other denominations are rare.

KAMPEN Town in the Netherlands, and an important mint since the 15th century. There is an extensive series of *siege pieces both of the 16th and 17th centuries.

KANEI TSUHO The main bronze coin of Japan during the period 1626–1863.

KANN, EDWARD (1880–1962) American numismatist, whose *Illustrated Catalogue of Chinese Coins* is the standard work for the modern coinage of the country.

KAPANG *keping.

KARAN *kran.

KARLSTEEN, ARFVID (1654–1718) Celebrated Swedish coin engraver and medallist, who worked first at the *Avesta Mint, then pursued his studies with *Warin in Paris and *Roettier in London. Though he worked for most of the remainder of his career in Stockholm, he received many commissions from foreign monarchs owing to the excellence of his work, among them Louis XIV of France and the King of Prussia.

KAS The Danish for *cash; as such, a copper coin struck for the Danish colony of Tranquebar (India) from 1677–1845.

KASTPENNING A Swedish coronation and burial jeton, thrown to the crowd. At first it had medallic character only, but from 1654–1772 it had the size and value of 2-Mark pieces, and from 1778–1818 it was valued at one-third of a Thaler. There are 25 different kastpennigar (pl.) of monetary character.

KASU A copper coin of the princes of Mysore (India) from the mid-18th century. It is also known as "elephant cash", after its distinctive obverse type.

Kasu of Mysore, 16th century

KAZBEGI A copper denomination of Persia, under the Safavid dynasty (1502–1736). Halves are known, also multiples of 2, 4 and 8 (the last very rare). There are a great number of different types; and since they also varied much in weight, they were a local rather than national currency, of full value only in or near the issuing town.

KELLOGG & CO. This company was the last to produce private gold coinage in San Francisco, during 1854–5, and actually continued to do so for some time after the establishment of a United States branch mint there. It struck pieces of $20 and $50 only, the last exceedingly rare.

KELSO An uncertain Scottish mint. There is a penny of Alexander II (1214–49) with the moneyer's name WILLEM and the inscription KAWLS, which is believed to stand for this town in the Lowlands.

KEMPSON, P. A Birmingham issuer of medals and tokens, active during the first thirty years of the 19th century. He was especially prolific in making spurious tokens for sale (e.g. a series of famous London buildings) as collectors' objects rather than a genuine medium of exchange. However, there are also genuine pieces, especially during the shortage of silver from 1811 onwards, when among others he made a sixpence for Poole and a 1-shilling piece for Dublin (Irish Bullion Company). For his die engravers, Kempson often used members of the *Wyron family.

KENGEN DAIHO The smallest and most debased of the twelve types of bronze *sen, cast in Japan *c.* A.D. 958.

KEPING A copper coin current throughout the Malay pensinsula and Sumatra during the 18th and 19th centuries. There are many issues and varieties; historically the most significant are undoubtedly those struck by Matthew Boulton's *Soho Mint in 1786. This was the first contract coinage made by Boulton with his new steam-driven machinery.

KIEV City in Russia. It was here that the first Russian coins were struck, just under a thousand year ago, in imitation of *Byzantine models.

KILKENNY MONEY Rough issues of copper farthings and halfpennies, issued by the Catholic Confederacy of Ireland (council set up at Kilkenny, 1642) during the Civil War. The Catholics proclaimed their loyalty to the King, not Parliament. The royalist character of the coinage is emphasised by a crown on both the obverse and the reverse: the first with two sceptres, the second above a harp.

KIMON Arguably (together with *Euainetos) the finest coin engraver who ever lived. His signed *decadrachms of *Syracuse are perhaps the most beautiful coins that have come down to us from the ancient world and fetch enormous prices on the rare occasions when they appear on the market today. His finest productions can all be dated to the decade from 410–400 B.C.

KING'S NORTON MINT This is a private mint, situated just north of Birmingham. Apart from the *Heaton Mint, it has probably executed more contract coinages than any other such establishment, both on its own account (for foreign governments) and as a sub-contractor for the Royal Mint in London. The mint-mark is KN. It is today part of the Imperial Chemical Group, called Imperial Metal Industries Ltd.

KIPPER UND WIPPER An extremely complex series of bebased silver coins which proliferated throughout the German states of the early 17th century. This debasement—turning silver more and more into copper (with admixtures of other base metals

Gold maravedi of Alfonso VIII of Spain, 1158-1214

Gold Venetian ducat of the Doge Giovanni Delpino, 1356-61, showing the
Doge kneeling before St Mark, patron saint of Venice

Gold leopard or half-florin of Edward III, 1327-77

Gold pavillon d'or of Philip VI of France, 1328-50

Unique uniface gold 10-shilling siege piece struck at Colchester, Essex, in 1648. It shows a schematic view of the castle, which is the largest Norman keep in England

Above: Chased silver plaque by Stuart with a portrait of Thomas Simon; the unknown original from which this is taken dates from *c.*1665

Right: Gold Japanese gory oban, 1837-43

American silver dollar piece of 1863

American gold 20-dollar piece of 1898

Koban: Late issue, c. 1860

such as lead)—started c. 1590 and reached its climax during the opening years of the Thirty Years' War (1619–22). Clipping, i.e. issuing coin under the specified weight, was another aspect of this monetary chaos, cynically indulged in by princes determined to reap profits from the unsettled conditions prevailing. The term "Kipper und Wipper" is derived from the swaying of the balance while coin was being weighed; any translation must miss the alliterative tartness, with dishonesty implicit, of the original.

KLIPPE The name for a square or lozenge-shape coin, common above all in Germanic series of Thaler-size coins; also in emergency coinages of many countries. Sometimes the same denominations were struck on round and square flans at the same date. The reasons for this are still a matter of controversy; but as Klippen are often of finer, commemorative types (often also multiples of Thalers), the most likely explanation seems that they were meant as presentation pieces.

KLIPPING Swedish for *Klippe. The type is less common than in the German series and does not appear in parallel with regular round strikings, but only in the 16th-century emergency issues of Sweden. There are also some rare Danish gold pieces, of both the 16th and the 17th centuries.

KNIFE MONEY A primitive bronze currency of China, current in the northern provinces from the 7th to the 4th centuries B.C. The earliest are larger than later ones (about 7 inches long as against 5) and are uninscribed. Later ones carry place names and sometimes even values.

An attempt was made under the usurper Wang Mang (A.D. 7–22) to revive this knife money almost three centuries later, but it failed to outlive him. Specimens from his time are only about 3 inches long.

KOBAN Japanese gold coin, one-tenth of the *oban. Ten separate issues are known from 1591–1860, the first experimental and exceedingly rare. The gold content gradually deteriorated from .856 to .209 fine. The coins differ from the oban not only in their much smaller size, but in having no guaranteeing inscription in ink.

KOEHLER, JOHANN DAVID (1684–1755) This remarkable German professor, who taught history and divinity at the University of Göttingen, published as a side-line the first regular weekly numismatic magazine. In twenty-two years (from 1729–50 inclusive) this one-man band did not miss one issue. He generally concentrated on a single coin (sometimes on a group of closely related ones), giving the most elaborate descriptions and historical background. Koehler corresponded with the most erudite collectors and museum curators and took special pleasure in showing and describing hitherto "unpublished" rarities. His bibliographical references are exhaustive (for their time) and refer us to many almost forgotten books and learned periodicals of his own and earlier centuries. The magazine enjoyed enormous popularity and was reprinted ten years after his death with a two-volume index. Koehler dubbed it "Historische Münzbelustigung" (Historical Coin Amusement); and though there were many similar attempts later during the 18th century, none was able to rival Koehler in range.

KOOKABURRA PATTERNS Square, round-cornered coins struck at the Melbourne Mint, Australia, from 1919 to 1921 in denominations of penny and halfpenny; with patterns in nickel, these were part of an abortive attempt to replace the current bronze coins. There are two types of the halfpenny struck experimentally only during 1920/21, and nine of the penny with dates between 1919 and 1921. They are among the most sought-after by Australian collectors, not only because of their rarity but because of the reverse type, showing the attractive Australian bird in various forms.

KOPEK   A Russian silver coin, derived from the Novgorod *denga, the first introduced in Moscow in 1535 at a value of 100 to the heavy (Novgorod) *rouble. It is thus the precursor of all modern decimal currencies, and continued to be struck in silver until 1719 (the main type showing the Tsar on a horse) until superseded by the copper kopek of Peter the Great in 1719. An earlier experimental copper kopek (1656–63) failed because its weight was no more than that of the silver issue, yet it was supposed to have the same value. Issues of the copper piece continued to be sporadic until the reign of Catherine the Great (1762–96), when it became firmly and regularly established. There are some very beautiful and rare patterns of Catherine I, Peter the Great's widow (1725–7).

KORONA   Name given to the Hungarian equivalent of the Austrian *Krone. Basically a silver coin, it is best known today in the form of the 100-korona gold commemorative piece issued in 1907, often found as a restrike. A more remarkable production, but likely to be overlooked because of its relatively small size, is the korona of 1896, commemorating a thousand years of the kingdom of Hungary, with a superb equestrian reverse by Philip O. Beck. This, like so many superlative pieces of the past 600 years, was struck at the *Kremnitz Mint.

KORUNA   Unit of value of the Czech state since 1922, when it was first struck in cupro-nickel. Since then, it has often been struck in multiples of 10, 20, 50 and 100 as a silver commemorative coin. All Czech coins are struck at the state mint of Kremnica (Kremnitz), one of the few to have preserved during this century the highest artistic standards of earlier times.

KRAN   Persian silver coin to the value of 1,000 *dinar introduced by Fath Ali Shah in 1826. Struck by hammer at a number of mints until 1877, it became known as the taze kran (new kran) when machinery was introduced at Teheran.

KRAUWINCKEL, HANS   A famous maker of *jetons at the turn of the 16th/17th centuries. He worked at Nuremberg c. 1580–1620 and among his counters (of which over a hundred different ones have been traced) are some with English themes, e.g. Queen Elizabeth on horseback.

KREMNITZ   A famous mint since it was opened as such by Charles Robert of Anjou as King of Hungary, c. 1324. It lay close to rich gold and silver mines and struck coins in these metals for Hungary, the independent dukedom of Transylvania, the Austrian Empire and (since 1922) Czechoslovakia.

KREUZER   First struck at Merano in the southern Tyrol in 1271, to the value of one *grosso, and so-called after the two crosses (one superimposed diagonally over the other), which was its distinguishing feature. Originally of silver, it was later struck in *billon and finally in copper, surviving as small change in the Austrian currency system until 1891.

KRONA   A silver coin of both Denmark and Norway, which has been their chief monetary unit since 1875. It was adopted by Iceland in 1925.

KRONE   Monetary unit of Austria since 1892, struck as a silver coin until 1916. Multiples of 2 and 5 were also struck in silver; larger ones of 10, 20 and 100 in gold.

Kopek:

Silver, Ivan IV, 1533–47

5 kopeks, copper, Catherine the Great, 1789 (slightly reduced)

Krauwinckel: The personal jeton of Hans Krauwinckel (a kind of metallic trade-mark, perhaps?), bearing his name and NUR, short for Nuremberg

KROON   Monetary unit in the revised (1928) currency system of Estonia. For general circulation, it was struck only once, in aluminium bronze (1934); but there is a commemorative silver piece of 1933 and 2-krooni pieces, also in silver, of 1930 and 1932.

KRUGERRAND   *bullion pieces.

KRUISDAALDER   A distinctive crown-size piece, introduced in the Netherlands under Philip II of Spain in 1567. Its name is derived from the obverse type: a cross of Burgundy, separating the figures of the date.

KUBLAI KHAN (1214–94)   The great Mongol ruler is notable in being perhaps the first successfully to impose a paper currency (fully described by Marco Polo) on his subjects. No examples have been found, the earliest Chinese paper money to survive dating from about a century later.

KÜCHLER, CONRAD HEINRICH (d. 1810)   The artist, whose place and date of birth are uncertain, is above all famous for the years he spent in *Boulton's service at the *Soho Mint (1793–1810). It was the excellence of his engraving as much as the efficiency of Boulton's machinery that gave Boulton his international prestige. His best known coins are probably the *cartwheel penny of 1797 and the *Bank of England dollar of 1804. The patterns he cut for coins of Alexander I of Russia and Christian VII of Denmark are as beautiful as they are rare and helped Boulton to obtain contracts for supplying minting machinery to these two countries. His medallic work—totalling thirty-four pieces at Soho—has been exhaustively analysed by Graham Pollard *(Numismatic Chronicle,* 1970).

KUTTENBERG   The richest silver deposits in Europe were discovered at this Bohemian town (approximately 50 miles east of Prague) during the latter part of the 13th century, and a mint for its exploitation was established in 1298. The distinctive type known as *Prager Groschen was struck here. The mint remained active until 1726.

KWANTUNG (CANTON)   A provincial mint of modern China since 1889. It was one of the major foreign installations of the Birmingham firm Ralph Heaton & Sons, who completed (in less than two years) a building with ninety coining-presses capable of producing over 2½ million coins per day.

KWARTNIK   The chief coin of Poland for over a century (c. 1350–1450), valued at half a *Groschen. Introduced by Casimir the Great (1333–70), it showed the ruler seated with orb and sceptre, and a Polish eagle on the reverse. The obverse type was replaced in 1399 by one showing a crown, whence the coin took its popular name of coronat.

L

LABBÉ, PHILIPPE (1607–67) French scholar, whose *Bibliotheca Nummaria* (1664) was the first attempt at a numismatic bibliography.

LAFAYETTE DOLLAR Issued in 1900, this shows the *jugate busts of Washington and Lafayette on the obverse, with Lafayette on horseback as the reverse design. It is the first commemorative United States coin of $1 denomination, and the first also to show the portrait of a president. Sold initially on behalf of the Lafayette Memorial Commission at $2 each (mintage figure 36,026), it is worth well over two hundred times that amount today.

LAGRANGE, JEAN (1831–1908) Prolific coin engraver who was chief engraver at the Paris Mint from 1880–96. Apart from French coinages of that period, he was responsible also for coins of Guatemala, Tunis and—perhaps finest of all—Ethiopia, cut in 1894.

LAHORE Town in northern India and a mint at various times; notably for the Gheznavid princes of the 10th century A.D., the sultans of Delhi a century later, the Moghul Emperor Akbar in the 16th century and the Sikh League under Rajit Singh (1799–1839).

LALIQUE, RENÉ (1860–1945) Though we tend to think of this great French craftsman chiefly as a superb jeweller and artist in glass, he did in fact also engrave several fine portrait medallions, notably of his first patron, the actress Sarah Bernhardt.

LAMPSACUS A town on the Hellespont, notable above all for the wide variety of gold *staters struck here during the first half of the 4th century B.C. Earlier, the town had struck coins in *electrum.

LANDESMÜNZE A German town, signifying a coin (generally of base silver or copper), the circulation of which was restricted to its own 'Land'', i.e. state or county.

LANDRY, FRITZ (1842–1927) Swiss sculptor and medallist, whose most famous and long-lived design was that for the ever-popular ''Vreneli'' of 1907–1949 (the Swiss 20-franc gold piece, representing the head of a young Swiss girl, wearing a necklace of Edelweiss).

LA PAZ A mint of Bolivia since 1853.

LAPETHUS A Phoenician settlement (and kingdom) on the island of Cyprus, more or less on the site of present-day Kyrenia. The main type is that of Athena: at first in profile, then full-face, finally standing, with shield and spear (480–350 B.C.).

LARGE CENT The early years of United States coinage found the mint concentrating on the minting of cents, the coin most needed for daily transactions. From 1793–1857 this was a large copper piece, the earliest issue of which showed on the obverse the head of Liberty facing right, and on the reverse 15 chains linked to form a circle (symbolising the 15 states then forming the USA) and surrounding the words ONE CENT. A wave of criticism caused this issue to be withdrawn almost at once, as the chain link was widely interpreted not as representing the solidarity of the states, but as chains of bondage, only recently thrown off.

The very same year, therefore, saw the introduction of a new type, with a similar obverse but with the chain link replaced by a wreath. A variation of this type again followed, still in 1793: this time the obverse was slightly changed, with the flowing hair of the original Liberty head replaced by a more sober design of braided hair, and showing the liberty cap behind the head. From 1796 onwards the bust was draped. This design was replaced in its turn in 1808 by a new turbaned head facing left, with 7 stars forming a quadrant facing bust and 6 stars behind. The coronet type (still facing left) followed in 1816: this time, 15 stars practically encircle the bust, with the date below. With minor variations (braided hair, and the number of stars reduced to 13) this type continued until 1857, the wreath reverse remaining constant all the time.

Among collectors today, the earliest cent is by far the most sought-after, as it rightly should be. Its recorded mintage was only 36,103 pieces, and the reverse design is artistically much more satisfactory, both as regards proportion and lettering, than the cluttered wreath.

LARI   Name given to the silver *wire money of Persia of the 16th and 17th centuries. Later (from the early 18th century onwards) the same word was applied to copper coins of the Maldive Islands in the Indian Ocean, where it continues as a denomination to this day (100 lari = 1 rupee). Most were struck locally, but an issue of 1913 is known to have been made in Birmingham.

LARISSA   Principal city of Thessaly in ancient Greece, and place of an important and beautiful coinage from c. 480–344 B.C. (after which date only bronze coins were struck here). Among the interesting reverse types of the early period is the sandal of Jason, said in legend to have been lost by him while crossing the river Anaurus. Later we find a variety of types with the nymph Larissa, culminating in a very fine full-face portrait of the best style, reminiscent of the full-face Arethusa portrait by *Kimon of Syracuse.

LAT   Local name for the silver currency of Siam; for details *tiger tongue money.

LATIN MONETARY UNION   First formed in 1865 between Belgium, France, Italy and Switzerland, to harmonise their gold and silver coinages with regard to shape, size and metal content, in an endeavour to create a European currency easily understood and universally acceptable. Gold was fixed at .900 fine, silver at .835, and the French franc with its multiples and sub-divisions was adopted as the model. The main pieces were 20, 10 and 5 in gold, and 5, 2 and 1 in silver (the 5-franc silver being a crown-size piece). Greece joined the Union in 1868 and she was followed by various South American republics of the former Spanish and Portuguese empires, though many of these, while accepting the sizes and weight standards of coins, preferred to retain the familiar peso name.

Like all similar attempts, the Latin Monetary Union ultimately failed because of fluctuations in the relative value of gold and silver. Indeed, it was doomed when the First World War practically put an end to gold coinages. Nor was the fact that England (at that time the world's greatest trading nation) resolutely stayed outside a help: there was no easily calculable relationship between the Union's gold coins and the ubiquitous English sovereign. The most successful period was from 1870–95.

LAUNE, ETIENNE DE (c. 1519–83) Celebrated French goldsmith. He engraved, together with Jean *Erondelle, some of the very first coins to be struck by machinery at the Paris *Moulin des Étuves in 1551–2. He also made a number of fine medals and *jetons. Later he went to Strasbourg and Augsburg, where certain German medals may be his handiwork.

LAUREATE Head shown wearing a laurel wreath. (Also *diademed, radiate.)

LAUREL The 20-shilling piece of James I, introduced in 1619. It takes its name from the *laureate, Roman-type bust of the King of which there are five variants (the last, smaller, exceedingly rare).

LAUSANNE Town on Lake Geneva in Switzerland, which enjoyed coinage rights as a bishopric only, from the 10th to the 16th century. There are some excessively rare gold ducats, undated but c. 1500.

LAVY, AMADEO Mintmaster and die engraver at the mint of Turin, c. 1796–1826. During the Napoleonic occupation of Italy, Lavy first struck the *marengo, and later (besides many other coins) a medallion of the Emperor. After the restoration of the House of Savoy he continued to work, now for King Victor Emanuel I; the 20-lire gold piece of 1821 is one of particular beauty.

Laurel of James I, 1619

LAW, JOHN (1671–1729) Scottish financier and speculator. Finding little enthusiasm in his native country for his theories (*Money and Trade Considered, with a Proposal for Supplying the Nation with Money,* Edinburgh, 1705), he later found a patron in the Duke of Orleans, which led to an astonishing and ultimately disastrous career as financial dictator of France from 1716–21. Beginning in a purely advisory capacity, he founded first the Banque Générale, then the Banque Royale (both responsible for early French banknotes). His Compagnie des Indes, also known as the Mississippi Company, issued shares for the development of Louisiana and laid the foundations of New Orleans. In July 1719, Law was appointed *fermier-général des monnaies* responsible for all revenues whether from notes or coin, and six months later he introduced two new denominations: the *quinzain d'or and the *livre de la Compagnie des Indes.

Law at first enjoyed almost unprecedented success; but confidence soon waned when he sought to make acceptance of his paper money compulsory by calling in gold coin only just issued, with heavy penalties for those refusing to surrender it. The crash, when it came a bare six months later, was absolute and he was forced to flee the country. He died in Venice eight years later, poor and almost forgotten.

LAYANG A mint in the province of Honan, northern China, from the early Tang dynasty (7th century A.D.).

LEAD Because of its softness, this metal has hardly ever been used for coinage. The one notable exception is an extensive series of coins of the Andhra dynasty (India c. 100 B.C.–A.D. 200). Also *tesserae.

LEAGUE COINAGES *alliance coins.

LEAKE, STEPHEN MARTIN (1702–73) English antiquarian and numismatist, whose *An Historical Account of English Money* (London, 1726, second and enlarged edition, 1745) was the first systematic attempt to classify this series.

LEAKE, WILLIAM MARTIN (1777–1860) An inveterate traveller and collector, with a great eye also for archaeology. His collection of Greek coins is now in the *Fitzwilliam Museum.

LEATHER MONEY Various medieval uses of this are attested by documents, the most detailed one being in respect of pieces stamped by the Emperor Frederick II at the siege of Faenza, later to be exchanged for an *augustalis. This particular pledge or promise to pay had the Emperor's picture stamped in silver on the leather. None has survived, the earliest pieces known being those of the siege of Leyden (1574), where both leather and cardboard were used.

LEBERECHT, CARL (1749–1827) Gem and coin engraver of German origin, who spent most of his working life in Russia and was principal engraver at the St Petersburg Mint from 1796–1810.

LE BLANC, FRANCOIS (d. 1698) French scholar, whose *Traité Historique des Monnoyes de France* (Paris, 1690) is the first scientific and still indispensable study of French regal coinage.

LEEUW, LEEUWENDAALDER, LEEUWENGROOT The first of these was struck in gold, by Anthony of Brabant, in 1409; the others were silver coins of Thaler and groat size issued in 1576. All have taken their name from the lion which is a prominent feature of the design.

LEGEND Numismatic term for the inscription(s) to be found on a coin. This may vary from a few words in the *exergue or around the circumference and/or edge to taking up the whole surface of the coin on both sides. This is fairly rare—much more so than coins which are *anepigraphic.

LEGIONARY COINS Coins of the Roman series, bearing the name and number of some particular legion; often made of base metal rather than pure silver, and very rarely in gold. They were probably used as a "token" payment to troops while campaigning, to be exchanged for true coin later. By far the most extensive series is that of Mark Antony, embracing most of his thirty legions (though there is doubt about the authenticity of numbers XXIV–XXX).

Legionary denarius of Mark Antony, 31 B.C.

LEIJCESTERDAALDER The Earl of Leicester, as governor-general of the Netherlands, reformed the Dutch coinage system in 1586. Coins of Thaler size and their halves bore his laureate bust—a type which continued, because of its popularity, well into the 17th century.

LEITZMAN, J. J. (d. 1877) German numismatist, founder and editor of the periodical *Numismatische Zeitung* (1834–63), of an important numismatic bibliography (1867) and a detailed guide to German mints (1865–9).

LENINGRAD *St Petersburg.

LEONARDO DA VINCI (1452–1519) The craft of coin engraving was one of the few which this almost universal Renaissance artist did not practice. He did, however, design the coinages of Milan from 1481–99 (engraved by *Caradosso) and was among the first to design coining machinery; a reconstruction of his planchet-cutting machine is to be seen in the Smithsonian Institution, Washington, D.C., and of his press for striking coins in the museum of his home town, Vinci, in northern Italy.

LEONE A Venetian silver coin to the value of 10 *lire, struck under two doges for the Levant trade towards the end of the 17th century. It bears a large lion as its reverse design, from which it takes its name.

LEONI, LEONE (1509–90) Renaissance goldsmith, coin engraver and medallist. He began his career at the Papal Mint of Rome in 1537, but was chiefly active at Milan for the emperors Charles V and Philip II, from 1550 almost to his death. His work, together with that of Antonio *Abondio marks the climax of the later 16th-century school of art in these fields. In the service of the Emperor he also travelled to the Netherlands, to Augsburg and to Spain and influenced medallic art in these places.

LEONI, POMPEO (c. 1533–1608) Son of the above, author of a few medals, but active chiefly as a sculptor at the Spanish court.

LEOPARD A rare and beautiful gold coin of England, introduced in 1344, to the value of 3 shillings. The beast shown on the coin is really a lion: the appellation leopard rests on a fine heraldic distinction, signifying that the head is turned toward us.

LEPTON Originally a very small weight of ancient Greece, the term was used to describe small copper coins in general, varying widely in value. It was reintroduced in the coinage of the Ionian Islands as a British protectorate in 1834, to the value of one-fifth of an *obol. Since 2 oboli were equivalent to a British penny, the lepton was one-tenth of this, though never actually expressed as a decimal fraction. There was a silver denomination of 30 lepta, equivalent to the 3-penny piece as struck at the same time for the West Indies, and in size the same as the copper unit.

LESBOS An island off the coast of Asia Minor, remarkable for its long series of *electrum *hectae (one-sixth of a *stater), struck every alternate year with those of *Phocea. Together with *Cyzicus, these two localities are the most important centres of electrum coinage of the ancient world.

Lesbos: one-sixth stater of Mytilene, 5th century B.C.

The most important mint was *Mytilene, where in Greek imperial times (2nd to 1st centuries B.C.) an interesting small bronze was struck showing on the obverse the draped bust of the poetess Sappho, and on the reverse a lyre.

LETTERING ON COINS Almost invariably, the lettering of modern coins, since the Renaissance, has been carried out in Roman capitals. Cursive italics are almost unknown; a somewhat mannered kind of script appears on certain Czech gold coins of the 1920s and 1930s. The circular setting around the portrait of the ruler (obverse) and the heraldic device (reverse) is by far the most common. Lettering as an integral part of the design is rare; a notable exception, again, is to be seen in the coins of Danzig in the 1920s.

The above applies only to Western and modern coinages, largely modelled during the Renaissance on Roman types. Medieval lettering follows various Gothic manuscript styles and of Arabic and oriental scripts (not to mention ancient ones) there are far too many even to outline, let alone detail. An interesting and largely unexplored field is the transition from Gothic to Roman types during the period 1450–1550. This takes place at different times in different European countries, and often bears little relation to the iconography of portraits or other pictorial themes. Letter punches were often entrusted to craftsmen other than those who designed the main features of a coin.

LEU Romanian currency unit introduced in 1890, the equivalent of the French franc.

LEUCAS A town in Acarnania and a colony of ancient *Corinth, basing its coinage on the Pegasus type.

LEV (pl. LEVA) Monetary unit of Bulgaria and principal coin of that country from 1880 onwards. It was modelled on the French franc and that coin's equivalent in silver value and weight within the Latin Monetary Union, though Bulgaria did not ac-

Liard of Louis XIV. The "A" in the centre of the reverse indicates the Paris Mint

tually belong to this. Like all such silver coins, it was devalued in 1946 and henceforth struck in base metal instead of silver.

LEVANT DOLLAR A generic term applied to crown-size silver pieces meant for trade with the Middle East. The most famous by far is the *Maria Theresa Thaler, but there are others: e.g. that issued by Frederick the Great of Prussia in 1766–7.

LI Currency unit of China until the Communist Revolution, the 1/100th part of the *tael or ounce.

LIARD Introduced by Louis XI of France, this was a small silver coin to the value of 3 *deniers, and of *delphinal type. The series was extended under Francis I to include types with a salamander and a crowned F. Louis XIV struck a liard de Lyon and one with a Maltese cross (both rare and dated 1655 only). He had previously (1649) introduced the copper liard, which exists in a large number of varieties, especially during the troubles of the Fronde in 1654, when it was struck with nine different provincial mintmarks, representing in all eleven temporary mints. The copper liard continued to be struck until 1786, and it remained legal tender until 1845.

LIBERTY CAP Based on the old Roman *pileus libertatis* (the hat worn by a slave when being given his freedom) this type became a favourite symbol on revolutionary coinages, especially French and South American. A little-known earlier example is a Dutch coin of 1681.

LIBERTY HEAD NICKEL Charles E. Barber executed the designs for this coin introduced in 1883. His initial design offered only a large V inside the wreath (on the reverse) as indicating the denomination. This was too easy for those of deceitful intent, who, finding the coins so similar in size to the *half-eagle, gave them a reeded edge and gold plating so that they might be passed on to the unsuspecting as $5 instead of 5 cents. This fault was quickly corrected with the addition of the word CENTS below the wreath in place of E PLURIBUS UNUM.

The coin was regularly struck until 1912 and five specimens are known with the date 1913. The story of these is not exactly edifying, for they were produced clandestinely at the instigation of Samuel Brown, a one-time mint official, simply for the purpose of creating a rare collectors' piece. He succeeded only too well, aided and abetted by the numismatic promotions conducted by the coin dealer B. Max Mehl, who offered to pay $50 (a large sum at that time) for any specimen, well knowing that they all rested in collections. Naturally, therefore, altered dates are frequent; and a "genuine" piece—if that is the right word for something basically spurious—was sold in 1967 for $46,000 by one coin dealer to another. (Readers may draw their own moral from this.)

LIBERTY SEATED DIME *dime.

LIBRA The Roman pound, still commemorated by the symbol £ in the modern British monetary system. A coin with the name libra has been struck only once: as a gold piece of Peru from 1898, showing the head of an Inca chieftain.

LIGHT-WEIGHT SOLIDUS A Byzantine coin struck from the reign of Justinian I (A.D. 527–65) to the first reign of Justinian II (A.D. 685–95), not of full weight (24 *siliquae), but clearly distinguished as an official issue with marks denoting 23, 22 and 20 siliquae (in one unique instance also 21 siliquae). In the absence of any official Byzantine mint records, their precise use is still a matter for conjecture. Trade with neighbouring countries has been suggested, but it is difficult to see just why such a varied range should be needed for this. Their most extended use (judging from the number of surviving types) was under Maurice Tiberius, Phocas and Heraclius (i.e. a period covering the sixty years from A.D. 582–641); strikings, with very rare exceptions (Rome and Ravenna under Maurice Tiberius) appear to have been confined to Constantinople and *Antioch. (Also *tetarteron nomisma.)

LILLE   A regal mint of France from 1686 with the mintmark LL, changed from 1693–1858 (when the mint closed) to W.A. crowned. Single L also occurs, 1686–99. In medieval times, the town had been a mint of Flemish counts, and there are also siege coins of 1708. During the reign of Louis-Philippe (1830–48) the output of this mint rivalled and sometimes exceeded that of Paris.

LIMA   An important mint, first of Spanish America (1565–1821) and then of Peru (1821 to the present day). A fine series of coins commemorating the mint's 400th anniversary was struck in 1965, reproducing exactly the 8-reales piece as struck there in 1565.

Early coin types followed those of *Mexico City and *Santo Domingo, but no copper was struck here. Gold was not introduced here until 1696, with the royal bust type from 1751. The earliest coins bore the mintmark P (for Peru), from 1659 LM, and later still L, LIM, LMA and LME (in monogram forms) were employed.

Lima half-crown of George II

LIMA COINAGE   English gold and silver coins of 1745–6, bearing the word LIMA below the bust of George II. This money was struck from coinage and bullion of Spanish South America, captured by Anson off the coast of Peru, and in the Peruvian port of Paita, during the course of his voyage round the world.

LIMERICK   An Irish mint from the late 12th century onwards. Various trade tokens are known from the period 1658–77, and there are siege pieces with the name of James II of 1691, consisting of halfpennies and farthings overstruck on *gun money.

LINCOLN   An English mint from Saxon times to the reign of Edward I, but most prolific during the period A.D. 865–1066, when the names of almost a hundred different moneyers are recorded.

LINCOLN CENT   In 1909, on the occasion of the 100th anniversary of Abraham Lincoln's birth, the introduction of Victor D. Brenner's Lincoln Cent ended the life of the Indian head cent after fifty years. It is still current, and still shows Lincoln's bust facing left. The reverse, however, was altered in 1959: instead of showing ONE CENT in large letters and half-encircled by two ears of corn, it now displays the Lincoln Memorial as erected in Washington. This new design was engraved by Frank Gasparro.

Enormous quantities of the Lincoln Cent have been struck over the years at the Philadelphia, Denver and San Francisco Mints, in some years exceeding 1,000 million specimens. There are thus many obvious mint and die varieties, as well as some less obvious ones and errors. It is thus a natural "starter" for young American collectors, and for all whose pockets run only to items in the lower price range.

LINLITHGOW   A Scottish mint that struck *groats only, and active only under James I and II (1406–60).

LION   The traditional royal beast appears on coinages throughout two-and-half millennia, from the very earliest Greek *electrum coins onwards. Not unnaturally, there are a number of denominations actually called after it. The best known of these are the lion of Scotland, a gold coin to the value of 5 shillings, first struck under Robert III at the end of the 14th century; the lion noble, of 1584, another Scottish coin; the French lion d'or, struck by Philip VI in 1338; and the lion heaumé (i.e. helmeted) of Louis de Mâle issued for Flanders from 1364–70. In all but one of these, the lion is the dominant feature of the design, the exception being the French piece, where he acts as a footstool for the King shown seated on his throne.

LIRA   Derived from the Roman *libra, and a money of *account in Italy from early medieval times. As a coin it was first struck by the Doge Nicolas Tron of Venice in 1472—incidentally one of the very few Venetian portrait coins and the first to be given the name *testone (a head) for that reason. The lira remains the monetary unit of Italy to this day, being adopted as the equivalent of the French silver *franc when Italy joined the Latin Monetary Union. The lira is also the monetary unit of the Vatican (since 1929), of the independent Republic of San Marino, and was occasionally struck in Italian colonies (Eritrea, Somaliland). Finally, it is another name for the Turkish pound or *yuzlik.

LIRA TRON   *lira.

LIS   Denominations in both gold and silver of this name (lis d'or and lis d'argent respectively) were decreed in December 1655 under Louis XIV of France. Patterns for these coins had been struck as early as 1653, but in the event the issue proved short-lived and unable to displace the popular *louis in gold and silver.

LITAS   Lithuanian currency unit established in 1922. Silver pieces of 1, 2, 5 and occasionally 10 litu (pl.) were struck from 1925–38.

LITRA   A Sicilian unit of weight, of 12 ounces, corresponding to the Latin *libra. As a coin it is known from the 6th century B.C. in silver (Sicily and Campania), slightly lighter than, but in practice almost equivalent to the Greek *obol. In the 5th century B.C. it was also struck in bronze; and in the 4th century B.C. there are particularly beautiful 50 and 100 litrae strikings in gold of *Syracuse.

LIVRE   The French for a pound (from Latin *libra). The currency system of Charlemagne maintained itself in Great Britain until 1971 (12 deniers = 1 sol, 20 sols = 1 livre) and we are reminded of its French origins in the abbreviation l.s.d. The pound as a unit remained in France chiefly as a money of *account. Denominations to the value of 20 sols were struck on only two occasions. These were the *lis d'argent of 1656 and the *livre de la Compagnie des Indes in 1720. On both occasions the emissions were called in almost as soon as issued.

LIVRE DE LA CAMPAGNE DES INDES   Created by John *Law in 1720, this piece is often erroneously classed among French colonial pieces. It was, in fact, a coin of the realm (and the only one ever to bear the official designation of livre), deriving its name from Law's company, which at that time held sway over all French finances. An extraordinary decree, dated 13 January 1720, entitled the company to have this piece struck at any mint it chose, even the Medal Mint established in the Louvre.

LOEHR, AUGUST OKTAV VON (1882–1965)   Leading Austrian numismatist and director of the great Vienna collection. Loehr was among the first to treat of monetary history as a whole, publishing pioneer studies on paper money and banking documents of all kinds, and greatly adding to the Viennese holdings in these fields.

LONDON   An occasional mint in Roman times and the principal mint of England from the time of the Norman Conquest onwards. Its history from A.D. 287 to 1948 has been told in a 450-page volume by Sir John Craig, while detailed annual reports have been published regularly since 1870 by the mint itself. The mint's activities have not been confined to Great Britain and her dependencies. Its first foreign contract (silver coin for Philip II of Spain) is dated 1555; it struck pieces for Louis XVIII of France and the payment of Hanoverian troops in 1815; and during the past century it has taken a pre-eminent place among the mints of the world executing coinages for other countries. In 1966 the mint gained a Queen's Award to Industry for Export Achievements: during the year, 774 million coins in 109 denominations were struck for thirty-five Commonwealth and foreign countries, rather more than for home consumption. Though the administrative headquarters remain in London, the chief place for coin manufacture in Great Britain today has been transferred to Llantrisant in Wales. While most coinages in London were executed at the *Tower Mint (at first within the Tower, later on Tower Hill), there were supplementary mints at *Southwark and in *Durham House off the Strand during Tudor times.

LONG-CROSS PENNY Introduced under Henry III of England in 1247, this coin took the design of the *voided cross (reverse) to the very edge, so as to make the task of the clipper more difficult. No less than twenty different mints, with eighty different moneyers, were involved in the "great recoinage" of 1247–50, the first such event to have been recorded in detail by contemporary chroniclers. The issues were enormous; figures have been preserved which show that Shrewsbury alone issued 1,720,080 pennies in under two years. Issues from 1250 onwards are distinguished from early ones by showing the King with a sceptre; quite apart from mint and moneyers' varieties, collectors distinguish between seven types in the first group and ten in the second. An almost identical issue, still reading HENRICUS (for Henry III) continued during the first seven years of the reign of Edward I, from 1272–8.

The long-cross pennies in Edward's own name, struck from 1279–1310, present an even more extensive series divided into ten main classes and thirty-four varieties excluding mints and moneyers. Ecclesiastical issues also figure here, and the cross is now no longer voided but *patté. The introduction of halfpennies and farthings made the cutting of these new coins into halves or quarters unnecessary.

Long-cross penny: Early type of Henry III, *c.* 1350

LOOS, DANIEL FRIEDRICH (1735–1819) German medallist and coin engraver, who served the Prussian court for over sixty years, first at Magdeburg (1756–67) and from 1768 at Berlin. His medallic work is perhaps more notable than his coins, and certainly easier to identify; only during the reigns of Frederick William II and III, from 1786–1813, do we find an L by way of signature on most of his coin dies. His son Gottfried Bernhard opened his own die-sinking establishment at Berlin in 1812, famous throughout the 19th century for the quality and variety of its medallic productions.

LOOS, GOTTFRIED BERNHARD (1774–1843) *Loos, Daniel Friedrich.

LORD BALTIMORE COINAGE *Baltimore, Lord.

LORRAINE, CROSS OF A cross with two bars, most familiar to us as the emblem of the Free French during the Second World War. It has, of course, frequently figured on the coins of the old duchy of Lorraine from the 16th century onwards, and was also to be seen on coins of Mary Queen of Scots during her brief marriage to Francis (1558–60).

LOTTERIEDUKAT A ducat showing the naked figure of

Louis d'or of Louis XIII, 1641. The "A" in the centre of the reverse identifies the Paris Mint

Fortuna, goddess of luck, struck by Duke Charles Theodore of the Palatinate on the setting-up of the Mannheim city lottery in 1767 (and possibly in subsequent years also). The coin is undated.

LOUIS D'ARGENT Introduced in 1641, to follow the *louis d'or of 1640, this was to remain the standard crown-size piece of France until the French Revolution. No less than twenty-six main types (with many minor varieties of dates and mintmarks) are known during the seventy-one years of Louis XIV's long reign.

LOUIS D'OR Introduced in 1640 under Louis XIII and struck under his successors until 1793 (by a curious oversight of the revolutionary "terror" regime, even after Louis XVI had been executed). There are superb multiples of 10, 8, 4 and 2 louis struck in its introductory year, the 10-louis piece being the largest and most valuable coin in gold ever struck in France. Among later issues, those struck during the minority of Louis XV (1715–23), no less than six different types are especially notable for beauty of execution.

LÜBECK An important German trading port on the Baltic, which struck an autonomous city coinage from the 13th to the 19th centuries, and episcopal coinages from the 16th to the 18th centuries. During the 17th century there were extensive multiple ducat issues (10, 5 and 4 ducats) based on the Hamburg *Portugalöser.

LUCCA Town in Italy and an important mint for over a thousand years. It struck *tremissi for independent Lombard counts in the 7th and 8th centuries A.D. and one of the very rare golden *sous of Charlemagne. A prevalent type from medieval times to the 18th century is that of *Sanctus Vultus*, a crowned and bearded effigy most probably representing the Emperor Otto IV, who had granted numerous privileges to the city in 1209. During the early 19th century (1805–14) it formed part of Napoleon's dominions, with his sister Elise and her consort Felice as nominal rulers; and from 1814–47 it was ruled by Maria Louisa, widow of the King of Etruria.

LUCERNE Swiss canton and town, with its own coinage from the 15th to almost the middle of the 19th century. Splendid Thalers and their multiples were struck from 1518 onwards, many with city views also showing the lake and wooden bridge (which still exists). There are gold presentation strikings of such pieces which now fetch astronomical prices among Swiss collectors.

LUESTER, CHRISTIAN (d. 1871) A native of Denmark, Luester entered the service of the Rio de Janeiro Mint in 1855 and from then until 1870 engraved the dies for many important coins and medals of Brazil.

LUIGINO *Timmin.

LUND A Danish town and mint from the time of Cnut the Great (1018–35). The similarity of its name with that of London, and the fact that English coin dies of the time were sometimes taken to Denmark by his moneyers, makes confusion between issues of these two towns not only possible but likely—especially as the King was apt to put his title of REX ANGLORUM also on his Danish issues. Lund continued to strike coins all through medieval times, later also as an archbishopric.

LUSCHIN VON EBENGREUTH, ARNOLD (1841–1932) Noted Austrian scholar, who published what is perhaps the best "synoptic" view of monetary history ever written.

LUSSHEBOURNE Base foreign coins imported into England (mainly from Luxembourg, hence the name) by merchants during the reign of Edward III.

LUTWYCHE, WILLIAM   One of the largest of Birmingham token manufacurers active at the end of the 18th and beginning of the 19th centuries. His own advertisement token shows a contemporary coin-press on the reverse.

LYDIA   *Sardes.

LYON   A mint from Roman times; later one of the most important in the French regal series. Like Birmingham, it was a centre for button manufacture; and the skill of its designers and die-sinkers is shown by patterns for coins in *bell money submitted during the revolutionary period. (*Mathieu, Mercié & Mouterde.)

M

MACATA   *Guatemala.

MACE   A Chinese unit of weight, one-tenth of the *tael. It figures on certain pre-Revolutionary Chinese coins, the silver dollar being expressed as 7 mace 2 *candareens.

MACEDONIA   For early *autonomous coinages of this region of northern Greece, *Acanthus, Amphipolis and Mende. The great influence of this region numismatically throughout the Western world dates from the reign of King Philip II (359–336 B.C.), who began to exploit the rich gold mines of Pangaeum around 355 B.C., issuing a gold *stater (obverse: head of Apollo; reverse: two-horse chariot) which was to become the first major gold currency of the ancient world after the Persian *darics almost two centuries earlier. The type was extensively imitated for centuries to come. Similarly, Philip's silver *tetradrachms, showing a bearded head of Hercules on the obverse and a youth on horseback as the reverse design, spread via the Balkans and Danube valley throughout western and central Europe. Finally, the conquests of Philip's son, *Alexander the Great, caused the silver types to spread east as far as the Indus and south to Phoenicia and Egypt.

Macedon: gold stater of Philip II, c. 350 B.C.

MACUQUINA   *cob.

MACUTA   Portuguese copper to the value of 50 *reis, struck only for the African colonies from 1762 onwards. Fractions of the half and quarter macuta were also struck in copper, while multiples of 2, 4, 6, 8, 10 and 12 macutas were struck in silver until the end of the 18th century.

MADAI, DAVID SAMUEL (1709–80)   German numismatist who published during the years 1756–74 an extensive listing (in four volumes) of *Thalers of Germany and neighbouring countries.

MADER, JOSEPH VON (1754–1815)   Austrian numismatist and professor at Prague University, who was the first to establish scientific principles for the study of medieval coinages. These had, until his day, been almost entirely neglected in favour of Greek and Roman numismatics. Apart from two essays on *bracteates, he published a six-volume general compendium from 1803–13.

MADRAS   A mint of the East India Company from the last quarter of the 17th century onwards. With the exception of one issue at the beginning of the 19th century, which bears the arms of the company and the name in English, all coinages are of local types and denominations. Of particular interest is the "pagoda" coinage of 1807–11, which bears marks of value in no less than four languages: English, Persian, Tamil and Telugu.

MADRID   The capital of Spain has not, like most other European capitals, always enjoyed the position of chief mint. It did not begin to strike coins until the reign of Sancho IV (1284–95) and was dropped again in 1497 (*Medina del Campo). A century was then to pass before it was reinstated (mintmark M, crowned from 1728). From 1943 onwards, the Madrid Mint has been responsible not only for all Spanish coinage but banknotes and stamps as well, as its name implies (Fabrica Nacional de Moneda y Timbre).

MAGDALON A special type of gold *florin struck in Provence only during the period 1476–81 at the mints of Aix and Tarascon. The type of St Mary Magdalen bearing a vase or oil vessel has remained unique.

MAGDEBURG A place of coinage from the 10th to the 17th centuries as a town and a bishopric. The patron saint, Mauritius, appears in a fine series of *bracteates of the 12th century and again on a rare gold ducat issued by the cathedral chapter in 1638.

MAHÉ *biche.

MAINZ Town on the river Rhine and a seat of coinage from *Merovingian times. There is an uninterrupted series of gold pieces of the archbishops from the late 14th to the end of the 18th century. Of special note are a 2-ducat piece of Queen Christina while the town was under Swedish occupation in 1634 and a Rhine-gold ducat of 1772. There is French occupation money dating from the period 1688–9 and siege pieces of 1793–4. (Also *St Albansgulden.)

MALER, VALENTIN & CHRISTIAN Father and son, who dominated the Nuremberg medal trade during the last quarter of the 16th and the first quarter of the 17th centuries. Valentin received an imperial privilege or monopoly (the nearest thing to copyright known in those days) and various medals with the inscription C.PRIV.C. (cum privilegio Caesaris) are known. Both father and son also cut dies at the mints of Nuremberg and Würzburg.

MALTA Seat of the Knights of St John after their expulsion from Rhodes by the Turks (1523). An extensive coinage in all metals is known from Peter del Ponte (1534–5) to Ferdinand de Hompesch (1797–9). There are exceedingly rare *ingots of gold and silver dating from 1799–1800 while Malta was occupied by the French and besieged by the British fleet. The English money for Malta is, by contrast, confined to a series of one-third farthings struck at intervals from 1827–1913 and a solitary 3-penny piece of 1840. A decimal coinage was adopted in 1972.

It should also be noted that the Knights of St John are continuing to issue commemorative pieces annually from an independent mint at their present headquarters in Rome (since 1961); though these do not enjoy status as legal tender, they are of historical interest and some artistic merit.

MANCUS An early European name for the Arab gold *dinar, equal (in the time of Charlemagne) to 30 silver *deniers. It remained very largely a money of *account so far as European strikings are concerned. The name has sometimes been given to the unique copy of an Arabic dinar by King Offa of Mercia (A.D. 757–96), now in the British Museum; also to gold coins with Arabic inscriptions by counts of Catalonia during the 11th century.

MANDAT TERRITORIAL French paper money of 1796–7, which met with an even more rapid and drastic devaluation than the previous *assignats.

MANEEN TSUHO Bronze denomination of the coinage issued in Japan A.D. 760. It was tariffed at ten times the earlier copper pieces (*wado kaiko).

MANGHIR The first copper coin of the Ottoman Empire, introduced under Murad I (1360–89).

Manghir

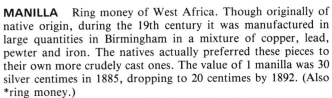

Marabotino of Alfonso VIII of
Castille, 1158–1214

MANILLA   Ring money of West Africa. Though originally of native origin, during the 19th century it was manufactured in large quantities in Birmingham in a mixture of copper, lead, pewter and iron. The natives actually preferred these pieces to their own more crudely cast ones. The value of 1 manilla was 30 silver centimes in 1885, dropping to 20 centimes by 1892. (Also *ring money.)

MARABOTINO   Spanish imitation of the Arab *dinar, struck in the kingdoms of Castile and Leon during the 12th and 13th centuries.

MARAVEDI   An alternative name for the above; but from 1497 a money of *account in the new coinage system of Ferdinand and Isabella, the gold *excelente being tariffed at 375 maravedis. As a coin, the maravedi was not revived until 1558 as a *billon denomination, and from 1680 was struck in copper. Pieces of 4 and 2 maravedis were also struck in copper as part of the first Spanish-American coinage (Mexico City Mint, 1537), but this proved an unpopular experiment; they were soon withdrawn and are today exceedingly rare.

MARCHANT, NATHANIEL (1739–1816)   An extremely able engraver of gems, employed from 1797 at the Royal Mint with the title of probationer or designer. He did not engrave coin dies but modelled them for others to copy.

MARCO POLO (1254–1324)   We owe to this Venetian traveller and explorer the first Western account of Chinese currencies, more particularly of the paper money then already in use there (though the earliest surviving specimens date from a century later).

MARENGO   A 20-franc gold piece struck in 1801–2, to celebrate the French victory at the battle of the same name, and the establishment of the Subalpine Republic. It was struck at the Paris Mint and not (as is often erroneously stated) at Turin. The error has probably arisen from the fact that it bears the initials of Amadeo *Lavy, engraver at the Turin Mint.

MARESCOTTI, ANTONIO (fl. 1444–62)   Nothing is known of the life of this medallist, except that he was active during the above years at the court of Ferrara and its mint. Apart from various cast medals, we owe to him the first portrait coin of the Renaissance: a gold ducat of Borso d'Este, engraved and struck in 1452. (*Pisanello.)

MARIA THERESA THALER   Possibly the best known and most widely diffused silver crown-size piece ever struck. It is based on a type first struck at the Günzburg Mint in 1773, which proved so popular in the Middle East it continued to be made after Maria Theresa's death, with the date "frozen" at 1780. When the Günzburg Mint was closed in 1805, the coins continued to be struck at Vienna with Günzburg mintmarks and the same date (for the Arabs would accept no other); and demand continued to increase throughout the 19th century. Milan and Venice, whilst under Austrian rule, were other mints to strike the coin. In the 20th century, strikings have been recorded at Paris, Brussels, Rome, London, Birmingham and Bombay; and Vienna also continued to strike the coin into the 1960s. There are minute differences by which these can be identified, classified by M. R. Broome in a paper published in the *Numismatic Chronicle* of 1972.

MARIENGROSCHEN   A coin first struck at Goslar, in the Harz mountain district of Germany, during 1503 (type: standing Virgin with Christ-child in her arms). It was of base silver, which became progressively baser over the years at other mints. It was finally stabilised at one-thirty-sixth of the *Reichsthaler and continued as part of the Brunswick coinage until the early 19th century, though not with the same design.

MARK   Currency unit of the German Empire, first struck as a silver denomination in 1873 (until 1927); from 1933–9 in nickel, and from 1950 in cupro-nickel. Multiples of 10 and 20 Marks were struck in gold until the First World War. Commemorative pieces of 3 and 5 Marks have continued to be struck in silver at intervals. As a weight and money of *account, the Mark goes back another thousand years, being valued at first at two-thirds of the Roman pound. There were, however, so many different weight standards throughout medieval Europe, from the Paris "troy" Mark of nearly 245 grammes to the Cracow Mark of 198 grammes, that its intricacies cannot be pursued here.

MARKKA   The Finnish equivalent of the Mark, struck there under Russian denomination from 1864 as a silver coin to the value of a quarter-*rouble. It was divided into 100 *pennia.

MARK NEWBY HALFPENCE   *St Patrick's token.

MARONEIA   Town on the southern shore of Thrace (northern Greece), famous for its wine, which was celebrated by means of a vine as the reverse design of its coinage from the 5th century B.C. The constant obverse type was a prancing horse (often its forepart only).

MARRAKESH   A mint of the Marinid dynasty (Arabic) in Morocco, from the late 13th century for almost two hundred years.

MARRIAN & GAUSBY   Birmingham firm of die-sinkers whose main claim to fame is a series of decimal patterns made in 1846 (value 10, 5, 2 and 1 cent), bearing on the obverse the firm's name below the Queen's head, and on the reverse the words SMITH ON DECIMAL CURRENCY. These patterns were originally offered in boxed sets by a parliamentarian of that name, together with a pamphlet with the same title, as propaganda for the decimal system.

MARS-EAGLE GOLD   Coins issued by Rome in 211 and 209 B.C. during the war against Carthage, in denominations of 60, 40 and 20 *asses. They show the head of Mars on the obverse, and an eagle on a thunderbolt as the reverse design.

MARSEILLES   As Massalia, one of the earliest Greek colonies in the western Mediterranean, this town struck coins from the early 6th century B.C. Its position at the mouth of the river Rhône made it a great entrepôt for trade; and through it, the gold *staters of *Macedonia spread among the *Celts of western Europe. The town has since acted successively as a Merovingian, Carolingian, Provençal, Aragonese and French regal mint. From 1853–7 it struck great quantities of the bronze coinage of Napoleon III, on new machinery specially supplied and installed for that purpose by Ralph *Heaton & Sons of Birmingham.

MARTIN, GUILLAUME   French engraver of coins and medals, active at the Paris Mint from 1558. Among the pieces he made there, a pattern *teston with facing busts of Mary Queen of Scots and the Dauphin Francis will be of special interest to British collectors. Disappointed in not being chosen to succeed *Bechot as engraver-general, he later worked for the court of Navarre, acting as engraver-general there for Jeanne d'Albret from 1564–71.

MARTIN, SIR RICHARD (1534–1617)   Goldsmith, Lord Mayor of London, and successively Warden and Master of the Tower Mint from 1559 until his death, a period of almost sixty years. This stewardship is the longest on record, and Martin can claim much of the credit for the excellence of the coinage during that time. He was among the first to suggest a copper coinage for England (1600) and left, among many other papers, a manuscript tract on mint organisation which is today in the British Museum.

MARYLAND *Baltimore, Lord.

MAS A small gold coin, containing less than ½ gramme of pure gold, current in Sumatra for almost five hundred years under the sultans of Atjeh (1297–1760).

MASLITZER, HANS (fl. 1538–74) A Nuremberg goldsmith and medallist of whom little is known except by way of a contemporary account which suggests that he was one of the most skilful artists and technicians in everything relating to coinage, not only engraving and striking but also assaying. A medal which shows him as a young man may well be by his own hand. But his signature is not on it, nor on any other piece which has come down to us.

MASSACHUSETTS The earliest coinage for English colonies on the American continent was struck here, near Boston, in 1652. They are plain silver pieces bearing merely the letters NE (for New England) in a rectangular stamp, and the denominations (shilling, 6 pence, 3 pence) in Roman numerals XII, VI and III.

MASSE D'OR French gold coins, struck only under Philip IV from 1308–10 and demonetised in 1313. It proved unpopular because it was not, like other gold coins of the time, of 24 carat purity, but fluctuated between 21 and 22 carat. The King is shown seated on his throne holding a sceptre (mace).

Earliest type of matapan, turn of the 12th and 13th centuries

MATAPAN Another name for the Venetian *grosso, as struck from 1202 onwards. The immediate occasion was for payment of troops on the fourth crusade, which also explains the Levantine origin of the popular name (Cape Matapan in Morea). The coin was extensively copied, both in Italy and the Levant, and continued to be struck by Venice herself until the middle of the 14th century.

MATHIEU, MERCIÉ & MOUTERDE Button-makers and die-sinkers of Lyon in France, and part of a group of "artistes réunis" of that town who presented pattern coinages in *bell metal to the French revolutionary assembly during 1791–2.

MATONA Coinage unit of Ethiopia under the Emperor Haile Selassie before the Italian invasion of 1936. Values to 1 and 5 matonas were struck in copper at King's Norton and Addis Ababa Mint respectively; higher values (10, 25 and 50 matonas) were struck at Addis Ababa in cupro-nickel. All show the crowned bust of the Emperor facing right, with the Lion of Judah on the reverse.

MATTHIASGROSCHEN Introduced by a convention between the town of *Goslar and the Bishop of Hildesheim in 1410, and named after its reverse type showing St Matthew. Originally intended to replace base silver, the coin in turn soon degenerated, becoming ever thinner and, by 1437, of single-sided, *bracteate fabric. A fresh attempt to make a "good" Groschen was made by Goslar (now on its own) from 1496, but this met with a similar fate; none the less, the type proved so popular that it was taken over by several neighbouring states. In one form or another, the "Mattier" or "Matier" survived until the middle of the 18th century—the final curiosity being a coin struck by Brunswick for French occupation troops, bearing on one side the designation 1 DENIER, and on the other 13 EINEN MATTIER (i.e. 13 deniers to 1 Mattier).

MATZENKOPF FAMILY Three generations of engravers, all
with the Christian name of Franz, dominated the Salzburg Mint
during the 18th century. Their artistry can be seen on both coins
and medals of the archbishopric from 1727 until 1807, when the
mint closed.

MAUNDY MONEY The Maundy ceremony—when the British
monarch distributes largesse to needy old men and women—is
said to date back to the reign of Edward II. It was not, however,
until Charles II that silver pennies began to be distributed and not
until around 1800 that Maundy Money as we know it today (4,
3, 2 and 1-pence pieces specially struck in silver for this
ceremony) was instituted. Before that, ordinary silver coins, more
often than not limited to the penny denomination, were used.

Maundy money: Full set of
George III, 1763

Recent issues of Maundy Money are scarcer than earlier ones.
Until 1909, one could order these special coins through a bank.
Then, following an express command of Edward VII, numbers
struck were strictly limited to those required to be distributed
each year, with a very few over for the Royal family and officials
taking part in the ceremony. Since the number of coins
distributed is directly related to the monarch's age, it follows that
those of the first regnal year are the scarcest and most valuable.

MAZEROLLE, FERNAND (1868–1941) French numismatist
and scholar, specially notable for his researches into French
Renaissance and early baroque coin and medal makers.

MAZUNA Coinage unit of Morocco from the late 19th century
to 1921, struck in bronze. The prevalent type of six-pointed star
is in some later issues varied to a more rounded form, i.e. as if
shaped of two interlacing trefoils. Values of 1, 2, 5 and 10
mazunas were struck.

MEA Mis-spelling of the Portuguese word *meia,* which occurs
on the *esphera of Goa. The word means half, implying that this
coin was to the value of one-half *cruzado.

MEDAL, MEDALET, MEDALLION The terms are to some
extent interchangeable, a medalet being a small medal and a
medallion a large one. Such pieces generally commemorate some
person or event, and may be either cast or struck. There are,
however, certain distinctions other than size. The medal may be
a military or other award, in which case (however small) the word
medalet is never used. And medallions are often uniface, i.e. one-
sided, with a distinctive pictorial and not just commemorative
appeal.

Mazuna: The date shown (1288)
is the Hegira one and
corresponds to 1871

MEDICINA IN NUMMIS A theme that has had its own
adherents (and even catalogues) for a long time. There are coins
showing Aesculapius, god of medicine, in ancient Greek times—
but it is the medal rather than coinage that is the main field, with
famous doctors figuring from the 16th century onwards.

MEDINA DEL CAMPO Town in Spain where Ferdinand and
Isabella proclaimed their famous edict of 1497 reforming the
Spanish coinage. This saw the introduction of the gold *excelente
and the silver *real. Strict controls were instituted over the seven
regal mints of Spain, with assayers' marks as well as mintmarks
ordered to be engraved on all gold and silver coins, each coin to
be weighed individually.

MEISSEN Town in what is today East Germany, situated
between Leipzig and Dresden. Famous for its porcelain from the
18th century, it has made many commemorative medallions in
this over the years. There were also emergency coins made in
porcelain here during 1922–3. Much earlier, during the second
half of the 12th century, Meissen had struck some particularly
fine *bracteates.

Mende: Tetradrachm, late 5th century B.C.

MELLE A mint of Poitou in France from Carolingian times. It has been suggested that the name, which sometimes appears on coins as METALLUM, itself refers to silver mines in the neighbourhood. There is an interesting *denier of Louis the Pious (A.D. 814–40), one of the very few coins to show actual coining implements.

MELOS An island in the Aegean, the most westerly of the Cyclades. Coins were struck here from about 500 B.C., the prevalent type being that of a pomegranate. There are varied reverses such as a wine-cup, trident and ram's head. Bronze coins, struck from about 300 B.C., often have a lyre on the reverse.

MENDE Wine-growing town on the coast of Macedonia, which in the 4th century B.C. struck some of the most beautiful among ancient Greek coins. A favourite obverse type is that of Dionysus (the god of wine) reclining on the back of an ass; while the reverse shows a vine with bunches of grapes.

MERCURY DIME *dime.

MEREAU A French word denoting token, ticket or pass. Such pieces were made in their thousands from early medieval times onwards by ecclesiastical foundations, corporations, guilds, etc. They served various purposes: sometimes as counters or even currency within a closed community; as fund raising or advertising media (e.g. sold as charms to pilgrims); or as admission tickets to places where security was essential (e.g. mines, mints). Numismatically, among the most interesting are moneyers' passes showing coining instruments: these are found in various regions of France from the 13th century onwards.

MERK Like the German *Mark originally a weight, then a money of *account, the merk became part of the Scottish coinage with the *balance half-merk struck in 1591. The *thistle merk followed in 1601.

MEROVINGIAN COINAGE An immense number of coins—mainly varieties of the gold *triens—were struck in post-Roman times within the confines of what is today France during the period of the 5th to the 7th centuries A.D. Such coins are known from over one thousand localities, which are not mints in the ordinary sense, as moneyers travelled from place to place, striking coins as and where needed (generally for tax purposes).

The absence of any contemporary written documentation makes this a field as hazardous to the amateur as that of *Celtic coinages; and although the localities are so very numerous, coins from individual ones are almost invariably rare and expensive. It is likely that many were re-converted into gold bullion once they had served the tax-gatherers' purpose and reached the king's coffers. Future finds and hoards may, however, conversely devalue what are now thought to be very rare pieces. A group of 37 pieces with no two from the same mint was found in a purse in the Sutton Hoo ship burial, buried c. A.D. 625 (discovered in 1939).

Merovingian gold coin

METALS While gold, silver, copper and bronze have been the most common coinage metals throughout the ages (all these, and platinum, having separate entries in this encyclopedia), there is almost no metal or *alloy which has not at one time or other been tried. During the past fifty years, the use of precious metals has been almost entirely abandoned, cupro-nickel being the favourite substitute for silver.

METAPONTUM Town in Lucania, near the "heel" of Italy, which struck a distinctive coinage from the 6th century B.C. At first the design consisted merely of an ear of corn, which was repeated in *incuse form on the reverse. This incuse design was, however, produced by a separate *relief die and not (as in the case of *bracteates) made by hammering the obverse design through the coin's thin fabric. Later coins are smaller and thicker, and the incuse design disappears. Later still, the ear of corn is relegated to the reverse of the coin, with the head of Leukippos, the city's founder, on the obverse.

METCALFE, PERCY   *Ireland.

METROVIC   *Ireland.

MEXICAN DOLLAR   A popular name for what is correctly described as the *peso.

MEXICO   The first country of the Americas to be extensively colonised by the Spaniards. Curiously, *Mexico City remained its only mint until 1810; but 10 branch mints were added during the 19th century, besides 11 emergency mints striking coins intermittently during the revolutionary war from 1811 to 1814. From the end of the 19th century, Mexico City was again the only mint, although now often supplemented by strikings from the US Mint at Philadelphia. A peso/centavo monetary system gradually superseded the old Spanish escudo/real denominations from 1870 onwards (first tried experimentally under the ill-fated Emperor Maximilian, 1864–7); for a time, both existed side by side. The series is intensively collected not only by its own countrymen but also by US citizens (more especially Texans, whose state once formed part of Mexico). The modern Mexican 50-peso piece was struck as currency until 1931 and has a slightly higher gold content than the US $20 (double eagle); it was then restruck as a *bullion piece from 1943 to 1947, the first date omitting the denomination and stating only the pure gold weight of 37.5 grammes. A similar silver bullion piece, with the stated weight of 33.625 grammes (one troy ounce of pure silver), was issued in 1949 only.

MEXICO CITY   The principal mint of the Spanish-American Empire from 1535–1821. Early coins struck here closely followed those struck in Spain, for both silver and copper denominations, with an "odd man out" in the shape of the 3 *reales (replaced, however, by the 4 reales in 1537). Gold was not struck until 1675. While the early coins until 1556 were round, they were replaced by the *cob type for almost two centuries, mechanical striking with protective serrated edges not being introduced until 1732. The same year saw the introduction of the King's portrait bust on gold coinage, and of the famous large "Pillar Dollar" which was to be struck in enormous quantities throughout the 18th century and became its principal international currency, both in its own right and in innumerable *overstruck or *countermarked shapes—not infrequently cut up into *bits. The mintmark, almost throughout the entire period of Spanish rule, was a distinctive M.

Mexico City has, of course, remained the principal mint of the modern Republic. Perhaps two aspects of its 20th-century coinage call for special comment. The silver is often marked not only with the denomination, but with the weight of the coin and the fineness of silver content. The 50-peso gold piece, struck intermittently since 1921, is the largest such piece struck for regular circulation; for some reason best known to dealers and collectors, it commands less of a premium over its gold content value than the USA *Saint-Gaudens $20 piece, though the latter was struck in much larger quantities over a longer period.

MEYBUSCH, ANTON (d. 1701)   Danish coin engraver and medallist, said to have been of German origin. He worked at the

Mexico:

Mexican dollar, Charles III, 1774. *(Photo courtesy R. Lobel)*

Group of modern Mexican coins. *(Photo courtesy R. Lobel)*

Milled shilling of Elizabeth I by
Eloye Meystrell

Copenhagen Mint from 1667–76, then at Stockholm, from 1684–90 in Paris (where he worked on the medallic series of Louis XIV, not on coinages), and finally once again at Copenhagen. He would appear to have been something of an engineer as well as an artist, for there are records of a payment to him in France in respect of a medal-striking machine. He was a very fine portraitist and produced many splendid dies especially during his final period at Copenhagen, for Christian V.

MEYSTRELL, ELOYS (d. 1578) French engineer and engraver, who introduced the mill and *screw-press to England from Paris, just ten years after they were first installed there. *Milled money was struck by (or under) him from 1561–71 and is notable for the neatness of its design and lettering. The jealousy of the traditional moneyers caused Meystrell to be dismissed; possibly he was something of a rogue anyway, for he was found guilty of counterfeiting and hanged at Norwich in 1578.

MIKHAILOVICH, GRAND DUKE GEORGE II (1863–1919) Cousin of Tsar Nicholas II and the most important Russian collector of his day. His collection (from Peter the Great to 1890) was published in twelve huge volumes from 1888–1914 with detailed documentation and is still the chief source of reference for the period.

MILAN Probably after Rome the most important place of coinage in Italy. A mint of both western and eastern Roman empires from c. 385–485, then successively for Goths, Lombards, Franks, Carolingians, German emperors, the Visconti and Sforza families, French Valois kings and Spanish and Austrian Habsburgs. The mintmark M first appears under Maria Theresa in the 1770s and continues as such until the final closure of the mint about a hundred years later. Ralph *Heaton of Birmingham struck here a great deal of copper coinage for the provisional Italian government of 1862. (Also *Caradosso.)

MILITARY GUINEA The final striking of the guinea denomination in 1813 (so called because it was struck for the payment of troops rather than general circulation) after an interval of fourteen years (though half and third-guineas had been struck in the meantime). The reverse is a shield within the garter, with the inscription HONI SOIT QUI MAL Y PENSE, already adopted on half-guineas from 1801. The type is scarce.

MILLED COINAGE As opposed to hammered coinage, struck by machinery. The etymology of the term is somewhat obscure, but it most likely derived from the fact that horse-driven watermills supplied power for the machinery. The term is sometimes used to describe the standard type of edge serrations on coins, but *grained* (vertical or diagonal) is a much more accurate term for these.

MILLES, CARL *Ireland.

MILL SAIL TYPE The pattern produced by punch-marks on reverses of very early Greek coins, resembling the sails of a windmill.

MILREIS Literally, 1,000 *reis; and since 1854, upon adoption of the gold standard, the Portuguese currency unit. Gold coins to the value of 5, 10 and 20 milreis were struck until the First World war in Brazil, first as part of the Portuguese Empire, and from 1889 as part of the Republic. In Portugal itself the denominations struck were smaller, 10, 5, and 2 and very occasionally 1 milreis.

MILTON, JOHN Gifted young engraver at the Royal Mint, who designed the Barbados penny in 1788. He was discharged in 1796 for supplying forged dies of foreign coins (French louis d'or and Portuguese joannes) to counterfeiters. He then carried on his own die-sinking business, mainly for the manufacture of tokens, at Rolls Buildings, Fetter Lane, in London. Most of his work was done to the order of collectors and in limited editions, so that all his fine pieces are today very scarce.

MINAS GERAES   Province of Brazil which, as the name implies, is rich in mines, and where a mint (with mintmark M) was established in 1724. It struck gold for ten years only, after that nothing but silver.

MINERS' BANK   A short-lived firm during the California gold rush, which issued one $10 piece only during the autumn of 1849. As it was found to hold less gold than face value, it was not readily accepted, and the Miners' Bank ceased trading early in 1850.

MINIM   From the Latin *minimus,* meaning smallest. The term is applied to minute bronze coins of the late Roman and early Saxon era on some of which *diademed or *radiate heads can be discerned. They are of no known or attributable denominations, some of them being no larger than a pin's head. A large hoard of them was found at Lydney Park, Gloucester, in 1929.

MINING COINS   Basically, all coins that show by design or inscription the source of the metal from which they were struck. They are known from Roman times to the present day, but 18th-century Germany is especially rich in them. Also *Flussgolddukaten, provenance marks, territorial gold.

MINT   The place where a coin is struck; more precisely, the building in which all the processes of coinage may be carried out, from the smelting of ingots to the final release of coins to banks. Nor are the activities of mints necessarily confined to the above: they have produced (and in some parts of the world still produce) paper money, revenue and postage stamps, lottery tickets and other kinds of documents where security is of importance as a safeguard against forgeries.

In ancient Greek times, the mint was probably little better than a smithy—which did not prevent the Greeks from turning out coins which remain unsurpassed in artistry. Today, administrative procedures and controls mitigate alike against fraudulence and excellence. The very processes by which a coin passes from design to manufacture almost inevitably ensure that little remains of what original artistic inspiration may have lain behind it; while the same elaboration of machinery (in all senses of the word) guarantees as nearly as is humanly possible that all coins passing from production line to the public are as alike as two pins. Nor are they, with rare exceptions today, any more interesting.

Apart from today, mints were probably most highly organised under the Roman Empire (*officina). At other times the structure has varied from the practically non-existent (*Merovingian) to the leasing of rights to entrepreneurs. These rights might pass from father to son, depending upon the conditions of the "lease". Such arrangements were not uncommon until well into the 18th century, since when governments have tended more and more to keep minting affairs in their own hands, and to regard those employed there as civil servants. None the less, private mints of one kind or another have flourished since the industrial revolution, under a system of *contract coinages farmed out by the government. This tends to be a two-way traffic, i.e. the central mint may send to the private mint dies ready for striking, or the private mint may supply blanks or dies to the central authority. Profit margins being as strictly controlled as everything else

Anonymous French jeton showing implements of Châlons-sur-Marne Mint, 1591. *(Photo courtesy the Paris Mint)*

pertaining to coinage, such contracts are today probably accepted by private mints only for their publicity value, the lucrative side of their business being to sell series of medals to the public.

MINT CONDITION   *fleur de coin.

MINTMARK   Literally, any mark on a coin which helps to identify the mint in which it was struck. This may be a letter or some other kind of symbol. The initial letter of a town is not uncommon (e.g. P for Prague). A favourite modern system has been that first instituted by Francis I of France in 1540, by which the principal mint of a country is given the letter A, and subsidiary mints are allotted other letters of the alphabet.

A great number of letters or symbols to be found on coins are not mintmarks in the strict sense of the word at all, but belong to officials such as mintmasters, mint wardens, engravers or even designers of coins. This can cause confusion or be helpful, as the case may be; and reference to documentary sources is usually essential. Quite often mints as such do not carry distinguishing marks, in which case identity marks of personnel known to have worked at a certain mint during a certain period help to "place" the coin.

MIONNET, THÉODORE-EDME (1770–1842)   French scholar, who compiled what was at that time the largest catalogue of Greek and Roman coins (from specimens in the Cabinet des Médailles, Paris), totalling over 52,000 pieces in fifteen volumes (1806–37). It was unique at the time also, for a scholarly work, in concerning itself with degrees of rarity and commercial values for various types. To ease classification of coins, Mionnet invented what is still known as the Mionnet Scale. This consists of a series of nineteen circles growing from a common base with varying diameters, taking in all the common denominations of ancient coins.

MISCAL   Originally, a Muhammadan weight standard for bullion transactions, the miscal was introduced as a silver coin equivalent to the Spanish *piastre towards the end of the 18th century. Very rarely, it was also struck as a small gold coin (1.9 grammes of gold as opposed to 28.5 grammes of silver). A century later, the miscal reappears as a coin of Chinese Turkestan (value one-tenth of a *tael); multiples of 2, 3, 4 and 5 miscals were also struck from 1892–1916.

MOCENIGO   A type of *lira introduced under the Venetian Doge Pietro Mocenigo (1474–6), showing on the obverse St Mark and the kneeling Doge, and on the reverse Christ standing. It was struck for a century and copied at Mantua and Modena.

MOCO   The centre-bit of the cut Spanish dollar, used as a coin in its own right, as used in San Domingo towards the end of the 18th century (counterstamped with a D).

MODEL PENNY   Designed and struck by Joseph Moore of Birmingham c. 1844 (some being dated, others not), these were small copper pieces with a silver "plug" in the centre. Though popular with the public, they were never adopted by the Royal Mint, which went to some trouble to disclaim all responsibility for them, and to point out that they were a publicity stunt only, not legal tender.

MODENA   Italian town, established as an autonomous city mint under the Emperor Frederick II c. 1226, and from 1294 a fief of the d'Este family, which also owned the duchies of Ferrara and Reggio. The coinage throughout the period from the Renaissance to the end of the 18th century (when the mint was finally closed) has great artistic merit. Foreign occupations and strikings include some by the Emperor Maximilian (1513), three popes (Leo X, Hadrian VI and Clement VII during the period 1514–27), and Louis XIV of France, whose troops occupied the town from 1702–6, during the War of Spanish Succession.

MODULE   The size of a coin, generally expressed in terms of its diameter (when it is round), or by the largest length and breadth (when it is irregularly shaped, e.g. oval, lozenge-shaped).

MOFFAT   *Humbert.

MOHUR   The standard gold coin of the Indian sub-continent, introduced by the Moghul emperors during the 16th century. It has been struck in most Indian native states since, and was adopted also as the gold unit of the East India Company from 1675. It survived as a gold piece of British India with the titles of Victoria as Queen (until 1870) and as Empress (1870–91).

The Moghul types, like all Muhammadan coins, were largely inscriptional. There are, however, some notable exceptions during the early periods, from Akbar (1556–1605) who introduced the coin, to Jahangir (1605–27). Figurative pieces include a hawk and a duck under the former and some actual portraits under the latter, apart from the famous series of twelve *zodiacal pieces (also struck as *rupees in silver). Dating each coin by month had already been the practice under Akbar.

Mohur of Jahangir (Moghul Empire), early 17th century

MOIDORE   Portuguese, a contraction of the words *moeda de ouro,* meaning simply gold money or coin. As such, quite a number of different denominations from the 500 *reis of 1575 onwards have been given the name; but it ultimately "stuck" to the 4-cruzado piece struck in large quantities during the period 1663–1722, which came to be as much the principal gold piece of the Western world as the ubiquitous Spanish "pieces of eight" were its chief silver currency. The piece, which was tariffed at 4,000 reis, was struck in even larger quantities in Brazil, especially during the years 1695–1700 at both Bahia and Rio mints, and again during the period 1751–77. All these coins show the crowned arms of Portugal on the obverse and a cross on the reverse.

MOKKO   Bronze drums, varying from 30 to 70 centimetres in height and 3½ to 7 kilograms in weight, and used as currency on islands in the East Indies (chiefly Solor, Pantar Allor and Tim.) from the 17th century to 1914. Even during this period their value fluctuated according to their age and beauty; by the end of the 19th century, the finest were valued at around 1000 Dutch gulden. Since many were melted down after the Dutch colonial office ceased to accept them for tax and other official payments from 1914 onwards, they are avidly collected by connoisseurs of ethnic art as well as by collectors of primitive money.

MOMMSEN, THEODOR (1817–1903)   German scholar, the first to examine thoroughly the legal and administrative bases of Roman coinage, and to attempt an assessment of Roman mint organisation. First published in 1860, his researches have warranted reprinting as recently as 1956.

MONACO   This independent principality, on the south coast of France near the Italian border, has struck its own coinage intermittently since the early 16th century. The gold pieces struck by Honoré II between 1649–61 are among the rarest in the European series.

MONETA   Juno 'moneta', the watchful one, had her temple on the Roman Capitol. The first Roman mint is said to have been established within its walls; and moneta became the word for both money and coinage. The origins of the word are com-

Moneta of T. Carisius, *c.* 45 B.C., showing coining implements on the reverse

memorated on a *denarius which shows on its obverse the head of the goddess with the inscription MONETA, and on the reverse an anvil, die, hammer and pincers with the name of the then (48 B.C.) moneyer, T. CARISIUS.

The figures of no less than three monetae (symbolising gold, silver and copper coinage) appear during the reign of the Emperor Septimius Severus: they each hold a horn of plenty and a balance. A single moneta again appears on coins of later Roman emperors (Diocletian among others), shown dropping coins on to scales.

Since then, the word *moneta* has appeared countless times on European coinages, most frequently in conjunction with the word *nova* to indicate a new coinage struck from old coin melted down.

MONEY The substance which has been called the root of all evil is the subject of this book. It comes in all shapes and sizes, from the *minim to the stone discs of *Yap, from the *cowrie to pressed bricks made from tea.

The reasons why different people attach a certain value to different substances remain obscure. At a basic level, there are obviously substances which we all need; and barter remains, to a much greater extent than many people realise, a common form of trading. True, it is not carried out by haggling in the street whether one cow is worth two sheep, but over the telex, with sophisticated switches of goods via perhaps three or four intermediaries who never see the goods they deal in.

Nor do such people ever handle money in the sense that you or I fish small change out of our pockets, or notes from our wallets. Money to them is a unit of value against which various goods are measured. It follows that at some point along the scale there must be something that everyone believes in, which is thought to be always "negotiable" for goods or services.

For all the efforts of economists to find something better, that substance remains gold. At government level, it is still shifted around in vast quantities, not as coin but as *bullion. So valuable is it to governments that very many will not allow their populations to keep it, except in the form of ornaments on which exorbitant taxes are levied. But gold coinage, in the sense that 2,500 years of human history knew it (i.e. pieces struck to the value of the gold content of the coin, with a minimal percentage taken by the government by way of a production fee) is a thing of the past and likely to remain so. Such coins as are today struck in gold, for commemorative purposes, are usually sold to the public at several times their metallic face value. The krugerrand is the most notable exception.

Even such *token money as we possess today is rapidly disappearing and will probably have done so completely by the end of the century. Plastic takes the place of cupro-nickel more and more; where previously we had coins of different sizes we now have credit cards of different colours. At the moment, we can still run into trouble if we use them indiscreetly. Soon, computers will instantaneously measure the "money" (such as it is) in our accounts as we present our plastic badges, and will give the shopkeeper a green or red light as the case may be. Whether all this—or any of it—is an improvement over what the human race has so long been used to only time will show.

MONEY OF ACCOUNT   *account, money of.

MONEY OF NECESSITY   *emergency money.

MONNAIE DES MÉDAILLES The French Medal Mint, as established under Louis XIV as a more or less autonomous part of his Paris Mint, with a quite separate function and constitution

from that of the coin mint. In Louis' own day, it existed chiefly
for the monarch's glorification, celebrating alike military and
civil events. It was responsible also for the striking of *jetons,
which continued throughout the "ancien régime". But during the
last year of Louis XVI's reign we find the Monnaie des Médailles
already taking on outside contracts: both Franklin and Jefferson,
for example, while envoys to France, commissioned American
revolutionary medals. Under Napoleon, the Medal Mint
reassumed its function as a propaganda machine (*Denon) in a
more marked degree than ever before. More recently, though still
striking official medals and orders of all kinds, it has become
more and more of a "collectors' mint", striking everything under
the sun from communion tokens to enamelled pieces that could
be called jewellery rather than medals; and outside contract work
continues to grow in scope. Exhibitions on various aspects of
medallic art are held regularly in the magnificent Hôtel de la
Monnaie, the mint's headquarters in Paris; their catalogues
are superbly produced by the Imprimerie Nationale and tend to
become standard works of reference. Special limited editions of
certain medals are produced solely for members of the *Club
Français de la Médaille.

Among the mint's many productions, the most sought-after are
probably those commemorating royal and other historic visits
both to it and the coin mint proper. The first such was that of
Tsar Peter the Great of Russia on the occasion of his Paris visit
in 1717, and the series continues to this day with presidential
visits and those of foreign royalty. Very few specimens are struck,
for presentation only, in gold; but the public is given the opportunity to purchase copies in silver and bronze. The mint has kept
most of its old dies and maintains a historic catalogue of items
still available (among them the one commemorating the 1717
visit). All such reproductions are carefully marked to distinguish
them from earlier strikings.

MONNERON TOKEN   The Frères Monneron were merchant
bankers in Paris toward the end of the 18th century. They had
handled *Boulton's business affairs in France for some years
when the French Revolution put an end to regular coinage. Consequently they turned to him to strike a series of copper *tokens,
in value of 5 and 2 *sols during 1791–2. Various designs are
known, with (as on English tokens) different edge-markings to
show places where tokens could be cashed. There are rare patterns in silver and copper-gilt. The pieces ceased to be legal tender
when the French revolutionary government brought out its own
copper pieces to the value of 2 and 1 sols in 1793 and prohibited
all tokens (*sol aux balances).

Bronze 5-sols piece by
Monneron, 1792

MONOGRAM   A device consisting of two or more interwoven
letters generally representing the initials of some ruling per-
sonage, and often designed in such a manner as to make an artistically pleasing pattern on a coin. In fact, collections can be
(and have been) built up of coins that are identifiable only by
their monograms and/or dates. A detailed German catalogue lists
over 2,500 of them.

One cannot help but notice that the elaboration of a monogram
tends to grow in inverse proportion to the importance of the ruler
employing it. Petty German princelings tend to outdo each other
in convoluted (and often indecipherable) squiggles and
flourishes, while the powerful ruler is content to be clear and
dignified. Nothing could be simpler than the monogram of the
Emperor Otto the Great; nothing more preposterous and preten-
tious than that of the wife of a 17th-century Saxon duke. It is also

an interesting study in psychology to compare designs such as those of Frederick II (the Great) of Prussia at different periods of his rule: young and flamboyant in 1753, the grand old monarch of 1783 no longer has any need to show off on his coinage.

The record for variety in monograms is held, not unexpectedly, by a monarch of the Baroque era: King Christian V of Denmark. No less than fifty-one different designs and sizes of C5 or CV are known on his coins. (Also *tughra.)

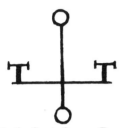

A Otto the Great, German Emperor, on a document dated A.D. 937

B MS—for Magdalena Sybilla of Saxony, on a coin of 1676

C FR—two monograms of Frederick the Great of Prussia, on coins dated 1753 and 1783 respectively

D C5 and CV—three of the very many different monograms to be found on coins of Christian V of Denmark (1670-99)

E CWAZ—Carl Wilhelm von Anhalt-Zerbston (1667–1718), on a coin of 1690

F GGzSWvH—Gustav Graf zu Sayn, Wittgenstein und Hohnstein, (Count of Sayn-Wittgenstein, 1657-1701), on coin of 1676

G WFzY—Wolfgang Fürst zu Ysenburg (Duke of Isenburg, 1907–18), private coinage n.d.

E-G: A group of particularly convoluted monograms, the last being an interesting example of Art-Nouveau style

MONTREAL A great number of *tokens were issued in this city, chiefly during the period 1837-9. The most sought-after are the *bouquet sous and bank tokens of the Bank of Montreal, which has also been a notable issuer of paper money from 1823-42 (and earlier as Montreal Bank from 1817-22).

MONTROSE One of the many mints opened by Alexander III of Scotland to coin his new type of *long-cross pennies. There is no record of its activity after 1286.

MORABITINO Early Spanish gold coin, struck under Alfonso VIII (1158-1214), showing on each side both circular and linear inscriptions in Arabic. The obverse relates that it was struck by Alfonso, son of Sancho, at Toledo; the reverse is an affirmation of the Christian faith as a challenge to Arab incursions into Spain, with the cross plainly visible to underline the linear inscription.

MORBIDUCCI, PABLO *Ireland.

MÖRIKOFER, JOHANN MELCHIOR (1706-61) Famous Swiss medallist and coin engraver, in charge of the Berne Mint from 1755 until his death. Many fine ducats, Batzen and Kreuzer are due to his talent.

MORMON GOLD Gold was issued from a small mint at Salt Lake City during 1849-50, in denominations of $2.50, $5, $10 and $20. The $20 piece was the first of that denomination to be struck in the USA. All carry as the obverse type the inscription HOLINESS TO THE LORD surrounding a bishop's mitre with the Eye of Providence beneath. The reverse shows a pair of clasped hands with the date below, surrounded by an inscription reading sometimes PURE GOLD (and denomination), or sometimes the initials G.S.L.C.P.G. (Great Salt Lake City Pure Gold). A further coin ($5) of very different type was struck in 1860 only. This shows on the obverse a lion facing left, surrounded by a legend in the Mormon alphabet (Holiness to the Lord). The reverse shows a beehive with an eagle holding a laurel branch and arrows in its talons; the surrounding legend reads DESERET ASSAY OFFICE PURE GOLD. ("The State of Deseret" was the first name given to Mormon territory, the word deseret meaning a honey-bee.) All Mormon gold is very rare.

MORSE CODE A single coin is known to have a series of irregularly spaced dots around its edge (rather than the continuous "pearly ring"). It is a Canadian 5-cent piece struck in 1943 in tombac and in 1944-5 in chrome-plated steel. The Morse code reads "We win when we work willingly"—a message reinforced by showing the denomination 5 as "V" surmounted by a torch.

MOSCOW The principal mint of Russia since the late 14th century, and its only mint under Peter the Great until he established a second one at his new capital of St Petersburg in 1718. The latter was, however, closed again soon after Peter's death for a period of ten years (1728-38); after its reopening, Moscow and St Petersburg shared in striking coins about equally throughout the 18th century. This balance was finally altered in St Petersburg's favour when new machinery imported from England (*Boulton) was installed there.

The history of the Moscow Mint—or rather mints—is a complex one, especially under Peter the Great. No less than eleven different *mintmarks have been noted during the period 1700-24 and coinage is known to have been struck in at least four different buildings. Copper was always struck quite separately from the precious metals.

MOTT TOKEN   William and John Mott were fashionable jewellers in New York during the late 18th century and issued a token in 1789 as an advertising piece, not as currency. One of the earliest American pieces of its kind, it was almost certainly manufactured in Birmingham.

MOULIN DES ÉTUVES   The first regular coinage establishment using machinery, installed on the Île de la Cité in Paris during 1551 and used intermittently for machine-struck coins until the last decade of the 16th century. A similar establishment was later in use at the Louvre. The word *moulin* derives from the water-mill which was used to activate the machinery.

Teſtons au pourtraict cy deſſus, du poix de ſept deniers dix grains, trebu chans, pour vnze ſolz quatre deniers tournois.

Demis teſtos au pourtraict cy deſſus du poix de trois deniers dixſept gr. pour cinq ſolz huict deniers tourn.

Moulin des Étuves: Page from a French coin proclamation of 1551, showing new testons and halves as first struck at the *moulin*

MOUTON D'OR   *agnel.

MULE   A kind of "hybrid" coin, made of obverse and reverse dies not originally meant to be used together. This may be either accidental or deliberate. Absentmindedness and/or haste may be an excuse for the former; but a close system of inspection generally ensures that no such hybrid leaves a reputable mint. As regards the latter, we must distinguish between official issues and artificial "concoctions" (of which some of the Russian *novodels are a typical example).

Deliberate mules that are at the same time official are mainly to be found at the beginnings of reigns, where the effigy of the new monarch is prepared for the coinage as soon as possible while it is not thought necessary to create a new reverse type at once. This happens not infrequently with the Norman kings of England; dies are even known to have been interchanged by different mints. Confusion could occur with this practice once coins began to be regularly dated during the late Renaissance: coins are known with dates (not always the same) on both the obverse and the reverse.

MÜLLER, PHILIPP HEINRICH (1655–1718) Noted German engraver and medallist, born at Augsburg but mainly active at Nuremberg. His initials are also found on *roubles of Peter the Great dated 1718–23, the dies for which are probably his last work.

MULTIPLE THALERS German Thalers are known in multiples from 1½ to 16 and fall into two quite separate categories. There are those which are broader than the single piece (Breit-Thaler) and those which are thicker (Dickthaler). In each case the weight would, of course, correspond to the exact value in silver proportionate to the unit as required under coinage statute.

Obviously, it would be cheaper to strike multiples simply on a thicker *flan, since the same dies could be used. Broad Thalers (on a thinner flan) would require different dies to be cut; they are therefore scarcer, being struck mainly for special commemorative purposes (weddings, funerals, shooting festivals, etc.).

MUNICH Capital of Bavaria and a mint since the 15th century, first of the dukedoms, later of the kingdom (until 1918). With the mintmark D, Munich continues to be one of the four mints of the German Federal Republic to this day.

MURAJOLA A generic name in Italy for any *billon coin of low silver content (moro = dark). It was first applied to papal coins struck in 1534 at the mints of Bologna and Piacenza, followed by Modena, Ferrara and others. The type was generally that of the local saint. During the 18th century they were struck in denominations of 2, 4, 8 and 16 *baiocchi or *bolognini.

MYTILENE Principal town on the island of *Lesbos (to which refer for coinage in ancient Greek times). During the Middle Ages, it was an outpost of Genoa, whose governors struck here in the early 14th century copies of Venetian types.

NAGAPATNAM   *pagoda.

NAMES   The etymology of coin denominations awaits a special study, especially as regards the many popular names or nicknames by which coins have been known at various times. Meanwhile, Stückelberg's general classification remains the best available and is summarised here:

(1) derived from the name of the ruler—e.g. DARIC
(2) derived from the title of the ruler—e.g. AUGUSTALIS
(3) derived from the dynasty—e.g. MARAVEDI
(4) derived from the name of the mintmaster—e.g. HANON
(5) derived from the place name—e.g. TOURNOIS
(6) derived from the coin design—e.g. KREUTZER
(7) derived from the inscription—e.g. DUCAT
(8) derived from the countermark—e.g. KELCHBATZEN
(9) derived from the name of the mint—e.g. ZECCHINO
(10) derived from the locality where the coin circulated—e.g. VIERLANDER
(11) derived from the colour of the coin—e.g. ALBUS
(12) derived from the metal—e.g. AUREUS
(13) derived from the provenance of the metal—e.g. GUN MONEY
(14) derived from the value of the coin—e.g. CENT
(15) derived from the edge—e.g. SERRATI
(16) derived from the size—e.g. PICCOLO
(17) derived from the thickness—e.g. DICKEN
(18) derived from the sound—e.g. CLINKAERT
(19) derived from a special occasion—e.g. MARENGO
(20) derived from the age—e.g. NOVA CONSTELLATIO
   (Classification from Stückelberg, *Der Münzsammler,* 2nd edition, 1919; but I have occasionally substituted other examples, more likely to be familiar to English and American readers.)

NANCY   A mint of the dukes of Lorraine from the middle of the 12th century onwards. Many fine pieces were struck here, especially during the period from 1500–1620. In 1796, during the revolutionary period, a certain Thuillie cast here a piece of one *décime in *bell metal.

NAPLES   An early colony of the Greeks in Campania, Naples struck coinage almost without intermission from the 5th century B.C. until 1870. The most notable issues are perhaps the gold *salutes struck under Charles I and II of Anjou during the latter part of the 13th century.

NAPOLEON   Common name for the 20-franc gold pieces struck in enormous quantities by both Napoleon I and III.

NARTOV   *reducing machine.

NASSARO, MATTEO DAL (fl. 1515–47)   Renaissance engraver from Verona, Italy, but attached for a long period to the court

of Francis I of France, for whom he made some particularly fine
*pattern pieces in gold.

NATTER, JOHANN LORENZ (1705–63)   One of the most
skilful of 18th century gem engravers, Natter is perhaps more
noted for his cameos and medals than for the engraving of coin
dies. None the less, he held for a time the post of chief engraver
at the Utrecht Mint and was an assistant engraver at London's
Royal Mint for some years from 1751. It was in London that he
published his *Treatise on Gem Engraving* in 1754. He is also
known to have worked at Copenhagen, Stockholm and St
Petersburg.

NAXOS   (1) Town in Sicily, famous for its wines in ancient
times, and celebrating this in most of its coin types (Dionysus,
Silenus, bunch of grapes, etc.). (2) Island in the Cyclades, also
given up to the cult of Dionysus, but with the wine-cup as its most
common type.

NECESSITY, MONEY OF   *emergency money.

NEGENMANNEKE   *gigot.

NEICKELIO, KASPAR FRIEDRICH   German antiquarian of
the early 18th century, who in 1727 published his *Museographia*,
a guide on how to arrange museums or collections, both public
and private. His advice is as sound today as when it was written:
avoid copies, collect only the finest specimens, and build a collection that tells a story.

NEUCHÂTEL   Chief town of the Swiss canton of the same
name. It did not obtain independence until after the Napoleonic
wars, being subject previously to the house of Orléans, the
kingdom of Prussia, and Alexander Berthier, one of Napoleon's
marshals. Its numismatic history is therefore rich and varied; and
its museum today has also the finest collection of coins and
medals engraved by Jean-Pierre *Droz, born nearby at La-
Chaux-de-Fonds.

NEWARK   Town in the English Midlands, not far from
Nottingham, and a place where a notable series of *siege pieces
was struck during the Civil War (dated 1645 and 1646). Known
values include the half-crown, shilling, 9 pence and 6 pence, all
in silver.

NEWFOUNDLAND   This island did not join the Dominion of
*Canada until 1949, but coins were struck for it as a crown col-
ony at the Royal Mint from 1865 in Canadian denominations of
50, 25, 10 and 5 cents silver, and 1 cent bronze. A unique additional piece is the $2 coin in gold, with inscription TWO HUN-
DRED CENTS—ONE HUNDRED PENCE, for which there
exists no parallel elsewhere in the British Empire. It was struck
intermittently from 1865 to 1888; only those dated 1882 carry a
minute H for "Heaton Mint" (another unique feature, since this
sub-contractor was generally entrusted by the Royal Mint in
London only with minor denominations, not gold). The accession
to the Dominion in 1949 led to a special commemorative dollar
(now as part of Canadian coinage), with the reverse showing the
Matthew (the sailing ship in which John Cabot discovered Newfoundland in 1497), and an inscription in tiny letters beneath this:
FLOREAT TERRA NOVA.

NEW JERSEY CENT   Coins struck by the authority of the New
Jersey legislature from 1786–8. The earlier varieties—especially
one with Washington's head—are exceedingly rare; later, more
common ones show a horse's head with the legend NOVA
CAESAREA on the obverse and a shield with the legend E
PLURIBUS UNUM on the reverse.

Naxos coin showing the head of
Dionysus on the obverse

Newark: A half-crown specimen
(XXX = 30 pence)

A selection of New Zealand coins; the top one is the rare Waitangi Crown

NEW ORLEANS   Capital of Louisiana and a US branch mint from 1838. Only *dimes in silver were struck in its first year of operation, but other larger silver denominations, and gold, were soon added. The mint was closed from 1861 (for the Civil War period, *Confederate half dollar) until 1879; from that date until 1909, it continued to strike coins with the mint letter O, the final issue being a very small one of the Indian head half-eagle (gold).

NEWTON, SIR ISAAC (1642–1727)   It is little known outside numismatic circles that the great mathematician and scientist spent the last thirty years of his life as Warden and Master of the Royal Mint. Newton discharged his duties punctiliously and was, among other things, responsible for fixing the value of the *guinea at 21 shillings in 1717. His enormous mass of Mint papers survive and are today in the Public Record Office.

NEW WESTMINSTER MINT   Rich deposits of gold were found in British Columbia in 1858; and the Governor, Sir James Douglas, approved the project for a mint in connection with a government assay office and refinery. Buildings were erected and machinery supplied in 1862; and dies for $10 and $20 pieces were engraved by Albert Kuner of San Francisco. Suddenly, the whole project was abandoned and the coinage remained in the pattern stage. Not more than four specimens of each denomination are known to survive, of which two are in the public archives of British Columbia, the others in private hands.

NEW ZEALAND   Many currencies, including the inevitable Spanish "pieces of eight", circulated here until 1850, when British coins were established as the official currency, but because of a persistent shortage of small change, many traders issued their own private *tokens from 1857 to 1897. From 1910 onwards, Australian coinage became recognised alongside the British, and it was not until 1933 that New Zealand had its own coins. These were designed along traditional lines until 1967, when New Zealand went decimal and, at the same time introduced an attractive series based on local fauna. The only great rarity in the New Zealand series is the Waitangi Crown of 1935, issued to commemorate the Treaty of Waitangi (1840) between the British and the Maori; the obverse shows George V as King-Emperor, with crown and Garter robes, and the reverse shows the British governor and the Maori chief shaking hands. Paper money occurred earlier and is also rare, notably that of the Maori chief Tawhio (Bank of Aotearoa).

NICAEA   A short-lived independent Byzantine empire, established in Asia Minor after the Crusaders had conquered Constantinople (1204). Coins of Byzantine type were struck here from 1208 onwards, and also in the cities of Magnesia and Thessalonika. By 1260 its ruler Michael VIII Palaeologus had become so powerful that he was able to reconquer Constantinople and restore the "legitimate" Byzantine empire, which his successors subsequently ruled until 1453, when it was finally destroyed by the Turks. Coins of Nicaea are known in gold, silver and bronze. The obverse generally displays two figures, that of the Emperor and one of the saints; the reverse shows Christ or the Virgin Mary. Their fabric shows such similarity with the immediately preceding Constantinople issues that it is assumed moneyers from there established the mint.

NICKEL   Discovered and used for coinage as long ago as 200 B.C. in Bactria, nickel was then neglected until the 19th century, when the Swiss began to use it once more—at first alloyed with copper, later in its pure state. Towards the end of the century, huge deposits were discovered in North America and Canada; and the metal has given its name to the 5-cent piece of the USA. Alloyed with copper (i.e. cupro-nickel), it does service as today's "silver" coinage. (*Buffalo nickel, Jefferson nickel, Liberty head nickel, shield nickel.)

NINEPENCE   No regular issues were struck to this value. There are, however, emergency pieces (*Newark in England and *Inchiquin money in Ireland) struck during the period of the Civil War, and pattern bank tokens struck in 1812.

NINI, JEAN BAPTISTE (1717–86)   Of Italian birth—he came from Urbino—Nini was much in demand throughout Europe both as an engraver on glass and a modeller in terracotta. From 1772 until his death, he was in charge of the pottery works at Chaumont, near Blois, and about sixty terracotta medallions made there are from his hand. The most famous is perhaps that of Benjamin Franklin, which exists in numerous varieties and on which even more numerous medals were based. Though he was never directly associated with coin designs, there is some evidence that Nini's medallion of Louis XVI served as a model for the dies of that monarch's early coinage.

NOBLE   English gold coin introduced by Edward III in 1344, to the value of 6s. 8d. Half and quarter-nobles were issued at the same time. The obverse shows the King standing in a ship and is believed to commemorate the victory over the French fleet at Sluys (1340); while the name of the coin reflects its very high gold content, with only ½ a grain of copper alloy. More than most coins, the early noble shows the shifting fortunes of the war with France, Edward omitting his French title during the period of the Treaty of Brétigny (1360–9) and laying claim only to the province of Aquitaine. During the treaty period, coins of the Calais Mint also make their first appearance, marked by a C on the centre of the reverse cross and a flag at the stern of the ship. There are many minor varieties of the six issues during Edward III's reign. For the later history and foreign copies of this large, handsome and popular coin *ryal.

NOMISMA   A Greek generic term for money; later used to denote the cup-shaped gold coins of Byzantium (*scyphate).

NONSUNT   Popular name for the 12-penny groat issued during 1558–9 during the reign of Mary Queen of Scots. It shows the crowned monogram FM on the obverse (Mary being at that time married to Francis II of France) and takes its name from the legend IAM NON SUNT DUO SED UNA CARO (now they are no more two but one flesh).

NORRIS, GRIEG & NORRIS   Possibly the earliest of all the Californian private gold issues: a newspaper account of 31 May 1849 mentions a $5 piece by this firm struck at Benicia City but inscribed SAN FRANCISCO. The initials N.G. & N. on this piece were not identified until 1902. Pieces, all dated 1849, exist with plain and reeded edges, and there is also a unique specimen dated 1850 with STOCKTON instead of SAN FRANCISCO.

NORTHUMBERLAND SHILLINGS   Two thousand shillings of King George III were specially struck for the Duke of Northumberland's entry into Dublin as Lord Lieutenant of Ireland. No further shillings were struck in this reign until 1787; the coin is consequently much sought-after by collectors.

NOVA CONSTELLATIO   Silver patterns bearing this inscription were struck in 1783 as experimental decimal pieces for the American Confederation, soon to become the USA. All are very rare; but copper pieces without denominational values of similar

Indian head nickel, 1936

Gold noble of Edward III

design circulated in large quantities from 1783–5. They are believed to have been struck as a speculative venture in England, most probably by *Wyon of Birmingham.

NOVGOROD   Independent principality of Russia until 1478, when it was subdued by Ivan III, Duke of Moscow, and first to take the title "Tsar of all the Russias". Coins were struck here from the late 14th century onwards and continued to be after its subjection. The town was the most important westerly outpost of Russia until the foundation of St Petersburg almost a century and a half later, and was the principal trading post for imports of silver from the West.

NOVODEL   A series of Russian coins (or imitation coins) that still awaits thorough exploration and classification—though perhaps the latter will never be entirely possible. Under a law of 1762, any collector could order restrikes of coins no longer in circulation from the St Petersburg Mint, in any quantity he chose. This state of affairs continued until 1890, when it ceased owing to representations of Russia's then most celebrated numismatist, the Grand Duke *Mikhailovich.

Such restrikes were by no means confined to coins struck from original dies and in the same metal. Old dies were recut when they were worn out and where the collectors' demand justified it, and special strikings were made in gold of what were originally silver coins. Nor did the abuses stop here: there is an extensive series of *mules. As the Russian series from about 1720 onwards is specially rich in its variety of inscriptions and edge-markings, Russian collectors seem to have vied with one another to create their own "unique" pieces. Thus you may find a "coin" concocted from an obverse die of 1705, a reverse of 1715 and an edge-inscription belonging to yet another year. These are, of course, pure *fantasy coins and have their place only in a collection of numismatic freaks.

Where a coin has been restruck from an original die and in the metal as intended for circulation, a novodel may well call for attention by a serious student. Some pieces are of such exceeding rarity that true "originals" are only to be found in Leningrad's Hermitage Museum. Of such "genuine" novodels, about 190 have been listed from the period of Peter the Great to Nicholas I (or roughly 1705–1855); and they are generally listed as such in fixed price or auction catalogues issued by reputable firms of professional numismatists. The identification is, however, not easy and mistakes can occur. No novodel with a date later than 1861 is recorded.

NUMISMATIC LITERATURE   References to numismatics go back to Herodotus for Greek and Pliny for Roman times; a spate of books begins with the Renaissance and the flood has grown ever since. A *Select Bibliography* published in 1965 lists nearly 5,000 titles, while the *Dictionary Catalogue* of the American Numismatic Society has well over 50,000 entries. The total of books in all languages is probably nearer double this—especially if we are to include under this heading printed ephemera such as occasional pamphlets, edicts, proclamations concerning forgeries or coins withdrawn from circulation, etc.

In recent years, the scholar's task has been much eased by a half-yearly book list issued by the American Numismatic Society, compiled by editors in thirty-five countries. Each issue lists close on 1,000 titles and is especially valuable for its abstracts of numismatic material appearing in journals throughout the world (whose special theme may range from archaeology to zoology).

Of "coin magazines" as such there are probably around fifty more or less serious; recently, these have been joined by specialist journals for collectors of paper money, orders and medals, even cheques.

There is a marked absence of magazines such as cater for the connoisseur in other branches of collecting (e.g. antiques). An attempt was made in the 1920s in France to run a coin magazine which was at the same time an art magazine. It was called *Aréthuse* and embraced such related topics as sculpture, gem engraving and goldsmithing. The "depression" killed it in 1931; the nearest equivalent today is again French—the quarterly bulletin of the *Club Français de la Médaille.

Reprints—good, bad, and indifferent—proliferate. On the assumption that numismatic scholarship has not stood still during the past hundred years, one might hope for more additions and revisions rather than straight facsimiles, even when these are excellent.

The earliest illustrated numismatic book: Andrea Fulvio's *Illustrium Imagines*, octavo, Rome, 1517 (reduced)

NUMISMATICS   The question "What is numismatics?" permits of no easy answer. Fifty years ago, perhaps the answer *was* easy: by and large, it meant the study of coins and medals in their historical context. Today, the scope—as hinted at in the previous entry—has broadened immensely. Money may or may not be the root of all evil, but it is endlessly fascinating to an ever-growing number of people. Whereas in previous generations the numismatist was primarily a historian, more often than not with archaeological leanings, he is today a member of any one of many professions (C. Wilson *Peck).

More and more, we begin to realise that we cannot study coins in isolation (*printing and numismatics). In one respect, this was always so: the relationship to seal and gem engraving, and to the sculptural arts, was always understood by numismatists. But certain divisions remain: while at the Smithsonian Institution paper money is now fully admitted into the fold, there is a separate department still for philately. One hopes these divisions are not watertight, and that numismatists will take some interest in the first "blind stamps" made for the Italian posts of the 15th century (their dies were almost certainly cut by the same artists as cut the coin dies)—or of such special "currencies" as postal orders, revenue stamps, etc., often produced to order by government mints (*postal currencies).

All this is one aspect of what one might call "comparative" numismatics. Another is to take certain limited periods—perhaps even years or months—under the microscope and study them on a world-wide basis. Too little of this has yet been done: the tendency both among museums and collectors being to think of "series" in terms of countries or reigns or mints.

The same tendency has caused collections to be built around people *for* whom money was struck rather than *by* whom. For every thousand people who collect or study the coins of the Popes, is there even one who collects and studies the coins of the *Hamerani family? Not only in relation to papal coins and medals (and the Hameranis dominated the papal mints for about a century and a half), but the many other courts of Europe where they were active.

To sum up: as we see how much has been achieved, we see even more clearly how much more remains to be done. Traditionally, the numismatist has dealt in minutiae, in observing and classifying tiny differences. New paths demand new but no less exacting standards of scholarship.

NUMISPHILATELY   An as yet little explored field, except in the most obvious connections such as *postal currencies, coins on stamps, etc. Postal numismatics, in fact, can be pursued as far back as Roman days, when an early imperial sestertius shows a postal coach. Since the appearance of the adhesive postage stamp, mints have often collaborated in their production; thus the Royal Mint produced all dies for British stamps from 1910–33, as well as revenue stamps for cheques, legal documents, etc. In some countries, this collaboration is closer and more permanent: the Spanish state mint in Madrid is, in fact, called the Fabrica Nacional de Moneda y Timbre to make this quite plain. The first French postage stamps were designed and engraved by Jean-Jaques Barre, engraver-general to the French mint.

NUMMIUM   The unit of bronze coinage of the Byzantine era following the reforms of Anastasius in A.D. 498. The plural is nummia, and the standard denominations were 5, 10, 20 and 40 (*follis). Odd denominations, such as 33, 16, 12, 8, 6, 4, 3 and 2 nummia, were struck at certain times by certain mints only.

NUREMBERG   Like *Augsburg, this southern German city was one of the centres of the goldsmith's art; and it struck an extensive coinage both for its own use and many surrounding smaller civic and ecclesiastical authorities, because of its artistic and technical skills. Perhaps its most famous issue was that of the commemorative "lamb ducats" of 1700, struck on both round and square flans, and so popular as to be several times restruck at later dates. Nuremberg was also the leading centre for the production of *jetons (*Krauwinckel).

NÜRNBERGER, GEORG FRIEDRICH (d. 1721) Active as a mintmaster at Nuremberg from 1677–1716 and responsible for the ''lamb ducats''—mentioned in the previous entry. His work is also indicative of the wide reputation which the Nuremberg Mint possessed, his initials GFN being found on coins of Hall, Schwarzenberg, Bamberg, Mainz, Hohenlohe and Nostitz, besides Nuremberg itself.

OAK-TREE COINAGE Early coinage of Massachusetts, dated 1652, though known to have been struck at various times from 1660–7. There are shillings, 6-penny, 3-penny and 2-penny pieces. All bear the legend MASSATHUSETS around an oak-tree on the obverse, with the date and figures XII, VI, III or II surrounded by the legend AND NEW ENGLAND, on the reverse.

OAXACA This province of Mexico, which remained royalist during the struggle for Mexican independence, produced from 1811–14 silver 8, 1 and ½ reales of a quite distinctive type. The obverse shows a cross of Jerusalem, bearing between the upper angles of the cross a lion and a castle, and in the lower angles the initials of the ruler F°. 7°. The reverse shows a rampant lion on a shield. In addition, all 8-real pieces are countermarked with a control letter and crowned pillars of Hercules (i.e. the device of the famous "Pillar Dollar"). As a mint of the later Mexican Republic, Oaxaca continued in operation until 1893, with some rare gold from 1853 onwards. The basic mintmark was an O, sometimes Oa, and sometimes with the small a within the large O.

During the second revolutionary period of Mexico, a century after the first, the "Free and Sovereign State of Oaxaca" produced a most extensive series. These ranged from provisional 1 and 3 centavos to the largest gold coin ever struck in Mexico, valued at 60 pesos, in 1916.

OBAN Largest of the oval-shaped Japanese gold coins, to the value of 10 *ryos. They were struck at intervals from 1591–1860 and are among the most decorative of gold pieces, with several seals punched into the metal and an Indian ink inscription giving the value of the coin together with the mintmaster's signature.

OBOL Derived from the Greek *obelos*, a spit (in pre-coinage times used as currency), the obol became a small silver coin valued at one-sixth of the *drachm. Though fractions of it were also struck, these turned out to be really too small for practical use; indeed, by the 2nd century B.C. the obol itself was struck in copper.

OBSIDIONAL COINS Derived from *obsedere*, to sit on, hence to besiege. Siege coins are a division of *emergency money, and are certainly the most avidly collected ones, as they form part of military history. European history from the 15th to the 19th centuries has preserved monetary records of well over one hundred besieged cities; English issues are confined to the period of the Civil War, 1644–9 (*Carlisle, Colchester, Newark, Pontefract, Scarborough).

OBVERSE When we today call "heads or tails", heads would be the obverse. This rule may be said to apply to most Western coinages since Roman times: i.e. the ruler's head or figure is what we take to be the more important side of a coin. The distinction is by no means as clear in ancient Greek coinage (e.g. *Rhegium), or in certain modern coinages showing on both sides of the coin other devices than portraits.

OCTADRACHM An 8-drachm piece struck only occasionally and within a limited geographical area, chiefly under Seleucid and Ptolemaic rulers, in Syria and Egypt (3rd to 2nd centuries B.C.). Though principally a silver denomination, it was also struck in gold under some of the Ptolemies, the gold octadrachms of Arsinoe II being particularly fine and sought-after.

OCTAVO Sometimes spelt ochavo, this was the eighth of the Spanish *real and first struck in silver under Ferdinand and Isabella from 1497. It has also been an occasional copper coin of Mexico since 1812.

OFFA Though rulers do not figure much in this encyclopedia, Offa, together with one or two others, presents a special case. This King of Mercia (A.D. 757–96) shows a larger range of types in his coinage than any subsequent British monarch, and its general standard is so far ahead of its time that it is evident he took some trouble and personal interest in finding the best engravers. Basically, Offa took over the French *denier as introduced by the Frankish ruler Pepin on the Continent some twenty years earlier, and which was to be known in England as the *penny. There are portrait and non-portrait types, both notable for their decorative elegance and the former of two main groups: one stylised copies of Roman types from the era of Constantine and his successors, the other much more naturalistic and showing what is obviously a Saxon king with long, flowing hair. Another Roman influence may be seen in that Offa struck a rare series of coins with the portrait bust of his wife, Cynethryth. Finally, we have by him a unique gold penny and a *dinar, also unique, copied from the coinage of the Caliph Al Mansur, with Arabic date 157 A.H. (A.D. 774) and OFFA REX on the reverse.

Offa: Portrait type, after A.D. 785, with the reverse showing a floreate cross and moneyer's name

OFFICINA The Roman word for a workshop in which coinage was struck. Each mint was divided, if its importance justified it, into two or more officinae, with a responsible superintendent for each. Their designation on coins varied, though the letters P, S, T, Q for *prima, secunda, tertia,* and *quarta* (i.e. first, second, third and fourth) are perhaps the most commonly seen. At the Eastern mints, Greek capital letters were used, starting with A for the first officina, and so forth. Nor is there any fixed rule where officina letters may be found on a coin. It may be in the field, in the *exergue, and before or after the main mintmark. Thus Trier (or Trèves) and its first officina are found variously as PTR or TRP. Eastern mints had many officinae: Antioch had fifteen, Constantinople eleven at times, and Alexandria as many as twenty. Rome never had more than twelve.

OLBIA A town on the northern coast of the Black Sea, and an important trading centre in ancient Greek times. There were found some interesting early bronze pieces which are cast instead of struck; one variety of this is in the shape of a dolphin. More orthodox struck money in both silver and bronze appeared during the 4th century B.C.

OLIVIER, AUBIN French coining engineer who in the early 1550s perfected a three-segmented collar in which to strike coins, and by means of which the edges of coins could first be mechanically inscribed.

ONCIA Derived from the Roman *uncia this is first mentioned as an Italian gold weight in the 10th century and *c.* 1335 became a money of *account in Florence (100 oncia = 5 florins). As a gold coin, it was struck in 18th century Italy at Palermo from 1720–59 under Charles II and III, with a phoenix as the reverse type.

Onlik of Ahmad III (Ottoman Empire), 1703

ONE-TENTH OF A PENNY   This curious denomination was struck for British West Africa during most years from 1907–57 in a variety of metals: aluminium, cupro-nickel and bronze. It is "curious", because other denominations of West African currency are not specifically decimal: the 3-pence and 6-pence pieces are retained and so is the halfpenny. One might therefore have expected smaller fractions to be the farthing and its half—but no!

The historical interest of this issue does not end here: it is one of the few from which genuine currency issues (not just *patterns) of Edward VIII may be collected; and, what is more, in three different strikings—Royal Mint, King's Norton Mint and The Mint (Birmingham) Ltd. The last is the rarest of the three and still not exorbitantly priced; as a set, this is more collectable than most nowadays.

ONLIK   Turkish silver coin to the value of 10 *paras, originally, of varying fineness, sometimes only *billon, but finally stabilised at 12.02 grammes and .830 fine during the 19th century.

ONZA   Another name for the gold 8-escudos piece of Spain and Latin America.

ØRE   Under the Scandinavian Monetary Union (Denmark, Norway, Sweden, 18 December 1872), which adopted a uniform decimal system, the øre was the smallest denomination, 100 øre equalling 1 *krona. It has been struck at various times in bronze, zinc and iron.

Prior to this, the øre had a history going back to the 17th century as a denomination—and even further back as a weight unit (one-eighth of a Swedish mark). Its first appearance as a coin is under Gustav I Vasa in 1522: pieces were then struck in silver, with (later) various multiples up to sixteen.

OREGON EXCHANGE CO.   The State of Oregon adjoins California to the north. At the time of the gold rush, many Oregon settlers (whose chief livelihood was trapping the beaver) joined the trek to the south to try their luck in the San Francisco region. A private mint was established late in 1849 at Oregon City to strike coinage from the gold dust brought back by returning settlers. Pieces of $5 and $10 were coined in pure gold without any alloy, the obverse type showing a beaver facing right on a log. The $5 pieces were carelessly engraved: they carried beneath the beaver the initials T.O. instead of O.T. (Oregon Territory), and above the initials K.M.T.A.W.R.G.S., supposedly those of the partners in the Oregon Exchange Company (but G should have been C for Campbell). The $10 pieces are finely engraved, with the beaver surrounded by stars and the initials K.M.T.R.C. only. Because of their unadulterated gold content many of these pieces were melted down; and the attractiveness of the $10 one, quite apart from its rarity, makes it one of the most desirable treasures among territorial gold issues. The pieces are commonly known as "Beavers".

ORESME, NICHOLAS (1320–82)   A great scientific figure of the late medieval period and the first to treat of money in a broad, economic context.

ORICHALCUM   Not quite *brass and not quite *bronze, this mixture of copper and zinc was used throughout the Roman Empire for the large base-metal coin known as the *sestertius.

ORLEANS   A regal mint of France in medieval times, and then again from 1700–90. It is also the place where Etienne *Bergeron struck the curious *teston morveux of Charles IX in 1562–3.

ORMONDE MONEY   All coins struck in Ireland under the authority of the Earl of Ormonde, appointed Lord Lieutenant in 1643. There are three distinct series: silver issues of 1643–4,

Ormonde Money: Shilling (XII = 12 pence)

exceedingly rare gold *pistoles of 1646, and more silver (actually issued by Ormonde after the execution of Charles I) in 1649. The earlier silver issue was by far the more plentiful, both as regards quantity and denominations, consisting of crowns, half-crowns, sixpences, shillings, groats, threepences and twopences. Of the posthumous Charles I issues, only crowns and half-crowns are known, both scarce.

ORMSBY, J. S. A firm at Sacramento, California, which operated a private mint and assay office there during the early days of the gold rush. Very rare coins of both $5 and $10 are known; the latter show thirty-one stars, which suggest they were struck in 1850 when California was admitted as the 31st state of the Union. These stars surround the value 10 DOLS on the reverse; the obverse shows the initials J.S.O. in the centre, with the circular legend UNITED STATES OF AMERICA (no mention of California!).

ORT A German word denoting one quarter, and often used to describe actual quarter denominations—thus Ortsthaler, Ortsgulden, etc. Coins can be found throughout the German series of the 16th and 17th centuries with a 4 or 8 (the latter denoting one-eighth Thaler or half an Ort) and sometimes with the inscription "1 Halb Reichsort".

ØRTUG A medieval Swedish coin, first struck in Gotland around 1320, and on the Swedish mainland by Albrecht of Mecklenburg (1363–95). Its value fluctuated until, in 1522, Gustavus Vasa introduced the *øre currency, when it became stabilised as that unit's half; it was last struck in 1591. During its first 150 years, it remained Sweden's principal silver coin, roughly equivalent in value to the north German *Witte, and used extensively for trade with the Hanseatic League towns. Its main type showed, on the obverse, the Swedish royal arms (shield with three crowns), and on the reverse, the ruler's initial and a cross.

Ørtug of Christopher of Bavaria, 1439-48

OSELLA Venetian presentation coin, issued at the New Year from 1521–1796. Its value gradually rose from 33 to 78 *soldi. The name is derived from ucella (a bird), since these traditional New Year's gifts had earlier been wildfowl. There is a very wide variety of reverse types and occasional gold strikings are known. The famous glass-producing island of Murano near Venice received the right to strike its own osella from 1711.

OSNABRUCK The bishopric of this town exercised the right of coinage for 800 years, until secularised and absorbed by the neighbouring Hanover in 1802. The prevalent type throughout the medieval period was that of St Peter on the obverse with a wheel on the reverse. Gold was struck from the early 15th to the late 17th centuries. For the town, there is the ducat of Gustavus Adolphus of Sweden when he occupied it in 1633. Hazlitt (*Coinage of the European Continent*) mentions an interesting series of pennies and multiples in copper, including the very odd denomination of 9 Pfennige.

OSTIA Town in Italy, the port of Rome, and adopted as a mint by the usurper Maxentius from A.D. 306–12. Constantine the Great continued to strike money here for a time after Maxentius's overthrow.

OSTROGOTHIC COINAGE Name given to the coinage of the Goths in Italy after the overthrow of the last Roman emperor in A.D. 476 and until the reconquest of the country by the Byzantine general Narses in A.D. 553. The Ostrogothic kings established themselves at Ravenna, which became their capital and principal mint. Coins were struck in gold, silver and bronze and generally followed well-established Byzantine types, with the portrait and title of the emperor on the obverse and Victory on the reverse. Under Theoderic the Great (A.D. 493–526), the King's monogram was sometimes added; there is also, under this ruler, a magnificent triple *solidus with facing bust bearing his full name. The most distinctive piece of the series is perhaps the 40-nummi bronze of Theodahad (A.D. 534–6), which is a thoroughly realistic portrait (even detailing the King's moustache), and which introduces for the first time a closed crown (instead of a diadem) as the ruler's headgear.

OTMANI *akce.

OTTAWA Seat of the Royal Canadian Mint since its establishment in 1908. Sovereigns were struck here until 1919, rare dates being 1908, 1913 and 1916. In recent years, many *proof sets have been issued by this mint for collectors, the most notable being that of 1967 including a $20 gold piece—the only example of the striking of this denomination within the British Commonwealth today. (Also *canoe dollar.) The Maple Leaf Dollar, a unique gold coin in that it is the only *bullion piece today struck to a standard of .999 fine, was introduced in 1979.

OTTOMAN MINTS The most important mints of the Ottoman Empire were Adrianopolis, Aleppo, Algiers, Baghdad, Cairo, Constantinople, Damascus, Tiflis, Tripoli and Tunis. Omitted in earlier coinages, the mint name appears regularly from the reign of Murad II (1421–51).

OVERSTRIKE Old coin recalled to the mint was not always melted down. Often it was simply overstruck, and traces of the old design can still be seen.

OWLS *Athens.

OXFORD CROWN Designed by Thomas *Rawlings and struck at Oxford in 1644, this is the only English coin to show a city view. It is as rare as it is beautiful.

Pattern Oxford crown of Charles I by Rawlings

P

PACIFIC CO.   A unique type (for USA) of private gold was struck by the Pacific Company, California ($5 and $10, all dated 1849). The legend, with the date and name of the company, surrounds the usual type of American eagle on the reverse. The obverse, however, shows a *liberty cap, with rays and stars radiating from it, reminiscent rather of South American coinages. At least two different Pacific Companies are known to have set out from eastern states during 1849 (Richmond, Virginia, and Boston, Mass.); but there is no direct evidence to link these issues with either of them. They remain among the obscurest and rarest of Californian private gold.

PADMA-TANKA   An early gold coin of Mysore, southern India. Its exact date is uncertain; but it is generally attributed to the later era of the Kadamba dynasty, during the 2nd and 1st centuryies B.C. The type shows an eight-petalled lotus flower.

PADUANS   *Cavino.

PAESTUM   An ancient city on the west coast of Italy, south of Naples, with magnificent temple ruins. Before its capture by the Lucanians in 390 B.C. it was known as Poseidonia, and the sea-god Poseidon with his trident was the principal type. The coining history of the city extends into Roman times, when it continued to strike small bronze coins, including one very rare issue showing the actual striking of a coin—the only such representation known in ancient coinages.

Paestum: Early type, *c.* 550–470 B.C.

PAGODA   The principal gold coin of southern India, characterised by a thick, somewhat dumpy, fabric, usually showing Hindu deities. It was also issued by the East India Company, by the Dutch for Nagapatnam and by the French for Pondicherry. The coinage issued by the East India Company for Madras in 1811 shows an actual pagoda surrounded by stars. Halves and quarters of similar type were issued in silver.

A special type, known as the Porto Novo pagoda, was struck by the Dutch at their trading post of Nagapatnam on the Coromandel (east) coast of southern India. This coin weighed 3.4 grammes and showed a four-armed deity on the obverse, while the reverse had a plain granulated surface. It was issued from 1745–84.

Pagoda: Type from Vijayanagar, southern India, *c.* 1570, with three unidentified deities

PAHANG   *hat money.

PAHLEVI   Persian dynasty which assumed power under Reza Shah in 1925. The gold unit of Persia first struck in 1927 is known as the pahlevi and has been struck at various times since then, also in multiples up to 5 pahlevis. The type followed the earlier *toman in showing a Persian lion striding, with an inscribed reverse. Latterly, when the portrait of the Shah figures as the obverse, the lion is seen on the reverse.

PAISA   *pice.

PALA Another name for the *deka of Ceylon.

PALESTINE The coining history of this area belongs in part to Persia, in part to the Alexandrine coinage and to the Ptolemies, until the late 2nd century B.C. Jewish coinage proper extends from John Hyrcanus I (135–104 B.C.) to the time of the second revolt of the Jews against the Roman occupation under the Emperor Hadrian, A.D. 132. Associations with the early history of Christianity make issues of Herod the Great and Pontius Pilate much sought-after by collectors.

Coins and banknotes of the modern state of Israel date from 1948. The coinage is notable for its many fine commemorative issues.

PALLADIUM A metal of the platinum group, but lighter in weight than platinum itself. Its only recorded use in English coinage is an exceedingly rare proof sixpence of William IV dated 1831.

PANTICAPAEUM Ancient Greek city on the northern shores of the Black Sea, founded by emigrants from Miletus in the 6th century B.C. The earliest coins are silver drachms with the type of a facing lion's head. It is, however, the prolific gold coinage of the 4th century B.C. for which the city is chiefly famous. These show, on the obverse, the god Pan in profile (or semi-facing bust), most exquisitely engraved in the finest style. The reverse shows a mythical beast, half panther, half gryphon, thought to represent the guardian of the golden treasure for which the region was renowned. The silver coins of the same period carry the Pan obverse with a bull or lion's head reverse. The bronze coinage is similar to the silver.

Panticapaeum: gold stater, 4th century B.C.

PAOLINO Another name given to the silver *scudo, as struck under Pope Paul III.

PAOLO Name first given to the papal *grosso as struck under Pope Paul III, replacing the *giulio. The name was later adopted by a number of other Italian city states for coins of similar size and value.

PAPADOPOLI, NICOLO (1841–1922) Italian numismatist who devoted thirty years of his life to compiling what is still the standard catalogue of the coins of *Venice.

PAPAL COINAGE The Popes have struck money since the reign of Hadrian I (A.D. 772–95) with few intervals until the present day. At one time or another, their sovereignty has extended over forty mints. In addition, papal medals have been struck regularly since Nicholas V (1447–55). The vastness of this material allows only a few hints here of its riches as a collecting quarry. A single piece by every pope known to have struck coins would already total over a hundred. The first 200 years show the name of both popes and emperors on coins. One may collect by mints, of course, or by popes of one family (e.g. Borgia, Farnese, Medici, Rovere). There are special categories of coins, such as *sede vacante pieces or *ducati di camera. There are the coins of the popes at Avignon, or of their legates; there are popes as patrons of the arts, employing practically every engraver of note through the centuries. There is papal emergency money (Castell San Angelo 1527, Gaeta 1848). And there is a fascinating series struck while the Fugger merchant-banking firm held the lease of the Roman Mint, at intervals from 1508–27. These are but a few of the special possibilities open to the collector, apart from the more common ones of denomination or reign. (*Jubilee coins and medals.)

Civita Vecchia 2½ baiocchi, 1797.

Coin of Hadrian, c. 772–95

Portrait medal of Pope John
XXIII (1958–63) by Giampaoli
(slightly reduced)

Coin of John XXII (1316–34)   Coin of Benedict XII (1334–42)

Coin of Clement VI (1342–52)   Coin of Innocent VI (1352–62)

PAPER MONEY   This is almost certainly as old as the invention of paper itself, Chinese records referring to it from *c.* A.D. 650 onwards. The earliest notes that have come down to us are from the Ming dynasty, 14th century. Around the same time we can date certain promissory notes of Florence which, when transferable, would be valid as legal tender. Banknotes as such date from the early 1660s (Stockholm). The Banks of England and Scotland followed thirty years later. Huge fortunes were made and lost in France under the paper money financial regime of John *Law, 1716–21. Country after country followed during the course of the 18th century, more often than not with disastrous results, culminating with the second and even greater French fiasco during the Revolution (*assignats). Forgers flourished when not caught and hanged: not till the mid-19th century did security printing reach a more or less reliable state. If today paper money is almost universally accepted, this is not to say that it is also trusted. Recent increases in the price of gold, despite all efforts of the world's most powerful governments, show that people still prefer something more solid. (Also *playing card money.)

PARA   A Turkish denomination, originally of silver (value one-fortieth of the *piastre), more recently of copper or nickel. Through Turkish domination of the Balkans, it also became a denomination of kingdoms like Serbia and Montenegro, and remains the monetary unit of Yugoslavia to this day.

PARDAO   *xeraphim.

PARIS   Capital city of France and its principal mint during the past 1,000 years—indeed, Hugues Capet struck coins here as Duke before assuming the title of King. It was an *Anglo-Gallic mint under Henry VI of England from 1422–37, with the mint-mark a crown. When Francis I reformed the French coinage in 1539–40, Paris was given the mint letter A, which it has retained ever since. Many coins in the French series exist only with this mark, though over thirty provincial mints were active during the reigns of Louis XIII and XIV. When *Bordeaux closed in 1878, Paris became the only French mint (except for war-time emergencies); but Bordeaux has now taken its place, in the sense that all French coins are struck at a new establishment there, while the Paris Mint concentrates on medallic art.

PARISIS D'OR   The first of the extensive series of gold coins struck by Philip I of France (1328–50) in 1329. It was struck in 24 carat gold to the exact value of 1 livre parisis, weighing 7.42 grammes. Gothic art is seen in this coin (1¼ inches diameter) at its most splendid: the King is shown seated on an elaborate throne, with two lions at his feet.

PARMA   Italian town in the province of Emilia, which has a coinage history going back to the days of Charlemagne. After various intermittent autonomous coinages during the medieval period, it passed to the Papacy in 1512 and struck money under Julius II, Leo X, Hadrian VI, Clement VII and Paul III. From 1547 onwards it was the principal place of coinage for the dukes of Parma and Piacenza and is especially notable for its fine series of multiple gold coins of the 16th and 17th centuries. In 1815, the duchy passed to Marie-Louise, Archduchess of Austria and wife of Napoleon, who continued to strike coins here intermittently until 1832.

PAROS   An island of the Cyclades group in the Aegean, famed for its marble. The coinage is, however, chiefly interesting for a

Facing page:
Papal coinage

type of the 4th century B.C., showing us Archilochus, an early lyric poet of Greece, playing the cythera.

PARPAGIOLA A type of *grosso known in northern Italy, western Switzerland and the kingdom of Savoy from the late 14th to the early 17th century.

PARSONS, JOHN, & CO. *Colorado gold.

PASCO A town in Peru, and a short-lived mint there during the 1840s, used only for striking silver 2 and 4 reales. None the less, three varieties of mintmark are known: Pasco spelt out in full, Paz and Po.

PASSE, SIMON DE Medallist of the second half of the 17th century, who specialised in thin, engraved oval-shaped discs—quite different from medallic techniques practised until this time. These were obviously individual pieces, not lending themselves to duplication by means of a press. They are therefore rare and much sought-after.

PATACA Authorities differ about the origin of this word: but it and various derivatives (e.g. Patacon, Patagon, Pataga and Pataque) have been used for money of *account and silver denominations almost world-wide since the 17th century. A short list of the connotations which can be traced would include an Arabic and Portuguese name for the Spanish *piastre; an 18th century silver denomination of Brabant and Westphalia; a Brazilian coin to the value of 320 *reis introduced by Peter II of Portugal in 1694; a currency unit of Macau and Timor; money of account in Algiers during the 18th century; and a common name for the *Maria Theresa Thaler in North and East Africa.

Brazilian pataca under Peter II, 1696

PATAGON Silver, Thaler-size coin of the southern Netherlands, first issued by Albert and Isabella in 1612 and tariffed at 48 *stuivers. It weighed just over 28 grammes and was of .875 fine silver. Its obverse showed the Burgundian St Andrew's cross; and the reverse, the Spanish arms below a crown and surrounded by the chain of the Order of the Golden Fleece. Large quantities were struck until c. 1700 (i.e. the end of Spanish sovereignty in the Netherlands). For its influence in Germany, Denmark and as far afield as Russia, *Albertusthaler.

PATARD A silver piece of the Burgundian Netherlands, first struck by Philippe le Beau in 1496 and equal to the double *gros. The same name was given in France to the half-liard (3 deniers) in the duchy of Dauphiné. The etymology of the name is uncertain, but it is most likely derived from Peter, as pieces so-called show the saint's emblem of crossed keys.

PATINA An incrustation on the surface of *bronze, due to oxidisation of the metal. The quality of the patina largely determines the value of ancient bronze coins, especially that of the Roman *sestertii. While it can be almost as unpleasant as a fungus, a delicate patina scintillates with rainbow shades from green to red and is much prized by collectors. Such coins should never be cleaned.

PATTÉ A form of the Greek cross (i.e. four sides of the same length), with the ends flattened or broadened out. It is also called the Maltese cross, since it was adopted by the Knights of Malta on their arms.

PATTERN A coin design not adopted for general circulation, but struck only in small quantities for the consideration of mint and/or government officials. Patterns tend to be sought-after and valuable for that reason; another is that they are often more beautiful than the final design adopted, where utility is more of a criterion than attractiveness. (Also *piéfort.)

PAU   Town in the western Pyrenees and the capital of the old kingdoms of Béarn and Navarre. A mint was installed there in medieval times; but its real importance dates from 1554, when Jean *Erondelle left the *Moulin des Étuves in Paris, taking with him all his secrets and installing similar machines at Pau for Jeanne d'Albret, mother of the future King Henry IV of France. Erondelle was joined five years later by Etienne *Bergeron, whose experience of the new mechanical striking processes was unrivalled. The mint remained unique in that—contrary to other *moulins* at Troyes and Paris—it did not have to compete with the jealousy of local moneyers working by the old hammered process. Many fine coins were produced here, first for Navarre, later for the French kingdom, until 1789. They show a small cow as the mintmark.

PAVIA   A mint of the Goths in Italy, later of the Lombard kings, the Carolingian and other German emperors. After a republican interlude it became subject to the Sforza family from 1350–1464. There is an exceedingly rare siege piece of 1424, when the town was blockaded by French troops.

PAVILLON D'OR   A gold coin of France, introduced by Philip VI in 1339. It is named after the type, which shows the king seated under an elaborate, tent-like canopy.

PAX   Peace, either personified or as an inscription, has figured in coinage since the Greek coinage of the 4th century B.C. It became more common in Roman coinage and frequent (as an inscription) on European coins from the early Middle Ages. Pax type pennies are known in the English series from Canute to Henry I. The word is sometimes written across the field of the reverse, sometimes distributed (with an S added) among the four angles of the cross.

Pax penny of Harold II

PEACOCK RUPEE   A spectacular silver coin introduced by the kingdom of Burma in 1852 and struck at the *Heaton Mint in Birmingham. The design, with the peacock's tail in splendour taking up almost the whole of the field, is particularly handsome and was repeated in later gold coinages (with multiples of 2 and 5 rupees), in 1880.

PEÇA (PEZA)   The half-*dobra of Portugal, as struck since the reign of John V (1706–50), valued at 4 *escudos or 6,400 *reis. This gold coin and its half were the only ones to retain validity after 1822, when all other Portuguese gold was withdrawn to be melted down, to make way for new types introduced by John VI from 1818 onwards.

PECK, C. WILSON (d. 1969)   By profession a research chemist, Peck produced one of the outstanding works of numismatic scholarship of this century in his study of the British copper coinage. His own unrivalled collection of *Soho Mint issues is today in the Birmingham City Art Gallery and Museum.

PENGO   Silver unit of Hungarian coinage since 1925, with occasional multiples of 2 and 5; later struck in aluminium.

PENNI (pl. PENNIA)   Copper currency unit of Finland since 1864 (as a Grand Duchy of the Russian Empire), and of the Republic of Finland since 1919. Multiples of 5 and 10 were struck in bronze and 25 and 50 pennia in silver.

Peacock rupee

PENNY   For details of the English silver coin, *agnus dei, benediction, crux and Hand of Providence types; also Offa and pax. The silver penny was the cousin of the Carolingian *denier, itself descended from the Roman *denarius; hence its abbreviated form as d. until the recent introduction of decimal currency. The copper penny dates from 1797, and from 1860 the penny was struck in bronze. Also *long-cross and short-cross pennies.

The penny is the longest-lived of all British denominations, continuing into the present decimal era as the "new penny" from 1970 onwards. But it is now both smaller in module and larger in value than it used to be: where the old two-shilling piece or *florin contained 24 pence, its contemporary equivalent (i.e. one-tenth of a pound) contains only 10 new pence, yet the coin is only a fraction of the size and weight of the former bronze one. There are many who would see in this simultaneous upgrading and degradation of the penny both a symptom and a cause of the inflation which has hit Great Britain during the 1970s. It took very little time indeed for the purchasing power of the new penny to be but the same as for the old one, despite its ratio of 2.4 to 1. The main reason for decimalisation, a harmonisation of the British currency with that of its continental neighbours, has proved to be hardly less expensive (or disastrous, according to one's viewpoint) than its ostensible reason: a necessary preliminary to the UK's entry into the European Economic Community.

Silver penny of Alfred the Great

PENTADRACHM There are references to a 5-drachm silver piece of Chios c. 406 B.C., but none has been found. As a gold denomination, such a coin was certainly struck by Ptolemy I, II and III of Egypt (323–221 B.C.). Finally, and as one of the most fascinating pieces of information to come down to us from ancient times, Heron of Alexandria (c. 150 B.C.) cites a 5-drachm *copper* piece as being used to set in motion what were almost certainly the first automatic vending machines on record—in this case, to supply ceremonial water to pilgrims. *(Pneumatics, I, 21).*

Silver penny of Edward the Confessor

PENTECONLITRA The Sicilian name for the *decadrachm, expressed at 50 *litrae instead of 10 *drachms.

PERGAMUM Town in Mysia, Asia Minor, more important for the relatively late *cistophori (from 200 B.C.) than the earlier portrait coins of its kings.

PERKIN WARBECK GROAT A medalet of doubtful authenticity, supposedly struck by the Duchess of Burgundy for Perkin Warbeck on his setting out for England in 1494.

Gold penny of Henry III

PERPER A silver coin of Ragusa, to the value of 12 *grossi, during the 17th and 18th centuries. The coin was revived as the silver unit for the kingdom of Montenegro in 1910, with multiples of 2 and 5 perperi also struck in silver and others of 10, 20 and 100 in gold, at the Vienna Mint.

PERPIGNAN Capital of the old province of Rousillon in southwest France, which has a varied numismatic history, since France and Spain disputed the territory over several centuries. There is a copy of the Paris écu d'or as early as 1349, but with the Paris mint-letter A standing on its head. In 1493, Roussillon was ceded by Charles VIII of France to Ferdinand II of Aragon and became a part of Catalonia. None the less Perpignan preserved a local coinage type (i.e. quite different from that of Barcelona), with the obverse showing John the Baptist; and the reverse, two interlinked Ps. Such types continued until the middle of the 17th century, and Louis XIV, when he regained the province in 1645, simply added a lily (putting it right in the middle of the Aragon arms on large silver pieces). From 1710 onwards, Perpignan was active as a regal French mint, striking current coins with the mint-letter Q, and also several issues for the colonies. The mint was finally closed in 1837. The small Musée Joseph Puig has an excellent collection of local issues, including tokens from surrounding monasteries, from medieval times onwards.

PERTH As befits Scotland's former capital, this town shows a

Copper penny of Queen Victoria, 1839

longer period of activity as a mint (from William the Lion to James III) than any other apart from Edinburgh. All medieval silver denominations (groats, half-groats, pennies and half-pennies) are known from here.

PESETA Monetary unit of Spain to this day, divided into 100 centimos when Spain joined the Latin Monetary Union in 1868 and adopted a decimal currency. The word is an obvious diminutive of *peso and its origins can be traced back to the early 18th century, when a ''pesata provincial'' began to be struck for internal Spanish circulation only. This was struck at a lower content of fine silver than the full peso as well as being much smaller, being worth one-quarter of the peso from 1728–72, and one-fifth from 1772 onwards. *Cut money in Mexico and other parts of Spanish America may have been called peseta much earlier; and the quarter of the full ''piece of eight'', to the value of 2 *reales and of the same type, was struck in Mexico from 1772 with the name peseta mexicana.

PESO Short for peso de á ocho, i.e. piece of eight, as its value was that of 8 *reales. This, one of the most famous and widely accepted of all silver coins, was introduced by Ferdinand and Isabella of Spain as part of the monetary reforms of 1497. Few such pieces or their halves were in fact struck until the time of Charles V, and then in Spain with the royal arms on both sides and the figures VIII or IV respectively. The famous type with the Pillars of Hercules and legend ''plus ultra'' was struck in Spanish-American mints from 1537 in vast quantities.

The peso was adopted as a gold coin by most South American countries during the second half of the 19th century. The 50-peso piece of Mexico was the largest and heaviest gold piece to be struck for general circulation until recently (1947), exceeding the American $20 by about 20%.

PEST THALER A medallic piece of large size struck from the 16th to the 19th centuries (mainly in Bohemia), issued during or immediately after periods of pestilence or plague.

PETITION CROWN The most famous *pattern in English coinage history, submitted by Thomas *Simon in 1663 for the new *milled money, in competition with the Dutchman Jean *Roettier. The piece is remarkable not only for the splendour of its engraving, but for the technical skill, unique at that time, that managed to squeeze two lines of text (one beneath the other) on to the edge of the coin. The edge inscription reads:

(1st line): Thomas Simon most humbly prays your Majesty to compare this his Tryall Piece with the Dutch
(2nd line): and if more truly drawn and emboss'd more gracefully order'd and more accurately engraven to relieve him.

Despite this plea and the undoubted superiority of Simon's art, Roettier's dies were preferred and used throughout Charles II's reign. It is most probable that the King never forgave Simon for his equally fine work during the Cromwellian period.

PETRARCH (1304–74) The great poet was as great a scholar, and one of the first to use coins (chiefly Roman) to help illumine classical history and texts. He is on record as presenting a selection from his own cabinet of Roman imperial portrait coins to the Emperor Charles IV at Mantua in 1354, with an injunction to study and learn from them (leading one modern scholar to comment that he hoped the less reputable emperors were not included in the gift).

PETSCHUT The Russian word for stamp or seal. It appears often on the early coins (14th–15th centuries) of the duchies of

Petition crown of Thomas Simon, 1663

Muscovy, Novgorod, Tver, etc.—an interesting reminder of the close relationship between sillography and numismatics.

PEWTER Rarely used for coinage because of its relative softness, this metal is for the same reason a favourite for the striking of *patterns, minimising as it does the risk of accidentally cracking the die. Malay and Chinese currency has, however, sometimes been struck in pewter despite its rapid wear.

PFENNIG The smallest German denomination, 100 of them being equivalent to 1 *Mark since the adoption of the decimal system in 1873. It thus bears little relation to the modern English bronze penny except in derivation of name. In the Middle Ages, however, it was struck in silver, like the latter, both being derived from the Roman *denarius, and was the chief circulating currency until the 13th century.

PHOCEA Town on the mainland of Asia Minor (Ionia) and one of the earliest mints known. Around the year 400 B.C. it entered into a monetary convention with *Mytilene (details of which have been preserved on a stone inscription), the two cities striking a similar type of *hecte in alternate years.

PHOENICIA Though a great trading nation, the Phoenicians adopted coinage later than many other Mediterranean countries (not until the early 5th century B.C.). The coinage reflects in its types both the seafaring character of the Phoenicians (war galleys, etc.) and their many local gods (Astarte, Baal, etc.). The most important mints were Byblos, Sidon, Tripolis and Tyre; though arguably the Phoenician coinage of the colony at *Carthage was the most extensive both in commercial and artistic influence.

PHOENIX The mythological bird rising from its own ashes occurs on Alexandrian and Constantine bronzes in ancient times. During the modern era, there have been at least two denominations given this name after their reverse types: a Sicilian gold piece of 1 *oncia value struck at Palermo from 1720–34 and a Greek silver coin to the value of 100 *lepta, struck from 1828–31.

PIASTRE The name given throughout Europe and the Middle East to the Spanish *peso, and hence to its almost innumerable derivative coins. There have been, at one time or another, Cypriot, Egyptian, Lebanese, Moroccan, Tunisian and Turkish piastres, to mention only a few. Large Italian silver coins at Bologna, Florence, Genoa, Leghorn and Rome (Papal States) have also been called by this name. The Cypriot piastre, struck in the island until 1949, bears no relation to issues elsewhere, being a small bronze denomination, with 45 piastres equal to 1 English crown of 5 shillings value, and struck as a silver piece in 1928.

PIASTRE DE COMMERCE The French term for *trade dollar.

PICCIOLO The smallest copper denomination in Malta's currency from the mid-16th century onwards.

PICE A small fraction (one-sixty-fourth) of the Indian *rupee until comparatively recently. With the adoption of a decimal system by the Republic of India in 1957, the rupee was divided into 100 pice.

PIE The twelfth part of the *anna, or one-third of the *pice, in the East India Company's currency system as established by an act of 1835.

PIÈCE DE PLAISIR French term denoting a coin struck for the King's pleasure rather than for currency—generally in gold. Many *patterns of Louis XIV fall into this category.

PIECE OF EIGHT *peso.

Silver 2-piastre of Egypt, 1917

East India Company pice, Bombay Mint, *c.* 1780

PIÉFORT   Coin struck on an especially thick *flan, which may be twice or even three times the normal thickness and weight. It is probably the one piece which may be described as both a *pattern and a *proof, though these terms are not generally interchangeable. It is a proof in the sense that it portrays the design of a coin as adopted for circulation; it is a pattern in that it is not the coin as issued, but is both thicker and heavier, and sometimes struck in a different metal (often gold). The extra thickness was often used for edge-inscriptions or decoration, also often lacking on the coin as issued for general circulation. Though certain English piéforts are known, they are much commoner in the French series, especially from Henry II onwards, and are struck for presentation and collectors' purposes by the Paris Mint to this day. After several centuries' lapse, the Royal Mint has again also begun to strike piéforts for collectors: first, of the 20p piece in 1982, then of the new pound piece in 1983 (both in silver).

PIERCED COINS   There are various types or kinds of pierced coins. The only good reason for piercing a coin is that it may be hung on a string or chain around the neck. That was, of course, the practical reason for the unchanging design over many centuries of Chinese *cash. In European coinages there is none struck offically at mints with this purpose in mind; but pierced coins are none the less frequently found. People would wear coins as amulets (*touchpieces) or quite simply as jewellery.

In the West Indies, we often find pierced coins in the so-called *cut money. The Australian *ring dollar is another example.

The most elaborate pierced coin ever made is probably the rare pattern half guinea devised by the Birmingham manufacturer Sir Edward Thomason at the request of Sir William Congreve. The piece is the size of a normal guinea, but exactly half the gold has been pierced out in what is best described as a decorative fretwork design.

PILLAR DOLLAR   *peso.

PILON, GERMAIN (1537–90)   Great French sculptor, who was given the post of "Controller of the King's effigy" in 1573. Among his duties was to prepare wax models for coin engravers at the mint. Pilon also cast many splendid medals of his own, especially of Charles IX, Henry III, and the Chancellor René de Birague.

PINCHBECK   An alloy of zinc and copper which, when polished, resembles gold. It is named after its inventor, Christopher Pinchbeck (1670–1732). His son, Edward Pinchbeck (1713–66), struck a series of medals in it, chiefly during the years 1739–41, to celebrate the naval victories of Admiral Vernon.

PINCHES (FAMILY)   The family of medallists can be traced back to Birmingham in the 18th century but did not really come into its own until the latter half of the Victorian era, after establishing a factory in Clapham. It still bears the name of John Pinches (b. 1852), though some years ago it was acquired by the *Franklin Mint of Philadelphia as part of their European expansion programme.

PINETREE COINAGE   Early coins of Massachusetts, dated 1652 but known to have been struck mainly from 1667–74 (when shillings were struck on a large *flan) and 1675–82 (small flan). There are also silver sixpences and threepences of the same period.

PINGO, LEWIS (1743–1830)   Assistant engraver at the Royal Mint from 1776, and chief engraver there from 1779–1815. He cut the dies for notable pattern guineas in 1787, and also for the general issue of spade guineas from 1787–99. A pattern half-guinea of 1798 is modelled on the cartwheel pennies of *Boulton (i.e. incuse lettering on a raised band). Pingo's last notable work was the engraving of *bank tokens for 3 shillings and 1s. 6d. from 1811–12. He designed relatively few medals, but those of the actor David Garrick (1772) and the antiquarian and numismatist Thomas Snelling (1773) deserve notice. Also *wire money.

He was the son of Thomas Pingo (c. 1692–1776), a medallist of Italian origins who came to England during the 1740s. Contrary to his son's later career, Thomas at first made his mark as a medallist, and did not obtain employment at the Royal Mint until towards the end of his life. There he engraved the "shield" guineas current from 1774–86. Among his medallic work are pieces commemorating the Battle of Culloden (1746); Society for Promoting Arts & Commerce (1757); Lord Chatham, and the Repeal of the Stamp Act (both 1766); and the Royal College of Surgeons' Medal (1767). He is known also to have made no less than two medals of the unfortunate Prince Charles Edward Stuart (Bonnie Prince Charlie) from 1750 onwards, but obviously did not advertise that fact.

PINGO, THOMAS   *Pingo, Lewis.

PISANELLO (c. 1395–1455)   Earliest and in the opinion of many the greatest medallist of the Italian Renaissance. His medal of John VIII Palaeologus, made in 1438 on the occasion of the Byzantine Emperor's Italian visit to attend the Council of the Two Churches at Ferrara, ushered in the style of modern realistic portraiture, leading to the first portrait coin (also at Ferrara) fourteen years later. The man who engraved that coin, *Marescotti, has also given us Pisanello's portrait on a medal.

All Pisanello's medals were cast (not struck) in bronze or lead, and are as remarkable for the richness and variety of the reverse designs as for the striking heads of d'Este, Malatesta and other families on the obverse.

PISTAREEN   Name given to the quarter-*peso, chiefly in the West Indies.

PISTOLE   A name familiarly given to the gold double *escudo introduced by Charles V of Spain in 1537, and which continued to be struck until the monetary reforms of Isabella II in 1847. In England, it was more commonly known as the *doubloon. There is a rare pistole of Scotland (1701) under William III and an even rarer one in Ormonde's gold emergency coinage for Ireland (1646). Other pistoles are those of various German states (e.g. Prussia, Brunswick) to the value of 5 Thaler from the 18th century onwards, and one of Geneva struck to the same value as the French *louis d'or.

PISTRUCCI, BENEDETTO (1784–1855)   Perhaps the last of the great coin engravers who were principally cutters of precious stones, cameos, etc. After working in Rome, Florence and Pisa, Pistrucci came to London from Paris after the Napoleonic debacle and owed his introduction to the Royal Mint here to the good offices of Sir Joseph Banks. He subsequently cut the dies for the new coinage of 1817–18, his most famous design by far being the St George and Dragon reverse, first introduced on the crowns of 1818 (see following entry). He also cut dies for the coronation medals of all British sovereigns from George IV to Queen Victoria. His masterpiece is undoubtedly the great Waterloo Medal, on which he worked from 1817–50. The dies of this are still preserved in the Mint Museum: the medal as such was never struck, for fear of cracking the huge dies, but some plaster

Pistrucci crown of George IV, 1821

impressions were taken from it.

PISTRUCCI CROWN   One of the most celebrated of English crowns, by the famous Italian engraver who redesigned the English coinage of George III in 1816 and originated that of George IV in 1821. The St George and Dragon reverse first seen on this crown was later adopted for many other coins, including a long series of *sovereigns, until today.

PITI   A tin coin of Java, Bantam, Sumatra and other East Indian states during the 17th and 18th centuries, with a centre hole (round or hexagonal) and of insignificant value (4,000 to the Spanish *real).

PLACK   A Scottish *billon coin, introduced under James II c. 1470 and struck until 1590. The name is derived from the French *plaque* meaning a thin plate of metal, and the coin varied in value from 2 pence to 4 pence during different reigns. The obverse shows a crowned shield of Scotland, the reverse varies from a floreate cross in early issues to a crowned thistle under James VI.

PLAPPART   A *billon coin current from the 14th century in various Swiss cantons (e.g. Berne, Lucerne, St Gallen, Zurich), to the value of 15 Heller.

PLAQUE   Like the Scottish plack, less a denominational value than a generic term for broad coins of thin fabric struck in Brabant and Burgundy during the 15th century; also a *billon coin of certain Dutch towns from the 14th to the 17th centuries. The first mention of the word in a coinage connection would appear to go back as far as 1342, when they were struck as part of a league coinage between the duchies of Bar and Luxembourg.

PLAQUETTE   A *billon coin to the value of 14 *liards, struck for the Austrian Netherlands and the bishopric of Liège from 1755–93.

In a more general sense, the word plaquette is used to describe any large medal which is *uniface and suitable as wall decoration rather than lying hidden in a cabinet.

A great many of the finest medallists of the Italian and German Renaissance made such sculptured pictures, cast in bronze and often gilt, and much prized as art objects. There was a marked revival of interest in this art during the half-century before the First World War, especially during the "art nouveau" period.

PLATED COINS   Any coin the exterior "skin" of which is of a different metal from the core. A favourite forger's trick has been to plate base metal coins with gold or silver; this is easily detected today. But there have also been quite official plated issues, from certain Roman *denarii to modern USA issues.

PLATE MONEY   Large copper plates were issued in Sweden from 1644–1722, as part of the regular currency system. The values were expressed in terms of silver *dalers, the first (and largest) issue being for 10 dalers, later ones (from 1649) in denominations of 8, 4, 2 and 1. The largest and earliest such coin weighed 19.7 kilograms and was of rectangular shape (625mm x 320mm). Just how impracticable it proved may be gathered from the fact that of 26,552 pieces known to have been struck only three remain today.

Of later issues, which are more plentiful, there are many varieties, with markings showing both mints (six different ones known) and provenance of the copper (a dozen different sources). There is also a variety struck—or rather cast in this instance—from 1714–16 in Stockholm only, not of copper but from the bronze of cannon.

PLATINUM   Discovered as a metal in Spanish South America *c.* 1725, platinum has frequently been an experimental coinage metal in *patterns and presentation pieces. For regular currency, it has been used only once, in Russia from 1828–45, for pieces of 3, 6 and 12 *roubles. It is intriguing to ponder that such pieces were, later in the 19th century, sometimes plated with gold, then considered the more valuable metal. Such "forgeries in reverse" are a lucky find for collectors today, when all platinum coins are exceedingly scarce. Since nearly one and a half million coins were struck by Russia in platinum over sixteen years, such a find may still occasionally turn up.

Among coinage issues more properly listed as patterns, Spain easily holds the record: eighteen between 1747 and 1904.

PLATMYNT   The Swedish word for *plate money.

PLAYING CARD MONEY   An *emergency money first documented as being used in Canada 1685, for the payment of troops when coin was in short supply. The first known notes date from *c.* 1714, and the habit persisted into Napoleonic times in French Canada, despite edicts at various times calling in such cards.

PLUG   The central or cut-out part of a coin, in the *cut money of the West Indies and parts of Central America. (Also *dump, ring dollar.) Such a plug often has a value quite independent of that part of the coin from which it is taken.

PLUGGED COINS   Coins which have been pierced and have then had the hole stopped up again. The piercing may have been done purely for practical purposes (e.g. to wear the coin as a piece of jewellery); in any case, its value is much diminished, however carefully the hole has been repaired.

Occasionally, coins are given a central plug of a different metal from the rest of the coin: *bi-metallic coins.

Plugged farthing of William and Mary

POGH   A small copper coin of Armenia while this was an independent Christian kingdom (1080–1375).

POINTS SECRETS   The medieval French system of identifying the mint in which a coin was struck: a dot was placed under a particular letter of the *legend. It began *c.* 1380 in the province of Dauphiné and was extended in 1389 to all twenty French regal mints. Paris set its dot (from 1411 an *annulet) under the eighteenth letter. In 1540, this system was superseded by Francis I's reform introducing *mint letters (with A for Paris as the principal mint); and there is an interesting transitional period during which both "points secrets" and mint letters may be seen on coins.

POITIERS   A French regal mint from the Middle Ages; also active for King Edward III as Duke of Aquitaine, and for the Black Prince until 1370.

POLTINA   Russian name for the half-*rouble.

POLUIMPERIAL   *imperial.

POND   The South African *pound. It was equivalent in weight and fineness of metal to the English gold *sovereign, and was first struck in a very small number only (837 pieces) with the effigy of President Burgers in 1874. Almost 2 million Kruger ponds were struck from 1892–1900. (Also *veld pond.)

Kruger pond of South Africa, 1896

PONDICHERRY   A French possession in India, on the southeast coast, first settled in 1674. Coins were struck here from 1736–1839, except for short periods of British occupation. They consisted of silver *fanams of European type (obverse depicts a crown, with five lys on the reverse), and gold *pagodas and silver rupees copying local Moghul types.

Pontefract siege piece in the name of Charles II

Silver portcullis trade dollar of Elizabeth I

PONTEFRACT This town was a royalist stronghold, besieged by the Roundheads from June 1648 until March 1649. It issued *emergency money in silver, chiefly shillings, and continued to do so, in the name of Charles II, after Charles I's execution, for almost two months.

POPAYÁN A mint of Spanish America established in 1729, in a rich mining area of what is today the Republic of Colombia. Gold was struck here abundantly, while silver was only struck as and when obtained and refined from the gold ore locally mined. A 2 escudos of 1732 is the earliest coin known from this mint; more regular issues of 8, 4, 2, 1 and ½ escudos did not begin until the 1760s under Charles III. All the silver is scarce today, especially the 8 reales. The mintmark was at first P, later Pn. The mint continued to operate under the Republic.

PORCELAIN COINS, TOKENS AND MEDALS The first known examples of porcelain as currency date from Siam during the middle of the 19th century. They were, in fact, made for use in gaming houses but during times of small change shortage are known to have enjoyed local currency status. The only other example of porcelain coins is their use as *emergency money during the German inflationary period 1921–2. Most of these were made at the Meissen porcelain factory, for a considerable number of towns. There are also some examples of stoneware rather than porcelain coins. As regards medals, medallions and plaquettes, porcelain has been a favourite medium since the early days of the Meissen factory; there are Worcester and Wedgwood examples in England, and Sèvres ones in France.

PORTCULLIS COINS The portcullis or drop-gate has figured often on English coinage as a *mintmark, and on two occasions at least has been used as the main reverse design. The best-known is the brass 3-penny piece of Elizabeth II; and her illustrious ancestor Elizabeth I used the design for a special series of crowns, half-crowns, shillings and sixpences, struck for the East India Company 1600–1. There are also portcullis groats and farthings during the reign of Henry VIII, but their extreme rarity and careful striking suggests that these were *patterns only.

PORTO NOVO PAGODA *pagoda.

PORTUGALÖSER A large gold coin, based on the *portuguez, and struck to the value of 10 *ducats in a number of German cities, usually for commemorative purposes. The most extensive is that struck in Hamburg from 1553–1673. There is another Hamburg series, dating from the foundation of the city bank in 1667 until the mid-19th century, but these "Bankportugalöser", as they are called, are more properly classed as medals.

PORTUGUEZ A large Portuguese gold coin, to the value of 10 *cruzados, struck from 1499–1557. It commemorated in its legend Portuguese discoveries, conquests and trade.

POSEIDONIA *Paestum.

POSTAL CURRENCIES The use of postage stamps as currency is a meeting-point for collectors of stamps, banknotes and coins. In fact, it is a very substantial collecting field in its own right and—like most categories of *emergency money—almost impossible to catalogue fully. The most recent and certainly most comprehensive attempt is that by Albert Pick *(Briefmarkengeld,* 1970). His 66-page catalogue lists no less than twenty-seven countries where stamps have been officially issued as currency, and sixteen others where in times of necessity postage stamps encased in windowed capsules of one sort or another were unofficially accepted as small change in times of regular currency shortage. Pick lists no less than thirteen main varieties, ranging from ordinary stamps merely stuck to special paper, or even loose in a special envelope, to what are in fact small banknotes using stamp designs and printing plates. Though the practice was worldwide, the English or Commonwealth collector will find little here: known issues are confined to Ceylon and Rhodesia.

POTIN   A base metal consisting of much brass mixed with various other metals, of a blackish grey colour. It is often confused with *billon, whereas its use was in fact largely confined to cast coins of certain Celtic tribes.

POTOSI   Silver mines of enormous richness were discovered here by the Spaniards in 1545; it is somewhat surprising, therefore, but none the less a fact, that a mint to exploit this silver was not established until some time between 1573–5. The earliest coins can be dated to 1574 from references in the correspondence of the Viceroy. The output here was immense, second only to that of Mexico City, and continued for almost exactly 250 years, until 1825. It was almost entirely confined to the locally mined silver; copper was not struck at all here, and gold in relatively small quantities only from 1778 onwards. The mintmark is P.

POUND   The major currency unit of Great Britain, retained in the new decimal system. For the gold coin, *sovereign. A pound and its half were struck in silver at the Shrewsbury and Oxford Mints for Charles I during the Civil War, with figures XX and X respectively. A new pound coin—the first ever to be struck in a base alloy—was issued in the UK during 1983 and is proving unpopular.

PRAGER GROSCHEN   A special type of *Groschen struck for Bohemia at the Kuttenberg Mint from 1298. It is the first of the larger silver coins to be struck in central Europe and takes its name from the legend "grossi pragenses", which encircles the rampant lion on the reverse.

PRAGUE   The principal mint of the kingdom of Bohemia from the 10th to the 18th centuries. Coins were struck here from the time of Boleslav I, A.D. 950.

PRETENDER COINAGES   These are of two kinds; (1) struck by or on behalf of a pretender to the throne during his lifetime, or (2) struck posthumously as a commemorative piece. The English series has only a very few (Empress Matilda, Lambert Simnel, Perkin Warbeck) which are known actually to have circulated; so-called "coins" of the Old Pretender both as James VIII of Scotland and James III of England are known only as *patterns. The French 19th century is fairly rich in mythical monarchs, Bourbonites and Bonapartists alike indulging their fancies with coinage for Louis XVII (who died as an infant), Napoleon II (who died in exile as Duke of Reichstadt—the "Aiglon" of Rostand's play) and Henry V (1820–83), who might well have reigned in fact as well as fiction but for his intransigence (he refused to accept the *tricolore* as the national flag when offered the crown in 1873). The Russian series has a few rare coins of the "False Dmitri" during the reign of Boris Godounov, and the Portuguese have a fairly extensive one for Antonio, who disputed the throne with Philip II of Spain from 1580–89, and struck coins as far apart as Paris, Gorcum (Holland) and the Azores.

PRIMITIVE MONEY   A fairly loose term, comprising almost every medium of exchange that is neither coin nor negotiable paper of some kind or other. It has ranged from cattle (from the Latin word from which the word pecuniary is in fact derived) to *cowrie shells. One might perhaps add that the term is slightly

Silver crown of the Old Pretender (James VIII of Scotland)

unfortunate, in that (a) the forms of such money are by no means always primitive but may be highly artistic, and (b) certain highly sophisticated civilisations used it—or no money in our sense at all—for centuries (e.g. the Phoenicians, who came to coinage late, preferring to trade in pure gold dust weighed out by the shekel or its fraction).

PRINCE EDWARD ISLAND Not unlike *Newfoundland, for a long time this was a kind of odd man out among British possessions in North America. For some peculiar reason (perhaps British shame at its long neglect), the island was suddenly given its own coinage of 1 million copper 1-cent pieces, struck in 1871 only at the *Heaton Mint. Two peculiarities of this unique issue should be noted: it does not carry the H mintmark (and is the only Canadian issue not to do so), and it carries the unusual legend VICTORIA QUEEN instead of REGINA. Only two years later, in 1873, Prince Edward Island joined the Canadian Confederation to become (and remain) its smallest province. It also adopted, of course, the by then well-established Canadian coinage, so that its own cents rapidly went out of circulation to become collectors' pieces.

PRINTING AND NUMISMATICS One's initial reaction to such a heading might well be that it should find treatment under *banknotes; but in fact the association is both wider and closer than that. Technical links are very close indeed between minting and printing from the Renaissance onwards. Gutenberg, the inventor of printing with moveable type (at any rate in the Western world) was the son of a Mainz mintmaster and himself trained as a goldsmith. The invention of the coin-press followed very closely upon that of the printing-press and is obviously closely related to it. In 1458 Nicolas Jenson, then mintmaster of Tours, was sent by Charles VII of France to investigate Gutenberg's invention at Mainz; he reappears in 1470 at Venice as one of the finest of early Italian printers. In the same year, a German printer set up the first press at another Italian town, Foligno—significantly in the house of the mintmaster there, one Emiliano Orfini. The first book printed at Florence, in 1471, is the work of the celebrated goldsmith Bernardo Cennini: he was not only the first native Italian typefounder but also cut coins for the Florence Mint. Philippe Danfrie, who cut several "civilité" types for the Paris bookseller and publisher Richard Breton from the late 1550s onwards, later became chief engraver at the Paris Mint; he was also a famous maker of astronomical instruments and towards the end of his life combined all these skills in a book of his own on a surveying instrument of his own invention, the "graphomètre". For this he not only cut a new type but also engraved the illustrations. This constant interchange of technique in printing and minting continues into the 19th century, with figures such as Anthony Bessemer (who at the time of the French Revolution left the Paris Mint to come and engrave minute "diamond" types for Caslon) and *Andrieu, a famous French medallist of the revolutionary and Napoleonic eras. Among Americans, Jacob Perkins is probably the best-known figure: a Massachusetts goldsmith and coin engraver who later settled in England and helped found the firm that printed the first postage stamps in 1840. (Also *lettering on coins.)

PRIVATE GOLD Any pieces purporting to be for circulation as currency and not issued by any government authority. The attempt has only once been made in England (*Thomason-Reading bank token), and was promptly prohibited. Coinage—

and especially gold coinage—remains a prerogative of the crown. Even though under common law anyone until quite recent times could take gold bullion to be coined, that coin had to be of the standard pattern and design of the realm, not some fantasy that pleased the owner.

Such fantasy pieces are not uncommon abroad; a great number, for instance, were made for the late King Farouk of Egypt (quite apart from his official Egyptian coinage in gold). In India, various banks have struck coins in gold for use (or invest-ment) by their customers (*tola coinage). Such bank coinages (also *ingots), however, are not generally accepted in circulation. A different category is that of US* territorial gold, often issued privately to meet the needs during gold rushes; some of such issues developed into at least semi-official coinages (*Humbert).

PRIVATE MINTS   Too little is known about the organisation of ancient Greek mints for us to say to what extent, if any, private mints operated in city states. Only of the very earliest coins is it believed that they may have been privately issued, by merchants, with their own guarantee marks. The centralised Roman Empire certainly did not tolerate any such thing, nor did Byzantium. But from early medieval times onwards, private mints (or at any rate moneyers) were not uncommon. Over very large parts of Europe, the privilege of striking coins was leased or farmed out to private individuals for profit.

Yet it could not be said that such mints were truly privately owned (though they might pass from father to son by right of suc-cession). The first and still in many respects greatest model for such a mint dates from the industrial revolution and is that established by Matthew *Boulton at his *Soho works in 1785. Birmingham has continued ever since to be a centre for *contract coinage, purely by virtue of its manufacturing skills, which often enabled it to produce the goods cheaper than government-operated establishments. Only in very recent years has British supremacy in this field begun to be challenged by American com-petition, notably by the *Franklin Mint of Philadelphia; yet even this has to date produced far more medals than government con-tract coinages.

PRIVY MARKS   A peculiar feature of English coinage from the period of Edward III to the Commonwealth. They are, as their name suggests, secret marks, identifying (but only to those in the know) a distinct period within which a coin was struck—sometimes even workshops or particular workmen. Their twofold purpose was to keep a strict control on coinage standards and to make forgery more difficult.

PROCLAMATION PIECES   An extensive series of Spanish-American coins and medals issued by most of the Central and South American mints as commemorative pieces to proclaim new rulers. The series extends from the reign of Philip V in 1701 to Ferdinand VII in 1808. Pieces are known in gold, silver and copper, with a solitary platinum specimen also for Ferdinand VII. The earlier pieces were purely medallic, but later ones from Charles IV in 1789 onwards show various values (on pieces of various sizes), ranging from a half to 8 *reales.

PROOF   A coin struck on a specially prepared *flan, by means of a specially polished *die. New denominations when introduced are often issued by mints in proof sets, specially cased for collectors, and at a premium price above face value. Such items lose much of their value if they show the slightest scratch or even finger-mark. A proof is always basically the same as a coin issued for general circulation; if the design differs, even in minor detail, we call it a *pattern.

PROVENANCE MARK   Many coins carry a mark, sometimes a word, phrase, or even picture, to denote the source of the metal from which the coin has been struck. Such sources have included particular mines, rivers, countries, trading companies, captured treasure and church or other plate melted down in time of emergency. Words and phrases tend to be self-explanatory (e.g. *China ducats, Lima, Vigo); and indications are very plain on various German mining Thalers and river ducats. In the English series, provenance marks first occur in 1621, when the Prince of Wales's plumes denoted coins struck from the silver of Welsh mines; later examples are roses to indicate West of England silver, and the elephant for gold or silver imported by the African Company. The letters EIC, SSC and WCC stand for East India Company, South Sea Company, and Welsh Copper Company. Such markings often have considerable bearing on the value of a particular piece: thus a shilling of George I of 1723 with the letters WCC below the bust is worth three times that of the same type and year with the letters SSC.

PSKOV   An independent city republic of Russia which, during the 15th century, issued its own coinage, and one in conjunction with Moscow after 1510.

PTOLEMAIS-ACE   *Acre.

PU   Early Chinese currency, derived from the still earlier *spade money but differing in detail and much smaller.

PUFFIN   An unauthorised bronze issue by the self-styled "King" of Lundy Island, Martin Coles Harman, in 1929. The coin (of penny size and value) bore Harman's portrait on the obverse and a puffin on the reverse. It led to a prosecution under the Coinage Act of 1870 and was quickly withdrawn.

PUL   A Russian copper coin, first issued during the 15th century and current until the end of the 17th. It also became the copper unit of Georgia after its annexation by Russia in 1800.

A pul of Tver, struck under the Grand Duke Boris Alexandrovich (1425–61), is one of the rare coins actually to show a moneyer at work.

PUNCH   The celebrated humorous English weekly may seem an unlikely entry in an encyclopedia of this kind. But *Punch,* especially during the Victorian era, was very alive to monetary changes. It carried on a positive vendetta with the Master of the Mint at the time of controversy around the *Godless florin, sent amusing reports on the California gold rush in the early 1850s, in both verse and prose, and on occasion sketched coinage and medal patterns hardly likely to meet with official approval.

PUNCH-MARKED COINS   A punch is, of course, the most elementary tool for marking a piece of metal. Punch-marked coins are those of which only a small part is stamped with such a tool. Often, too, such pieces are irregularly shaped. Such pieces are particularly prevalent in the early coinage of India, but are to be found throughout history in times of emergency.

PUNNING TYPE   A coin design whose pictorial representation puns on the name of a person or place. Thus, for instance, the monk who appears on medieval coins struck at Munich.

PYX, TRIAL OF THE   From the Greek *pyxis,* a box or vase with a lid. By derivation, the Trial of the Pyx in Britain is the testing of certain gold and silver pieces put aside in special boxes from all monies coined. This trial takes place annually in Goldsmiths' Hall; formerly it was held in the Chapel of the Pyx at

Puffin of Lundy Island, 1929

Westminster Abbey. The jury consists of members of the Goldsmiths' Company, who must report to the Lord Chancellor on whether these coins—always picked at random—meet the required standards of weight and purity of metal within the *tolerances as laid down by law. Although gold sovereigns are no longer legal tender, the ceremony still takes place in years when they are struck by the mint.

QUADRANS The quarter of the *as in the Roman republican coinage. Since the latter was divided into 12 *uncia, the quadrans bore three dots as a mark of value.

QUADRATUM INCUSUM Name given to the rough punch-marks seen on the reverses of some of the earliest Greek coins, four of which often formed a square.

QUADRATUM SUPERCUSUM Name given to a raised square containing initials, which originated at the mint of Hall in the Austrian Tyrol on the *Heller coinage, but is most commonly found on Bavarian coins struck at Munich during the later Middle Ages.

QUADRIGATUS Another name for the didrachm of the *Romano-Campanian coinage, so-called after its main type, a chariot drawn by four horses or quadriga.

QUADRUPLA A multiple of four in the Italian coinage, and hence a name of a long series of gold 4-scudi pieces (Papal States, Sicily, Mantua among others).

QUART D'ÉCU Introduced by Henry III of France in 1578, this was a silver coin to the value of 15 *sols. It enjoyed wide popularity throughout Europe and was struck by subsequent French kings until 1720, when the *écu was divided into thirds, sixths and twelfths instead of quarters and eighths. When the Tower Mint was closed owing to the plague in 1625, an edict proclaimed the quart d'écu legal tender in England, at a value of 19½ pence.

QUARTER (USA) The quarter-dollar is perhaps the most interesting of all USA denominations. Its first issue, in 1796, was without indication of value (with the draped bust design); the designation 25 C was added at the base of the reverse when the heraldic eagle design was introduced in 1804 and continued throughout the life of the liberty cap design (1815–38). Ever since the introduction of the Liberty seated design, i.e. 1838 onwards, the popular name "quarter" has also figured as the official designation on the coin itself, first as QUAR.DOL. and from 1892 onwards in full as QUARTER DOLLAR. Alone among the principal coinages of the world, the quarter has maintained its popularity against the almost universal 20-cent piece of other decimal coinages, and bears witness to the practical and pragmatic sense of Americans; for it is certainly easier to reckon in halves and quarters than it is in fifths.

The Barber Quarter of 1892 carries on the obverse the same Liberty head design as the *dime, but with a heraldic eagle reverse. In 1916, this was superseded by Hermon A. MacNeil's beautiful standing Liberty design, with an equally fine flying eagle reverse. Unfortunately, the obverse was very susceptible to wear, and was for this reason several times reworked in an effort to provide better wearing qualities. The first and most obvious change was in the flimsy drapery around the bust of the standing figure, replaced by chain mail armour. The date on the pedestal was at first raised, and later recessed (1925 onwards). On the reverse, the eagle had been repositioned in 1917, slightly higher, with 3 stars added beneath.

The Washington Quarter introduced in 1932 is still current today. On it, Washington's bust faces left, with the word LIBERTY above it and IN GOD WE TRUST in small letters below the chin. There is a new heraldic eagle reverse. Since 1965, this coin has been struck in nickel-clad copper instead of silver.

QUARTER-EAGLE The quarter-eagle or $2.50 gold piece, along with larger multiples of $5 (*half-eagle) and $10 (*eagle) was authorised by the original US coinage law of 2 April 1792. Its stipulated weight was 67.5 grains of .916 fine gold, where it remained until the standard was changed to 64.5 grains at .899 fine by an act of 28 June 1834, this being revised to .900 fine by a law of 18 January 1837.

The first design, by Robert Scot, the liberty cap type, did not carry a designation of value and was struck from 1796–1807. A new design by John Reich, introduced in 1808 and struck at intervals until 1834, shows on the obverse a turban head design and carries the designation 2½D. on the reverse. A new issue of 1834 was designed by William Kneass, featuring a liberty band holding the hair, but with the turban removed. Previous issues had been small as well as irregular; this one could be counted in hundreds of thousands.

The next issue, known as the coronet quarter-eagle and designed by Christian Gobrecht, was introduced in 1840 and continued largely unchanged until 1907. There is a very rare 1848 piece overstamped CAL (for California) above the eagle's head on the reverse, made from a consignment of gold sent by the state's military governor to the Secretary of War.

The final issue, known as the Indian head quarter-eagle from its fine obverse type designed by Bela Lyon Pratt, lasted from 1908–29, with an interval of ten years between 1915–25.

QUARTINHO The quarter of the *moidore of 4,000 *reis, as introduced in 1677. The name was applied equally to the *escudos in the new portrait coinage of Portugal from 1722 onwards.

QUARTO Name of the silver coin of Spain to the value of one-quarter *real, introduced by Ferdinand and Isabella in 1497; *cuarto. Copper quartos were struck early in the 19th century during the French occupation of Barcelona and Catalonia. The same denomination was also adopted in Gibraltar under British sovereignty: in 1802 as *tokens, and as a regal coinage in 1842 (the name then abbreviated to quart). Halves and doubles were also struck, and were equal to a farthing and a penny respectively.

QUATREFOIL The four-leafed clover, often used as a mint-mark. For almost two hundred years, it was placed in the central joint of the cross as the distinguishing mark for York archiepiscopal coinages (1331 onwards).

QUATTRINO In a number of Italian city coinages the quarter of the *grosso. It occurs in both copper and *billon, with the most extended use in the Papal States, where it remained current until 1854.

QUEDLINBURG A town near Halberstadt in the Harz mountains, and the seat of a famous abbey. The abbesses struck coins here from the 11th to the 18th centuries; there is a particularly fine series of *bracteates during the 12th century and a splendid 2-ducat gold piece of Anna Dorothea (1704), the last abbess to strike coins.

QUINARIUS One half of the *denarius, as introduced in the first Roman silver coinage, *c.* 211 B.C. It was equal in value to 5 bronze *asses.

QUINZAIN D'OR A piece projected by John *Law towards the end of his rule as French financial dictator, around 1720. Although mentioned in an edict of the time, and illustrated in the *Almanach des Monnaies* of 1784, no further trace of it has been found, even as a *pattern.

ALMANACH
DES
MONNOIES
ANNÉE 1784.

Nummus quæsitus et comparatus est, ut omnium rerum quodam modo sit medius seu mensura.
(*Aristote. Etich. Nicoma. Lib. V. Cap. 8.*)

A PARIS.
Chez Méquignon, Libraire au Palais.
Avec Approbation, et Privilège du Roi.

R

RADIATE Word denoting beams of rays around the head. The most famous type on coins of antiquity is that of Helios, the sun-god; and its most famous representation is that on coins of *Rhodes. For Roman coinage, *Antoninianus; for British and Celtic copies, *barbarous radiates.

RAMATANKA A Hindu *amulet of brass (but sometimes silver-plated), sold in temples as a good-luck charm. There are many varieties; and these pieces, mostly of modern manufacture though made to look antique and picturesque, are often mistaken for coins.

RAND Decimal unit of the coinage of the independent Republic of South Africa since 1961. It has been struck in both silver and gold.

RAPPEN The smallest unit of Swiss coinage in common use since the Middle Ages. It was at first equivalent to 2 *deniers, and struck in *billon. When the Swiss went over to the decimal system in 1850, the name *Rappen was retained instead of *centime throughout the German-speaking cantons and is in use to this day.

RAPPENMÜNZBUND Name of a league coinage uniting a large number of southern German mints, which in 1403 adopted a uniform type of *Groschen, valued at 6 *Rappen. The first attempts to create this "monetary union" were made in 1387 and 1399; but the treaty was not finally signed until 24 February 1403. Signatories were Duke Leopold of Austria (through the Governor of his territories of Alsace, Breisgau and Sundgau) and a number of free cities on both sides of the upper Rhine. Whole and half Rappen were for many years the only silver coins of this territory, supplemented by gold *Gulden. The league ran into difficulties from 1559 (*Basel) and was finally disbanded in 1584.

RAVENNA A Roman, Byzantine and Lombard mint where coins were struck from the early 5th century A.D. onwards. During the Roman period, Ravenna struck coins in all metals for both Western and Eastern emperors, though with a preponderance for the former, since Ravenna was virtually the capital after the first sack of Rome by the Goths under Alaric in A.D. 410. After the final overthrow of Rome, Ravenna became the capital and principal mint of the Ostrogothic kings Odovacer and Theodoric the Great. After Italy had been reconquered under the Byzantine Emperor Justinian I by Belisarius and Narses, Byzantine coinage of distinctive types was struck here from the mid-6th to the mid-8th centuries. The gold *solidi are characterised by a spread fabric with broad raised rim. There was struck here a unique series of silver coins under Justinian I, expressed in terms of the bronze *nummium, in multiples of 120, 125 and 250 nummia.

Brass ramatanka, 20th century

Ravenna: Gold solidus of
Constantine III, A.D. 421

Real: Earliest silver type, as struck for Peter I for Castile and León, 1350–68

The later history of the mint is one of more sporadic coinages, among which we may single out some *papal coins under Leo X.

RAWLINS, THOMAS Coin engraver and medallist to King Charles I during the time of the Civil War, chiefly at the Oxford Mint, where he struck a famous *pattern crown with the only city view known on any English coin, and the equally famous *triple unite. His work shows the influence of Nicolas *Briot, whose pupil he may well have been. He was equally distinguished as a medallist of royalist notables.

REAL A silver coin introduced almost at the same time (mid-14th century) in both Spain and Portugal. It remained the standard unit of Spanish silver coinage for over four centuries (though many more of the multiple 8-reales pieces were struck, *peso). In Portuguese coinage, however, it became a copper coin in the 16th century and multiples up to 10 reas (Portuguese spelling, later changed to reis) were struck. Gold coins, especially larger denominations, were often expressed as *milreis, e.g. 4 milreis rather than 4,000 reis.

REAL DE CATORCE A rare silver 8 reales of 1811 only is known from this Mexican mint, or rather mining centre. It is without a portrait bust of Ferdinand VII, simply bearing a legend which gives the place-name, date and value.

REDDITE CROWN A famous *pattern crown by Thomas *Simon, similar to his *Petition Crown, but with a single-line edge reading QUE CAESARIS CAESAI & CT. POST, followed by a sun appearing out of a cloud. The coin is rarer than the Petition Crown and there is an even rarer version with the edge reading in English RENDER UNTO CAESAR THAT WHICH IS CAESARS.

REDUCING MACHINE Prior to the invention of this, all coins and medals were engraved by hand. The reducing machine could take a large plaster model and from this trace the original design reduced to any scale in steel. It should be added that it does this three-dimensionally: i.e. it reproduces to exact scale not only the outline but the height of relief of the sculptured model.

There have been many different inventions of this kind; indeed, new and improved models of exactitude are still being produced. But the earliest known (upon the principle of which all others are based) was invented by Konstantinovitch Nartov (1680–1756), a protegé of Tsar Peter I of Russia and an employee from 1712–25 at the Moscow Mint. The exact date of his invention is not recorded but must have been before 1717; for in this year Peter visited Paris and presented one of these machines to the eminent French scientist Pajot d'Ons-en-Bray, whose "mechanical museum" was then world-famous. On Pajot's death, his entire collection passed to the French Academy of Science; and his first reducing machine, together with others constructed between 1767 and 1927, is now on display at the Conservatoire des Arts et Métiers in Paris.

As an aid to modern mass-produced coinage the reducing machine is today indispensable; but by the same token, it has removed from modern coinage much of the artistic validity which has distinguished it in the past. A design which may look splendid in a model 4 inches in diameter often loses much of its effect in miniature.

REGENBOGENSCHÜSSELCHEN A coinage peculiar to the Danubian Celts, roughly dated to the 1st century B.C., and of a strong concave fabric (the German *Schüssel* meaning bowl).

These miniature bowls are decorated on what may be called the inside with a variety of patterns hitherto unexplained, though probably of religious significance, whereas the outside is most often plain, only infrequently carrying other patterns or inscriptions. The coins are found both in gold and *electrum, which explains their popular name, for it was an ancient superstition that a rainbow shed drops of gold as it passed.

REGENSBURG   Town in Bavaria, on the river Danube, and the seat of an important coinage from the 10th to the early 19th century. At first, the mint was operated jointly by the bishops and the dukes of Bavaria. From 1230, Regensburg struck its own coinage as a free city of the Holy Roman Empire. Gold was first struck here in 1512, and regularly from the 17th century onwards. There are many fine ducats and Thalers with city views. The episcopal as well as city coinage continued until 1809; secularisation and full integration into Bavaria followed a year later.

REICHSTHALER   *Thaler.

REIS   Plural of *real (also *milreis).

RELIEF   That part of the coin design which is raised from the surface of the *flan when struck.

REMEDY   In numismatics, a technical term signifying the amount by which one coin may vary from another in weight or fineness of metal. Such tolerances are minute, and any coin not meeting them is liable to be rejected. Samples are taken at random during coining operations at every mint and there is also the Trial of the *Pyx.

RENAISSANCE   The marvellous flowering of painting and sculpture seen during the period 1450–1600 had its counterpart in a coinage unmatched in splendour since ancient Greek times. The large, sculpted medals of *Pisanello gave an impetus to experiments on a smaller scale for coinage. Here the initiative was taken by goldsmiths (*Camelio, Caradosso, Cellini) who at the same time revived the parallel art of engraved gems. And if art flourished, so did techniques. The invention of the printing-press was followed within a few years by that of the *screw-press for coinage, with a collar to ensure perfect roundness and a little later still, adding devices for lettering to be impressed on the edges of coins.

RESTRIKES   Coins or medals restruck later, but from the original dies. For the very extensive Russian series, *novodels. In the English series, the most important are copper coins and patterns of Matthew Boulton's *Soho Mint. C. Wilson Peck has distinguished not only between the later 19th-century strikings by W. J. Taylor (a London die-sinker who purchased the Soho dies after the closure of the mint) and Soho strikings, but between "early" and "late" Soho. There are also *proof restrikes by the Royal Mint of certain gold coins for British India.

REVERSE   The other side of the *obverse of a coin. The most common type by far in all coinages since the Middle Ages is some sort of heraldic design. But pictorial representations of one kind or another have been frequent, with city views a special favourite in continental coinages of the 16th to the 18th centuries.

RHEGIUM   Town in southern Italy, opposite the straits of Messina, and the seat of an ancient Greek coinage. It struck at first *drachms of *incuse fabric with the type of a man-headed bull. Later, a lion's head facing becomes the principal type; because of its persistence, this is deemed to be the *obverse even when, c. 400 B.C., there is a series of *tetradrachms featuring the head of Apollo on the other side.

RHODES   Island in the eastern Mediterranean. In the 6th and 5th centuries B.C. small coins in *electrum and silver were issued by the independent towns of Camirus (fig-leaf), Ialysus (forepart of winged boar) and Lindos (lion's head). Around 408 B.C. these three towns founded the new capital, Rhodos, in the extreme north of the island, which now alone issued coinage and of an entirely new type; the obverse depicted the head of the sun-god Helios (sometimes *radiate), to whom all the island was sacred, with the reverse type showing a rose (often with vine tendrils and a bunch of grapes as additional features). These types—with, of course, frequent changes of style—persisted throughout the ancient history of Rhodes, right through Roman republican times to 43 B.C. To Rhodes belongs one of the earliest and most lovely of gold *staters in the ancient Greek series, a superb specimen of which is in the British Museum collection.

From the 13th to the 16th centuries, until captured by the Turks in 1522, Rhodes was the headquarters of the Knights of the Order of St John of Jerusalem. They struck here a quantity of coins which were mostly derivative: *ducats of Venetian type, *grossi on Byzantine models and others.

RIAL   An obvious corruption of the Spanish word *real, this is a silver denomination which has during the current century been adopted by Morocco and Zanzibar in Africa, and also by Persia.

RIDER, RIJDER   An obvious name for an obvious type, showing a figure on a galloping horse (also *franc á cheval, the prototype of both). It occurs in the Scottish coinage during the reigns of James III and James VI (the latter a rather tame version, hardly more than a trot) and—spelt rijder, as above—in a long sequence of the United (Dutch) Provinces stretching from 1581 until the latter part of the 18th century.

RIGA   In the Middle Ages, a mint of the Teutonic Knights, the city was later under the sovereignty of Poland and Sweden. There are many fine and rare pieces in both gold and silver from the late 16th to the early 18th century, including some splendid city views. No coins were struck for or at Riga under Russian rule; but a

Rider: Gold type, as struck for Scotland under James III, *c.* 1485

mint was re-established there after it became a capital of the independent Republic of Latvia, and the high standards of earlier coinages were reflected in those from 1922–39.

RIGSDALER, RIJKSDAALDER, RIKSDALER   *Thaler.

RING MONEY   The first coinage of Australia. It was authorised by proclamation of Governor Macquarie of New South Wales dated 1 July 1813. About 40,000 Spanish dollars were bought at 4s. 9d. each and had their centres cut out. The remaining "ring" was then marked on one side with the value FIVE SHILLINGS, and on the other side NEW SOUTH WALES 1813. The centre part (known as *"dump") was issued as a piece of FIFTEEN PENCE (reverse inscription); while the obverse showed a crown with again the legend NEW SOUTH WALES 1813.

These ring dollars are also commonly known as "holey" dollars. They were called in from 1822 onwards and finally ceased to be accepted in exchange for sterling coinages from 1829. Fewer than 200 of the "rings" and 1,000 of the "dumps" are believed to exist today and they command increasingly high prices as coin collecting attracts more and more Australians.

RIO DE JANEIRO   A mint of Portuguese Brazil from 1654 (mintmark R), and still the country's most important place of coinage. In former centuries, both Bahia and Minas Geraes often exceeded its output, which from 1703–1822 was confined to gold coinage.

RITTENHOUSE, DAVID (1732–96) The first director of the USA mint at Philadelphia. A man of outstanding mechanical genius, he had attained a nation-wide reputation as an instrument-maker—chiefly of fine clocks. He was appointed to the office of director when already sixty and in failing health, but none the less remained for three years to see it through its teething troubles and firmly established. By the time he resigned in June 1795, the mint had struck coins in all metals, including the very fine first silver *dollars and gold *eagles. Rittenhouse's earlier distinctions had included the presidency of· the American Philosophical Society (in which office he succeeded Benjamin Franklin) and the professorship of astronomy at the University of Pennsylvania.

RIX DOLLAR A corruption of the Dutch word *rijksdaalder, this denomination was struck only for Ceylon from 1803 onwards. It first followed the Dutch currency system in being struck to a value of 48 *stuivers, but from 1825–69 was absorbed into the sterling system at a value of 1s. 6d. It then disappeared, making way for a decimal currency.

ROCHE *voce populi.

ROCHELLE, LA Town on the western sea-coast of France, a little north of Bordeaux. Under the Black Prince, it was an *Anglo-Gallic mint. Both as this and a later French regal mint, it used the mintmark R until the coinage reforms of Francis I of 1540, when the letter H was assigned to it. Under this it remained active until 1835, striking money in all metals.

ROETTIER (FAMILY) A celebrated family of coin and medal engravers, of Flemish origin, but employed because of their skill at the courts of England, France and Spain among others. The father of the family, a goldsmith of Antwerp, had assisted Charles II financially during his exile from England; and the King showed his gratitude after the Restoration by engaging all three of his sons (Jean, Joseph and Philippe) at the Royal Mint in preference to Thomas *Simon. Jean remained in English service until his death in 1703 (when he was buried in the Tower) and was responsible for most of the regal coinage in the meantime. In such work as he assigned to others at the mint, he tended to favour his sons, Jacques and Norbert, rather than his brothers. So Joseph went to France, where he worked on the medallic history of Louis XIV; and Philippe went via Flanders into Spanish service, where his son Jean Charles followed him. Various offspring remained active until well into the second half of the 18th century.

ROLLER DIES Mechanical coinage by means of this established itself around the same time as the *screw-press. There were advantages in economy, in that several dies (up to six for crown-size pieces and eighteen for smaller coins) could be engraved on the rollers, between which whole sheets of metal were then pressed and the coins then cut out. Dies were engraved in slightly ovoid form, so as to compensate for the curvature of the rollers and enable the coins to emerge fully round. But the actual curvature, however slight, is still to be noted on specimens produced by this method, which was adopted throughout the Holy Roman Empire by imperial decree of 1566 and remained in use there for a full 200 years (though experiments with the screw-press began towards the end of the 17th century). Such roller dies are still preserved in the mint museums of Vienna and Augsburg. Spain, too, adopted this method at the Segovia Mint under Philip II from 1586 onwards.

ROLLER-PRESS As the name implies, a coin-press in roller form rather than the more familiar up-down version. Such presses were almost universally adopted throughout the Holy Roman Empire from 1566 onwards, and examples are extant at the Augsburg museum. The dies were engraved on these rollers and strips of softened metal were passed through them (rather like washing might be passed through a mangle for drying, but of course under much greater pressure). Coins manufactured by this process usually show very slight curvature. *Briot is known to have used both a roller-press and a *screw-press. The latter was not adopted in Habsburg lands until the time of *Warou.

ROMAN COINAGE Roman coinage is generally divided into republican and imperial; but such division does scant justice to its complexity. With their passion for order and organisation, the Romans evolved a monetary system which—perhaps even more than the Greek—must come down to a study of individual mints and, within these, of the *officinae or workshops.

The mintage was controlled by an elaborate system of markings on coins which is, even today, imperfectly understood and classified. Modern "date collecting" is made to look rather silly when we remember that the coinage of a single moneyer in a single year may show about 10,000 different control or sequence marks. Handbooks and catalogues of Roman coinage have tended to concentrate on well-worn paths such as the above- mentioned republican and imperial series. Perhaps the most rewarding field for further study is the immense variety of provincial issues, and more especially those with Greek rather than Latin inscriptions. A useful checklist of almost two hundred Graeco-Roman mints was compiled by L. Isztimery in the second coin catalogue to be issued by the Bayerische Vereinsbank, (Munich, December 1972).

ROMANO-CAMPANIAN Term applied to a series of the earliest Roman silver coins, believed to have been struck between 269–211 B.C. They may be divided into two main groups. The first, bearing the word ROMANO, was struck on the weight standard then ruling in the cities of Magna Graecia (southern Italy), to the value of a didrachm (7.5 grammes). This group was struck until around 235 B.C. at mints which have not yet been identified with certainty. The second bears the word ROMA. Perhaps this group contains some of the earliest coins actually struck (as opposed to cast bronzes) within the city of Rome. Both series are of fine style, with dies probably engraved by Greek artists.

ROME The principal mint of the Roman Republic and Empire (*Roman coinage), Rome ceded supremacy to *Ravenna during the 5th century A.D. and was then, until the death of Theodoric the Great (A.D. 526), an Ostrogothic mint. Revived under Justinian I as a Byzantine mint, it was never more than a subsidiary one until the Popes (*papal coinage) began to strike money here in Charlemagne's time. The coinage then was characterised for two centuries by denarii carrying names of both Pope and Emperor. During the 12th and 13th centuries there was little or no coinage struck here, and there are only very sporadic issues throughout the 14th century, when the Popes resided at Avignon. But from 1431, during the papacy of Eugenius IV, there was an uninterrupted series of papal money from Rome until the 1870s, and then again from 1929. For the past century, the Roman Mint has also acted as that of the unified Italian state.

ROOSEBEKER A rare gold denomination, struck only for Brabant and Flanders during the joint rule of Philippe le Hardi and Jeanne (1384–9). Its proper name was the grand écu d'or; the

Silver Romano-Campanian didrachm with the head of Mars and a horse

popular appellation derives from what might be taken for a crown or bunch of roses above the shield of Brabant and Burgundy on the obverse type.

ROOSEVELT DIME *dime.

ROSA AMERICANA Struck by William Wood in 1722–4 under the same patent that gave him the right to strike a coinage for Ireland (*Wood's halfpence). The laureate bust of King George I is similar here; but the reverse shows, instead of Hibernia with her harp, a large rose and the legends ROSA AMERICANA and UTILE DULCI. The denominations are halfpenny, penny and 2 pence, with some exceedingly rare varieties. American interest has tended to inflate prices for this series. The coinage was struck in *Bath metal, an alloy invented by Wood.

ROSENOBEL Name given in the Netherlands to the many copies made there of the *ryal of Edward IV. There is also a Danish gold coin of this same name, struck only under Christian IV from 1611–29, but of an entirely different type, showing the half-length figure of the crowned King facing right as the obverse type, with a large elephant on the reverse. This coin is rare—and its half, struck only in 1611, even more so.

ROSE-NOBLE *ryal.

ROSE RYAL A gold denomination to the value of 30 shillings, occurring only in the second and third coinages of King James I of England, from 1604–25. It shows the King enthroned holding the orb and sceptre on the obverse, while the reverse has the royal arms on a square shield superimposed on a large Tudor rose. (This reverse differs on the third coinage, which shows the shield encircled by a band of lys, lions and crowns; but the name rose ryal was none the less retained.)

ROSKILDE An early Danish mint, active from the 10th century. There are a number of issues of Cnut the Great with his English title REX ANGLORUM.

ROSTOCK A city of the Hanseatic League on the Baltic coast, which enjoyed and exercised coinage rights from 1325–1869. The prevailing type was a rampant griffin. Coins in all metals were struck here, and there are some fine commemorative Thalers. Besides its own city coinage, Rostock struck pieces for the duchy of Mecklenburgh in the 17th and 18th centuries.

Gold double rouble of Peter I of Russia, 1721

ROTHSCHILD It is not perhaps as widely known as it might be that the rise of this world-famous banking house began in the late 18th century with dealing in coins and antiquities. Some of the early catalogues have survived; and the satisfaction which the earliest Rothschild gave to the Duke of Hesse-Kassel led to his rapid advancement as court factor and general financial adviser.

ROTY, LOUIS OSCAR (1846–1911) French coin and medal engraver, who also made many fine *plaquettes in the art nouveau style around the turn of the century. His most famous design is undoubtedly that of "La Semeuse", a symbolic female figure of the French Republic sowing the fields. First used in 1898, it is still to be seen on French coinage today and has also figured on postage stamps.

ROUBLE The principal silver denomination of Russia, introduced by Peter the Great in 1704 (though the name was earlier applied to silver bars: the Russian *rubitj* meaning to chop off). Its value was fixed at 100 *kopeks, and to Russia belongs the distinction of introducing the first decimal monetary system of any modern state. The very first roubles were overstruck on foreign Thalers or other crown-size pieces: there is one known in

Gold 15-rouble piece of Czar Nicholas II, 1897

the Hermitage collection, Leningrad, which still shows the English crown's edge reading DECUS ET TUTAMEN.

Enormous numbers of roubles have been struck, including many fine commemorative pieces. Multiples of 3, 6 and 12 roubles were struck in *platinum from 1828–45 and are the only extended regular currency series known in this metal. Among earlier roubles, perhaps the most remarkable series of varieties is that of no less than sixty, recorded during the single year of 1725 for the Empress Catherine I.

ROUEN   Town in northern France and a mint since Carolingian times. Apart from French regal coinage, it has been active for the Dukes of Normandy and as an *Anglo-Gallic mint. It operated from 1540 under the mint letter B until 1857, when it was closed.

ROUILLE, GUILLAUME (1518–89)   Publisher and antiquary of Lyon, who in 1553 issued his *Promptuaire des Médailles,* one of the first popular coin-books with woodcut illustrations. It mixed fact and legend in a charming if irresponsible manner, containing besides much genuine material, imaginary portraits of such figures as Adam, Noah, Agamemnon and others. Sometimes Rouille even takes a genuine coin and adds a fictitious legend— as, for example, when he turns the river-god Gelas (from a Sicilian tetradrachm) into the Cretan Minotaur.

ROXBURGH   Probably one of the earliest of Scottish mints, dating from near the beginning of David I's reign (c. 1135). These early issues also bear the moneyer's name, HUGO, while Roxburgh is generally spelt ROCASBURG. The mint remained an important one throughout the early medieval period; there are also some exceedingly rare *groats of James II, most probably struck at Roxburgh Castle for the payment of troops after its recapture.

ROYAL D'OR   Documents suggest that a coin of this name was first struck under Louis IX of France; but the first known specimen is from the reign of Charles IV, dating from 1326 and of a distinctive type showing the King standing under a Gothic carved screen and holding a long sceptre. This was then struck under successive monarchs until the reign of Charles V, though this last issue is known only as a *piéfort in a unique specimen of the French national collection.

ROYAL FARTHING TOKENS   *Harrington farthings.

ROYALIN   Silver coins struck for the Danish colony of Tranquebar from 1755–1807. The dies were cut in Copenhagen but coins were struck at a mint within the colony. They show the ruler's crowned monogram on the obverse, with the Danish coat of arms and the inscription 1 ROYALIN or 2 ROYALINER (for the double denomination) on the reverse.

RUBA   A quarter dinar as struck by the Fatima Dynasty, principally for Sicily, from the latter part of the 10th century A.D. for about a century.

RUDING, THE REV. ROGERS (1751–1820)   The author—or rather compiler—of a remarkable series of documents, which he collected together from various archives under the general title *Annals of the Coinage of Great Britain and its Dependencies,* first published in 1819. It was amplified after his death (a fourth edition being published in 1840) and is still our chief source of original material for a study of Britain's monetary history.

RUPEE   The principal silver coin of India: like the Roman *pecunia* (money), the word is derived from cattle (Sanskrit *rupa*), a medium of payment still in use among primitive peoples. The coin as such dates back to the 10th century: but the collector

Rupee: Sher Shah, Sultan of Delhi (1540–45)

today will probably limit his interest to the modern period, beginning with the issues of the Bombay Mint (1676), authorised for the East India Company by King Charles II. The coin continued to be struck in silver until 1945, but is today struck in nickel.

RUPIA The Portuguese version of the Indian *rupee, struck for her colonies of Diu and Goa from 1725 onwards.

RUPIE A silver coin of German East Africa from 1890 to 1914 at the Berlin and Hamburg Mints (mintmarks A and J respectively). The helmeted bust of the Emperor Wilhelm II is seen on all obverses, but the reverses change after 1902 from the shield of the Deutsch-Ostafrikanische Gesellschaft (German East African Company, which until then had administered the country) to a plain inscription DEUTSCH OSTAFRIKA under direct administration by the German foreign office as a colony.

RUSPONE Gold coin of Florence, introduced in 1719, to the value of 3 ducats or 40 lire. It continued to be struck for the Grand Duke of Tuscany until the beginning of the 19th century and was one of the few gold coins to be struck to a standard of 1,000 fine, i.e. of pure gold, without any alloy at all.

RYAL An English gold coin first struck under Edward IV in 1465, to the value of 10 shillings. It became known as the rose-noble from the large rose which decorates the side of the ship on the obverse. There is a Scottish gold denomination, to the value of £3, struck during the period 1555–8 only. This is a portrait coin of the young Mary Queen of Scots, exceedingly rare, and bearing no relation to its English namesake. Mary also struck a silver ryal late in her reign (1565), valued at 30 shillings, commonly known as the *Crookston Dollar.

RYO Standard monetary unit of Japan. The gold *koban was its equivalent and the *oban was valued at 10 ryos. There was also the shu (a word meaning fraction) at one-sixteenth of the ryo.

Ryal of Edward IV (1464–70)

S

SAIGA Thickish small coin of the *Merovingians, of apparently varying weight and value. There are many issues, the most notable perhaps for Charles Martell (A.D. 685–741) at Arles and Marseilles.

ST ALBANSGULDEN Gold coins struck at the abbey of St Alban, Mainz, from the 14th to the 16th century. Only one carries a date (1584), and has a special reverse type (angel with the arms of the abbey). The usual reverse is a shield, with a wheel in an enclosure. The obverse type is always St Martin on a horse.

ST ANDREWS Scotland's only ecclesiastical mint, active for Bishop Kennedy from 1452 onwards. The coins show an orb surmounted by a cross, which device is also found on the mace and other objects of St Salvator's College there. Prior to recent researches, these coins were sometimes assigned to Crossraguel Abbey on the west coast of Scotland, owing to a find of them there; but there is no evidence that the abbot there ever enjoyed coinage rights. Bishop Kennedy's right to coinage, however, is established by a royal charter of James II; the pennies are, moreover, more often found in eastern than western Scotland. Three main types are known.

SAINT-GAUDENS, AUGUSTUS (1848–1907) Great American sculptor, born in Dublin of French-Irish parents (his mother was a Guinness). The family emigrated to the USA while Saint-Gaudens was in his infancy and, after some months in Boston, settled in New York. By the mid-80s, Saint-Gaudens had established himself as the most celebrated of all American sculptors, chiefly through monumental work (e.g. statues of Sherman and Lincoln). His medallic output was small but distinguished (Columbus Medal, Chicago Exhibition 1892); his numismatic fame rests mainly on the $20 gold piece which bears his name, commissioned by President Theodore Roosevelt himself in an unprecedented, direct, presidential initiative as regards coin design. Saint-Gaudens also designed the $10 piece (Indian head eagle); both pieces were first issued during the year he died, 1907, and continued to be struck for more than 20 years thereafter.

ST PATRICK'S TOKENS Halfpennies and farthings brought to America by the Irish immigrant Mark Newby in 1671 and accepted by the General Assembly of the then colony of New Jersey as an official circulating medium. The pieces are of good copper; there is also a very rare farthing of silver. Most probably, they were struck in Dublin, but this is uncertain both as regards the artist and the minting establishment. (The American numismatist Don Taxey has suggested that the original dies may have been made by *Briot as early as the 1640s for a Civil War coinage.) The piece takes its name from the effigy of the Irish saint shown preaching on the obverse. The reverse shows a kneeling Irish king, playing the harp with a crown above. Among the many varieties, perhaps the most interesting is that which has a small brass plug inserted, making the crown seem to be of gold.

ST PETERSBURG   Little more than a village at the beginning of the 18th century, this was developed by Peter the Great of Russia and designated his capital from 1712 onwards. (It remained Russia's capital city until 1922.) From 1718 onwards it also superseded Moscow as Russia's principal mint; it was here that the country's first edge-engraved coins were struck, and here that *Boulton erected an entirely new building with the most up-to-date machinery at the turn of the 18th/19th centuries, some ten years before London was to have similarly modern facilities. Today, though Moscow is once more Russia's capital, the mint in Leningrad (as it is now called) remains Russia's state mint.

SAINT-URBAIN, FERDINAND DE (1658–1738)   French coin and medal engraver, born in Lorraine, where he was trained and first worked at the mint of Nancy. At an early age he was called to the papal mint in Bologna, and from 1683 worked at Rome for successive popes from Clement X to Clement XI in 1704. Apart from cutting many coin dies, he is also known for a fine series of papal medals, and another featuring the dukes and duchesses of Lorraine; in these, done during his later years (after his return to Nancy from Rome), he was much assisted by his son Claude Auguste (1703–61).

SALT MONEY   A form of primitive currency. Salt being a biological necessity in man's diet, it has always been prized as a medium of exchange. In its simplest form, such exchange took place merely by weight (e.g. in sacks); but it has also been pressed into bars (rectangular or cylindrical). Its most extensive use has been in Africa, especially Ethiopia, but it has also been known in Asia (Burma and Borneo). One cannot speak of ''denominations'' here; its value has fluctuated widely, sometimes even seasonally.

SALUT D'OR   One of the earliest gold coins of medieval Europe, first struck by Charles I of Anjou for Naples *c.* 1276, and continued under his successor Charles II. In both these, the Salutation of the Virgin by Archangel Gabriel is shown in full-length figures. When the type was taken up later by Henry V and Henry VI as part of the *Anglo-Gallic coinage, the figures appear in half-length only, above the shields of France and England.

Salut d'Or: Anglo-Gallic type of Henry VI, *c.* 1430

SALVATORTHALER   A fine Swedish Thaler type, struck under rulers there from 1542 to 1653: the obverse depicts the King; the reverse shows the figure of Christ with the legend SALVATOR MUNDI ADIUVA (or SALVA) NOS. Halves and quarters are also known for certain dates.

SALZBURG   Among ecclesiastical coinages, only the Papacy has exceeded that of the archbishopric of Salzburg in length and splendour. The series extends for nine centuries (the mint right was granted in A.D. 996 under Emperor Otto III) to the secularisation of 1803. From the Renaissance onwards, there is an uninterrupted series of magnificent gold, often multiple ducats in value up to 50. For special occasions, these were struck both round and as *Klippen (e.g. dedication of Salzburg cathedral under Archbishop Paris Lodron in 1628, type showing two saints carrying the cathedral, of which no less than thirteen are listed in values ranging from 3 to 20 ducats). The Thaler series is equally impressive. The expulsion of Protestants from Salzburg under Archbishop Leopold Anthony during the years 1731–3 gave rise to a great number of interesting medals, not least in countries where these 20,000 were welcomed (e.g. Prussia and the Netherlands).

SAMPIETRINO   Copper coin of the Papacy to the value of 2½ baiocchi; struck between 1795–9 at a great number of mints in the Papal States under Pius VI and showing St Peter's head in profile on the obverse, and the value in three lines across the reverse.

SANESE D'ORO   The principal gold coin of Sienna (N. Italy), struck from 1340 to the precise weight and fineness of its Florentine equivalent. A large ornamental initial S takes up the whole of the obverse, while the reverse shows a cross. This continued until 1553 (no change even while the city was occupied by Charles V).

SAN FRANCISCO   The gold rush of 1848 led to a great number of private gold issues here, until a mint was opened in 1854 (mintmark S). These will be found described under the names of their issuers: *Baldwin, Dubosq, Humbert, Moffat among others. An Assay Office under Augustus Humbert preceded the actual mint by two years; here large octagonal ingots were marked with actual fineness (e.g. .880, .887) before exact .900 standard was finally established. San Francisco remained active as a United States mint until 1955, and then resumed striking ten years later, chiefly for the many *proof sets now required by collectors. The old mint building of 1874 is today a museum of earlier coining history, especially gold rush days.

SANTA FÉ DE BOGOTÁ   This Spanish-American mint was established in 1626 as the result of an agreement between Philip III and D. Alvaro Turrillo de Yerba, who offered to establish a mint at his own expense in Cartagena (1620). No coins struck there appear to have survived; the mint is known to have been transferred to Bogotá by 1626, the earliest dated coin known being of the year 1627.

A remarkable feature of this mint established by private initiative is that it was the first in the New World to be authorised to strike gold. The first such coin to survive is the 2 *escudos of 1633. This anticipates other Spanish-American gold coinages by nearly fifty years (*Mexico City). Copper was never struck here. The mintmark has been, at various times, NR (Nuevo Reino), B, Ba and BOGOTA spelt out in full.

The varied fortunes of the country first named by the Spaniards Nuevo Reino de Granada may be followed after the Spaniards' withdrawal (1813) at the mint of Bogotá. What we know today as the Republic of Colombia appears first on Bogotá coins as República de la Nueva Granada, becoming successively Confederación Granadina, Estados Unidos de la Nueva Granada, Estados Unidos de Colombia and finally República de Colombia.

SANTIAGO DE CHILE   Representations to establish a mint here were made by the local authorities from the late 17th century onwards, but it was not authorised until 1743 and then only because certain individuals undertook to bear the entire cost. (It remained private property until 1772, when all such mints became Crown property.)

Gold is known from 1749 (8 and 4 escudos) and silver from 1751 (8 reales). The royal bust appears on all denominations from 1773. Copper was not struck here, nor was *cob money, all issues from the earliest being of round, well-struck types. The mintmark is S, sometimes with a small circle above the letter.

SANTIMS   Smallest coin unit of the Latvian Republic from 1922–39: 100 santims = 1 lats in the decimal system of that country. Struck also in denominations of 2, 5, 10, 20 and 50 (the last three in nickel, the smaller denominations in bronze). Distinguished in design and execution, in the best traditions of the famous *Riga Mint.

SANTO DOMINGO The second mint of the New World, opened by the Spaniards on the island of Santo Domingo (today divided into Haiti and the Dominican Republic) very soon after the one at Mexico City. An edict of 1542 mentions—besides the more common denominations of ½, 2 and 4 reales—unusual ones to the value of 5 and 10. Of these, only the 10-real piece appears to have been struck (at any rate, none of the 5 reales has been found); it is among the great rarities of numismatics and often referred to as "the first crown piece of the New World". Its silver content and value corresponded exactly to that of the Spanish *escudo.

SAN TOMÉ (THOMÉ) Gold coin of Portuguese India, struck from 1545 at Diu and Goa; the type is named after the figure of the standing saint on the obverse. The main reverse type of the coin (struck until well into the 18th century) shows the Portuguese shield of arms, but there are variants with a ship or a cross of Jerusalem. Weight and fineness vary also, owing to primitive local mints.

SAN VINCENTE Portuguese gold coin first struck in 1556, the obverse showing the standing figure of the saint, holding a ship and palm to symbolise Portuguese discoveries, together with the inscription ZELATOR FIDEI USQUE AD MORTEM—a reminder of the title "zelator fidei", given to King John III by Pope Paul III for his support of the Inquisition. The reverse shows the Portuguese coat of arms. The type was continued under Sebastian (1557–78) with modifications; a half was also struck.

San Vincente, John III, 1521–57

SAPÈQUE *dong.

SARDES Believed to have been one of the earliest mints of Lydia striking an *electrum coinage; certainly a mint under Croesus and later Persian kings for gold coinage.

SARRAZZINO A gold coin of the Crusaders, copied from the Arab *dinar, but with Cufic script, and with inscriptions as "propaganda" for the Christian cause. They often bore a small cross in the centre.

SASSANIAN COINS Persian dynasty of A.D. 226–641. The rulers throughout struck a rather thin coin on a broad flan, showing on the obverse usually a bust of the King, and on the reverse two priests at a fire altar. At first naturalistic in the Greek and Roman portraiture tradition, the coins became more and more abstract through the centuries—even more so when the coinage was continued, after the fall of the dynasty, under Arabian suzerainty. Recent research has made the series accessible to average collectors for the first time; it is particularly attractive to those wishing to delve deeper into as yet unsolved problems concerning date sequences and mints.

Obverses of Sassanian silver drachms

SATIRICAL COINS AND MEDALS The former are exceedingly scarce and are generally accidental rather than deliberate (certain testons of Francis I might be deemed portrait caricatures, but this is due to the incompetence of local die cutters at provincial mints rather than anything else). The great period of the satirical medal is the Baroque, Christian *Wermuth being its master and producing sometimes quite scatological comments on everything from peace (so-called) signed with Louis XIV, to the financial adventures of John *Law. Smeltzing and *Dadler were other noted medallists that practised the genre. In the 20th century, it was revived by Karl Goetz of Munich. It is an oddity of numismatic history that Bonaparte, a favourite subject of printed satire and caricature, never appears mocked in metal (though Napoleon III, after the fiasco of Sedan, does).

SAXONY Numismatically important German state, today forming part of East Germany, with a mint at Dresden. Complicated by many minor earldoms, etc., from the 16th century onwards (e.g. Sachsen-Coburg, Sachsen-Eisenach) most of which also struck coins. The "main line", however, was that of the Electorate from 1547, which became a kingdom in 1806 and as such continued to mint until 1918. The great period of Saxon coins and medals is the Baroque, beginning with Sebastian *Dadler and ending with Christian *Wermuth, who worked for both Dresden and *Gotha. Much splendid gold was struck under Frederick Augustus "The Strong" (1694–1733) of Meissen porcelain fame. The series is also notable for its many *Klippen and *shooting Thalers.

S.C. "Senatus consulto"—by decree of the Senate. The letters appear on the base metal coins of imperial Rome. The Senate was responsible for their striking; the Emperor had responsibility for precious metals.

SCARBOROUGH This town issued by far the most extensive series of siege coins during the English Civil War, with many odd values such as 5s. 8d., 2s. 4d., 1s. 9d., 7 pence, etc., all of which are very rare. There are no denominations in the usual sense: the pieces were roughly cut, weighed, and stamped with the intrinsic value of the silver content (1644–5).

SCEAT (pl. SCEATTA) Name given to the Anglo-Saxon coins of England after the departure of the Romans and before the adoption of the silver penny, *c.* 650–770 A.D. They were originally of base silver but later degenerated into copper. Stylistically, these small pieces present much interest, since they combine Roman-Byzantine models with Germano-Celtic symbols, a mixture not found elsewhere. The above remarks apply to southern England only: in the north—where the sceat was the circulating medium both of the kings of Northumberland and the archbishops of York—they were of a simple cross or pellet type, with circular inscriptions giving the name of the ruler (obverse) and the moneyer (reverse).

SCELLINO Word derived from shilling, this has been the Somalian currency unit since 1962, struck as a coin since 1967 in the decimal system of that country (1 scellino = 100 centesimi).

SCHAFFHAUSEN Town which is the capital of the Swiss canton of the same name, and with the mint-right dating from 1333. There are even *bracteates of an abbey there dating from a century before this, but the main period of production falls in the 15th–17th centuries. The arms show a prancing chamois. Very rare gold ducats were struck only towards the end of Schaffhausen's coinage period; there is an exceedingly rare 20-ducat multiple of 1656 with the obverse type showing a chamois jumping out from the city gate. Smaller silver denominations (e.g. "oertli" or quarter-Thalers) predominate. A brief postscript to the town's coinage history occurs during 1808–9 when *Batzen and their halves, as well as 1-Kreuzer pieces, were struck in its name at the Berne Mint.

SCHEGA, FRANZ ANDREAS (1711–87) Rococo coin engraver and medallist, die engraver at Munich Mint from 1738 and from 1751–74 official Court Medallist to Bavarian rulers (who were also Electors of the Palatinate). Much admired, even by *Hedlinger, the greatest of his older contemporaries who

Scarborough siege piece

Sceat with runic inscriptions, 8th century

dubbed him "first among Europe's die cutters". His signature appears sometimes in full, sometimes as initials.

SCHLÖSSER, E. Mint warden at Hanover, where he published in 1883 his book *Die Münztechnik* (Coining Technique), which still remains the standard manual. With over a hundred detailed drawings, Schlösser describes all that goes on in a modern mint, from the alloying of metals to the final inspection and sorting of coins.

SCHLÖZER, AUGUST LUDWIG VON (1735–1809) Eminent German philosopher and historian, who spent many years in Russia and published an invaluable survey of the Russian monetary system in 1791. It remains our chief source of knowledge for economic and mining background to Russian coinage since Peter the Great, as well as going into early paper money history from 1762 under Catherine the Great.

SCHRÖTTER, FRIEDRICH FREIHERR VON (1862–1944) German numismatist and keeper of Berlin Coin Cabinet from 1927. Apart from standard surveys of Brandenburg and Prussian coinages, Schrötter is famous as the editor of *Wörterbuch der Münzkunde* which, nearly fifty years after its appearance in 1930, still remains unrivalled for range and depth of scholarly detail. The illustrations do not live up to the quality of text, however.

SCHULTZ & CO. Established at San Francisco in 1851, this was principally a brass foundry and die-sinking establishment; and it is believed that most of the dies for private gold coinages after this year (except those of *Moffat & Co) were made here. The firm also struck one $5 piece on its own account, the engraver managing to mis-spell the name SHULTS.

SCHWARZ, HANS (c. 1492–?) Greatest among the German school of Renaissance medallists, this artist was born at Augsburg and was active from *c.* 1521–32. All his medals are cast from models carved in wood. The original carving for what is perhaps his most celebrated medal—that of his fellow-artist Albrecht Dürer, signed and dated 1520 and belonging to the days when he worked at Nüremberg—is still extant and today preserved at the Braunschweig Museum. Schwarz became widely famous during 1518, the year of the Diet of Augsburg, when he modelled no less than twenty-five portraits of local citizens and notable visitors attending this event. To the best of our knowledge, he never cut any coin dies, but certain medallic Thalers (e.g. Salzburg 1521) are based on models of his. Among the most famous of his sitters were the Emperor Maximilian, George Duke of Saxony, Hans Burgkmair and the merchant banker Jakob Fugger.

SCHWYZ One of the three original cantons of Switzerland, with its own coinage from 1424, continuing with intervals until 1848. A gold ducat of the early 17th century, showing St Martin with a beggar on horseback on the obverse and the Madonna on the reverse, is particularly fine. Later types show a lion holding a shield with the cantonal arms.

SCOT, ROBERT (d. 1823) Chief engraver to the Philadelphia Mint almost from its beginnings in 1793 until his death. He was of English birth but had certainly settled in America at an early age, for by 1781, as a watch engraver in Philadelphia, he already advertised himself as "late engraver to the State of Virginia". At the mint, he succeeded Joseph Wright, who had been the first engraver there but died of yellow fever within a few weeks of his appointment. There is still controversy about Scot's ability, and as to which of the early USA coinages he actually engraved, since neither Wright nor Scot signed any dies.

SCOTLAND Scottish coin issues began with the silver pennies

A group of Scottish coins:

William the Lion
(1165-1214)

Robert II (1371-90)

Robert III (1390-1406)

James III (1460-88)

James V (1513-42)

of David I (1124–53), which were derived from English types. A more specifically Scottish design was first used under William I (the Lion), showing a profile portrait and struck at Edinburgh. Its French legend, LE REI WILLAME, was to remain unique. The first *groats and the first gold piece (noble) are again derived from English types (David II, 1329–71). A more original gold coin followed in the shape of the *lion (or *St Andrew) under Robert III (1390–1406). More gold types (*rider and *unicorn) appeared during the late 15th century, and also the *plack, a *billon coin. Under James V (1513–42), the *bawbee was introduced, as well as Scotland's first dated coin (1539)—a gold ducat commonly called a *bonnet piece after its obverse type. The coinages of Mary Queen of Scots and her son James VI, from 1542 to 1603, are especially profuse: no fewer than five separate issues under the former and eight under the latter, with many gold types under James. The gold *unite celebrated Scotland's union with England in 1604, and Edinburgh continued to strike coins until 1709. A number of local mints had been active during the medieval period, but none coined gold and only Stirling remained open after James III's reign, to strike a rare issue for Mary.

The numismatic history of Scotland does not end with coins: it is rich in medals from the 16th to the end of the 18th century, the Old and Young Pretender series from their exile days being particularly noteworthy. Paper money began to be signed by the Bank of Scotland in 1696, while the Royal Bank of Scotland has the distinction of having brought out the first three-colour note in the British Isles (a guinea note of 1777, with words in blue and the King's head in red). As an interesting sidelight for those who collect series by denominations, it should be noted that the National Bank of Scotland issued guinea notes until 1833, although the last gold coin to this value had been struck for general circulation in 1799 (the "military" guinea of 1813 being a very limited issue for troops).

SCREW-PRESS Invented soon after the printing-press, i.e. towards the end of the 15th century, the screw-press at first made only little progress against the hammered coinage as struck since ancient Greek times. The invention is usually credited to the Italian architect Bramante, whose likeness by *Caradosso is probably one of the earliest machine-struck medals. It is obvious from Cellini's *Treatise on Goldsmithing* that by the mid-16th century the screw-press was well known in Italy, but all attempts to introduce it for regular coinage on a permanent basis failed until a century later (France 1640, England 1662). Yet even early experimental efforts, such as Cellini's own *testone of Duke Alessandro of Florence (1633), the Paris *Moulin strikings from 1552 and *Meystrell's "milled" issues for Queen Elizabeth of England a decade later, showed clearly that this invention must sooner or later supersede older and cruder methods. The situation was certainly complicated by the almost simultaneous invention of the *roller-press, preferred throughout Habsburg and Spanish territories until the beginning of the 18th century.

SCRIPULUM The English "scruple", i.e. a tiny weight which was in Roman coinage mainly a money of *account, being equal to one-twenty-fourth of an ounce. A gold piece to the value of 1½ scripula was struck under the Emperor Valentinian I (A.D. 364–75).

SCUDO Italian for a shield, and originally any gold or silver denominations with an heraldic device on the reverse. The gold coin soon began to lose its importance (except for multiple scudi struck for presentation purposes); and gradually, during the course of the 16th century, the silver scudo became the Italian equivalent of the Thaler, i.e. the principal large silver coin, irrespective of the design on the reverse. Scudi are known from, among other Italian towns and principalities, Ancona, Bergamo, Bologna, Florence, Genoa, Mantua, Milan, Modena, Turin and Venice. The series of papal scudi extends over 250 years from the mid-16th century onwards. Outside Italy, the scudo is found in Ragusa (Dalmatia) and Malta among other places.

SCYPHATE   The term is derived from scyphus, meaning a cup, and is applied to concave coins which began to be struck in the Byzantine series during the 10th century. The habit spread to neighbouring states and as far as Cyprus. Though the most notable series is that of the gold *nomisma, there are also scyphates in electrum, silver and copper. The reasons for adopting this peculiar technique of striking coins remain obscure. Professor Grierson *(Numismatic Chronicle,* 1971) has queried the wide generic use of this term, pointing out that *nummi scyphati* were before the mid-11th century a clearly defined category of gold coin, and suggesting the use of the word concave (or the Greek word *trachy*) in the wider context.

Gold scyphate coin of Michael VII, 1071–8

SEAL   The same artists who engraved gems and coins were often responsible also for a ruler's seals. In England, Thomas *Simon and Thomas *Wyon are notable examples. The study of seals, as that of heraldry, is so closely related to that of numismatics as to be almost indispensable. Indeed, what may be called the very earliest numismatic documents to have come down to us are Babylonian cylinder seals. Impressed by rolling on a soft clay tablet, they were used to sign debtors' notes and other banking transactions as well as to attest ownership.

SEDE VACANTE   A term used to describe any coinage issued during an interregnum between the death of one ecclesiastical ruler and the appointment of his successor. While there are quite a number of these in various European episcopal series, by far the most important and extensive are the sede vacante coins of the Popes, which always carry the arms of the papal chamberlain. The first of these dates back to the late 13th century, and they become a regular feature of papal coinage soon after 1500, continuing to the present day. In Germany, the Electors of the Palatinate and Saxony fulfilled much the same function upon the death of an emperor, for northern and southern Germany respectively. (*Vicariatsthaler.)

SEIGNEURAGE   A fee on coinage belonging to the ruler. In normal times, it has been a very small proportion to the coinage; but monarchs like Henry VIII vastly increased their revenue by the expedient of debasing the coinage and pocketing the difference between nominal and real value of coin. In France, seigneurage was abolished from the time of Francis I's coinage reforms (1540) onwards: the French monarchs made good its loss by high regular taxation.

SEMIS   In early Roman republican coinage, one half of the *as. The obverse of this cast bronze coin shows the head of Jupiter, the reverse the prow of a galley and the letter S. In the later Roman imperial coinage, the semis was, first, half of the *aureus, and later of the *solidus (though for the latter, the late Latin word *semissis* is more commonly used).

SEMISSIS   *semis.

SEMUNCIA   One half of the *uncia in the *aes grave series of early Roman coinage.

SEN   The principal copper coin of Japan, introduced in 708 A.D. in imitation of the Chinese *cash, i.e. a round coin, cast not struck, and with a square centre hole. Production ceased in the 10th century, and until the 16th century imported Chinese pieces circulated freely. Beginning in 1636, the locally cast sen was reintroduced; it now consisted of two-thirds copper and one-third pewter. Later alloys varied, with a preponderance of iron during the 19th century. When a European-style decimal coinage was introduced in 1871, the sen remained a currency unit as the 100th part of a *yen, and now of pure copper.

SENT Fairly obviously derived from *cent, this was the smallest denomination of the reformed Estonian coinage introduced in 1929, with 100 senti equal to 1 kroon. The single unit was struck (in bronze) during 1929 and 1939 only; but at various times there were multiples of 2, 5, 10, 25 and 50 senti.

SEQUENCE MARKS A feature of Roman denarii during the 1st century B.C. in particular, most probably (hence their name) concerned with some sort of output control of the mint and/or different *officinae. It is also possible that they were used to give a detailed check on the life of each particular die (cf. the series of *die-numbered coins in late Victorian England). Because of their complexity, they have never yet been properly classified, but fall into various groups such as letters of the Greek or Roman alphabet, besides Roman numerals and symbols. Sometimes they appear singly, sometimes in combinations on the obverse or the reverse or even both. Of a single coinage in 89 B.C., that of L. Calpurnius Piso, it has been calculated that more than 10,000 die varieties exist. This enormous number gives some idea as to the scale on which Roman coinage was struck during the years of civil strife—and possibly also as to the poor quality of the dies. For the collector it is a subject for study which makes modern date-collecting seem altogether elementary.

SEQUIN English colloquial form of *zecchino, and for the equivalent gold coins of the Ottoman Empire.

SERINGAPATAM A mint in Mysore, India, which was especially active during the rule of Tipu Sultan (1782–99).

SERRATED COINS Coins with indented or "nicked" edges. They were first seen just before the turn of the 2nd century B.C. and became fairly regular in certain Roman series after 117 B.C. Their precise purpose has not been documented. Possibly they were meant to circulate among foreign tribes (Celts), who might attach to them a religious significance similar to that of their own serrated ring-amulets. The suggestion that they were issued for the purpose of making the detection of debased silver more difficult does not hold up in view of the fact that many of the serrated coins are, like others of the same period, only silver-plated.

SESINO An Italian coin of copper or *billon, to the value of 6 denarii or half a *soldo, issued in a number of principalities until towards the end of the 18th century. It was first struck in Genoa during the 14th century, with Milan and Perugia following soon after. Papal sesini were struck at the Avignon Mint during the rule of Urban V (1364) and Gregory XI (1371), and at Parma under Paul III (1535 and 1544).

SESTERTIUS This coin was an infrequent silver denomination in the early Roman republican series, equal to a quarter-*denarius. Later, and tariffed at the same value, it became the principal bronze coin of the Roman Empire from Augustus onwards. These coins, with their large *flans, allowed much variety of artistic expression and have therefore always been coveted among collectors. This artistry is at its best and most varied during the 1st and 2nd centuries A.D. None of these coins

Sestertius of Claudius

Double sestertius of Trajan Decius

is cheap, and all with a good *patina command high premiums.

SESTINO   A *billon piece to the value of one-sixth of the
*tornese, introduced during 1498 into the coinage of Naples
under Ferdinand III of Aragon. It was taken up by Louis XII of
France during his brief occupation of the city in 1502–3, when it
was struck in pure copper.

SEVEN SHILLING PIECE   *third guinea.

SEXTANS   One-sixth of an *as in the cast bronze coinage of
early republican Rome. The obverse shows the head of Mercury,
with the prow of a galley as the reverse. Two large dots on each
side of the coin indicate its weight of two *uncia.

SHAKI   The smallest silver denomination of Persia from the
late 16th to the 19th centuries. It was valued at 10 *kazbegi.

SHEKEL   Originally a Jewish weight (1/3,000th of the *talent),
the shekel was struck as a silver coin from the time of Simon Mac-
cabeus (143–135 B.C.). The rarest and most sought-after issues
are those of the First and Second Jewish Revolts (A.D. 66–70 and
A.D. 132–5 respectively). In Phoenicia, and more particularly in
the city of Sidon, the shekel had been adopted as a coin already
in the late 4th century B.C. Here a double shekel was also struck,
and fractions as low as one-sixteenth, all in silver.

Shekels of the First Revolt

SHERRITT PRIVATE MINT   Established in Fort Saskatchewan,
Canada, in 1968, this mint has since then struck all Syria's
coinage. Its mintmark consists of a hexagon with a line across the
centre.

SHIELD NICKEL   Issue of the nickel was authorised by an act
of May 1866, as a companion piece to the nickel *three cent piece
introduced just over a year earlier. Originally approved as a
substitute for the *half-dime during the period following the Civil
War when all payments in gold and silver were suspended, the
issue ultimately brought on the demise of the silver coin.

There are two shield nickel designs, both the work of the US
Mint's chief engraver at that time, James B. Longacre. The
obverse is the same in both cases, showing the US shield with IN
GOD WE TRUST above and the date below. The reverse has a
large 5 surrounded by stars, interspersed with rays in certain 1867
issues. The coins were struck only at the Philadelphia Mint.

SHILLING   The silver shilling has been regularly struck as part
of the English series since introduced by Henry VII in 1504. It is
arguable that the first shilling remains the finest artistically, with
the splendid profile bust of the King by Alexander *Bruchsal. In
Scotland, where the shilling was introduced about half a century
later, the series is notable for the large variety of multiples struck.
These include, at various times, pieces of 2, 3, 4, 5, 6, 8, 10, 12,
16, 20, 22, 30, 40, 44, 48 and 60 shillings.

SHOOTING COINS AND MEDALS   Shooting festivals and
competitions have always been popular in Germany and
Switzerland, and a wide variety of pieces commemorate these
events. The collector should be careful to distinguish between
official and unofficial issues, the latter being far more numerous
and of much less value. As always, official commemorative
Thalers struck as currency in limited quantities take pride of
place. Occasional strikings in gold will command very high prices
indeed.

SHORT-CROSS PENNY   This type of English penny was
introduced by Henry II in 1180; the angles of the cross stop short
of the circular *legend surrounding the coin. The type was continued under Richard I, John and Henry III until 1247, when it
was superseded by the *long-cross penny. It is notable that the

Short-cross Penny: Early type
of Henry II, *c.* 1180–89

legend read "Henricus" even during the reigns of two monarchs whose names were quite different; a classification is therefore by no means simple.

SHREWSBURY   The first of the Civil War mints to be opened on behalf of Charles I by Thomas Bushell, previously in charge of the Aberystwyth Mint. Bushell took with him his mintmark of a Welsh plume and struck here, during 1642 only, silver pounds, half-pounds, crowns, half-crowns and shillings. At first certain obverses were struck with Aberystwyth dies; but all show the reverse *declaration type, also adopted at the Oxford Mint.

SHU   *ryo.

SICCA RUPEE   A popular name for the *rupee struck by the East India Company in its Bengal principality from 1773–1818, always with the same regnal year A.H. 1202, and always with the Murshidabad mint name, though often struck at other mints (e.g. Calcutta). The long life and constant type of this coin caused it to be called "sicca", i.e. current and acceptable everywhere.

SICILY   The numismatic history of this Mediterranean island has been dominated by the splendour of its ancient coinages, generally reckoned to be among the finest of the Greek world (*Acragas, Naxos, Syracuse). Yet it is worth pointing out, however briefly, that there are important Byzantine and Arabic issues later; that the Emperor Frederick II held court here in the early 13th century when he issued the decree which led to the *augustalis; and that under the Angevin and Aragonese kings of Naples and Sicily many important and fine coins were also struck. The Palermo museum conserves a good cross-section of this varied numismatic history.

Fatimid gold quarter-dinar, struck during the island's Arabic occupation, *c.* 1000

Copper tornese, for Victor Amadeus, 1717, while Sicily was part of the kingdom of Savoy

SICYON   Mint in the northern Peloponnese, close to the Gulf of Corinth. Coins were struck here during the 5th century B.C., the main type being a chimera (obverse) and a flying dove within a wreath (reverse). From *c.* 330 B.C. it ceased to issue independent types and struck coins for the ever-expanding empire of Alexander the Great.

SIDON The most important seaport of ancient Phoenicia, with trade and consequently coinage to match from the late 5th century B.C. onwards. It adopted a curious mixed type in that it used the Jewish *shekel as a weight-standard yet copied its design, at any rate on the reverse, from Persian models. A war galley is the prevalent obverse type. From 333 B.C. Alexandrian type *tetradrachms were struck here under Ptolemaic and Seleucid rulers. Interesting and varied bronze coinage continued well into the 2nd century A.D.

Sidon (Phoenicia): 2 shekels, late 4th century B.C.

SIEGE PIECES These form part of the general category of *emergency money, and may relate to either the besieged or the besiegers. The variety of metals and other substances (including leather, wood and cardboard) which have been used in such circumstances is only rivalled by the many irregular shapes and sizes which this type of emergency coinage displays. Metal, so long as it lasted, might include anything from church plate to church bells. The collector of purely English issues will find nothing here except some Civil War issues of Charles I's reign: exceedingly rare gold of Colchester and Pontefract, and silver of Carlisle, Newark, Pontefract and Scarborough. Nothing here is easy or cheap to come by, the Newark pieces being the least scarce. For other collectors there is much more: over 250 besieged towns in the Netherlands alone issued various kinds of emergency coins. A prize piece in any collection devoted to papal coinage would be anything struck by Pope Clement VII during the Sack of Rome (1525–7) at the Castell San Angelo. Because of their irregular shape, rough methods of manufacture and largely indeterminate metals and weight standards, siege coins lend themselves particularly well to forgery. Experience is the only guide and caution must be the watchword when buying from anyone except a dealer of international repute.

SIEGESTHALER Sieg is the German word for victory, and the term is therefore applied to large commemorative coins struck in celebration of famous battles won. The first is probably that of the 1546 retreat of the Schmalkaldian League before the forces of the Emperor Charles V, and there have been many examples since.

SIENNA Town in northern Italy and the seat of an important coinage since the days of Charlemagne. The main type was a large, decorative initial S on the obverse and a cross on the reverse. A gold piece of this type, to the same weight and standard as the gold florin, was struck from 1340. The mint closed in 1555.

SIERRA LEONE The coinage of Sierra Leone—or rather that of the independent Sierra Leone Company formed in 1791—deserves mention as the first British attempt at decimalisation. These issues are also notable for their fine design and technical excellence, both due to Matthew *Boulton and his *Soho Mint in Birmingham. There are silver denominations of $1, 50 cents, 20 cents and 10 cents, and copper ones of 10 cents and 1 penny (the latter most probably struck not for circulation, but for presentation to the company's English shareholders). All show a crouching lion ready to spring on the obverse, and clasped hands on the reverse. The fine criss-cross lines on one hand make it clear that it is meant to be dark. Coins are dated either 1791 or 1796 (in one instance, the 10-cent piece, also 1805).

SIGLOS The silver coin of ancient Persia from the 5th to the 4th centuries B.C. It was tariffed at one-twentieth of the gold *daric and is of similar type, showing the King as an archer. It

Siliqua: Type struck under
Magnus Maximus, A.D. 383-8

was last struck under Darius III (337–330 B.C.) prior to his defeat by Alexander the Great.

SILIQUA A silver coin to the value of one-twenty-fourth of the *solidus, introduced by Constantine the Great in A.D. 323. It was struck in large quantities until the reign of Heraclius, when—doubtless owing to the continual devaluation of the currency—it was largely superseded by the *hexagram. Large hoards of siliquae have been found in England.

SILVER Until comparatively recently, silver was by far the most important of the world's coinage metals. Except at the very beginning of coinage history, when electrum and gold were used, silver was the chief currency medium of the ancient world, both Greek and Roman. The Byzantine and Arab worlds see a resurgence of gold; but then again, from the time of Charlemagne onwards, silver takes over almost entirely for nearly 500 years. Silver and gold seem to go hand in hand from the late Middle Ages onwards and continued to do so until world shortages of this metal caused an almost universal substitution of cupro-nickel during the 1940s and 1950s.

From the collector's point of view, the large silver pieces—crown, scudo, Thaler—are by far the most attractive. Coinage is a miniature art, which does not mean that one wants to employ a microscope to appreciate its beauties. Large gold pieces (in any case most often struck for presentation rather than as genuine currency) are comparatively rare and today hideously dear as well. So, of course, are the large silver *decadrachms of ancient Syracuse on the few occasions that they are offered for sale. But other silver pieces of similar size if not quite similar beauty may still be had for a fraction of what one would pay for antique works of art of like quality (e.g. Renaissance bronzes or ivories). A silver *pattern of Elizabeth I has almost the delicacy of a Hilliard miniature—and may well be, although unsigned, from his hand. Yet its cost is still ludicrously low in comparison.

SILVER RIDER *ducatoon.

SIMON, ABRAHAM (c. 1617–?) Elder brother of Thomas Simon and an extremely skilled wax modeller who was almost certainly the inspiration behind many of Thomas's finest medals. For a time he was in the service of Queen Christina of Sweden; his English work dates mainly from the Civil War and Cromwellian periods. Possibly because of this, he seems to have fallen into disfavour soon after the Restoration, the last known work by him being dated 1662.

SIMON, THOMAS (c. 1618–65) By common consent, the greatest of English coin and medal engravers. He was almost certainly a pupil of Nicolas *Briot, but already at an early age showed independent mastery (Scottish Rebellion Medal, 1639). From 1645 onwards, he appears to have worked solely for the Parliamentarians; by 1648 he was asked to engrave the Great Seal of the Commonwealth, and in 1649 he became chief engineer at the mint. During the next ten years, he made all the seals of England, Scotland and Ireland, almost all the coinage and medallic portraits of almost every Puritan notable. His crown piece of Cromwell as Lord Protector (1658) is only exceeded in artistic splendour and technical skill by his *Petition and *Reddite Crowns (1663). Like his elder brother, he failed to re-establish himself in favour under Charles II, despite the excellence of his workmanship.

SINOPE A town in Paphlagonia, near the southern coast of the Black Sea, and the seat of an important and extensive coinage

from *c*. 500 B.C. Its early types show an eagle's head with a dolphin beneath on the obverse, with a simple *quadratum incusum* as the reverse; later we find the head of the nymph Sinope as the obverse type, and a flying eagle with a dolphin as the reverse. These types remain constant even when the city name is replaced by that of Persian satraps during the 4th century B.C. Later still (*c*. 200 B.C.) Attic tetradrachms show the head of Sinope with a turreted crown.

SIRIES, LOUIS (c. 1686–c. 1766) A celebrated gem engraver, at first goldsmith to Louis XV, but chiefly active in Florence and Pisa, where he doubled the role of ducal curator with that of engraver and mintmaster. A catalogue listing 168 gems by him was published at Florence in 1757.

SIRMIUM A Balkan mint of the Roman Empire, open intermittently only from A.D. 320–95. Gold *solidi were struck here in fairly large quantities, especially under Constantius and Gallus (A.D. 351–64) and Theodosius (A.D. 379–95), with the mintmark SIRM.

SIXAIN The half of the *douzain, e.g. a piece to the value of 6 *deniers. As a French billon coin, it was struck only during the reigns of Louis XII and Francis I; but it appears also under Charles V of Spain in his coinage for Perpignan, and as a siege coin during the French occupation of Barcelona (1642), this time struck in copper.

SIXPENCE Introduced in 1551 as part of the reformed coinage of Edward VI, the sixpence remained until decimalisation in 1971, and was legal tender until 1980, in the absence of any new coin to take its place. Like other English "silver", it was struck in cupro-nickel from 1947. Collecting English sixpences has much to commend it, quite apart from the question of prices, which still remain reasonable even for 16th–17th century pieces. Until the *milled coinage of Charles II, this was a handsome piece, as large as the *shilling and only distinguished from it by the figures VI instead of XII beside the monarch's bust. The three-quarter facing portrait of the earliest issue under Edward VI is attractive, and unusual in English coinage. Later issues have their own interest. Thus the sixpences of the great recoinage under William III (1696–7) may be collected in a larger number of mint and other minor varieties than any other denomination, while during the reign of Victoria there is a long *die-numbered series.

SKAR A copper coin of Tibet introduced in 1908. Multiples of 2½, 5 and 7½ were also struck.

SKIDMORE, THOMAS A manufacturer of *tokens during the last decade of the 18th century, with premises in Holborn, London. Medalets would perhaps be a better word than tokens for Skidmore's productions, for he specialised in attractive "London Buildings", and sold these small pieces for profit, at considerably higher prices than their currency value.

SKILLING The Scandinavian *shilling, struck as a silver coin from about 1445 in Denmark; gradually debased, it reappeared during the 18th century as a copper coin. In Sweden, the skilling appears until the end of the 18th century only as a money of *account and does not make its appearance as a denomination until 1802, as a copper coin only. There had, however, been some half-skilling and quarter-skilling "National Debt Office" tokens from 1799 onwards. A skilling "banco" appears in 1835.

Silver sixpences of Elizabeth I, 1562, Charles I, and George V, 1930

SLOANE, SIR HANS (1660–1753) Irish physician, first to Queen Anne and later to George I. His collection of more than 32,000 coins, chiefly Greek, formed one of the biggest bequests

ever made to the British Museum. There is a fine portrait medal of him by *Dassier.

SLUG Any rough piece of metal or mineral as found in its natural, unrefined state. In the United States, it is also applied by collectors to pieces roughly cast as currency during the period of the California gold rush.

SMELTZING, JAN (1656–93) A Dutch engraver of considerable skill, born at Leyden. During his comparatively short life he made a great many medals, of which a large proportion are relevant to British history (from the Duke of Monmouth Rebellion 1685 onwards).

S.M.V. Abbreviations for Standard Mint Value. These initials occur frequently on coins struck by private mints in San Francisco during the period of the gold rush (1848–52), to imply that the gold content was in accordance with standards as officially laid down.

SNOWDEN, JAMES ROSS Ninth director of the United States Mint at Philadelphia, from 1853–61. Snowden's tenure of the office was notable for some experiments with "German silver" (an alloy of copper, nickel and zinc), the first publication concerning the mint's own collections (under the title *The Mint Manual of the Coins of All Nations*) and, less savoury, the restriking of some rare coins and patterns. Even this, however, had the honest purpose of augmenting the modest sums allowed to Snowden to augment the mint's collection of Washington Medals, on which he was later also to publish a catalogue.

SOHO MINT Name given by Matthew *Boulton to the coining establishment which he ran in Birmingham from 1786 until his death in 1809. This was the first mint in which the coin-presses were operated by steam power, and James Watt was Boulton's technical partner in the enterprise. Despite the great advantages both as regards the quality of the coining and the economy of running costs, it was not until the year of Boulton's death that the Royal Mint in London ordered similar equipment. Meanwhile, Boulton himself had executed contract coinages for the British government from 1797 onwards (*cartwheel twopence), and foreign coinages, too numerous to list here, from as early as 1786 (East India Company). The mint employed many of the finest coin engravers of the time; the most celebrated and prolific was probably *Küchler, to whom we owe (besides many patterns and medals) the very fine *Sierra Leone coins.

SOL, SOU A denomination with many ramifications, in France, Spain, Portugal, the Low Countries, Italy and certain Swiss cantons among others. The word is, of course, derived from the Roman *solidus, but became under the Carolingian monetary reforms the 20th part of the pound (libra), while being itself divided into 12 deniers (pennies). There were vestiges of this old system in the British system of l.s.d. But just as the Carolingian sol or sou had little to do with the Roman solidus, so does the modern sou have little to do with the Carolingian one. In almost every case, from the late 18th century onward, it became a copper coin of low value. In France, the sou is still 5 cents; and "not worth a sou" has passed into common parlance in the same way as "not worth a brass farthing". The main exception to this low-value meaning of sol or sou is the Peruvian denomination introduced in 1863 (pl. soles), struck both in silver (25 grammes weight) and gold (1.45 grammes), with gold multiples struck to the value of 2, 5, 10 and 20 soles. Here was a more or less true reversion to the old Roman original. The unit was aligned with the French 5-franc piece originally; but in 1901 the English gold standard was adopted and gold 10-soles pieces were struck to the exact value of 1 gold sovereign.

SOL AUX BALANCES A type of sol (or sou) of the French Revolution, struck during 1793, sometimes carrying that date on the reverse, and sometimes only the inscription L'AN 2 on the obverse. The name is taken from the reverse design, showing a balance behind a wreath, with a liberty cap above. It is known from at least fifteen different French mints and was also crudely copied in the French West Indies on the island of Santo Domingo. Struck in both copper and *bell metal, the latter being rare in fine condition, as the soft bronze wore quickly

SOLDO The Italian for *sol or sou. Very rare gold soldi were struck under Charlemagne (e.g. at Lucca); as a silver coin, to the value of 12 denarii, it makes its appearance first at Bologna and later at Genoa during the 13th century. During the 14th century it was taken up by Venice and very early in the 15th at Verona and Vicenza.

SOLIDUS The standard Roman gold coin as introduced by Constantine the Great and tariffed at 72 to the Roman pound (*libra). It was first struck at *Trier c. A.D. 309 and only gradually taken up by other mints over the next fifteen years. It remained a by-word for full weight and value as long as it was struck, i.e. until well into later Byzantine times. (Also *light-weight solidus, stamenon nomisma, tetarteron nomisma.

Solidus of Emperor Constantius II (A.D. 317–37)

SOMBRERETE A mint in the Mexican state of Zacatecas, which produced an independent emergency coinage from 1810–12. Although loyal to the ruler Fernando VII, General Vargas displayed no royal bust on the coins (which ranged in denomination from the 1 to 8 silver reales). Instead, they carry his own name. The smaller denominations were struck from dies, the 8-reales piece has only an obverse die with the name VARGAS and the date engraved; four small punch-marks are shown on the reverse.

SOMER ISLANDS *hog money.

Henry VII sovereign

Mary sovereign

SOOKOO, SUKU A Malay word meaning a quarter. A silver piece to the value of half a Malay dollar (i.e. 2 sookoo) was struck by the East India Company at Fort Marlborough in 1783 and 1784. It bears the number 2, the words FORT MARLBRO and the date on the obverse and a Malay inscription on the reverse.

SOOTHE, J.C. VON German 18th century numismatist who published in 1784 what still remains the most detailed catalogue of gold ducats.

SOPHIENDUKAT Struck by Sophia, wife of the Elector of Saxony, for her children at Christmas 1616, with her initials CS and the inscription WOHL DEM DER FREUDE AN SEINEN KINDERN ERLEBT (Blessed is he that rejoices in his children). The coin was regularly restruck at the Dresden Mint until 1872 (with dies often renewed) and remained a favourite baptismal gift.

SOSLING A Danish silver coin to the value of 6 pennies, introduced by Eric of Pomerania early in the 15th century.

SOU *sol.

SOU MARQUÉ The habit of marking (or, as we would say more generally in numismatics, *countermarking) small change for colonial use was a regular habit of the French government. It began in the 17th century, when old *dixains were marked with a lily. Special 2-sou pieces were struck under Louis XV, with a crowned L and three lilies as the obverse type for colonial use; and though these coins were not countermarked in any way, they were none the less known as "sous marqués".

SOUTHWARK MINT A mint in London which was open for only a short time during the final period of the reign of Henry VIII (1544–7) and the first years of Edward VI's reign. It struck debased coin in gold and silver and was closed in 1549.

SOUVERAIN D'OR A gold coin of the Netherlands, its type closely copying that of the British *sovereign of 30 shillings as struck under Mary and Elizabeth. The type continued its popularity until the late 18th century, being continually restruck not only under Spanish but later also under Austrian rule—though the coin's size was then reduced from 38 millimetres to 30 millimetres in diameter. When a Belgian national coinage was established in 1832 under Leopold I, the souverain was discontinued, but maintained itself as the sovrano in the Lombardic territories of the Austrian Empire for another twenty years.

SOVEREIGN A gold coin of this name, and to the value of 20 shillings, was introduced under Henry VII in 1489. It is of magnificent ornamental style, showing the King enthroned and holding the orb and sceptre as the obverse type, with the royal arms in the centre of the Tudor rose as the reverse. There are four main types of this coin, with varieties in the shape of the throne and the size of the shield; all are very rare. The type was continued under subsequent monarchs, with many variations, until the first coinage of James I, 1603–4. Thus, for example, Henry VIII introduced a sovereign to the value of 22s. 6d. in his second coinage of 1526. In his third coinage, he reverted to a nominal value of 20 shillings, but in fact dropped the gold standard from 23 to 20 carat. During the reign of Edward VI, sovereign gold was raised again, this time to 22 carat (at which it has remained ever since); and in 1550 a "fine", or rather heavy, sovereign to the value of 30 shillings was introduced. This was struck under Mary also, and under Elizabeth (who struck also a 20-shilling piece, called a pound to distinguish it from the sovereign). Though there were other coins to the value of 20 shillings from time to time (e.g. *broad, unite), no coin offically designated sovereign appears again until 1817. This bears no relation in type (or size) to its famous ancestor, being merely a replacement for the *guinea current since 1663. The coin has been struck by every British monarch since George III, with the splendid *Pistrucci reverse of St George and the Dragon (sometimes replaced by the royal arms). It is known, from Victoria's reign onwards, also from mints in Australia, supplemented under George V by mints in Canada, India and South Africa. Though they ceased to be legal tender during the First World War, sovereigns continue to be struck to this day. (Also *die-numbered coins.)

SOVRANO   *souverain d'or.

SPADE GUINEA   The fifth type of guinea as issued under George III from 1787–99, so called after the shield on the reverse which is pointed like a spade. More spade guineas were struck than any other type, and they were widely imitated in brass or silver gilt as gaming counters.

George III spade guinea, 1787

SPADE MONEY   A primitive form of early Chinese currency, dating from the 7th century B.C. It reproduced the actual shape of tools formerly used in barter.

SPAIN   Greek, Carthaginian, Roman and Celtic influences all contributed to Spain's early numismatic history. Domination by the Visigoths followed, and then a much longer one by the Arabs, who began to occupy the country in the 8th century and were not driven out finally until 1492. Even when what may be loosely described as a "national" coinage was established in 1497, provincial issues continued for Catalonia, Valencia and Majorca until the end of the 17th century. Complexities arise at every turn: for instance, Catalonia was for a long time disputed between Spain and France, so there are Catalan issues for Louis XIV. Similarly, Spain during the 16th and 17th centuries occupied large parts of Italy and the Netherlands, and Charles V not only held vast possessions in Central and South America but was also German Emperor. A very few points can therefore here be picked out as of special interest, e.g. Arabic legends even on coins by Christian kings in medieval times, Europe's first "realistic" portrait coin (under Peter the Cruel, mid-14th century, a good 100 years before the Italian Renaissance), the facing portraits of Ferdinand and Isabella in the *excelente of 1497. From 1537, however, Spain was to abandon portraiture except for Netherlands and Italian possessions until the 18th century. The famous *pieces of eight established themselves as the principal silver trading coins of the world; the *doubloon did the same for gold. Not until the Spanish Empire began to crumble during the early 19th century was this currency supremacy seriously challenged. Spain adopted a decimal system in 1854, though at first retaining the names real and escudo: the peseta of 100 centimos did not become the official monetary unit until 1870, and so it remains now. The last genuine silver coin was struck to the value of 100 pesetas in 1966; as everywhere, "silver" is today just cupro-nickel. Specialist collectors will find *emergency coinages notably for the period of the Napoleonic wars and the Civil War of 1936 onwards.

At one time Spain had 7 mints; today all coinage is centralised at the Fabrica Nacional de Moneda y Timbre which—as its name implies—produces also stamps and banknotes.

SPANISH MINTMARKS   The coinage reforms of Ferdinand and Isabella of 1497 for the first time instituted a unified Spanish coinage, with seven regal mints. These were identified by their initial letters in five cases: Burgos, Cuenca, Granada, Seville and Toledo. Corunna and Segovia used symbols: the former a shell, the latter that of the famous Roman aqueduct which exists to this day.

SPARTA In the firm belief that money is the root of all evil, the Greek city of Sparta forbade it to be struck throughout the classical period which saw the finest flowering of coinage arts elsewhere throughout the Greek world. Legend has it they used iron spears instead. Such as does appear, from the 3rd century B.C., is both scarce and stilted in style. A century later still, and extending into Roman times, there is a plentiful bronze coinage. Types were copied from various sources (the earlier silver tetradrachms from those of Alexander the Great); but Spartan coins are easily identified by the letters S and A on the reverse, usually separated by a figure. (The Greek name for Sparta was, of course, Lacedaemon.)

SPECIES From the French word espèces meaning real or "ringing" money as opposed to money of *account. The word occurs most often numismatically when used in conjunction with Thaler, Speciesthaler being those struck to the standard proclaimed by imperial ordinance of 1566 (i.e. 9 to the Mark of silver, whereas other Thalers might be struck to a lower weight and value).

SPECIESDALER The double thaler of Denmark, so-called when struck in metal to distinguish it from the far more prevalent paper currency in Denmark during the first half of the 18th century.

SPERANDIO (c. 1431–1504) Medallist of Mantua, active throughout the latter half of the 15th century both in his native town and other Italian cities (Bologna, Faenza, Ferrara, Milan and Venice). As a master of the cast bronze medal, none exceeds him save *Pisanello. Goethe, in fact, preferred him to the earlier master; but few connoisseurs have agreed with this judgment, for though his portraits are generally fine, he does not show Pisanello's skill or imagination in the treatment of reverses. Of his almost fifty signed works, perhaps the most interesting is the three-quarters facing bust of Francesco Sforza of Milan, executed shortly before the Duke's death and showing on the reverse a four-cupola temple which has recently been identified as the Duke's projected mausoleum, based on plans of the architect Filarete.

SPEYER The glory of the town of Speyer in Bavaria is its cathedral; and the glory of Speyer's coinage are certain rare silver pennies, struck in the latter part of the 12th century when the cathedral had been partly destroyed by fire and was rebuilt by the Emperor Henry IV.

SPINTRIA More or less pornographic tokens, occurring in the bronze imperial series. Their precise use is not known, but they are known with numbers from I to XVI on the reverse, indicating value of some kind—possibly as gaming tokens, or as admission tickets to brothels.

SPUR RYAL Popular name for the half-*ryal as it appears in the second and third coinages of James I of England, i.e. 1604 onwards. The name is derived from the very sharp rays of the central sun on the reverse, giving this in effect the appearance of a spur. It was a gold coin tariffed at 15 shillings.

SRANG The principal silver unit of Tibet, first struck in 1909. Multiples of 1, 3 and 10 srang were also struck in silver, and there is a rare 20-srang gold piece.

SREBENIK   Name given to the earliest known Russian silver coins, dating from the time of Vladimir of Novgorod (A.D. 980–1015). Four different types are known from his reign; they bear no denominational value, only the words "this is his silver". The obverse shows the figure of St George, the representation of which is derived from Byzantine models of the 10th century.

S.S.C.   The initials of the South Sea Company. They occur, set in the angles between shields on the reverse, on crowns, half-crowns, shillings and sixpences dated 1723, denoting that these coins were made from the company's silver.

STAMENON NOMISMA   The official name of the heavy *solidus (full weight of 24 *siliquae) in the later Byzantine Empire, which during the 10th century took on a broad, somewhat cup-shaped form (*scyphate).

STAMPEE   Popular name for the Cayenne Islands (French West Indies) base metal *sous, as countermarked or "stamped" for use by British traders throughout British possessions there during the late 18th century.

STAMPFER, JAKOB (c. 1505–79)   By general consent, the greatest of Swiss coin engravers and medallists. He was the son of a Zurich goldsmith and mintmaster, and had his training first under his father, then at Augsburg. His first dated works, both of 1531, are portrait-medals of his father and of the Reformation theologian Zwingli. He came relatively late in life to coinage, but was responsible for a great many of Zurich's finest commemorative Thalers from 1558–75. He also worked at the mints of Zug, Chur and St Gallen.

STANDING LIBERTY QUARTER   *quarter.

STAR PAGODA   The type of *pagoda as struck in Madras under the East India Company. A five-pointed star was always a feature of this, whether as the dominant design of the earlier coins from 1758 onwards (reverse type) or a whole field of small stars surrounding the pagoda (obverse type), 1810–11.

STATER   A Greek word that can mean almost anthing: Regling (in Schrötter's *Wörterbuch der Münzkunde)* devotes a good two columns to showing that there is no such denomination, and that in the ancient world any number of different coins in different weights and even different metals (gold and silver) were called stater. By and large, however, the word seems to have been most often applied in the sense of meaning double. Certainly, the gold coins most usually referred to as staters are found to be roughly the weight of double drachms (varying from 8.1 to 8.6 grammes). As regards the silver unit, the position is less clear, for the word stater would seem to have been almost equally used of the *didrachm and *tetradrachm. Perhaps Frey, in his *Dictionary of Numismatic Terms,* makes as good a guess as anyone: that the stater was the principal currency unit of any particular city, and thus would vary in value and even metal according to a city's wealth and importance. This would explain why we even find many long series of *electrum coins referred to as staters.

STELLA ($4 USA)   First envisaged by John A. Kasson, US Minister to Austria, the stella was intended as an international coin issue which would tie the US coinage to the *Latin Monetary Union formed in Europe in 1865. The purpose of the LMU was to standardise coinage systems, within which the stella would have been equivalent to France's 20 francs, Austria's 8 florins, Holland's 8 florins, Italy's 20 lire and Spain's 20 pesetas.

The issue—*stella* is Latin for star, the latter being the central feature of the reverse design—materialised through the efforts of Dr W. W. Hubbell, who held the patent on the "goloid" coinage

S.S.C. crown of George I, 1723

Gold stater of Alexander the Great

metal (gold, silver and copper in combination) used in the coins. Two types of patterns were prepared in 1879 and again in 1880: a flowing hair Liberty head by Charles E. Barber and a coiled hair type by George Morgan, both facing left. Only the 1879 Barber flowing hair type, however, was produced in any quantity, 400 of 415 examples struck being prepared for the review by Congress. The other three varieties total not more than 35 specimens between them and hence are among the rarest of US pattern coins. A few examples of each were also struck in aluminium and copper, and in one case in white metal.

STERLING   There are several meanings to this word. The most common is that implying some kind of standard of purity, e.g. sterling silver. Pennies of the Middle Ages were often referred to as sterlings, and the word is generally accepted to have been derived from the French *esterlin*. Opinions differ, however, as to the origins of this word. Some take it to have connections with the East (in the sense that the coins were a favourite circulating medium in eastern Europe, or that moneyers from Eastern countries were employed during the 13th century in regulating the coinage); others see a connection with the word *stater.

What is certain is that the word sterling occurs in an ordinance of 1257, when the value of the gold penny was fixed at the rate of "twenty pennies of sterling", and that pennies of Scotland and Ireland of the medieval period were also frequently called sterlings. Finally, there is frequent evidence to denote the use of the word as a weight value; the silver mark was tariffed in England until 1526 at 160 penny-weight or sterling.

STETTIN   Town in Pomerania, notable for a rich series of *bracteates during the 12th and 13th centuries. Fine gold *Gulden began to be struck here towards the end of the 15th century, and there is a rare ducat of 1632 with the bust of the Swedish King Gustav Adolph. *Bugslawer were struck here under Polish rule.

STIGLMAYR, JOHANN BAPTIST (1791–1844)   German medallist and coin engraver, born near Munich, and equally skilled in the techniques of casting and die engraving. His best-known work is that for Ludwig I of Bavaria, notably the *Conventionsthaler of 1828, with an obverse portrait of the King and the reverse showing small portraits of the Queen and her eight children.

STIRLING   An intermittent Scottish mint from the reign of William the Lion to James II (*c.* 1190–1460). A century later, *c.* 1555, the mint was briefly reopened to strike *bawbees for Mary Queen of Scots with the legend OPPIDUM STIRLINGI. It was thus the only Scottish mint, apart from *Edinburgh, active during Mary's reign.

Half-stiver, as issued by way of a token for Essequibo and Demerara under George III

STIVER   A spelling of the Dutch *stuiver which appears both on English issues for Ceylon 1801–15 and West Indian tokens (Essequibo and Demerara) 1813–15.

STOCKHOLM   The principal mint of the kingdom of Sweden since early times. The mint name appears on the reverse of some 16th century copper coins as part of the circular legend, not just a small mintmark—an unusual feature in coinage.

STOLBERG   German princely family with a castle in the Harz mountains not far from Nordhausen. It enjoyed coining privileges from the 13th to the 19th centuries of which it made ample use, from early *bracteates to a long series of splendid gold and silver pieces including multiple Thalers and ducats. The main type was always that of a stag or stag's head. Local gold and silver mines furnished its requirements.

STOOTER   A base silver coin of the Netherlands, first issued during the last quarter of the 16th century, with the portrait of the then Governor General, the Earl of Leicester. Its value was one-twentieth of the *daalder, and it remained current throughout the United Provinces until the mid-17th century.

STORA KOPPARSBERG BERGSLAG The oldest still existing mining company in the world, founded in Sweden as long ago as 1347. It issued *tokens in copper during the 1720s, 1762–5 and 1790–1. These (and more particularly the final issue) enjoyed acceptance over a far wider area and for a longer period than is customary for tokens, remaining in circulation until a regular copper coinage was introduced in 1832.

STOTINKA The copper unit of Bulgarian coinage, introduced as part of the new decimal system when the country joined the Latin Monetary Union in 1880. Multiples of 2, 3, 5, 10 and 20 stotinki were struck at various times, also in copper; the 50-stotinki piece, in silver, was equivalent to half a *lev. The coins bear the inscriptions in Cyrillic script.

STRIATED From Latin *striatus,* meaning lined or furrowed. A pattern of lines is seen on the reverse of certain early Greek coins.

STÜBER *stuiver.

STUIVER A base silver coin of the Netherlands, first struck towards the end of the 15th century. Its types are as numerous as the provinces in which it was struck, and its name is retained to this day in popular usage for the 5-cent piece, though no denomination of this name was struck after the Napoleonic wars. Many stuivers are known both in the Dutch colonial series and as *siege pieces. The name was adopted, and adapted as Stüber, by the Germans, who struck a similar denomination chiefly in states or towns adjoining the Low Countries, and along the lower reaches of the Rhine.

STUTTGART Principal mint of the dukedom (later kingdom) of Württemberg since 1423, and today one of the four state mints of the German Federal Republic (mint-letter F). There are notable gold pieces commemorating royal visits to the mint in 1844, the latter showing as the reverse type the new mint building.

STYCA Base metal coins appearing only in the Northumbrian series from A.D. 670–875. They bear no relation to the regular pennies of the period; their value is indeterminate and they appear to have been used as local small change only. We must assume that they were official issues of some kind, as they usually show the names of both ruler and moneyer. Ecclesiastical issues (e.g. archbishops of York) are known.

SUCRE The crown-sized piece of Ecuador, struck in silver from 1884–97 to the same standard as the French 5-franc piece. It is named after a former patriot, General Sucre (1793–1830) who fought under Bolivar against Spanish rule. These coins were struck at various mints: Lima, Santiago and also Birmingham.

SUELDO Monetary unit of the Republic of Bolivia from 1827, struck as a silver coin to the value of 1 *real (8 sueldi = 1 peso). The word sueldo is the Spanish equivalent of the Italian *soldo, but the coin is unknown in the Spanish series, except for *emergency issues of 30 sueldos struck for the Balearic Islands and Tarragona 1808–9. Its only other appearance in coinage seems to be during the French occupation of Perpignan (1642–55), when it was the equivalent of the French *sol or sou.

SVORONOS, IOANNES N. The Greek numismatist who has written important works on Athenian and Ptolemaic coinages and—perhaps most useful for the average collector—made a synopsis of the thousand false coin dies of the counterfeiter Christodoulos.

Sueldo: Bolivian type of 1855, showing a profile of Simon Bolivar

SWITZERLAND In relation to its size, Switzerland had perhaps the most diverse coinage of any country apart from ancient Greece. Indeed, until the Federal Constitution of 1848, it is quite inaccurate to talk of "Swiss" coinage. In that year, the country could still boast seventy-five different minting authorities, including twenty-three cantons and half-cantons, sixteen cities, fifteen secular princes and twenty-one prelates. Between them, these issued 860 main types; but counting varieties of effigies and designs besides earlier issues then still legal tender, well over 8,000 different coins were current in Switzerland at that time. This in a country of 16,000 square miles only and a then population of under two and a half million.

No wonder the gnomes of Zurich are a by-word for astuteness in banking. They are descendants of a tribe that needed to handle daily at least half a dozen different monetary systems; florins expressed in such different values as 60 Kreutzer at Basel, 12 sols at Geneva, 40 Schillings at Lucerne—not to mention French francs and Brabanterthaler elsewhere.

It is undoubtedly in collecting "across the board" that the main interest and opportunity for the foreign collector lies. There is little chance of competing with Swiss collectors in the rarities of any particular series; but as pride is still very localised, a general Swiss collection avoiding such rarities and concentrating on a particular year or period rather than locality could be both historically rewarding and comparatively inexpensive.

SWORD DOLLAR Popular name for the silver *ryal of Scotland, as issued under James VI (first coinage, 1567–71). The obverse design shows a crowned shield between initials I and R, and the reverse, from which the coin takes its name, a crowned sword, between and pointing up to the value XXX (30 Scottish shillings). Two-thirds ryals (value mark XX) and one-third (value mark X) were also struck during the same period.

SYCEE SILVER One of the more interesting and widely used curious currencies of the Far East, the sycee is a boat-shaped pure silver ingot, usually stamped with one or more banker's marks as a guarantee of its weight and purity. Sycees are known in weights of from one-tenth of a *tael (3.75 grammes) to 100 taels. The name is taken from the Chinese word si-tse, meaning pure silk, and refers to the thread-like pattern which forms on the ingots when the silver is poured into the mould. They first made their appearance during the second quarter of the 19th century and remained current until the 1920s, when their value interest to collectors began to exceed that of their bullion content. Today, especially in the USA, the larger sycees are much sought-after by collectors of odd monies. Other cast forms of this native silver are known: e.g. shoes and miniature drums.

SYMBOL Coins throughout history abound in symbols. Many are easy to explain: the lion is perhaps the most widely used for a ruler, stressing his power. The trident was a favourite symbol in ancient coinage for Poseidon, the sea-god. Yet there remain many symbols which have not yielded their secret. This must remain especially true of where the symbol is a *punning type on the name of some mint official where records of mints are lacking.

SYRACUSE The coinage of Syracuse is, both artistically and historically, among the most interesting of the ancient world. Historically, it reflects the pattern of many changing conflicts and influences, from local tyrants to Carthage and Corinth and Rome. Artistically, it represents perhaps the crown jewel of all Greek coinages, more specially after the defeat of the

Syracuse: Decadrachm of the finest period, c. 400 B.C.

Carthaginians by Gelon in 480 B.C., which saw the first issue of large *decadrachms, and again after the defeat of the Athenians in 413 B.C., when similar large pieces bear the signatures of the two greatest known Greek engravers, *Euainetos and *Kimon. Not unnaturally, such pieces are among the most expensive in today's coin markets throughout the world; and even fine examples of the smaller *tetradrachms are well beyond the average collector's pocket. But coins of fine style continue into the reigns of Agathokles (317–289 B.C.) and even Hieron II (274–216 B.C.), and these may still be found reasonably priced. The bronze coins of Syracuse have, like most of the Greek series, been unduly neglected in favour of its more splendid silver; and the true numismatist may find an undervalued quarry here.

The mint has little of interest to show under Roman rule, but resumed activity under the Byzantine Emperor Constans II (A.D. 641–68), who left Constantinople to make Syracuse his capital for the latter part of his reign. The prolific coinage of gold *solidi (21 main types) exceeds that of any other provincial mint, and even that of Constantinople itself under any other emperor except Heraclius. The mint continued in operation, though with lesser output, until captured by the Arabs in A.D. 878.

T

TABRIZ One of the more important of the 120-odd Persian provincial mints which flourished from the 16th to the 19th century, until coinage reforms of 1877–8 concentrated all striking at Teheran, capital of the modern state of Iran. Copper coins with a large variety of obverse designs were struck here.

TAEL The standard silver weight in the Chinese monetary system, and the equivalent to 1,000 bronze *cash. Although the Chinese Republic officially adopted the *dollar as its currency unit in 1912, silver coins still occasionally expressed coin values in tael weight terms, and coins to the value of 1 tael were also occasionally struck (6.317 grammes). For multiple taels during the 19th century, *sycee.

TAIHAI GENPO A silver piece in the early coinage of Japan. No specimen has been found; it is known from documentary evidence only.

TAKOE One-eighth of the *ackey in the Gold Coast coinage. It was a tiny (16 millimetres) silver coin, struck in 1796 at the *Soho Mint, Birmingham. As usual, *Boulton struck some proofs for presentation purposes; these are known in bronzed copper and copper-gilt, the latter very rare. The obverse shows a crowned monogram GR, referring to George III; the reverse, the arms of the African Company.

TALAR A Thaler of Frederick Augustus of Saxony, 1807–15, struck for his dukedom of Warsaw, bears this inscription.

TALARI The Ethiopian silver unit of coinage, as introduced under Menelik II in 1892. This is a handsome coin, the same size as the *Maria Theresa Thaler, which was its obvious inspiration as the principal circulating medium in Ethiopia for the past century. Halves and quarters were also struck. All bear the crowned profile bust of the Emperor facing right on the obverse, with the Ethiopian lion striding to the left as the reverse type.

Talari: Quarter, struck in 1894

TALBOT An elusive and probably non-existent gold coin in the *Anglo-Gallic series. A warrant for its striking was issued to John Talbot, Earl of Shrewsbury, during the period that he held Bordeaux in 1453. This ordinance, dated 10 September, gives the coin's name as "talbot" and its value as 21 sols 8 deniers. With the defeat and death of Talbot soon after, English rule in France came (but for Calais) effectively to an end.

TALENT The largest standard unit of weight in the ancient world. Both in the Babylonian and Greek systems, the talent was equal to 60 minae; and with the mina generally worth 100 drachms, a talent of gold would be worth 6,000 drachms. We say "generally" because weight standards varied widely at different times and places.

TALLERO A fairly obvious Italian derivation of the German word Thaler, this first occurs during the late 16th century in coinages of Mantua, Messerano and Florence and is still to be found during our own century as a denomination of the former Italian colony of Eritrea. The Duchy of Savoy and the Republic of Ragusa are other territories which adopted it from time to time; and there is an extensive series of Venetian Talleri struck specifically for the Levant from the middle to the end of the 18th century. By and large, however, this coin never rivalled the *scudo as the principal silver denomination among the many Italian states and cities.

TAMPANG   *hat money.

TANGA   A coin first struck at Goa during the early 17th century for circulation in the Portuguese East Indies. It was tariffed at one-fifth of the *xeraphim, weighed just over 3 grammes and displayed the Portuguese shield with a cross above. Tangas were struck first in silver, from 1765 in copper.

TANGKA   The basic silver coin of Tibet. It has a chequered history from the mid-16th century, when it is first said to have been struck in Nepal. No coins earlier than 1696 are, however, known today with specifically Tibetan symbols, e.g. the hand drum (damaru), distinguishing them from the native Nepalese *mohur. Coining in the Tibetan capital of Lhasa began around the middle of the 18th century, and again imitated Nepalese types, but showing a wheel instead of a dagger in the centre of the obverse, and an ornamental flower instead of a trident on the reverse. Most of these Tibetan tangkas are of debased silver, and the weight fluctuates widely from nearly 7 to just under 4 grammes.

TANKAH   This word has been used to describe a number of coins. Its first use occurs for a silver denomination of the sultans of Delhi during the early 13th century. It was then applied to a gold coin of the same type and weight, also struck for Delhi later during the same century. Copies inspired by the above appeared in the coinage of Deccan from the 14th century onwards. The earliest type is the most interesting, showing the Sultan on horseback as the obverse type; later issues carried, according to prevalent Muhammadan usage, inscriptions only on both sides.

TANNER, JOHN SIGISMUND (d. 1775)   Coin engraver of German origin, who received his early training at *Gotha, came to England in 1728, and was for over thirty years chief engraver at the Royal Mint. As such, he was responsible for most of the coinage of George II from 1739 onwards and also engraved patterns for the gold coinage of George III until 1773. Among his medals, mention should be made of that of John Conduit, Master of the Mint, to whom he owed his appointment; the Jernegan Lottery Medal of 1736; and the Copley Medal of the Royal Society 1737. His copies of Thomas *Simon's patterns for Cromwellian coinage, partly utilising old dies still in the mint's possession, deserve notoriety rather than fame.

TARENTUM   An early Greek colony on the heel of southern Italy, and the seat of an important coinage in both gold and silver from the late 6th century B.C. Legend had it that the city was founded by Taras, son of Poseidon; and the prevalent type is that of a youth riding on the back of a dolphin. At first silver, the coins are of the peculiar fabric common to southern Italy, with the reverse repeating the obverse type *incuse; later a rider with a lance on a prancing horse is the most frequent design on the obverse of the coins, as the district was famous for its horses and horsemanship. The gold coins, which are much rarer and begin at a later period, show very different types, with the heads of gods or goddesses on the obverse and reverses such as Taras driving a chariot, an eagle on a thunderbolt and others.

Taro: 8-tari piece of 1723,
issued under Manoel de Vilhena

TARIN A heavy silver denomination introduced by Ferdinand II of Aragon as part of the coinage for his kingdom of Naples and Sicily towards the end of the 15th century. It was the double of the *carlin, and showed on the obverse the bust of the ruler, with an eagle on the reverse. This denomination was struck at Messina until the end of the 18th century.

TARO A small gold coin (weight about 1 gramme), current in the Campanian and Sicilian territories of the Normans from the 10th century onwards and continued by the Hohenstauffen and Anjou dynasties until the end of the 13th century. Tari, in multiples also of 2, 3, 5, 6 and occasionally even 10, were struck mainly at Amalfi, Brindisi, Messina and Palermo. They are of varying types, only rarely with a bust of a ruler, more often showing just an heraldic device and sometimes with legends only.

Much later, the name taro was given to the principal silver coin of Malta, where it was struck from 1530 until the end of the 18th century. Multiples of 2, 4, 6, 8, 12, 16 and even 30 tari were struck here at various times, the 12-tari piece being the equivalent of the *scudo. The most common type showed the portrait bust of the Grand Master of the Order of the Knights of Malta on the obverse, with the paschal lamb or Cross of St John as the reverse.

TARSUS St Paul's birthplace in what is today southern Turkey had an important coinage from early times. Silver coins of the 5th century B.C. are of Persian regal type, and satrapal coins of the next century bear witness to the worship of Baal. Later it became one of the principal mints of Alexander the Great in Asia Minor. A continuous stream of local types persisted throughout the Roman imperial period from Domitian to Caracalla.

TAYLOR AND CHALLEN From small beginnings by Joseph Taylor in 1850, this Birmingham firm rose quickly to importance in the manufacture of coining machinery. By the year 1855 it was sufficiently advanced to supply the entire plant, machinery, steam engines and presses for the Sydney Mint in Australia, a contract to the value of £10,000 which was completed within six months. Since then, the firm has supplied minting machinery to about thirty mints throughout the world. It is especially noted for its large variety of presses, ranging from the most rapid type for small change to individually hand-fed ones, exerting a pressure of over 400 tons and able to make medals in high relief up to 6 inches in diameter.

Among the more unusual contracts mentioned in the firm's records is one for highly finished and hand-operated coining machinery, presented by Queen Victoria to the King of Siam in 1857, and "one coining press for a London customer, which was found afterwards to have been used for (it is sad to relate) the manufacture of counterfeit coin (not English coin)".

Coining operations as such have not formed part of the firm's work, with one exception: it made the dies for and struck the first coinage of the independent Republic of Algeria in 1964.

TAYLOR, WILLIAM JOSEPH (1802–85) Born and trained in Birmingham, Taylor set up his own business as die-sinker, medallist and engraver in London during 1829. His output was prolific rather than distinguished, but he was responsible for one historically important coinage: the first copper pieces for the independent Republic of Liberia, 1847. He also made a number of tokens for Australia and had an ambitious plan for coining local Australian gold which, however, came to nothing. Finally, he is famous (or infamous, according to one's point of view) for restriking a great number of *Soho Mint patterns from original dies which had come into his possession.

TAZE KRAN *kran.

TEALBY COINAGE The coinage of Henry II of England from
c. 1158–80. Its obverse shows the King's facing bust, the reverse
a large cross with smaller crosslets set diagonally in its angles. It
takes its name from Tealby in Lincolnshire, where a very large
hoard of these coins was unearthed in 1807. They are mostly very
crudely struck and six main varieties have been distinguished.

TEMPLETON REID Little is known about this person, except
that he was a goldsmith and assayer and struck pieces of $2.50,
$5 and $10 in Lumpkin County, Georgia, in 1830, with the
inscriptions GEORGIA GOLD and the value on the obverse, and
his name, value and the word ASSAYER on the reverse. He is
unique in also striking very similar pieces but with the words
CALIFORNIA GOLD in 1849, having presumably joined the
gold rush there. One of these is further unique in being the only
known one to a value of $25. The only known specimen of this
piece was unfortunately stolen from the United States Mint
Collection in 1858 and has never been recovered.

Tealby coinage: penny of
Henry II

TENEDOS A small island off Troas, which struck an extensive
series of coins from about the mid-6th century B.C. The main
type of all values over two hundred years, ranging from
hemidrachm to tetradrachm, is a strange janiform head, one half-
bearded male, the other female. The principal reverse type is that
of a double-headed axe *(labrys);* a valued object from Minoan
and Mycenaean times onwards both in peace and war (*axe
money).

Tenedos double axe

TENTZEL, WILHELM ERNST (1659–1707) German
numismatist, who issued from 1689–98 a monthly periodical containing a great deal of useful information on coins and medals—
probably the first regular publication of its kind. His *Saxonia
Numismatica* remains the standard work on the numismatic
history of Saxony.

TEOS A town on the coast of Ionia in Asia Minor, which
struck a distinctive coinage from about 550 B.C., the obverse
type showing a griffin. Small coins only, from drachm
downwards, are known, the earlier ones being uninscribed, the
later ones having the city's name.

TERRITORIAL GOLD Coins struck from locally mined gold,
generally by pioneers without benefit of an official mint. The
USA series is the most prolific, beginning with Georgia in 1830,
continuing with North Carolina in 1832, and culminating with the
great Californian gold rush from 1848 onwards, when a whole
series of different bars or ingots were struck without government
authority before the opening of the San Francisco Mint. Other
USA territories include Colorado, Oregon and Utah. There is a
similar though much less extended occurrence of such pieces in
Australia. Further details may be found under *Baldwin & Co.,
Bechtler, Dubosq, Colorado gold, Humbert, Kellogg, Miners'
Bank, Mormon gold, Oregon Exchange, Ormsby, Pacific Co.,
Schultz, Templeton Reid, Wass Molitor.

TESSERAE Leaden tickets, tokens or counters in the Roman
imperial series which are largely unclassified and may have served
a variety of purposes (e.g. gaming, admission tickets and
possibly—during the later Empire when bronze coinage was in
short supply—small change transactions). (Also *spintria.)

TESTON, TESTONE, TESTOON The French, Italian and
English spellings of this word all refer to what was basically the
same coin, i.e. one showing the ruler's portrait bust. The name
appears first to have been attached to a silver coin of Milan struck

Teston:

Original type, as introduced in Milan under Galeazzo Maria Sforza in 1474

One of many French types during the long reign of Francis I (1515–47); this one is an early portrait

in 1474, and was quickly followed by similar coins in other Italian city states, notably Ferrara. Louis XII struck testones for his Italian possessions before introducing the coin to France in 1513; the French series then continues with very many varieties under Francis I, 1515–47. In England, the name testoon was given to the *shilling introduced by Henry VII in 1504. In Scotland, the denomination appears, obviously under French influence, during the reign of Mary Queen of Scots only.

TETARTERON NOMISMA A gold denomination introduced by the Byzantine Emperor Nicephorus II (A.D. 963–9), lighter by one-twelfth than the *stamenon nomisma. It was thus the exact equivalent of the much earlier *light-weight solidus of 22 *siliquae and probably served a similar purpose, or maybe circulated in Eastern territories newly conquered, where the Fatimid *dinar was formerly current.

TETRADRACHM The largest standard silver coin in the ancient Greek series, to the value of 4 *drachms. The Athenian tetradrachms of the 5th–3rd centuries B.C. were the international coinage of the ancient world. No indication of value is ever shown, except on an undetermined bronze coin (probably Adriatic) of a later period.

TETRATEMORION A minute Greek silver coin, to the value of one-quarter of an *obol. It weighed no more than 0.19 of a gramme. Such small silver denominations were found impracticable in everyday use and larger bronze coins took their place from the 3rd century B.C. onwards. None the less, some have survived and are occasionally listed in dealers' catalogues at reasonable prices, having little appeal to the average collector.

THALER A heavy silver piece, struck as the result of rich silver deposits being found during the Renaissance both in Austria and Germany. Deposits near Hall in the Tyrol encouraged the first striking of such a piece in 1486, while the first similar German pieces were struck in Saxony around 1500. These pieces, however, were then termed *Guldengroschen, implying that their silver content was equivalent to that of a gold *Gulden. Not until the enormous strike at Joachimsthal in 1519 and the consequent minting operations there did the generic term Thaler (an abbreviation of *Joachimsthaler) find acceptance. Even then, the word Guldengroschen or Guldiner continued to be used in official documents for years to come. The Thaler, as a specific denomination of fixed weight, is first mentioned in ordinances of Saxony dated 1534 and was not adopted by the Holy Roman Empire until the edict of 1566. By that time, there had been no less than eight various standards of value, from 60 to 72 *Kreuzer, and weights varying 24.6 to 32 grammes.

There were to be ten further variations of one sort or another over the next 300 years, until the 3-Mark piece finally took the place of the Thaler under the 1873 decimalisation laws (even then, the coin remained legal tender until 1908). Of these, the Bancothaler (Netherlands 1612), the Conventionsthaler of 1753 and the Vereinsthaler of 1839 are the most important in monetary history. To the collector (as opposed to the economic or numismatic historian) the series offers something approaching 10,000 different types, not counting multiples and divisions. German towns and principalities during the 16th century alone total close on 1,500 pieces. Attempts at a *corpus* have been made from the mid-18th century onwards and still continue (notably by the indefatigable Dr Davenport in the USA). (*Maria Theresa Thaler.)

Like the English *crown piece, which is its equivalent, the

Original Joachimsthaler, made of silver from a local mine, *c.* 1520

Saxe-Weimar, the so-called Achtbrüderthaler, 1611

Augsburg under Ferdinand III, 1642: imperial "free city" Thaler with a splendid town view and emblem (pineapple cone) on the reverse (slightly reduced)

Unflattering portrait of the Emperor Leopold I (known as "the hog-mouth"), Austria, 1682 (slightly reduced)

Thaler is avidly collected. Its large surface enables the coin engraver's skill to be displayed to best advantage, and appreciated without artificial magnification. So it is difficult, with today's inflation in coin prices as elsewhere, to find any Thaler worth having under two figures (£ sterling); and even pieces which may be considered common by some will fetch three figures if they catch some specialist collector's fancy at auction. To form an even moderately representative collection of Thalers today needs a long purse; but a Thaler of one sort or another should certainly form part of any representative coin collection.

THASOS Island in the northern Aegean, close to the Macedonian coast. Its prevalent type is that of a satyr carrying a nymph, at first crudely struck, later (after the island had come under Athenian rule) in fine style. In this later period, too, there are some very rare gold *staters.

THEBES The most powerful city of Boeotia, central Greece, with an important coinage from the 6th century B.C. The obverse always showed the distinctive Boeotian shield while reverses varied (bearded Dionysus, amphora, Heracles, etc.). Many magistrates' names are to be found during the middle of the 4th century B.C., some known to us from the accounts of contemporary historians. Local issues of surrounding towns show similar types to Theban currency and may well have been struck there.

THESSALIAN LEAGUE This confederate coinage began in 196 B.C., following the Roman declaration of the independence of Greece at the Peace of Corinth and continued for the next fifty years. There are varying obverse types showing the heads of deities (Zeus, Apollo, Athena) and a more constant reverse—at any rate on the silver coin struck to the value of 1½ Roman *denarii—showing Athena with a poised spear.

THESSALONICA Of only minor importance in Greek and Roman times, this mint achieved prominence during the Byzantine era, when it struck coins at intervals until well into the 14th century. It is especially notable under Justinian I (A.D. 527–65) for a series of bronze denominations peculiar to itself, in multiples of 2, 4, 8 and 16 *nummia.

THIRD GUINEA An English gold coin to the value of 7 shillings, struck almost every year from 1797 to 1813 (excepting 1805 and 1812), i.e. during a period when the full guinea was hardly struck at all (1799 onwards until 1813).

THISTLE CROWN Struck as part of the second coinage of James I from 1604, this gold coin was current for 4 shillings. By one of James's peculiar academic quirks, its value was raised by 10% in 1611, making it worth 4¾ pence more—scarcely a convenient denomination! It was not unnaturally discontinued when James's third coinage was introduced in 1619. Meanwhile, it had served its purpose to advertise the happy union of the two kingdoms of Scotland and England. The Scottish thistle is surmounted by a crown, and the legend TUCATOR UNITA DEUS means "May God safeguard our Unity".

THISTLE DOLLAR A popular name for the double *merk as issued in the third coinage of the reign of James VI of Scotland, 1578–80 only. The coin was tariffed at 26s. 8d. and took its name from the large thistle on the reverse. The obverse shows a crowned shield.

THISTLE MERK A silver coin in the eighth coinage of James VI of Scotland, 1601–4, tariffed at 16s. 8d. The obverse shows a crowned shield, the reverse a crowned thistle.

Facing page: A group of Thalers **THISTLE NOBLE** A large gold coin in the fifth coinage of

James VI of Scotland, 1588–90, its general type freely adapted from the English *rose-noble of a century earlier. It shows a large crowned shield (with the Scottish lion) on a ship as the obverse type; the reverse is an elaborate design incorporating thistles among sceptres, crowns and lions. The coin also reverted to the fine gold standard of .975, all other gold coins of James VI being struck to .916 or 22 carat. The coin's value was set at £7. 6s. 8d.

THOMASON, SIR EDWARD (1769–1849) Birmingham manufacturer of coins, medals and tokens—and a good many other things besides. He had been apprenticed to Matthew *Boulton at the age of sixteen and his enormous respect for Boulton's genius caused him not to compete directly with his master during the latter's lifetime. He concentrated rather on general manufacturing activities and exercised his ingenuity on improvements (often patented) to such devices as gun-locks, corkscrews, hearthbrushes and umbrellas.

Thomason was nothing if not a go-getter—what we would today call the aggressive salesman. With naive boastfulness he relates some of his exploits in his memoirs. He did not scruple to supply electioneering medals to both parties on the eve of the poll, or to offer a congratulatory medal to the self-styled "Emperor" Henri Christophe of Haiti. A great admirer of Wellington, he struck commemorative medals for all his victories, and on his appointment as Commander-in-Chief following the death of the Duke of York produced a medal which he had delivered to the Iron Duke within forty-eight hours of the official announcement.

His other medals and tokens are far too numerous to list and have never been comprehensively documented, apart from such mention as they receive in his memoirs and in *Forrer. But special mention should perhaps be made of the 40-shilling bank token in gold which he struck for J. B. Monck's Reading Bank. This piece is now very rare, as the "coinage" was stopped by the Prime Minister as infringing the royal prerogative. Among his more substantial productions was a whole series of sixty biblical subjects issued in a handsome presentation case.

THONNELIER French coining machinery engineer, who during the 1830s and 1840s improved upon *Uhlhorn's presses—especially as regards edge-marking. His presses remained in use at the Paris Mint for over a century.

THREE CENT (NICKEL) Faced with the fact that the silver trime was not circulating, Congress decided to replace it with a nickel piece in March 1865. The coin is undistinguished compared with its predecessor: it has a Liberty head facing left as the obverse, and the numeral III surrounded by a wreath as the reverse. Issues were small after 1873, with the exception of 1881 when over one million were struck. The coin was finally withdrawn in 1889.

THREE CENT (SILVER) The trime, as the silver 3-cent piece was originally known, was created as a direct result of a reduction in US first-class postage rates from 5 to 3 cents in 1851. Although the denomination today seems rather odd within a decimal currency structure, it was well conceived at the time and gained immediate popularity. During the first three years of issue it was produced at the then exceedingly high rate of about one million examples per month (as a basis for comparison, more than twelve times the rate of the 5-cent piece or half-dime). Struck to begin with at only .750 fine, it was brought into line with other US silver denominations (.900 fine) in March 1853. The chaotic economic conditions brought on by the Civil War drove the coin out of circulation: very few were struck after 1862, and though officially it remained a mint issue until 1873, it was to all intents and purposes driven out by a nickel trime (see previous entry) in 1865. The coin is elegant in appearance, showing a six-pointed star on the obverse with a shield in the centre, and on the reverse a florid capital C, within which is the figure III (Roman capitals), the whole surrounded near the edge by 13 stars.

THREE DOLLARS (USA)   Authorised by an act of 21 February 1853, this unpopular coin survived thirty-six years despite the fact that only in the first year of issue were more than 100,000 of it struck. The coin's only logical application was to purchase sheets of 3-cent stamps, the adoption of that postal rate having led to the introduction of the silver 3-cent piece two years earlier. The obverse design shows a Liberty head, with feathered headdress, facing left; the reverse shows the words 3 DOLLARS and the date within a wreath. James B. Longacre was the designer. In its first year of issue, 1854, the coin was also struck at New Orleans and Dahlonega branch mints, but later mainly at Philadelphia with very sporadic strikings at San Francisco branch mint only. Scarcest collectors' piece in the series is the 1870S, of which only two are known to have been struck and one survives.

THREE-FARTHINGS, THREE-HALFPENCE   Both these distinctly odd denominations appear first in the early coinage of Edward VI for Ireland, with the facing bust of Henry VIII. They appear again, as unexpectedly, in the English coinage of Elizabeth from 1561–81. The three-halfpence here is especially remarkable, showing as its obverse type a portcullis and bearing no legends whatsoever. The three-farthing piece was never again struck after this, but the three-halfpence was revived under William IV (1834) and struck intermittently through the reign of Queen Victoria until 1862 for use in certain colonies (Ceylon, Jamaica, British Guiana). The obverse of this showed the royal portrait, the reverse the figures 1 1/2 surrounded by a wreath.

THREEPENCE   The English silver threepenny piece first makes its appearance in 1551 as part of the fine silver coinage of Edward VI. Its type is similar to the *sixpence, but shows the figure III instead of VI to the right of the King's bust. Like the sixpences, these pieces were struck at York as well as London, distinguished by the inscription CIVITAS EBORACI. No threepenny pieces were struck under Queen Mary or Philip and Mary, but the denomination was resumed under Elizabeth from 1561–82 (there being a few *milled issues from 1561–4). No threepenny pieces were struck under James I and during Charles I's reign issue of the denomination was confined to provincial and Civil War issues (York, Aberystwyth, Bristol, Oxford and a few other mints). Charles II struck it regularly from 1670 onwards, as did subsequent monarchs until George III. Under George IV it appeared as a *Maundy coin only, under William IV also occasionally as a coin struck only for the colonies. From Victoria's reign onwards it was again struck regularly until the end of George V's reign.

The dodecagonal (twelve-sided) brass threepenny piece was first devised for Edward VIII; but although a few dated 1937 were struck, most were melted down and this is an exceedingly rare coin. The same type was continued under George IV and Elizabeth II until decimalisation.

THRYMSA   An English gold coin during the Anglo-Saxon period from c. A.D. 575–775, based on the *triens (i.e. one-third

Thrymsa, c. A.D. 650–700

of the *solidus). There are various types, all rare today.

TICAL   A monetary unit of Siam and Burma. For its history in Siam in spherical or skull-shaped form, *bullet money.

The modern coinage of ticals, in values from 2 down to one-sixteenth, began in 1861 with pieces struck at Birmingham's *Heaton Mint during the reign of King Mongkut. Gold ticals in multiples of 2½ to 8, were struck in 1863. All these coins are much rarer than earlier types, which were made and circulated during five centuries.

TIFFIN, JOSEPH   A 19th century Canadian merchant, resident at Montreal, who around 1825 imported a great number of English *tokens, made for him in Birmingham, to help alleviate the acute shortage of copper coinage in Canada at that time. His name passed into local folklore, "tiffins" being a popular name for tokens for years to come.

TIFLIS   A town in what is today the USSR State of Georgia. It had a mint going back to Sassanian times, from the 7th century onwards became an Islamic mint for about 350 years, and during the 11th and 12th centuries issued coins for the independent kingdom of Georgia. Its later and no less chequered history includes Persian, Ottoman and Russian rule; coins of local type, with the mint name of Tiflis, were struck until 1834.

TIGER TONGUE MONEY   A longish cast silver bar of varying size and weight, on the obverse of which are to be seen wart-like excrescences (said to have been achieved by stewing ants over it while casting the fluid metal). Such bars passed as currency (by weight) from the late 17th to the late 19th century in Cambodia, Laos and north-eastern Thailand.

TILLA   The Persian word for gold, but never struck as a denomination in Persia. The gold coin occurs in both Afghanistan and Turkestan during the second half of the 19th century; there are also some earlier issues in Bukhara from 1785–1800.

TIMBRE DE VALENCE   A gold coin struck only during the reign of Alfonso V of Aragon for his kingdom of Valencia, to the value of two-thirds of a ducat (weight 2.4 grammes).

TIMMIN   *Trevoux.

TIN   A metal rarely used in coinage, except for *emergency issues. Exceptions are the English farthings as issued under Charles II and James II from 1684 onwards, but even these had copper *plugs. Trademen's *tokens and colonial coinages are more frequently found in tin (especially Dutch colonial issues for Batavia, Ceylon, Java and Sumatra).

TIOLIER, PIERRE JOSEPH (1763–1819) & NICOLAS PIERRE (1784–1853)   Father and son, and successively engravers-general to the Paris Mint from 1803–16 and 1816–43. Between them they dominated French coin engraving from the *patterns of Bonaparte as First Consul to the issuers of Louis-Philippe. The elder Tiolier was brother-in-law to Benjamin *Duvivier, under whom he received his training. Between them, father and son were responsible for several hundred coins and medals, which all attest their high skill. Many improvements of coining machinery took place while they worked at the mint, and among the younger Tiolier's pieces there is a fine one of 1833 commemorating the installation of *Thonnelier's coining press.

TOKEN   A token is a pledge, the intrinsic value of which is less than what it purports to be. All money today is token money; but until about sixty years ago this was the exception rather than the rule. Previously—and certainly until the First World War—gold and silver coins had an intrinsic value only very slightly less than their face value; and that slight difference was all the government and the manufacturer made out of the coinage.

A token in coinage prior to this was, therefore, by and large, *emergency money issued privately when the government failed to provide sufficient coin. Tokens in silver, and even very occasionally gold, are known. The vast majority are, however, of copper or other base metal; and the English series is mainly concentrated in two periods. Commerce was only possible because private enterprise supplied the change for small, everyday transactions.

In some instances, there were "town" tokens of semi-official status; but the great majority were tradesmen's tokens of every description: butcher, baker, candlestick-maker, and so on. This is especially true of the 17th-century farthing tokens. In London alone, about 4,000 tradesmen issued tokens; and in view of the fact that most of these were struck before the great fire of 1666, they furnish not only a commercial directory of the time but also an index to streets and places many of which were soon to disappear.

While very few of such tokens are technically or artistically distinguished, many have a naive charm that appeals to collectors and social historians alike. Thus a coffee-house token might show a coffee-pot or (if this was its name) a Turk's head. The token of a scrivener might show a hand holding a pen, and that of a wine merchant a flagon or cup.

Such tokens may still be found for a few pounds and should certainly be represented in any general collection. Specialisation may take various different paths: by trades, by towns, by date, even (in London) by districts, streets and buildings.

Late 18th-century tokens show the influence of the Industrial Revolution in three respects: there are fewer tokens (more firms rather than small tradesmen); the principal unit is now the halfpenny; and tokens are, in general, better struck. One other main difference: many have edges inscribed with the names of places where they could be cashed, and such edge-inscriptions tend to change quite frequently on what is basically the same token. The collector here is therefore on the lookout for minor die varieties rather than variety of design.

The period 1811–12 saw the issue of a limited number of private silver tokens (also bank *tokens). There are also some oddities like the Reading 40-shilling gold piece (*Thomason) and a so-called half-guinea of Liverpool struck in copper. Such pieces are both rare and expensive. Also *Bristol town tokens, Tiffin.

TOLA COINAGE This remains an inadequately documented part of modern gold coinage. The tola is, in fact, an Indian weight of 180 grains, equal to 11.664 grammes. Various Indian banking houses have issued .995 fine gold pieces to this weight. It is incorrect to call these either tokens or bars: they belong rather to the category of *private gold coinages, being always redeemable at their full metallic value. They come in a large variety of shapes (round, square, scalloped, diamond), designs (often showing the bank or its heraldic device) and sizes (multiples up to 10 tolas and fractions down to one-quarter). Issues have not been systematically catalogued, even in India or Pakistan, and thus offer the enterprising researcher an almost virgin field.

TOLEDO A town in Spain, and an important mint from the 6th century A.D. onwards, when it was the principal mint of the Visigoths. Its influence declined during medieval times, but it took its rightful place again as one of the seven regal mints of Spain (with mintmark T) in 1797. It also struck coins for Joseph Bonaparte as King of Spain, 1808–10.

TOLERANCE   The permitted deviation from the standard of weight or fineness of metal for a particular coin as laid down by law. Such tolerances were fairly wide in former days, when coins were hand-struck and (in the case of silver) often not weighed individually (*al marco). But there has always been the strictest control over gold, ensured in England by the Trial of the *Pyx; and a variation of more than 1/1,000th would certainly not be passed. Tolerances in medieval Islamic coinages have been shown to be even stricter.

TOLSTOI, COUNT FEODOR (1783–1873)   Russian modeller and engraver, whose chief claim to fame is a series of nineteen magnificent medallions celebrating the events which led to the final defeat of Napoleon (1812–14). It begins with the arming of Russian volunteers and ends with the allies' entry into Paris. These medallions are not modelled realistically but in classical, allegorical style, and were later cast in bronze. Tolstoi himself published engravings of the medals with an explanatory text in 1818.

TOLSTOI, COUNT IVANOVITCH (1853–1915)   Russian collector and numismatist who specialised in the series of imperial Russian coins struck from 1725–1801, and in the early coins of Kiev. The catalogues of both these collections (which have since passed into the Hermitage Collection) remain standard works of reference. (Also *novodels.)

TOMAN   The principal gold unit of the Persian coinage from the reign of Aka Muhammad onwards (*c.* 1794). Previous to this, the toman had been a money of *account only, the chief circulating gold medium in Persia being the *mohur. During the whole of the 19th century, a great number of handsome tomans were struck, with multiples up to 25 and divisions down to one-fifth. There is a particularly fine series under Fath Ali (1797–1834), some showing the ruler on a galloping horse, others showing him seated on a throne. A more general type is that with a Persian lion on the obverse and an inscription on the reverse.

Half-toman of 1833, showing the ruler seated

TOMBAC   An unusual alloy (88% copper, 12% zinc), which has apparently been used in regular coinage only for the Canadian 5-cent pieces of 1942–3. This was at a period when the Ottawa Mint was experimenting with various metals; for the same piece, commonly struck in nickel, is found in 1944–5 struck in chromium-plated steel. Tombac has, however, been a favourite alloy for striking medals from time to time, and in the manufacture of military and other *buttons.

TOOLED   It is not uncommon, in auction or fixed-price catalogues, to find a description of a piece reading "Very fine, but has been tooled"—the implication being that this must somewhat (or somehow) detract from the full value of the piece.

Certainly, if the tooling (i.e. retouching with a graving tool after the coin has been cast or struck) has been done much later with the idea of bringing out details lost through wear and tear, this would be true. But it should always be remembered that a piece may have been cast or struck with the specific intention that it should be, as it were, hand-finished afterwards. Such a technique was not uncommon, especially in late-Renaissance German medals which were, almost invariably, made from a wooden mould. The natural softness of the wood tended to mitigate against sharp detail in the medal as cast (very different from a die

Tostao of Manuel I of
Portugal, 1495–1521

engraved in steel, for direct striking of a coin or medal); and the
craftsman might often wish to bring out detail in sharper relief.

TORNESE   The Italian name for the *gros tournois. The Italian
coin, as struck from the late 15th century onwards, had little in
common, however, with its French ancestor, being generally
struck in base metal. A pure copper denomination of the same
name was introduced in the Naples coinage *c.* 1560, and multiple
tornesi (up to 10) were issued until 1680.

TORNEZ A Portuguese silver coin, introduced by Peter I
(1350–69), directly modelled on the French *gros tournois of a
century earlier.

TOSTAO   This   Portuguese   coin   struck   under   Manuel
(1495–1521) took its name and weight (9.96 grammes) from the
Italian *testone. Yet this denomination was notable among
Renaissance pieces in *not* showing any head and is therefore, in
a pertinent respect, a complete misnomer. Like other Portuguese
coins of the period, including gold, it showed only a shield on the
obverse and a cross on the reverse.

TOUCHPIECES   Since kings were thought to rule by "divine
right", it is not surprising that divine properties of healing were
held to reside in their touch. As long ago as Roman times, we find
that the Emperor Vespasian was credited with this power (in
accounts of Tacitus and Suetonius). In England, the monarch's
touch was held to be efficacious in curing the scurvy, and the
"touching" ceremony is known to have been held from the reign
of Edward the Confessor to that of Queen Anne. Both coins and
medals were used at various times to hang round the necks of
those who presented themselves for healing; and the Tudors and
Stuarts until Charles II's reign invariably used the gold *angel. It
should, however, not be assumed that an angel was necessarily
used as a touchpiece just because it is today found pierced, since
any attractive gold piece was always prone to be worn as
jewellery. Gold medalets such as were specially struck for the
"touching" ceremony after the coining of angels had ceased are
a different matter: though the general obverse type is similar,
they bear on the reverse the legend SOLI DEO GLORIA (To God
alone be the Glory). A medalet of this type, formerly belonging
to Dr Johnson (who was touched by Queen Anne when he was
two and a half years old) is now in the British Museum.

TOULOUSE   A town in south-western France, and one of its
chief mints successively in Visigothic, Merovingian, medieval and
modern times. The coinage of its independent counts was
especially prolific during the 11th to the 13th centuries. It is also
noted for a large series of monetary weights dating from the 14th
century, which have the peculiarity of being dated. As a regal
mint, Toulouse was allotted the distinguishing letter M in the
coinage reform of Francis I (1540), which it retained until the
mint was closed in 1837. Gold was struck here until 1812 only.
A fine collection of regional coins is to be seen at the Musée Paul
Dupuy.

TOURNAI GROAT   In 1513 Henry VIII seized the town of
Tournai and struck there until 1518 a rare series of *groats. Two
types are known. The first shows a profile bust of the King on the
obverse, with a shield and the words CIVITAS TORNACENS on
the reverse. The second has a crowned shield as the obverse and
the initial H on the centre of the reverse surrounded by leopards
and lys. A unique specimen of the first type as a half-groat has
survived. This was the last coinage to be struck by an English
monarch on French soil.

TOURNOIS Of or pertaining to the town of *Tours. The word is more particularly used in conjunction with the *denier and *gros introduced there under Philip II (1206) and Louis IV (1266) respectively. The latter became one of the most widely copied coins of Europe, especially in German states under the name of Turnose.

TOURS An important town in the Loire valley of France, and an equally important mint from the days of Charlemagne at least. Not only the kings of France but also the abbots of the Abbey of St Martin struck coins here. The regal mint continued (with mint- letter E) until 1772. (Also *tournois.)

TOWER MINT With rare exceptions (*Durham House, Southwark), the principal mint of England has since Norman days always been situated in or around the Tower of London. The move from inside the Tower did not take place until the erection of a specifically designed building on Tower Hill early in the 19th century. From 1642 onwards, the Tower Mint was under the control cf Parliament and continued so throughout the Civil War, the King meanwhile using a wide variety of provincial mints (some very ephemeral). Today, the Royal Mint has transferred most of its coining operations to Llantrisant in South Wales.

TOYÉ, KENNING & SPENCER A firm of medallists which traces its English origins back to Guillaume Toyé, a Huguenot weaver who fled from France to Britain after the Edict of Nantes in 1685. While embroidery, ribbons and uniform trimmings still form an important branch of the firm's business, it has for well over a century also produced metal badges and insignia of all kinds. During the past twenty years, it has specialised in the making of large commemorative medallions in precious metals, many officially commissioned, among which those for the Royal Silver Wedding, the Tutankhamun Exhibition and the Chinese Exhibition deserve mention.

TRADE DOLLARS The most famous of coins falling under this general description is the *Maria Theresa Thaler. The success of this large silver coin throughout the Middle East was paralleled in the Far East by the popularity of the Mexican *peso. To compete with this, both the British and American governments struck large and handsome pieces of a similar kind during the latter part of the 19th century.

The American coin was first in the field, being struck regularly from 1873–8. (*Proofs, however, continued to be struck in small numbers until 1885.) It shows on the obverse the seated figure of Liberty, with the date below, and on the reverse an eagle, with the legend above UNITED STATES OF AMERICA and below 420 GRAINS 900 FINE, TRADE DOLLAR.

The English trade dollars were first issued in 1895 and continued to be struck intermittently until 1935. Most were made in India, at the Bombay and Calcutta Mints, only a few at London's Royal Mint. They show on the obverse Britannia standing, with a spear and shield, the words ONE DOLLAR and the date. The reverse consists of a Chinese labyrinth, the compartments surrounding which again show the words ONE DOLLAR, this time in both Chinese and Malay characters. Imitations of this coin exist, made at private mints in Canton, which are more or less identical but for the words FOR JEWELLERY in English on the obverse. (*Canadian trade dollar, United States trade dollar.)

TRANQUEBAR Town on the Coromandel coast in southern India. From 1620–1845 it was a possession of the Danish East

India Company, who struck here a number of coins with the initials DOC. First issues were crudely struck in lead, with dies manufactured locally. During the 18th century, when the colony was well established and flourishing, copper and even silver pieces were struck with dies made in Copenhagen. During the reign of Christian VII (1766–1808), a new coin (and the only gold one of the colony) was introduced: equivalent to the Indian *pagoda, it bore the King's monogram C7 on the obverse and the goddess Lakshmi on the reverse. A large number were struck (the mintage figure for 1789 alone is 18,375 pieces). Silver *fanams and copper kashas only were struck during the reign of Frederick VI (1808–38). These were the last-known coins for the Danish colony, which was sold to the British East India Company in 1845 for two million Kronen.

TREASURE TROVE   In the UK anyone discovering a *hoard of gold, silver or bullion should inform the local police at once. The Crown has the right to such treasure if the original owner cannot be traced, and the finder will be rewarded at current market values (more, probably, than he would get if he tried to dispose of the coins surreptitiously). He will also, of course, be allowed to keep, or sell in the open market, any items not purchased by public collections.

TREBIZOND   Town in north-eastern Asia Minor, on the south coast of the Black Sea, the seat of an independent empire under the Commenian branch of the Byzantine dynasty from 1204 to 1461, when it was captured by the Turks. The main coins struck here did not follow Byzantine types in the more or less rigorous fashion to be seen at *Nicaea, although the principal coin, the *asper, at first followed the fashion of showing standing the emperor on the obverse and a saint (mainly St Eugenius) on the reverse. However, from around A.D. 1300 both figures appear on horseback. As such they diverge sharply from any other Byzantine-related coinages. Specimens are not particularly rare, so that persistence rather than a great deal of money is required to collect the many interesting varieties produced during a period of over 250 years.

TREMISSIS   *triens.

TREVOUX   The principal mint of the principality of Dombes, in Burgundy, and for over two centuries (mid-15th to the late 17th) the place where a splendid series of feudal pieces were struck for the dukes of Montpensier. The small silver pieces struck for Marie de Montpensier during the 1660s, to the value of one-twelfth of an *écu, were the first Western silver to find extensive favour in the Levant, among Turks and Arabs, and are in that respect an interesting antecedent to the *Maria Theresa Thaler. Such was their success that they were much copied by a number of Italian states who traded with the Near East, where all such pieces were known as timmins and often used for jewellery.

TREZZO, JACOPO DA (c. 1515–1589)   One of the finest late Renaissance coin and medal engravers, born in Milan. Although he was by 1550 well known enough to receive a mention in Vasari's *Lives of the Painters*, his signed and dated work falls mainly between the years 1552–78. Indeed, it is as the court medallist of Philip II of Spain that he achieved his greatest fame, first in the Netherlands and later at Madrid. He may even have accompanied Philip during his brief sojourn in England: certainly, his medallic portraits of Mary Tudor are vivid likenesses. Among his earlier, Italian work, portrait medals of the Gonzaga family stand out.

TRIBUTE PENNY The common Roman *denarius in circulation within the Roman province of Judaea during the time of Christ. It was named so colloquially since the imposition of an annual poll tax of 1 denarius on each citizen, levied by the Romans. Generally identified as a denarius of the Emperor Tiberius, with a seated figure of the Empress Livia on the reverse.

Tribute penny, silver denarius of Tiberius

TRIENS Latin word meaning one-third. As a denomination, the triens occurs already in the *aes grave series of cast bronze coinage during the 3rd century B.C. The obverse showed a thunderbolt and four pellets (signifying 4 *uncia), the reverse a dolphin and again four pellets. In the struck coinage of a century later the obverse type is a helmeted Minerva head, the reverse a ship's prow, with four pellets above and below respectively. The triens disappears from the Roman republican coinage around 120 B.C. A later triens, also called tremissis (a late Latin word), is a gold coin worth one-third of the Constantinian *solidus. This was to remain the smallest gold denomination struck throughout the Byzantine period, and also widely struck by Goths and Celts in more or less barbarous imitations of Roman types. Weight and metal standards varied widely (*electrum specimens being known), so that the word triens is here no more than a convenient generic appellation for the many small gold coins struck during the Dark Ages throughout southern Europe from Spain to the Danube. Only in the independent dukedom of Beneventum in southern Italy, from the 6th to the 9th centuries A.D., were Byzantine models and standards more or less strictly obversed.

TRIER Town on the Moselle, and an important Roman mint from the time of Diocletian (A.D. 296) until Valentinian III (A.D. 450). It continued to strike coins according to Roman models after it was captured by the Burgundians in A.D. 458, and later still under the Merovingians. In medieval times, it became a powerful archbishopric, and there is an uninterrupted series of gold coinages from the late 14th century until 1770. The most common type is one showing St Peter; from the mid-17th century onwards the Archbishop's portrait is sometimes seen.

TRIME *three cent (silver).

TRIOBOL The half-drachm piece of ancient Greek coinage, sharing with the *diobol a particular function: it was the daily payment of any citizen acting as a judge.

TRIPLE UNITE The largest (in size, not weight or value) English gold coin ever struck, tariffed at 60 shillings. It is confined to a period of under three years of the Civil War, struck first at Shrewsbury in 1642, and at Oxford later in 1642 until 1644. The obverse shows a half-length figure of the King facing left, holding in his right hand a sword and in his left an olive-branch; the reverse is the *declaration type also known on other coins. The Shrewsbury Mint piece is exceedingly rare and no varieties are known; the Oxford Mint piece is known in some half-dozen minor varieties, of which one struck on a slightly smaller *flan and with OXON below the date 1643 is by far the rarest. But rare is a relative term here: any fine specimen of this magnificent piece would today be valued in thousands rather than hundreds of pounds. The portrait of the King is very much in the style of Nicolas *Briot; but the coin is unsigned and cannot, in the absence of documentary evidence during this troubled period, be attributed to him with certainty.

TROYES French regal mint from *c.* 1315, given a *point secret under the fourteenth letter of the legend in 1389. An *Anglo-Gallic mint under Henry VI with a mintmark of a rose (various designs). Under the mint reforms of Francis I (1540), it received the mint-letter S, which changed to a crowned S in 1690, and changed again to V from 1698–1772, when the mint was closed. Documents prove that mechanical coining was introduced at Troyes (*moulin) about a year earlier than in Paris. (Etienne *Bergeron.)

TUGHRA A distinctive feature of Ottoman coinage, displaying the Sultan's name and titles in *monogram form. It is first seen under Suleiman I (1520–26) but not used regularly until Muhammad III (1595–1603).

TUNG PAO Chinese for "current money" and the inscription which—with additions to describe the dynasty and sometimes place of coinage—is to be found on all Chinese *cash from the 7th to the 19th centuries.

TURNER *bodle.

TURTLES *Aegina.

TWENTY CENTS (USA) This shortest-lived of USA coins—it was actually issued in circulation quantities only in 1875—was launched at the instigation of Western states interests, but was too similar to the *quarter to survive after 1878.

TWO CENT Authorised by the same law (1864) which provided for the change to a bronze composition for the cent, the 2-cent piece had a weight (96 grains) exactly twice that of the cent. It served to fill the vital need for small change to replace the many *tokens then in circulation, but outlived its usefulness by the early 1870s and was finally withdrawn when a major revision of US coinage law took place in 1873. This coin, at the instigation of the Rev. Mark R. Watkinson, and with the support of Lincoln's Secretary of the Treasury, Salmon P. Chase, became the first to carry the motto IN GOD WE TRUST. The only notable die varieties occur, in fact, in the lettering of these words during the first year of issue (i.e. 1864) (small or large letters on the scroll above the obverse shield—the former by far the rarer).

TWOPENCE This denomination is, until the reign of Charles II, better known as the half-*groat; but a silver coin officially named twopence then continued until the reign of Queen Victoria, when it disappeared (except in the *Maundy series), its place taken by a silver *threepence. There is also the famous large copper *cartwheel of 1797, and the recent copper denomination in the new decimal currency.

Cartwheel twopence of George III, 1797, Soho Mint, Birmingham

TWO SHILLINGS A denomination coined for British West Africa from 1913–52. It never at any time bore the words *one florin*, always *two shillings*. The coin was struck at the Royal Mint, King's Norton Mint and The Mint (Birmingham) Ltd. A date likely to elude most collectors is 1928: although 7,900,000 are known to have been struck only a handful have so far been traced. Most were melted down and used for 3-pence and 6-pence pieces instead. Those making a technical collection of metals used in coinage may like to know that the 1920 date can be had in three different metals: (1) .925 fine silver, struck at the Royal Mint, (2) .500 fine silver, struck at The Mint (Birmingham) Ltd and (3) in brass, struck at King's Norton Mint.

TYMPF, ANDREAS A Polish mintmaster of German extraction, active at various mints from around 1650–67, whose name became a by-word for debased coinage. The base silver *Gulden, first struck in Posen during 1663 became known as the tympf. Similar coins were later also struck by the Electors of Saxony for their Polish possessions, and by the Electors of Brandenburg for both Polish and Lithuanian provinces. As late as 1752, we find a base silver coin of Frederick the Great of Prussia, struck at Königsberg, referred to as a tympf.

TYPE The word to describe, in coin collecting, the general design of a coin (e.g. obverse: portrait facing right; reverse: arms). The thrill of the hunt for many collectors lies in finding as many possible *varieties of one particular type of coin—not only of such obvious features as different dates, but minutiae such as *mintmarks.

TYPE MUET This French term takes *anepigraphic coins one step further. It implies that not only is there no inscription to help identify the piece, but other possible clues such as a portrait are also lacking. Such coins are said, quite aptly, to be dumb.

TYRE A Phoenician mint from the 5th century B.C., and active well into Roman times. Early types show the local sea-god Melkart riding a sea-horse or dolphin on the obverse, with an owl of distinctly Athenian aspect as the reverse. Later types often have a sea-horse and/or dolphin without the god. During the Ptolemaic period, Alexandrian-type tetradrachms were struck here. There is an interesting later history to the town as a mint in the time of the Crusades, when coins were struck here in imitation of the Arab *dinar and *dirhem. A few rare feudal French *deniers were also struck here during the same period, by Philip de Montfort and his son John, as Princes of Tyre.

U

UGORSKY Russian for Hungarian, and hence applied to the gold coin derived from the Hungarian ducat, as first struck *c.* 1475 under Ivan III. A unique specimen is preserved in the Hermitage Museum at Leningrad. It is most probably due to the influence of the Italian mintmaster and architect Aristoteles Fioravanti who was then employed by the Russian ruler, having previously worked at the court of Matthias Corvinus, King of Hungary.

UHLHORN, DIETRICH (1764–1837) A German technician and manufacturer of coining machines, who invented the lever-press which had its first public demonstration at Düsseldorf in 1818. It was an almost immediate success, being adopted by the Berlin Mint in 1820 and (at any rate experimentally) by the Royal Mint in London during 1828. Various rare commemorative trial pieces and advertisement tickets struck by Uhlhorn exist, including the 1828 London event, and the 200th machine made by the firm during 1876 (by then known as Uhlhorn & Sohn, his son having succeeded him in the business). With improvements by *Thonnelier, the Uhlhorn lever coining-press was also adopted at the Paris Mint during the 1830s and by the end of the century had generally superseded the *screw-press everywhere. It was driven first by steam, later by hydraulic power, and enabled both greater and more even pressures to be exerted, with less die wear, than earlier systems.

ULFELDTER These coins are named after the Danish Grand Chamberlain Corfitz Ulfeldt. Under his supervision, there were struck at the Copenhagen Mint from 1644–7, during the war against Sweden, certain coins with the legend JUSTUS JEHOVAH JUDEX (the word Jehovah engraved in Hebrew characters). In gold there is the ducat, its half and quarter; in silver, pieces of 2 Mark, 16 Shilling (1 Mark) and 4 Shilling.

UNCIA One-twelfth of the *as in the Roman *aes grave series. At first (from *c.* 260 B.C.) cast, with knuckle-bone as the obverse type and showing a single pellet on the reverse. In the struck coinage about a century later it appears with a helmeted head of Bellona to the left, and a pellet behind on the obverse; a ship's prow with ROMA above and a pellet below as the reverse.

UNCIRCULATED Numismatic term for a coin showing absolutely no traces of wear, with the possible exception of almost invisible hair lines caused by coins rubbing against each other while being transported in bags from the mint to a bank or other distribution point.

UNGARO Italian name for the Hungarian ducat, or rather its type as extensively copied (especially during the 17th century) at a number of mints in northern Italy, e.g. Modena, Parma, Tassarolo. This type is one showing a standing warrior-saint (in Hungarian coinage St Ladislas) and a reverse of either the Madonna or a shield.

UNICORN   A gold coin of Scotland, struck during the reigns of James III, IV and V during the period 1486–1517 only. There are a number of varieties, with a unicorn supporting the Scottish shield as the main type, sometimes with a crown. The half-unicorn also exists.

UNIFACE   Numismatic term for coins or medals struck on one side only, the other remaining blank.

UNITE   Gold coin of both England and Scotland, struck first by James I of England (James VI of Scotland) in 1604 to celebrate the union of the two kingdoms, with the legend reading FACIAM EOS IN GENTEM UNAM, i.e. "I will make them one people". The type (which was continued under Charles I) shows the half-length figure of the King holding the orb and sceptre. It was tariffed at 20 shillings. (Also *triple unite.)

UNITED STATES MINTS   Of the mints in the USA only Philadelphia has been active during the whole period 1793 to date. The other principal mint now is Denver, Colorado, which began operations in 1906. Prior to this the San Francisco Mint (1854–1955) has been the main subsidiary mint. Mints for the coinage of gold only were active in Charlotte (North Carolina) and Dahlonega (Georgia) from 1838–61. This was due to local lobbying after the discovery of gold nearby. New Orleans (Louisiana) laid claim to a mint at the same time (i.e. 1838) but struck both gold and silver and continued in operation until 1909. Carson City (Nevada) followed as a result of the opening-up of the West but had only a short lifespan (1870–93).

Mintmarks as shown below were used regularly by all the above mints except Philadelphia. This has shown the mintmark P only on one occasion for a USA coinage: that of the 5-cent pieces struck between 1942–5. There are, however, more examples of the initial P on coinages struck for foreign countries (e.g. Curacao, Surinam). Finally, it should be noted that the San Francisco Mint has again been active since 1965 for the striking of specimen sets for collectors.

C	Charlotte
CC	Carson City
D	Dahlonega (to 1861)
D	Denver (from 1906)
O	New Orleans
P	Philadelphia
S	San Francisco

United States Mints:

Kennedy half-dollar, 1972. *(Photo courtesy R. Lobel)*

Lincoln Cent, 1983. *(Photo courtesy R. Lobel)*

UNITED STATES TRADE DOLLAR   Issued in limited quantities only from 1873 to 1878, although some further proofs were struck until 1885. They are known from the Philadelphia Mint and also occur with Carson City and San Francisco mintmarks. None is common and some very scarce. They were legal tender in the USA until June 1876, after which they were valid for export trade only, mainly in the Far East. The obverse shows the seated Liberty figure and the date; the reverse has the legend UNITED STATES OF AMERICA above an eagle, below which, in small letters 420 GRAINS, 900 FINE and below this, in larger letters, TRADE DOLLAR. Although more than 35 million were struck over a period of five years, over 7½ million are known to have been returned to the US Mint for redemption and recoinage after they were demonetised, and many more were melted down for bullion in the Orient: hence their rarity today.

URBS ROMA   An inscription appearing on certain coins of Constantine the Great, during the period A.D. 330–35, to

Urbs Roma bronze coin of
Constantine, Siscia Mint

distinguish them from others celebrating the foundation of his
new capital of Constantinople. The reverse shows a wolf suckling
the legendary founders of the city, the twins Romulus and
Remus. The series is one of small copper coins only.

URSENTALER, ULRICH (d. 1562) Austrian coin engraver and
medallist, active at Hall, Salzburg, Augsburg and other mints.
Little is known of his early life and career, but he obviously
enjoyed high repute during the lifetime of the Emperor
Maximilian I (d. 1519), for he is mentioned as engraving the
Emperor's secret seal in 1518. Indeed his medal of the Emperor
on horseback, dated as early as 1509, is a superb production. As
late as 1558 he cut the dies for the new coinage of the Emperor
Ferdinand I.

URSULATHALER A type of Thaler struck at Cologne, with
dates 1512 and 1516, commemorating the martyrdom of St
Ursula, which took place in this city. The name is taken from the
reverse type showing St Ursula and her attendants in the ship
which took her up the Rhine to Cologne. The obverse shows the
Three Kings, patron saints of Cologne. There are many later
restrikes, generally undated.

UTRECHT Town in the Netherlands and an important mint to
this day. There was a very fine series of medieval episcopal money
struck here, and a short series of Napoleonic coins dating from
1812–13, when the kingdom of Holland formed part of the
French Empire. During the 18th century, this was the principal
mint of the Batavian Republic, and it also struck a great deal of
coinage for the Dutch colonies.

V

VACQUETTE A small cow, which was both the mintmark of the mint at Pau in the French Pyrenees and the popular name given to a *billon coin struck there by the Vicomtes de Béarn in the early 15th century. The type was continued in the regal coinage of Henry IV, on which the field was quartered with two crowned initial Hs and two cows.

VALENCIA Independent types continued to be struck in this Spanish town (and kingdom) after the union of Aragon and Castile until the War of the Spanish Succession at the beginning of the 18th century. The main type on both gold and silver is that of the ruler's profile bust (facing bust at first, during the 15th century), with a diamond-shaped shield on the reverse.

VAN LOON, GERALD (1683–1758) Dutch historian and numismatist, who published during the 1720s the basic work on Netherlands coinage from the date of the abdication of Charles V to 1716. The five volumes are notable for the many fine engraved plates.

VARIETIES The more obvious kinds of varieties that coin collectors look out for are briefly mentioned under *type. This game can be extended almost indefinitely—or, as one might say if one does not share the passion, *ad absurdum*. Thus, for example, the twenty-three die varieties listed by two American collectors of the 1862 silver *rupee (India) after "several years" detailed research. The present writer can think of more fruitful and pleasant forms of masochism.

VATICAN *papal coinage.

VEIC The initials of the United East India Company (the V form of capital U being common on coins during the 16th–18th centuries). They are found both on coins of Bombay and Java while under the company's rule: also on certain English guineas and half-guineas between 1729–39, signifying that these were struck from gold shipped to England by the company.

VELDDAALDER Dutch terms for *emergency money, used indifferently to describe *siege coins or those struck by a commander on the field of battle to pay his troops.

VELD POND A very rare South African gold coin, struck in 986 specimens only by the Boers during the 1902 campaign, to the value of a pound sovereign, at Pilgrim's Rest. It shows on the obverse the initials ZAR (Afrikaans abbreviation for South African Republic) and the date, and on the reverse simply the words EEN POND.

VENEZOLANO *bolivar.

VENICE The seat of an uninterrupted series of coins from the late 12th century until 1797. The mint was also active during the troubles of 1848–9 and for the kingdom of Lombardy-Venetia until 1866. The particular type of *ducat struck here from the late 13th century, which was copied throughout Europe, became

Venetian ducat (n.d., but known to be 1284 from other evidence)

universally known as the *zecchino. (Also *lira tron, Matapan, osella.)

VEREINSTHALER This Thaler was created by the Austro-German monetary union (Vereinigung) of 1857. The coin was henceforth struck to a uniform standard of .900 fine and weighed 18.5 grammes. Most of the German states adhered to it, with a general type of ruler's bust on the obverse and arms on the reverse. An exception was the city of Frankfurt, which showed a female portrait on the obverse (personification of the city) and an eagle on the reverse.

VERMEIL French term (not confined to numismatics) for silver *gilt.

VERONA A mint of the Lombard kings until the time of Charlemagne, who struck here (after his coronation as Holy Roman Emperor in A.D. 800) a denier with his profile bust. Under the Emperor Henry II (1013–24) one of the very rare gold pennies of medieval Europe was struck here. Later coins include autonomous issues, some struck under Venetian and Milanese sovereignty, and finally some more imperial coins for Maximilian I. The mint was closed in 1516.

VERTUE, GEORGE (1684–1754) English antiquary and line engraver, one of the founders of the Society of Antiquaries, whose official engraver he was from 1717 onwards. In numismatics, he is important for his pioneer monograph on Thomas *Simon with many illustrations of that master's coins, medals and seals.

VIANEN, PAUL VAN (d. 1613) Dutch artist, as famous for his goldsmith's work and line engraving as for his medallic productions. He was the successor of Antonio *Abondio at the court of the Emperor Rudolph II at Prague, and his various medallic portraits of this monarch are among the finest existing. A particularly magnificent and large cast medal shows on the obverse the Emperor on horseback, and on the reverse seated between the figures of Bellona and Pax, surrounded by six Electors. His elaborate designs mark the transition from late Renaissance to the Baroque.

VICARIATSTHALER A term used to describe the *sede vacante coins issued by the Electors of the Palatinate and Saxony during an imperial interregnum. It is derived from the inscription *vicarius*, meaning deputy (i.e. for the Emperor, until the election of a new one).

VIENNA Principal mint of the Habsburg Empire from the early 18th century and sole mint of the Austrian Republic since 1925. It has always been distinguished for the quality of its workmanship and has an academy for coin design attached to it. Many fine commemorative pieces have been struck here during the past sixty years, besides the perennial *Maria Theresa Thaler. Its high reputation has also led it to execute many foreign coinage contracts. Its mintmark is A, not always shown. The Vienna Kunsthistorisches Museum has one of the world's largest universal monetary collections, embracing all aspects of numismatics including banking documents of all kinds from early days. A unique collection of coin dies, dating back to the 15th century and formerly at the mint, is also housed there.

VIERER A silver denomination to the value of 4 *Pfennige, first struck at Strasbourg in 1397, later at Basel, Berne and Merano. Swiss types often carry the figure 2, since the Vierer was the equivalent of 2 *Rappen.

VIGO Town in Portugal, off which a famous naval battle was fought in 1702, resulting in the capture by the British fleet of enormous amounts of gold and silver *bullion from French and Spanish ships. Most of this, and also much plate, was melted down; and coins struck from it bear below the bust of Queen Anne the word VIGO. Any such issues in gold denominations (i.e. the 5-guinea piece, the guinea and its half) are rarer and dearer than ordinary ones. Silver issues bearing the word VIGO, however, tend to be more common than those without it. They comprise the crown, half-crown and shilling. None of these coins is known with a date other than 1702 or 1703.

VINTEM A Portuguese silver coin to the value of 20 *reis, introduced by John II in 1489. It showed a crowned Y on the obverse and the Portuguese shield of arms on the reverse. Under Manuel I (1495–1521) the letter M replaced Y. John III (1521–57) introduced the double vintem bearing, besides his initial, the figures (40 reis). In the Portuguese possessions in what is now Brazil, the vintem was struck as a copper denomination from the early 17th century. There are multiples up to 12 vintems.

VIOLET, THOMAS A somewhat disreputable London gold-smith, active c. 1634–62, who is important for publishing a pamphlet on *Trade and Mint Affairs* with details of the Cromwellian period, and especially *Blondeau's patterns during the 1650s.

VIRGINIA An official coinage for the Crown colony of Virginia was authorised by Royal Warrant dated 20 May 1773, which provided for the coining of 25 tons of halfpenny pieces. This coinage has the distinction of being the only one executed for the American colonies by the Royal Mint in London, and the dies for it are still preserved in the Mint Museum. Rare *proofs are known for a penny dated 1773 and a shilling dated 1774, but no such coins were ever issued. The obverse of this copper piece shows the King's bust facing right, with a crowned shield of the royal arms on the reverse.

VIS-À-VIS PORTRAITS *bajoire.

VISIGOTHS Tribe of Goths who ruled Spain from the 6th to the 8th century A.D. Their coinage consists almost entirely of *tremisses, based on Roman or Byzantine models. From about A.D. 580 onwards, during the final years of the reign of King Leovigild (A.D. 568–86), coins regularly bear the name of the King and of the mint (Toledo and Barcelona being the most important). A facing bust on both the obverse and the reverse was the most common type; but the reverse may carry a cross or a mint name in monogram form.

VLIES Gold or silver coins of the Netherlands, the type of which was modelled on that of the Order of the Golden Fleece (vlies), founded by Duke Philip of Burgundy in 1429. As a gold coin, it was first seen in Brabant in the latter part of the 15th century, showing the chain of the Order only; this was widely copied and also known under its French name of toison d'or. The jewel of the Order, showing the actual fleece, appears on the silver pieces to the value of 3 *stuivers, towards the end of the century; this type was copied as far afield as Italy and Spain.

V.O.C. The initials of the Vereenigde Oostingdische Campagnie, i.e. the United East India Company (of the Netherlands). They appear, often in *monogram form, on very many coins of the Dutch colonial series from the 17th to the 19th century.

VOCE POPULI Copper coins (or *tokens) bearing the words VOCE POPULI were struck in denominations of a halfpenny and farthing with the date 1760 by a button-maker of Dublin called Roche (or Roach). They show a laureate bust of George III

Vigo crown of Anne, 1703

Vlies: Issued under Philip the Fair, Holland, c. 1500

facing right, with an inscription as above on either side of it, and Hibernia seated, with a harp, on the reverse. Some authorities have tried to see the features of Prince Charles Edward Stuart in this portrait, suggesting that Roche may have been a Stuart sympathiser and pointing to a mysterious initial P (for Prince?) which appears before the face or below the bust as additional evidence to support this theory. These tokens are also known to have circulated in the North American British colonies.

VOIDED   This adjective is used to describe a certain type of cross, as current on the English penny from 1180 onwards. It consists of two thin, double lines rather than one solid one. At a time when coins are frequently cut into half or into four parts, to serve as halfpennies or farthings, the voided cross made such cutting easier.

VOIGT, HENRY (d. 1814)   First chief coiner of the United States mint in Philadelphia, appointed by *Rittenhouse in July 1792. He was a skilled mechanic (in fact, like Rittenhouse, originally a watchmaker), but a poor die engraver and soon entrusted this work to others. Today he is chiefly remembered for his *pattern Silver Center Cent, a copper piece with a small *plug of pure silver. The object of this was to reduce the large cent, as first mooted, to a more manageable size, the silver plug bringing the copper piece up to the full intrinsic value. The idea, however, was not adopted. Voigt remained in his post until his death in 1814.

VOIGT, KARL FRIEDRICH (1800–74)   Famous and prolific German medallist and die engraver, who studied for a time under *Pistrucci in London. He became chief engraver to the Munich Mint in 1829 and worked there for twenty-five years. During this time, he engraved most of the regular coinage for Bavaria, besides numerous *patterns and many medals of the Wittelsbach family. His work and fame, however, were not confined to Germany, but included coinages for the newly established kingdom of Greece (King Otto, 1832 onwards) and for the Papacy (Pius IX, 1858 onwards).

VOTIVE COINS   A term referring to those coins in the Roman imperial series that have on them inscriptions including the word VOTA in various combinations (e.g. VOTA PUBLICA, VOTA SUSCEPTA, VOTA SOLUTA), or in conjunction with numbers (VOTA V, VOTA X, VOTA MULTIS XX). The word is the plural of the Latin *votum*, meaning not a vote but a vow; and such coins refer to the solemn vows which emperors renewed from time to time. At the beginning of each year, such vows would be solemnised with a religious ceremony, shown on the coins by way of a sacrificial scene, or two figures of Victory inscribing the VOTA on a shield. Coins bearing the word *suscepta* refer to vows for the future (and the figures to the years ahead, which might be 5, 10 or even 20); those with the word *soluta* are in fact thanksgiving coins for promises (or victories) achieved. The practice began with Augustus but was not by any means followed by all the emperors on their coins; the types are most common during the late Constantine period.

VRENELI   *Landry.

VUURIJZER   A Dutch silver coin first struck under Charles the Bold (1467–77) at his new mint of Nijmegen in Gelderland. There were also halves and doubles; among the latter, that of 1474 is the first dated Netherlands coin. In French this coin is known as a briquet.

Silver votive coin of Honorius

W

WADO KAIKO   The first cast bronze coinage of Japan. It is closely modelled on Chinese coinage, but the four characters are read clockwise and may be interpreted as "first Japanese copper treasure". Believed to have been introduced around A.D. 708, the first issue is very crudely produced. A second issue (*c.* A.D. 720) shows better workmanship, probably by Chinese craftsmen.

WAPPENMÜNZEN   The earliest coins of Athens; the name was invented by German numismatists, because of the many varying designs on the obverse: e.g. wheel, triskelis, Gorgon's head, etc., which at the end of the 19th century were believed to represent the coats of arms (Wappen) of leading Athenian families. This theory is today discredited, but no other satisfactory explanation for the wide variety of symbols has been forthcoming. In any case, the period when these coins were struck was a brief one, *c.* 575–525 B.C.; at the latter date, the famous owl type superseded all others. (*Athens.)

WARIN, JEAN (c. 1604–72)   French medallist and coin engraver. He was a very fine technician, who succeeded where Nicolas *Briot had failed, i.e. in getting mechanised coining finally adopted at the Paris Mint in 1640 (and at other French mints from 1646). He was a protégé of Cardinal Richelieu and his portrait of that statesman is one of his best medallic productions. But no less remarkable are many of the dies he cut for the coins of Louis XIII and Louis XIV. The piece of 10 *louis d'or of Louis XIII (1640) is one of the great glories of French coinage.

WARK   A rare gold coin of Ethiopia, first struck (posthumously) in memory of the Emperor Menelik II (1889–1913) in 1916. The obverse shows his profile bust, the reverse the Lion of Judah. The double was also struck, and fractions down to one-eighth. There are even rarer issues by the Empress Zauditu (who struck multiples of 2 and 4 wark), and by Haile Selassie (1930 and 1931 only).

WAROU, DANIEL (1674–1730)   Swedish medallist and coin engraver, whose fame rests on his thirty years' work as chief engraver to the mint of *Kremnitz (1699–1729). The standard of his work there has never been excelled, and as a modeller in the whole Austro-Hungarian series Antonio *Abondio is probably his only equal. His was the first use of the *screw-press at Kremnitz, and of *edge-lettering. During one of his regular inspection tours of Transylvanian mints he was detained by the uprising of the Malcontents (1703–7) and cut dies for the insurgent Francis Racoczi. Only his medals are signed (D. WAROU or D.W.); but most of the fine Thalers under the reigns of Leopold I and Charles VI may be assigned to him.

WARSAW   Though the capital of Poland, this city was only an occasional mint, being much overshadowed in this respect by *Cracow. Its chief times of operation have been during the sovereignty of the Saxon kings (18th century), and from 1815–67, when the Russians struck coins for Poland here. Only in 1925 did the capital city become the sole mint of the then young republic. During that year, and to celebrate the 900th anniversary of the kingdom, gold commemorative pieces of ducat size were struck here, showing on the obverse the bust of Boleslaw (the first monarch) and on the reverse the crowned Polish eagle.

WASHINGTON QUARTER   *quarter.

WASHINGTON TOKENS   Struck during the early period of American independence, c. 1783–95, with numerous varieties of Washington's effigy. Some were undoubtedly of English origin, the reverse bearing a figure looking suspiciously like Britannia; and values of a halfpenny are known as well as the cent. Others, again, were meant to serve as patterns for the half-dollar and are known in silver strikings, with an American eagle reverse. The same dies were also used for buttons in more than one case; and there are straightforward advertising pieces for tradesmen besides true copper tokens.

WASS, J. MOLITOR & CO.   Wass and Molitor established a smelting and assaying plant in San Francisco very early in the 1850s. At first they did not themselves strike coins, but acted as consultants to others engaged in production. When they did undertake a coinage in 1852, it was a $5 piece of very high quality. $10, $20 and even $50 pieces followed at intervals until 1855, the largest denomination (an index to the times) also being struck in the largest quantity—up to $38,000 per day. All their coins follow the Liberty head/eagle pattern, but with the words CALIFORNIA and/or SAN FRANCISCO prominent on the reverse.

WATERFORD   An occasional Irish mint from the late 12th century onwards, and more regularly from the time of Edward IV to Henry VII. There is an extremely rare *groat of Lambert Simnel (the Pretender) as "Edward VI of Ireland" with the legend CIVITAS WATERFORD on the reverse. Later issues are confined to the 17th century tradesmen's *tokens, and a few farthing tokens of the period 1840–50.

W.C.C.   These initials are seen on certain shillings of George I (placed beneath the bust) dated 1723–6. They signify that the

pieces were made from silver mined by the Welsh Copper
Company.

WEDGWOOD, JOSIAH (1730–95) The famous Staffordshire
potter produced from *c*. 1776 onwards a huge series of portrait
medallions, mainly in his well-known jasper ware (white portrait
busts on blue or other coloured background), but also a few in
glazed cream ware and black basalt. Apart from a great number
of mythological and historical figures, there was (in his 1779
catalogue) the gallery of "Illustrious Moderns", including practically every contemporary of note, English, European and even
American. Some of these were modelled from the life by
Wedgwood's skilled craftsmen Flaxman and Hackwood, but the
majority were taken from silver and bronze medals which
Wedgwood's agents found for him (e.g. *Dassier's portrait of
Montesquieu). Originals are now scarce and expensive, but the
firm of Wedgwood continues to produce reproductions of certain
favourites to this day.

WEIDITZ (c. 1500–1559) German Renaissance goldsmith and
medallist, whose activity falls mainly between the years 1523–36.
Though he never signed his work (except for a jewelled dagger at
Dresden) stylistic evidence has caused more than a hundred
medals to be attributed to him. He worked at first in a number
of German cities (Augsburg, Ulm, Strasbourg and Nuremberg)
and around 1529 came into the employ of the Emperor Charles
V, whom he accompanied to the Netherlands, Spain and perhaps
even Italy. His work is therefore much more cosmopolitan than
that of most other German medallists of the period (who tended
to confine their subjects to local worthies): there are superb
medals of, among others, the Spanish conquistador Cortez and
the Genoese admiral Andrea Doria—also, of course, of Charles
V. He is perhaps the most 'classical' of all German medallists,
with refined detail and lettering.

WEIGAND, EMIL (1837–1906) Engraver and medallist at the
Berlin Mint from 1866–1904. Extremely prolific and able rather
than inspired, Weigand was responsible for the German imperial
coinages from William I to William II, and for the German colonial coinages of East Africa and New Guinea. But this was by
no means all: he engraved dies (for striking at Berlin) for eight
German principalities and for the coinage of Egypt.

WEISSPFENNIG *albus.

WENDENPFENNIGE German term for the type of *bracteate
(Bohemia, Poland) with a distinctive upturned rim.

WERMUTH, CHRISTIAN (1661–1739) One of the most prolific
of German medallists. Though he also cut coin dies for the house
of Saxony at the Gotha Mint (where he acted as chief engraver
for most of his working life), he is chiefly remembered today for
his extraordinarily lively satirical medals, which in their
frankness— and sometimes scurrilous crudity—recall nothing so
much as the work of Gilray and other Georgian caricaturists.
Scarcely a subject was sacred to him, and he could be as scathing
(and scatological) about peace treaties as about pietism, the Jews,
or the financial manipulations of John *Law.

Wermuth was the first to put the marketing of commemorative
medals on a mass production basis, offering them in printed
catalogues of several hundred items at a time, which he
distributed to a regular mailing list of collectors, dealers and
museums. What is perhaps his finest work, a series of 214 portrait
medals of the Roman emperors, is hardly ever found complete
today.

WEYMOUTH A mint for Charles I during the Civil War, 1643–4 only. Very roughly struck pieces, in denominations from the half-crown down, were issued here with the initial W to distinguish them.

WIELANDY, CHARLES (1748–1837) Swiss coin engraver and medallist who worked chiefly at the Geneva Mint, where he cut the dies for the *décime of 1794 and petit *écu of 1795. The coinage of Neuchâtel from 1797–1807 is also attributed to him, and he submitted *patterns for the French coinage contest of the First Consulate (i.e. the first coins to show a portrait of Bonaparte). Though his designs did not win the prize he was highly commended.

WIENER, CHARLES (1832–88) One of three brothers, all of whom achieved fame in their native Belgium as modellers of coins and medals. Charles, the youngest, is of more than passing interest to English collectors for his stay in London during the early 1860s. Here he held the post of assistant engraver at the Royal Mint and was responsible for some interesting *patterns, notably shillings with the unusual legend HALF FLORIN. In 1864 he went to the Lisbon Mint, where he was responsible for postage and revenue stamps as well as coinage. His later work is principally medallic and again includes work for England: twice he engraved the dies for the City of London Medal (1874 visit of Tsar Alexander II, 1884 gift of Epping Forest to the nation by Queen Victoria).

WIENER PFENNIGE The *Pfennig was first struck in Vienna towards the end of the 12th century and is mentioned in official documents by 1204, though none has been found prior to c. 1230. Since small coin was frequently called in (annually from the middle of the 13th century), over 150 different types are known to this early period. Only in 1400 was a uniform type introduced, with the Austrian shield of arms and the ruler's name. Their generally high metallic standard caused them to be widely accepted as trade coins, north as far as Bavaria and south as far as Florence.

WILDMAN COINS A common type of coin in the Brunswick series, showing a wild man with uprooted fir-tree (sometimes two such figures with shield of arms between). The type derives from a legend of the Harz mountain region. It is also (but much less often) found on Thalers of certain other German states, e.g. Prussia 1790–1809. The Brunswick issues begin already in the mid-16th century.

WILLOW TREE COINS Early coins of Massachusetts, struck in denominations of shillings, sixpenny pieces and threepenny pieces only. They show on the obverse a willow tree, on the reverse the date 1652 and the figures XII, VI or III. All belong among the rarest of early American coins, only three specimens having been found on the 3-penny piece.

WIRE MONEY (1) A curious form of currency, made of thin bars of silver, with one end often bent round in the shape of a fish hook; much in use in the Persian Gulf area from the 16th century onwards. Also known as *lari. (2) A name popularly given to the 1792 *Maundy issue engraved by Lewis *Pingo, on account of the extremely thin, wire-like look of the numerals. (Also *lari.)

WITTE A special type of *albus as struck in the Hanseatic League cities under a monetary convention of 1379. These cities, i.e. Lübeck, Hamburg and Wismar, were among the first to feel the need of a larger denomination than the standard *Pfennig and issued this coin to the quadruple value. By 1381 two other cities, Rostock and Lüneburg, had joined the convention. They all had a common reverse, showing a cross with a star at the centre and the inscription BENEDICTUS DEUS; while the obverse carried the issuing.city's badge and mint name (e.g. for Hamburg a tower and the inscription MONETA HAMBURG). These issues proved popular and continued until the mid-16th century.

WOLSEY GROAT A special *groat as struck by Cardinal Wolsey at his archiepiscopal mint at York from 1514–26, with initials T.W. on either side of the royal shield of arms and a cardinal's hat beneath (reverse type). While both York and Canterbury certainly enjoyed coinage rights, these were always confined to striking pennies; and Wolsey's presumption, both in striking this larger denomination and using his own initials and insignia on it, were later to be one of the indictments in his trial.

WON The currency unit of Korea after 1905 (1 won = 100 chou). As a unit, it was never struck; but a half exists in silver, and there are multiples of 5, 10 and 20 in gold.

Wolsey groat of Henry VIII, with Thomas Wolsey's initials on the reverse

WOOD, WILLIAM (1671–1730) English entrepreneur, merchant and ironmonger, and the inventor of *Bath metal. His sallies into coinage will be found described under *Rosa Americana and *Wood's halfpence.

WOOD'S HALFPENCE Struck by William *Wood at his Bristol foundry for circulation in Ireland during 1722. The coinage caused a scandal not only because it was struck in *Bath metal (there was only a half-crown's worth of copper in each pound's worth of coin), but because of the circumstances in which the patent for the coinage had been acquired by Wood from the King's mistress, the Duchess of Kendal. It gave rise to the famous *Drapier's Letters* of Dean Swift, and all production ceased in 1724. A great number of the coins were subsequently shipped to the North American colonies where they circulated alongside Wood's *Rosa Americana issues.

Both farthings and halfpennies were issued; four varieties of the former and eight of the latter are known. The obverse type shows the King's bust facing right, with the legend GEORGIUS DEI GRATIA REX; the reverse shows a seated figure of Hibernia with the legend HIBERNIA and date.

WORCESTER A half-crown only was struck here, or rather within Hartlebury Castle while the city was besieged from March to July 1646. It shows the King on horseback riding to the left (obverse), and the royal arms with the initials HC beneath (reverse).

WÜRZBURG Formerly in Franconia, today part of Bavaria, the town of Würzburg was an important bishopric whose ruler struck coins from the time of Bruno (1034–45) onwards. There is an uninterrupted and splendid gold series from 1506–1814. Early types show St Kilian, the town's patron saint, later ones more often show the ruler's bust, with St Kilian or a shield as the reverse.

WYON FAMILY (18th & 19th centuries) Perhaps the most talented family of coin engravers and medallists ever to work in England. The first Wyon we hear of came to that country during the reign of George II, from Cologne, doubtless because he was already distinguished in his profession there. He settled in Birmingham, which was therefore the "home town" of the English Wyons. Some of them remained there, working for (among others) Matthew *Boulton but also a great deal on their own account, as die-sinkers of tokens and medals. One branch of the family, however, went to London, where successive generations become chief engravers at the Royal Mint—a post that became a virtual Wyon monopoly from the beginning of George I's reign almost to the end of Queen Victoria's.

Forrer devotes well over a hundred pages of his *Dictionary of Medallists* to this family; but it is to be noted that three-quarters of this is taken up by two names only: William Wyon (1795–1851) and his son Leonard Charles Wyon (1826–91). It was they who were to dominate the mint during the period mentioned, though William had his brushes with *Pistrucci in the early days. When Leonard Charles took over from his father, his position was unassailable; the list of coin dies engraved by him reads like a gazetteer of the British Empire (Forrer, vol. VI, pp. 595–601). Apart from all this, he was also very much involved with the early history of British decimalisation of the currency, engraving numerous fine *patterns for cents, decimal pennies, etc., all to-day very rare.

Though other members of the family could not rival these achievements it is fair to add that Thomas Wyon (1792–1817) might even have exceeded them, had he not died from consumption at the early age of twenty-five. Two years running, in 1810 and 1811, he won the Society of Arts gold medal for medal engraving; and in the four short years from 1811–15 he rose at the Royal Mint from the grade of a mere probationer to the post of chief engraver. During this time, he was responsible for the *token coinages of England and Ireland 1812–13, similar coinages for Jersey, a few colonial pieces (Ceylon and British Guiana) and two interesting ''foreign'' coinages struck at the Royal Mint: *pistoles and *Gulden struck to pay the King's Hanoverian troops (1813–14) and 20-franc gold pieces with the effigy of Louis XVIII (1815) for the payment of British troops serving in France. Three superlative medals, too, date from these years: Manchester Pitt Club (1813), the King's Medal for Indian Chiefs (1814) and the Bombardment of Algiers (1816).

XERAPHIM A silver coin for the Portuguese Indian colonies, struck at Goa and Diu from 1570–1871. It was equivalent to 360 (later 300) *reis or the half-*rupee. At first it weighed 19.05 grammes with a silver content of 17.46 grammes and there were various obverse types of standing saints (John, Philip, Sebastian). In 1672 the Cross of St George became the dominating type, and from 1730 the bust of the Portuguese king. By 1850 the coin had much shrunk in size and weight (to 5½ grammes), and the word PARDAO now appeared on it. It was, however, still worth half a rupee and continued to be known popularly by its old name.
XVI *denarius.

Y

YANG A silver denomination of Korea from 1894, until the currency reform of 1905, when it was replaced by the *won. Pieces of 1 and 5 yang were struck.

YAP One of a group of islands in the South Pacific known as the Carolines. It has a unique and curious currency known as fei, dating from the Stone Age. These are limestone discs, varying in size from 6 inches to 12 feet in diameter. The biggest ones weigh nearly 5 tons. They have large centre holes to facilitate transport.

YEATS, WILLIAM BUTLER (1865–1939) Irish poet who, in his capacity as a senator of the young Irish Free State, chaired the Committee on Coinage which selected the designs of Percy Metcalfe for Ireland's first independent coinage. His report (published in 1928) still makes such interesting reading that an edited version was brought out in 1972 (Dolmen Press).

YEFIMOK The Russian term for the first attempts to create a large silver denomination, by *overstriking or *countermarking European *Thalers. The word is a Russian adaptation of the Polish Joachimik, itself from *Joachimsthaler. The earliest Yefimoks date from 1653–4.

Yefimok, Moscow, 1655 (Thaler of Mansfield)

YEN The gold unit of Japan since the institution of Western-type coinage in 1870. Multiples of 2, 5, 10 and 20 yen have been struck from time to time, all at .900 fine (i.e. the same standard as the USA dollar). There have been two main types. The first (until 1897) showed a dragon on the obverse, with a reverse of a wreath over crossed banners. The second shows a radiant sun on the obverse, with the value of the coin within a wreath on the reverse. Last strikings (as multiples of 5 and 20 yen only) were in 1930.

YEO, RICHARD (d. 1779) Assistant engraver at the Royal Mint from 1749, and appointed chief engraver in 1775. Among his many productions were the dies for the guineas of George III's reign until 1774 and the *Northumberland shilling. He also designed the official medal to commemorate the Battle of Culloden in 1746 and probably a number of Vauxhall Gardens admission tickets. The Culloden medal is particularly interesting in that it incorporates a decorative border topped by a suspension loop which is also part of the overall design—a distinct improvement on the normal soldered loop attached to medals.

YORK An important English mint from the time of Archbishop Egberth c. A.D. 750. It remained an archiepiscopal mint until 1545; and the most famous (or notorious) coin struck here was probably the *Wolsey groat. After the Viking invasions, York became also the principal mint of their Northumbrian kingdom. Its activity as an English regal mint from the time of Edward the Confessor onwards was intermittent, the most important period being the reign of Edward VI, the Civil War, and the great recoinage of 1696. The inscription EBOR or EBORACUM began to appear during Henry VIII's reign. Civil war coins here were better struck than at most other mints: there is evidence here for the handiwork of Nicolas *Briot.

YORK, MATTHEW (1771–1838)   A notable collector and later dealer and jeweller, who issued his own penny *token in 1798. He also struck from original dies which came into his possession 60-shilling pieces for the Pretender James VII of Scotland (dated 1686) and a crown of James VIII with the date 1716. The sale of Young's own considerable collection took place over a total of sixty-six days from 1838–41 and made over £9,000.

YUAN   The Chinese name for the dollar, named after Yuan Shi Kai who first struck the type in 1912, showing on the obverse his uniformed facing bust. Previous Chinese coins had never pandered to the cult of the personality.

YUZLIK   The largest Turkish silver coin, equal to 2½ *piastres or 100 *paras (*yuz* meaning one hundred). It was first struck under Selim III (1789–1807) to a weight of 32.40 grammes, but soon deteriorated from what was its original intent, i.e. to be the Turkish counterpart to the ever popular *Maria Theresa Thaler.

Z

ZANCLE   An important mint of ancient Sicily, later known as Messana (the present-day Messina). The earliest coins are *drachms showing a sickle-shaped representation of the harbour, within it a dolphin. These are believed to date from *c.* 500 B.C. They are followed by an attractive type of a running hare, with a dolphin below, and an alternative type of a facing lion's head. These coins are all *tetradrachms. The later coinage is particularly interesting in that it consists entirely of bronze, from about 288 B.C., when the city was conquered by a body of Oscan mercenaries called the Mamertini. This series, of many varying types, continues well into Roman times.

ZANETTI, GUIDO ANTONIA (1741–91)   Italian numismatist, whose five-volume work on Italian mints is still used today by scholars in advanced research, because of the many sources cited and documents often reproduced verbatim.

ZECCHINO   "La Zecca" was the name of the Venetian palace which housed the mint; and zecchino was the name given to the most famous coin struck here, i.e. the *ducat whose type, weight and fineness of gold standard continued virtually unchanged.

It was introduced under the Doge Giovanni Dandolo in 1284, showing the Doge kneeling before the standing figure of St Mark, and receiving the gonfalone, the sacred banner. The reverse shows the figure of Christ surrounded by stars within a printed oval. The reverse inscription reads SIT TIBI CHRISTE DATUS, QUEM TU REGIS, ISTE DUCATUS. Together with the *florin, this became the most widely copied gold coin of the Middle Ages. If the type did not change until the end of the Venetian Republic in 1797 neither did the weight standard: it remained constant at 3.49 grammes, holding 3.44 grammes of gold (i.e. .986 fine).

ZER MABUB   A light gold coin (2.6 grammes) of the Ottoman Empire, introduced during the first quarter of the 18th century. It remained current for over a hundred years.

ZINC   A metal used only rarely on its own in coinage but fairly frequently in *alloys. In pure state, it has the disadvantage of fairly rapid oxidisation and therefore tends to be confined to times of emergency. Its widest use was probably by the Germans in both World Wars in occupied countries: Denmark, France, Belgium and the Netherlands.

ZLATNIK   Name given to the earliest known Russian gold coins, and derived from the word *zoloto* meaning gold. They were struck after A.D. 988 by Prince Vladimir of Kiev and show his seated figure on the obverse, with the bust of Christ Pantocrator on the reverse. Only ten specimens are recorded. The coins are roughly equivalent in value to the Byzantine *nomisma, whose influence is also evident in their style.

ZLOTY   The word *zloty* is Polish for golden and was first applied in coinage to the gold *ducats as introduced under the

Zer mabub of Ahmad III
(Ottoman Empire), *c.* 1711

monetary reforms of Sigismund I in 1528. But just as the word *Guldiner in German might relate also to a silver coin standing in fixed relationship to a gold one, so also has the zloty in its time been many different things. In the 17th century it became a money of *account, constant in value at 30 *Groschen, however debased the actual currency might be. Later again, when Poland was under Russian rule, the zloty was revised both as a gold and silver coin: between 1833–41 the unit and multiples of 2, 5 and 10 were struck in silver and a 20-zloty piece in gold. Under a decree of 1924, the zloty is divided into 100 Groschen, and for commemorative purposes there have been special gold issues of 20, 25, 50 and 100 gold zloty, while the silver denomination has been struck as the unit and its half, and in multiples of 2 and 5.

ZODIACAL COINS   Signs of the zodiac are frequently shown on ancient coins, sometimes singly, sometimes with more than one or even all twelve together. By far the most famous series, however, is that of the twelve zodiacal gold *mohurs, issued by the Mogul Emperor Jahangir between 1618–22, chiefly at the mint of *Agra. Silver *rupees showing the same general types were also struck. All these coins are scarce, and sets of them take time, patience and money to assemble. Their popularity with collectors led to clever forgeries, especially in recent years. (Also *Alexandria.)

Zodiacal: Gold mohur of Jahangir, 1619, showing the sign of Aries

ZOLOTYE   A generic name for any gold coin in Russia since the 16th century. More specifically, it was applied to the three-quarter *chervonetz with portraits of the Tsarina Sophia and the child tsars, Peter and Ivan, which were issued to reward participants of the Crimean campaigns of 1687 and 1689.

ZUG   Swiss canton with principal town of the same name. It had its own regular coinage from 1564–1805, which has formed the subject of a separate and detailed study by Professor Friedrich Wielandt, published under the auspices of the Zuger Kantonalbank. There are many fine Thalers, and an official 5-franc silver coin commemorating the Swiss federal shooting festival held here in 1869. With the exception of a half-ducat dated 1692 the gold is exceedingly rare.

ZURICH   Largest—and richest—of Swiss cities, Zurich has a coinage going back to the 10th century, when silver pennies were first struck here by the abbesses of the Fraumünster-Abtei. Curiously, the city itself did not receive the right of coinage until 1514 (by cession of the abbey's right), which it then continued to exercise until the federal constitution and coinage were adopted in the mid-19th century. Its coinage corresponds to its importance and wealth, with a particularly rich series in gold. Multiples up to 15 ducats are known and 4-ducat ones are not infrequent. Often they show fine city views, as do many of the splendid Thalers. Although a lion with a shield and a sword is the city badge, many other types occur, including the somewhat morbid one of three saints carrying their heads. Among special commemorative pieces are ducats with the bust of the reformer Zwingli, 1719 and 1819, and federal shooting Thalers (5 francs) of 1859 and 1872. All pieces prior to the 18th century are rare, the gold especially so; and outsiders scarcely stand a chance against the proverbial "gnomes", who collect their own rarities avidly.

ZWEKKERT, JOHANN ANTHONIE (d. 1819)   A famous Dutch coin engraver, who served as mint-master at the Surabaya Mint, Java, from 1807–17. Owing to the fortunes of war in the East Indies, Zwekkert's initial mark Z appears not only on Dutch colonial coinages struck there during his administration, but also for French and British ones. Some of the French issues carry the monogram of Louis Napoleon as nominal ruler of the area during the year 1810. The gold half-rupees struck under British rule from 1813 are especially interesting in carrying Malay script and the Javanese date 1740 on the obverse, with an Arabic legend and the date 1668 of the Hegira era on the reverse.

BIBLIOGRAPHY

The following book list was compiled on a very simple principle: it mentions every book which the author had occasion to consult during his work, whether frequently or only once. The specialist scholar or collector will therefore be bound to note many omissions. Indeed, an adequate bibliography of coinage would today take up more than the whole of this book. Even way back in 1965, Elvira Clain-Stefanelli's *Select Numismatic Bibliography* contained in its 380 pages nearly 5,000 titles, while the *Dictionary Catalog* of the American Numismatic Society Library runs to 8 stout volumes. Meanwhile, the flow of numismatic books (many of them reprints of older standard works) continues at the rate of about 50 per month at least. To keep track of all this is a full-time job on its own.

The general reader may well seek for some guide around this maze. R.A.G. Carson's *Coins* remains the standard, indispensable general survey of the whole world and from the beginnings of coinage to the present day (or at least to 1960). Its bibliography is equally indispensable.

A synoptic view of *Numismatics* is given in brief but masterly form by Philip Grierson (Oxford University Press, 1975). I would place it with Carson as *the* other book you must have on your shelf for essential background reading, apart from any special field of interest you may have. Again, his "Suggestions for Further Reading" (in this case annotated) are alone worth the modest price of the book.

Really to study coins you must, of course, handle them. The next best thing is first rate illustrations; and here the six-volume series conceived jointly by Office du Livre (Fribourg, Switzerland) and Battenberg Verlag (Munich,

Germany) is unrivalled: the photos are so uniformly good that you feel you are almost touching the coins. Unfortunately, only the first three of the volumes (on Greek, Roman and Byzantine coins, by Jenkins, Sutherland and Whitting respectively) appeared in an English edition. For Philip Grierson's masterly account of the medieval period or Clain-Stefanelli's from 1450–1789 you must try and get hold of the French or German editions. For the sixth volume, the Swiss and German publishers chose different authors, so you must pick and choose according to your special interests.

For all the multiplicity of specialised works that have appeared over the past ten years or so (and more particularly in Roman and Byzantine studies) there remain some big gaps to be filled. Nothing practical exists for the coins of the Popes: Professor Muntori's magisterial 4-volume study is hardly a "collector's guide" in the manner of the Seaby or Yeoman catalogues. And while the estimable Dr Davenport has done sterling work on German Thalers from 1500 onwards, the Germans themselves have so far fought shy of really getting to grips with the coinage of the Holy Roman Empire from A.D. 800–1800—expanding, say, W.D. Craig's *Germanic Coinages* without running to extremes of length or expense. However, the indefatigable Günter Schön, the author of the *World Coin Catalogue* (4th edition 1983, Barrie & Jenkins, London), has published in 1983 *Die Deutschen Münzen, 1700–1806*, which, including Habsburg and Swiss, lists over 350 issuing authorities.

If the present volume encourages this or that collector to undertake this or that task, my own work will not have been in vain.

E.J.
August 1983

Facing page: Ballooning medal (anon.), enlarged, showing the first manned ascent over Paris, November 1783

A

ADAMS, E.H., *Catalogue of the Collection of Julius Guttag Comprising the Coinage of Mexico, Central America, South America and the West Indies,* New York, 1929.

AHLSTRÖM, B.A. and HEMMINGSSON, B., *Sveriges Mynt 1521–1977,* Stockholm, 1976.

AHLSTRÖM, B., BREKKE, B.F. and HEMMINGSSON, B., *Norges Mynter,* Stockholm, 1976.

AKERMAN, J.Y., *Coins of the Romans Relating to Britain,* London, 1844.

ALFÖLDI, A., *Die Kontorniaten,* Budapest, 1943.

ALLAN, J., *The Coins of Ancient India,* London, 1936.

ALLAN, J., *The Coins of the Gupta Dynasties, and of Sasanka, King of Ganda,* London, 1914.

ANDREW, A., *Australasian Tokens and Coins,* Sydney, 1921.

ANZANI, A., *Numismatica Auxumita* (reprinted from Rivista Italiana di Numismatica), Milan, 1926.

APPOLGRON, T.G., *Gustav Vasas Mynt,* Stockholm, 1933.

ATKINS, J., *The Coins and Tokens of the Possessions and Colonies of the British Empire,* London, 1899.

B

BABELON, E., *Description Historique et Chronologique des Monnaies de la République Romaine,* 2 vols., Paris, 1885–6.

BABELON, E., *Les Médailles Historiques de Napoléon le Grand, Empereur et Roi,* Paris, 1912.

BABELON, E., *Les Perses Achemenides,* Paris, 1893.

BABELON, E., *Traite des Monnaies Grecques et Romaines: 1ère Partie, Vol. I. Introduction,* Paris, 1901; *2me Partie, Vols I–IV. Description Historique,* Paris, 1907–32.

BABELON, J., *La Médaille en France,* Paris, 1948.

BAHRFELDT, E., *Brandenburgisch – Preussische Münzstudien,* 2 Vols., Berlin, 1913–30.

BAHRFELDT, M. VON, *Die Römische Goldmünzenprägung während der Republik und unter Augustus,* Halle, 1923.

BARNARD, F.P., *The Casting-Counter and the Counting-Board,* Oxford, 1916.

BELFORT, A.D., *Description Générale de Monnaies Merovingiennes,* 5 Vols., Paris, 1892–5.

BELLINGER, A.R. and GRIERSON, P., *Catalogue of Byzantine Coins in the Dumbarton Oaks Collection and in the Whittemore Collection,* 3 Vols., Washington DC, 1966–73.

BELTRAN MARTINEZ, A., *Curso di Numismatica, Vol. 1. Numismatica Antigua Clasica y de Espana,* Cartagena, 1950.

BENDIXEN, KIRSTEN, *Denmark's Money,* Copenhagen, 1967.

BERESFORD JONES, R.D., *A Manual of Anglo-Gallic Gold Coins,* London, 1964.

BERGHAUS, P., *Währungsgrenzen des Westfälischen Oberwesergebietes im Spätmittelalter,* Hamburg, 1951.

BERNAYS, E. and VANNERUS, J., *Histoire Monétaire du Comte Puis Duche de Luxembourg et ses Fiefs,* Brussels, 1910.

BERNHART, M., *Handbuch zur Münzkunde der Römischen Kaiserzeit,* 2 Vols., Halle, 1926.

BERRY, G., *Mediaeval English Jetons,* London, 1974.

BERRY, W.T. and POOLE, H.E., *Annals of Printing,* London, 1966.

BETTS, C.W., *American Colonial History Illustrated by Contemporary Medals,* New York, 1894.

BJØRNSTAD, O.C. and HOLSTE, H., *Norges Mynter Efter 1814,* Oslo, 1927.

BLANCHET, A., *Traité des Monnaies Gauloises,* Paris, 1905.

BLANCHET, A. and DIENDONNÉ, A., *Manuel de Numismatique Française,* 4 Vols., Paris, 1912–36.

BOBBA, C., *Super Manuale del Collezionista di Monete Decimali Italiane,* 16th Edition, 1980.

BOEHRINGER, E., *Die Münzen von Syrakus,* Berlin-Leipzig, 1929.

BOLIN, S., *State and Currency in the Roman Empire to A.D. 300,* Stockholm, 1959.

BORG, E., *Soumessa Katytetyt Rahat (Coins and Banknotes used in Finland),* 2nd revised edition, n.p., 1978.

BOSTROM, H.J., *Suonem Muistorahat (On Finnish Medals),* 2 Vols., Helsingfors, 1932–6.

BOSWELL, JAMES, *An Account of Corsica,* London, 1768.

BOTET Y SISO, J., *Las Monetas Catalanes,* 3 Vols., Barcelona, 1908–11.

BOYNE, W., *Trade Tokens issued in the Seventeenth Century in England, Wales and Ireland,* revised edition by C.G. Williamson, 2 Vols., London 1889–91.

BRAMAH, E., *English Regal Copper Coins,* London, 1929.

BRAUSE-MANSFELD, A., *Feld-Noth und Belagerungmünzen,* 2 Vols., Berlin, 1896–1902.

BREEN, W., *Encyclopedia of U.S. and Colonial Proof Coins 1722–1977*, n.p., n.d.

BRETT, A.B., *Catalogue of Greek Coins,* Museum of Fine Arts, Boston, 1974.

BROOKE, G.C., *English Coins,* 4th edition, London, 1966.

BROOKE, G.C. and HILL, G.F., *Guide to the Exhibition of Historical Medals in the British Museum,* London, 1924.

BROOME, M.R., *The 1780 Restrike Talers of Maria Theresia,* London, 1972.

BROWN, C.J., *The Coins of India,* Calcutta, 1922.

BROWN, I.D. and DOLLEY, R.H.M., *A Bibliography of Coin Hoards of Great Britain,* London, 1971.

BRUCE / DEYEL / RHODES / SPENGLER, *The Standard Guide to South Asian Coins and Paper Money,* Krause Publications, Iola, Wisconsin, 1981.

BRUUN, L.E., *Mønt-Og Medaille-Samling,* Copenhagen, 1928.

BRUUN, L.E., *Swedische Münzen,* 2 parts, Frankfurt, 1914.

BURGESS, F., *Chats on Old Coins,* London, 1913.

BURNS, E., *The Coinage of Scotland,* 2 Vols., Edinburgh, 1887.

BURZIO, F., *La Ceca de la Villa Imperial de Potosi y la Moneda Colonial,* Buenos Aires, 1945.

BURZIO, HUMBERTO F., *Diccionario de la Moneda Hispano-Americana,* 3 Vols., Santiago de Chile, 1956–8.

BUTAK, B., *Ressmli Türk Paralari,* Istanbul, 1947. With 2 supplements, Istanbul, 1948–50.

BUTTREY, T.V. and HUBBARD, C., *A Guide Book to Mexican Coins, 1822 to Date,* Racine, 1977.

BYRNE, RAY, *Mints of the Americas,* Numismatic Scrapbook Magazine, Feb. 1962.

C

CAGIATI, M., *Le Monete del Reame delle due Sicilie da Carlo I d'Angio a Vittorio Emanuele I,* Naples, 1911–37. *Corpus Numorum Italicorum,* Vols., I–XIX, Rome, 1910–40.

CAHN, J., *Der Rappenmünzbund,* Heidelberg, 1901.

CALICO, F.X., *Aportacion a la Historia Moneteria de Santa Fe de Bogota,* Barcelona, 1953.

CALICO, F., CALICO, X. and TRIGO, J., *Monedas Espanolas Desde Carlos II a Isabel II, anos 1665 a 1868,* 2nd edition, Barcelona, 1978.

CALICO, F., CALICO, C. and TRIGO, J., *Monedas Espanolas Desde 1868–1978,* Barcelona, 1978.

CARON, E., *Monnaies Féodales Françaises,* Paris, 1882.

CAROTHERS, N., *Fractional Money: A History of the Small Coins and Fractional Paper Currency of the United States,* New York, 1930.

CARSON, R.A.G., *Coins,* London, 1962.

CARSON, R.A.G. (ED.), *Mints, Dies, and Currencies,* London, 1971.

CARSON, R.A.G., HILL, P.V. and KENT, J.P.C., *Late Roman Bronze Coinage,* London, 1960.

CARSWELL, M.N., *Coins of the World by Location,* Decatur, Georgia, 1967.

CHALLIS, C.E., *The Tudor Coinage,* Manchester University Press, 1978, Barnes & Noble Books, NY, 1978.

CHALON, R., *Recherches sur les Monnaies des Comtes de Hainaut,* Brussels, 1848.

CHALON, R., *Recherches sur les Monnaies des Comtes de Namur,* Brussels, 1860.

CHAMBERLAIN, C.C., *Collecting Coins,* London, n.d.

CHAMBERLAIN, C.C., *Guide to Numismatics,* London, 1960.

CHARLTON, J.E., *1960 Standard Catalogue of Canadian Coins, Tokens and Paper Money,* Toronto, 1960 (and annually). (For Canadian Trade Dollars, *see* Pelletier.)

CHASE, P.H., *Confederate Treasury Notes: The Paper Money of the Confederate States of America, 1861–5,* Philadelphia, 1947.

CHAUDOIR, S. DE, *Aperçu sur les Monnaies Russes et sur les Monnaies Étrangères qui ont eu Course en Russie,* 3 Vols., St Petersburg, 1836–7 (reprinted 1974, 2 Vols., 654pp, 81 plates).

CHESTRET DE HANEFFE, J.DE, *Numismatique de la Principauté de Liège,* Brussels, 1890.

CHIJS, P.O. VAN DER, *De Munten der Nederlanden van de Vroegste Tijden tot aan de Pacificatie van Gend,* 9 Vols., Haarlem, 1851–66.

CIANI, L., *Les Monnaies Françaises de la Révolution à la fin du Premier Empire, 1789–1815,* Paris, 1931.

CIANI, L., *Les Monnaies Royales Françaises de Hugues Capet à Louis XVI,* Paris, 1926, reprinted 1973.

CLAIN-STEFANELLI, E.E., *Numismatics – An Ancient Science,* Washington, 1965.

CLAIN-STEFANELLI, E.E., *Russian Gold Coins,* London, 1962.

CLAIN-STEFANELLI, E.E., *Select Numismatic Bibliography,* New York, 1965.

CODERA Y ZAIDIN, DON F., *Tratado de Numismatica Arabigo-Espanola*, 1879 (reprinted 1977).

CODRINGTON, H.W., *Ceylon Coins and Currency*, Colombo, 1924.

CODRINGTON, O., *A Manual of Musalman Numismatics*, London, 1904 (reprinted 1970).

COHEN, H., *Description Historique des Monnaies Frappées sous l'Empire Romain*, 8 Vols., Paris, 1880–92.

COLBERT DE BEAULIEU, J.B., *Traité de Numismatique Celtique*, Paris, 1973.

COMENCINI, M., *Coins of the Modern World, 1870–1936*, London, 1937.

COOLE, A.B., *Coins in China's History*, 4th edition, Denver, 1965.

COOLE, A.B., *The Early Coins of the Chou Dynasty*, Boston, 1973.

COPE, M.E. and RAYNER, P.A., *The Standard Catalogue of English Milled Coinage in Silver, Copper and Bronze, 1662–1972*, London, 1972.

CORAGGIONI, L., *Münzgeschichte der Schweiz*, Geneva, 1896.

COUVREUR, R. DA COSTA, *Numismatica Indo-Portuguesa, Bazarucos*, Lisbon, 1943.

CRAIG, J., *Newton at the Mint*, Cambridge, 1946.

CRAIG, J., *The Royal Mint*, Cambridge, 1953.

CRAIG, W.D., *Coins of the World 1750–1850*, 3rd edition, Racine, 1966.

CRAIG, W.D., *Germanic Coinages: Charlemagne Through William II*, California, 1954.

CRAWFORD, M.H., *Roman Republican Coinage*, 2 Vols., n.p., 1974.

CRESSWELL, O.D., *Chinese Cash*, London, 1971.

CRESSWELL, O.D., *Tibetan Coins*, n.p., 1977.

CROSBY, S.S., *The Early Coins of America*, Boston, 1878.

CUNNINGHAM, A., *Coins of Ancient India from the Earliest Times down to the Seventh Century A.D.*, London, 1891.

CUNNINGHAM, A., *Coins of Mediaeval India from the Seventh Century down to The Muhammadan Conquest*, London, 1894.

CZESLAW, K., *An Illustrated Catalogue of Polish Coins 1916–1976*, n.p., 1977.

D

DALTON, R. and HAMER, H.S., *The Provincial Token Coinage of the Eighteenth Century*, 14 parts, London, 1910–18 (reprinted 1977).

DANAHER, M.A., *The Commemorative Coinage of Modern Sports*, n.p., 1978.

DANNENBERG, H., *Die Deutschen Münzen der Sächsischen und Fränkischen Kaiserzeit*, 4 Vols., Berlin, 1876–1905.

DASI, T., *Estudio de los Reales a Ocho*, 5 Vols., Valencia, 1950–1.

DAVENPORT, J.S., *European Crowns 1484–1600*, n.p., n.d.

DAVENPORT, J.S., *European Crowns 1600–1700*, n.p., 1974.

DAVENPORT, J.S., *European Crowns since 1800*, Buffalo, 1947.

DAVENPORT, J.S., *German Church and City Talers 1600–1700*, n.p., 2nd edition 1975.

DAVENPORT, J.S., *German Secular Talers 1600–1700*, n.p., 1976.

DAVENPORT, J.S., *German Talers, 1500–1600*, n.p., n.d.

DAVENPORT, J.S., *German Talers, 1700–1800*, Galesburg, 1958.

DAVENPORT, J.S., *German Talers since 1800*, Galesburg, 1949.

DAVENPORT, J.S., *Oversize Multiple Talers of the Brunswick Duchies and Saxe Lauenberg*, Galesburg, 1956.

DAVIS, N. and KRAAY, C.M., *The Hellenistic Kingdoms*, London, 1973.

DAVIS, W.J., *The Nineteenth Century Token Coinage of Great Britain, Ireland, The Channel Islands and the Isle of Man*, London, 1904.

DAVIS, W.J. and WATERS, A.W., *Tickets and Passes of Great Britain and Ireland*, London, 1922 (reprinted 1974).

DELMONTE, A., *The Golden Benelux*, Amsterdam, with supplement 1978.

DELMONTE, A., *The Silver Benelux*, Amsterdam, 1967.

DE MEY, J. and PAUWEIS, G., *European Crown Size and Multiples, Vol. I: Germany 1486–1599*, Amsterdam, 1975.

DE MEY, J. and PAUWEIS, G., *Les Monnaies de Belgique 1790–1977*, Brussels, 1978.

DE MEY, J. and POINDESSAULT, B., *Répertoire des Monnaies Napoléonides*, Paris, 1971.

DEMOLE, E., *Histoire Monétaire de Gèneve de 1535 à 1848*, 2 Vols., Geneva, 1887–92.

DENIS, C., *Catalogue des Monnaies Émises sur le Territoire de la Russie, 1914–25*, Paris, 1926.

DE SAULCY, F., *Recherches sur les Monnaies des Ducs Héréditaires de Lorraine*, Metz,1841 (reprinted 1974).

DE SAULCY, F., *Souvenirs Numismatiques de la Révolution de 1848*, Paris, 1849 (reprinted 1973).

DESNEUZ, J., *Les Tetradrachmes d'Akanthos*, Brussels, 1949.

DIEUDONNÉ, A., *Manuel des Poids Monétaires*, Paris, 1925.

DIEUDONNÉ, A., *Les Monnaies Françaises*, Paris, 1923.

DIVO, JEAN-PAUL, *Modern Greek Coins 1828–1968*, n.p., 1969.

DIVO, J-P. and TOBLER, E., *Die Münzen der Schweiz im 18. Jahrhundert*, Zürich, 1974.

DIVO, J-P, and TOBLER, E., *Die Münzen der Schweiz im 19. und 20. Jahrhundert*, Zürich, 1969.

DIVO, J-P, and TOBLER, E., *Die Taler der Schweiz*, Zürich, 1966.

DOLLEY, R.H.M., *Anglo-Saxon Pennies*, London, 1964.

DOLLEY, R.H.M., *Medieval Anglo-Irish Coins*, London, 1972.

DOLLEY, R.H.M., *The Norman Conquest and the English Coinage*, London, 1968.

DOLLEY, R.H.M., (ED.) *Anglo-Saxon Coins: Studies Presented to Sir Frank Stenton*, London, 1961.

DOMANIG, K., *Die Deutsche Medaille in Kunst- und Kultur-Historischer Hinsicht*, Vienna, 1907.

DOWLE, A. and DE CLERMONT, A., *Monnaies Modernes de 1789 à Nos Jours*, Fribourg, 1972.

DOWLE, A. and FINN, P., *The Guide Book to the Coinage of Ireland from 995 A.D. to the Present Day*, London, 1969.

DUGNIOLLE, F.J., *Le Jeton Historique des Dix-Sept Provinces des Pays-Bas*, 4 Vols., Brussels, 1876–80.

DUPRIEZ, C., *Monnaies et Essais Monétaires du Royaume de Belgique et du Congo Belge*, 2 Vols., Brussels, 1949.

DURAND, ANTHONY, *Médailles et Jetons des Numismates*, Geneva, 1859.

DURST, S.J., *Comprehensive Guide to American Colonial Coinage, Its Origins, History and Value*, n.p., 1976.

DUSHNICK, S.E., *Silver and Nickel Dollars of Canada, 1911 to date*, n.p., 1978.

DYER, G.P.. *The Proposed Coinage of Edward VIII*, London, 1973.

E

EINSIG, P., *Primitive Money*, London, 1949.

ELLIOT, W., *Coins of Southern India*, London, 1886.

ELMER, G., *Die Münzprägung der Gallischen Kaiser in Köln, Trier und Mailand*, Bonn, 1941 (reprinted 1974).

ENGEL, A. and SERRURE, R., *Traité du Numismatique du Moyen Age*, 3 Vols., Paris, 1891–1905.

ENGEL, A. and SERRURE, R., *Traité du Numismatique Moderne et Contemporaine*, 2 Vols., Paris, 1897–9.

ENGSTROM, J.E., *Coins in Shakespeare, A Numismatic Guide*, London, 1964.

ENGSTROM, J.E., *The Medallic Portraits of Sir Winston Churchill*, London, 1972.

EVANS, J., *The Coinage of the Ancient Britons*, London, 1864, Supplement, 1890.

F

FARRES, O.G., *Historia de la Moneda Hispanola*, Madrid, 1960.

FERRARI and PARDO, *Amonedacion de Cordoba*, Buenos Aires, 1951.

FERRARO VAZ, J., *Catalogo das Moedas Portuguesas:Portugal Continental 1648–1948*, Lisbon, 1948.

FEUARDENT, F., *Collection Feuardent: Jetons et Mereaux, Depuis Louis IX Jusqu'à la Fin du Consultat de Bonaparte*, 3 Vols., Paris, 1904–15.

FIALA, E:, *Berschreibung der Sammlung Bömischer Münzen und Medaillen des Max Donebauer*, 2 Vols., Prague, 1895–8.

FIALA, E., *Münzen und Medaillen der Welfischen Lande*, 7 Vols., Prague, 1906–19.

FLORANGE, J., *Armorial du Jetonophile*, Paris, 1902.

FORRER, L., *Biographical Dictionary of Medallists, Coin, Gem and Seal Engravers, Ancient and Modern, with References to their Works, 500 B.C.–A.D. 1900*, 8 Vols., London, 1902–29.

FORRER, L.S., *The Art of Collecting Coins*, London, 1955.

FORRER, R., *Keltische Numismatik der Rhein- und Donaulande*, Strassburg, 1908.

FREEMAN, M.J., *The Bronze Coinage of Great Britain*, London, 1970..

FREEMAN, M.J., *Buying and Selling Coins*, London, 1983.

FREY, A.R., *The Dated European Coinage Prior to 1501*, New York, 1916 (reprinted 1978).

FREY, A.R., *Dictionary of Numismatic Names,* New York, 1947 (reprinted with additions, London 1973).

FRIEDBERG, R., *Gold Coins of the World, A.D. 600–1958,* New York, 1958, 5th edition, 1979.

FRIEDBERG, R., *Paper Money of the United States,* New York, 1953.

FRIEDENSBURG, F., *Die Münzen in der Kulturgeschichte,* Berlin, 1926.

FROSSARD, E., *Franco-American Jetons,* New York, 1899 (reprinted 1977).

FUCHS, W., *Platinmünzen und -Medaillen,* n.p., 1975.

FURSE, E.H., *Mémoires Numismatiques de l'Ordre Souverain de Saint-Jean de Jerusalem,* 2nd edition, Rome, 1889.

G

GADOURY, V. and DROULERS, F., *Les Monnaies Royales Françaises de Louis XIII à Louis XVI 1610–1792,* n.p., 1978.

GAILLARD, V., *Recherches sur les Monnaies Royales de Comtes de Flandre,* Ghent, 1854.

GALBREATH, D.L., *Papal Heraldry,* 2nd edition, revised by Geoffrey Briggs, London, 1972.

GALEOTTI, A., *Le Monete del Granducato di Toscana,* Leghorn, 1930.

GALSTER, G., *Danske Og Norske Medailler Og Jetons, ca. 1553– ca. 1788,* Copenhagen, 1936.

GALSTER, G., *Die Münzen Dänemarks, bis Etwa 1625,* Halle, 1939.

GARDNER, P., *The Coins of the Greek and Scythic Kings of Bactria and India,* London, 1886.

GARDNER, P., *A History of Ancient Coinage, 700–300 B.C.,* Oxford, 1918.

GARDNER, P., *The Parthian Coinage,* London, 1877.

GARDNER, P., *Types of Greek Coins,* London, 1883.

GARIEL, E., *Les Monnaies Royales de France sous la Race Carolingienne,* 2 Vols., Strassburg, 1883–4.

GARRARD, T.F., *Akan Weights and the Gold Trade,* London, 1980.

GARSIDE, H., *British Imperial Copper and Bronze Coinage, 1838–1925,* 2 parts, London, 1920–35.

GARTNER, J., *The Australian Coinage,* n.p., 8th edition, 1977.

GAUBE, H., *Arabosasanidische Numismatik,* n.p., 1973.

GEBHART, H., *Die Deutschen Münzen des Mittelalters und der Neuzeit,* Berlin, 1929.

GELDER, H.E. VAN and HOC, M., *Les Monnaies des Pays-Bas Bourgonignons et Espagnols 1434–1713,* Amsterdam, 1960.

GLUCK, H. and HESSELBLAD, G.G., *Artalsforteckning over Svenska Mynt med Värderingspriser: Gustav Vasa- Gustaf VI, 1521–1959,* Stockholm, 1959.

GNECCHI, F., *I Medaglioni Romani,* 3 Vols., Milan, 1912.

GNECCHI, F. and E., *Le Monete di Milano,* with supplement, Milan, 1884–94.

GÖBL, R., *Antike Numismatic,* 2 Vols., Munich, 1977.

GÖBL, R., *Sassanian Numismatics* (tr. by Paul Severin), n.p., 1971.

GOODACRE, H., *A Handbook of the Coinage of the Byzantine Empire,* 2nd edition, London, 1957.

GRANT, M., *From Imperium to Autoritas,* Cambridge, 1946.

GRANT, M., *Roman Anniversary Issues,* Cambridge, 1950.

GRASSER, WALTER, *Bayerische Münzen,* Rosenheimer Verlag, 1980.

GRAY, J.F.C., *Tranquebar: A Guide to the Coins of Danish India circa 1620 to 1845,* n.p., 1974.

GRIERSON, P., *Coins and Medals, A select bibliography,* London, 1954.

GRIERSON, P., *Bibliographie Numismatique,* Brussels, 1966 (greatly enlarged ed. of above, in French).

GRIERSON, P., *Monnaies du Moyen Age,* Fribourg, 1976.

GRIERSON, PHILIP, *Numismatics,* London, 1975.

GRINSELL, L.V., *The Bath Mint.* n.p., n.d.

GRINSELL, L.V., *The Bristol Mint,* n.p., 1972.

GRUEBER, H.A., *Handbook of the Coins of Great Britain and Ireland in the British Museum,* London, 1899 (extensively revised edition, London, 1970).

GRUNTHAL, H. and SELLSCHOPP, E.A., *The Coinage of Peru,* n.p., 1978.

GUMOWSKI, M., *Handbuch der Polnischen Numismatik,* German edition, Graz, 1960.

GURDIAN, R., *Contribucion al Estudio de las Monedas de Costa Rica,* San José, 1958.

GUTHRIE, H.S. and BOTHAMLEY, M., *Mexican Revolutionary Coinage 1913-1917,* n.p., 1976.

H

HÄBERLIN, E.J., *Aes Grave: Das Schwergeld Roms und Mittelitaliens,* 2 Vols., Frankfurt, 1910.

HABICH, G., *Die Deutschen Schaumünzen des XVI Jarhunderts,* 2 Vols., Munich, 1929–34.

HAFFNER, S., *Judaic Tokens and Medals,* n.p., 1978.

HAMBURGER, L., *Cabinet de Monsieur Le Chevalier E. Gnecchi de Milan,* 3 parts, Frankfurt, 1901–3.

HANDS, A.W., *Common Greek Coins,* London, 1908.

HANKS, W.L., *The Comprehensive Catalog and Encyclopedia of Modern Mexican Coins,* n.p., 1976 edition.

HANS, J., *Zwei Jahrhunderte Maria-Theresien Taler 1751–1951,* Klagenfurt, 1950.

HARRIS, R.P., *A Guidebook of Russian Coins, 1725–1970,* n.p., 1974.

HAUBERG, P., *Myntforhold og Udmyntninger i Danmark Indtil 1146,* Copenhagen, 1900.

HAWKINS, E., *Medallic Illustrations of the History of Great Britain and Ireland to the Death of George II,* edited by Sir A.W. Franks and H.A. Grueber, 2 Vols., London, 1885 (reprinted 1977).

HAZARD, H.W., *The Numismatic History of Late Medieval North Africa,* New York, 1952.

HAZLITT, W., *The Coinage of the European Continent,* London, 1893, Supplement 1899 (reprinted in 1 vol.).

HEAD, B.V., *Historia Numorum: A Manual of Greek Coins,* 3rd edition, Oxford, 1911 (reprinted 1963).

HEISS, A., *Descripcion General de las Monedas Hispano-Cristianas Desde la Invasion de Los Arabes,* 3 Vols., Madrid, 1865–9.

HEISS, A., *Description Générale des Monnaies Antiques d'Espagne,* Paris, 1870.

HENNIN, M., *Histoire Numismatique de la Révolution Française,* 2 Vols., Paris, 1826 (reprinted 1976).

HEPBURN, A.B., *History of Currency in the United States,* 3rd edition, New York, 1924.

HERRERA, A., *El Duro: Estudio de Los Reales de a Ocho Espanoles,* 2 Vols., Madrid, 1914.

HEWLET, L., *Anglo Gallic Coins,* London, 1920.

HICKSON, H., *Mint Mark 'C.C.', The Story of the United States Mint at Carson City, Nevada,* Carson City, 1975.

HILDEBRAND, B.E., *Anglosachsiska Mynt i Svenska Kongliga Myntkabinettet, Funna i Sveriges Jord,* 2nd edition, Stockholm, 1881.

HILDEBRAND, B.E., *Sveriges och Svenska Konungahusets Minnespenningar Praktmynt och Beloningsmedaljier,* 2 Vols., Stockholm, 1874–5.

HILL, G.F., *Coins of Ancient Sicily,* London, 1903.

HILL, G.F., *A Corpus of Italian Medals of the Renaissance before Cellini,* 2 Vols., London, 1930.

HILL, G.F., *Historical Greek Coins,* London, 1906.

HILL, G.F., *Historical Roman Coins,* London, 1909.

HILL, G.F., *Imperial Persian Coinage,* London, 1919 (reprinted 1977).

HILL, G.F., *Medals of the Renaissance,* Oxford, 1920. Revised and enlarged by Graham Pollard, London, 1978.

HOFFMAN, H., *Les Monnaies Royales de France,* Paris, 1878.

HOLM, J.C., *Danmarks Monter 1848–1947,* Copenhagen, 1947.

HOUBEN, G., *European Coin-Weights for English Coins,* n.p., 1978.

HUSZÁR, LAJOS, *The Art of Coinage in Hungary,* Budapest, 1963.

HUSZÁR, L. and VARANNAI, G., *Medicina in Nummis: Hungarian Coins and Medals Related to Medicine,* Budapest, 1977.

HUTTEN-CZAPSKI, E., *Catalogue de la Collection des Médailles et Monnaies Polonaises (1871–1916),* 3 Vols. (reprinted Graz, 1957).

I

ILYIN, A.A. and TOLSTOI, I.I., *Russian Coins Struck from 1725–1801,* St Petersburg, 1901.

IVERSEN, J., *Medaillen auf die Thaten Peter des Grossen,* St Petersburg, 1872 (reprinted 1978).

J

JACOBS, N. and VERMEULE, C.C., *Japanese Coinage,* New York, 1953 (reprinted 1972).

JAECKEL, P., *Münzprägungen des Hauses Hapsburg 1780–1918 und der Bundesrepublik Österreich 1918–56,* Basel, 1956.

JAEGER, K., *Die Deutschen Reichsmünzen Seit 1871*, Basel, 1959.

JENKINS, G.K., *Ancient Greek Coins*, London, 1972.

JENKINS, G.K. and LEWIS, R.B., *Carthaginian Gold and Electrum Coins*, 1963.

JENKINSON / BARNES / HECTOR, *A Guide to Seals in the Public Record Office*, 2nd edition, HMSO, London, 1968.

JESSE, W., *Quellenbuch zur Münz- und Geldgeschichte des Mittelalters*, Halle, 1924.

JESSE, W., *Der Wendische Münzverein*, Lubeck, 1928.

JOSSET, C.R., *Money in Britain*, London, 1962.

JUDD, J.M., *United States Pattern, Experimental and Trial Pieces*, n.p., 5th edition, 1977.

JULIAN, R.W. and HARRIS, N.N. (EDS.), *Medals of the United States Mint. The First Century 1792–1893*, n.p., 1977.

K

KALGAN, SHIH, *Modern Coins of China*, 2 Vols., Shanghai, 1949.

KANN, E., *The Currencies of China*, Shanghai, 1927 (reprinted 1978).

KANN, E., *Illustrated Catalog of Chinese Coins*, Los Angeles, 1954.

KAPLAN, A., *Catalogue of the Coins of South Africa*, Germiston, 1977.

KARST, J., *Précis de Numismatique Georgienne*, Paris, 1938.

KELLY, E.M., *Spanish Dollars and Silver Tokens, An Account of the Issues of the Bank of England 1797–1816*, London, 1976.

KENT, J.P.C., *2000 Years of British Coins and Medals*, London, 1978.

KENT, J.P.C. and HIRMER, M.&A., *Roman Coins*, London, 1978.

KENYON, R. LLOYD, *The Gold Coins of England*, London, 1884.

KIRMIS, M., *Handbuch der Polnischen Münzkunde*, Posen, 1892.

KISCH, B., *Scales and Weights, A Historical Outline*, n.p., 3rd printing 1975.

KRAAY, C.M., *Archaic and Classical Greek Coins*, London, 1976.

KRAUS, F.F., *Die Münzen Odovacars und des Ostogotenreiches in Italien*, Halle, 1928.

KRAUSE, CHESTER L. and MISHLER, CLIFFORD, *Standard Catalog of World Coins* (annual), Iola, Wisconsin.

KROHA, TYLL, *Lexikon der Münzkunde*, Gütersloh, 1977.

L

LAFAURIE, J., *Les Billets des Banques de Law*, Auxerre, 1952.

LAFAURIE, J., *Les Monnaies des Rois de France, Hugues Capet – Louis XII*, Paris, 1951.

LAFAURIE, J. and PRIEUR, P., *Les Monnaies des Rois de France Francois I – Henry IV*, Paris, 1956.

LAGERQUIST, L.O. and NATHOORST BÖOS, E., *Mynt och Medaljer och Annam Numismatik*, Stockholm, 1960.

LAMAS, A., *Medalhasportuguesas e Estrangieras Referentes a Portugal*, Lisbon, 1916.

LANE-POOLE, S., *Coins and Medals: Their Place in History and Art*, 3rd edition, London, 1894.

LANE-POOLE, S., *The Coins of the Moghul Emperors*, London, 1892.

LANE-POOLE, S., *The Coins of the Mohammadan States of India*, London, 1885.

LANE-POOLE, S., *The Coins of the Sultans of Delhi*, London, 1894.

LANG, D.M., *Studies in the Numismatic History of Georgia in Transcaucasia*, New York, 1955.

LANGLOIS, V., *Numismatique de l'Arménie du Moyen Age*, Paris, 1855.

LE GENTILHOMME, P., *Mélanges de Numismatique Merovingienne*, Paris, 1940.

LEITAO, S., *Catalogo de Moedas Brasileiras de 1643 a 1975*, 13th edition, Rio de Janeiro, 1976.

LE MAY, R., *The Coinage of Siam*, Bangkok, 1932.

LE RIDER, GEORGES, *Monnaies Cretoises*, Paris, n.d.

LINDGREN, T., *Sveriges Mynt 1719–1776*, Stockholm, 1953.

LINECAR, H.W.A., *British Coin Design and Designers*, London, 1977.

LINECAR, H.W.A., *British Commonwealth Coinage*, London, 1959.

LINECAR, H.W.A., *Coins*, London, 1955.

LINECAR, H.W.A., *The Crown Pieces of Great Britain and the British Commonwealth of Nations, 1551–1961*, second, revised edition, London, 1969.

LINECAR, H.W.A. (ED.), *The Milled Coinage of England 1662–1946*, 1950, with Supplement 1958. Reimpression, London, 1966.

LINECAR, H.W.A. and STONE, A.G., *English Proof and Pattern Crown-Size Pieces*, London, 1968.

LISMORE, T., *The Coinage of Cuba*, Havana, 1955.

LJUBIC, S., *Opis Jugoslavenskih Novaca,* Zagreb, 1875.

LOCKHART, J.H.S., *The Currency of the Far East from the Earliest Times up to the Present Day,* 3 Vols., Hong Kong, 1895–8.

LOCKHART, J.H.S., *The Stewart Lochhart Collection of Chinese Coins,* Shanghai, 1915 (reprinted 1974).

LOEHR, A., *Österreichische Geldgeschichte,* Vienna, 1946.

LONGUET, H., *Introduction à la Numismatique Byzantine,* London, 1961.

LOW, L.H., *Hard Times Tokens,* n.p., reprinted 1977.

LUSCHIN VON EBENGREUTH, A., *Allgemeine Münzkunde und Geldgeschichte,* Munich, 1924.

M

MACDONALD, G., *The Evolution of Coinage,* London, 1935.

MACK, R.P., *The Coinage of Ancient Britain,* London, 1953, 3rd edition, 1975.

MACKENZIE, A.D., *The Bank of England Note,* Cambridge, 1953.

MADDEN, F.W., *Coins of the Jews,* London, 1881.

MANSFELD-BULLNER, H.V., *Afbildninger af Samtlige Hidtil Kjendte Danske Monter fra Tidsrummet 1241–1377,* Copenhagen, 1954.

MARIC, R., *Études de Numismatique Serbe* (in Russian with French summary), Belgrade, 1956.

MARSDEN, W., *Numismata Orientalia Illustrata,* 2 Vols., London, 1823–5.

MARSH, MICHAEL A., *The Gold Half Sovereign,* Cambridge, 1982.

MARSH, MICHAEL A., *The Gold Sovereign,* Cambridge, 1980.

MARTINORI, R., *La Moneta,* Rome, 1915.

MATEU Y LLOPIS, F., *La Moneda Espanola,* Barcelona, 1946.

MATTINGLY, H., *Roman Coins from the Earliest Times to the Fall of the Western Empire,* 3rd edition, London, 1962 (reprinted 1977).

MAURICE, J., *Numismatique Constantinienne,* 3 Vols., Paris, 1908–12.

MAY, J.M.F., *Ainos, Its History and Coinage,* London, 1950.

MAY, J.M.F., *The Coinage of Abdera,* n.p., n.d.

MAYER, L.A., *Bibliography of Moslem Numismatics, India Excluded,* London, 1939.

MAYS, JAMES O'DONALD, *The Splendid Shilling: A Social History of an Engaging Coin,* n.p., 1982.

MAZARD, J., *Corpus Nummorum Numidiae Mauretaniaeque,* Paris, 1955.

MAZARD, J., *Histoire Monétaire et Numismatique des Colonies de l'Union Française,* Paris, 1953.

MAZEROLLE, F., *Les Médailleurs Français du XVe au Milieu du XVIIe Siècle,* 2 Vols., and plates, Paris, 1904.

MEDINA, J.T., *Las Monedas Chilenas,* Santiago, 1902.

MEDINA, J.T., *Las Monedas Coloniales Hispano-Americanas,* Santiago, 1919 (reprinted 1975).

MEEK, W.T., *The Exchange Media of Colonial Mexico,* New York, 1948.

MEILLI, J., *Das Brazilianische Geldwesen,* 3 Vols., Zürich, 1897–1905.

MESHORER, Y., *Jewish Coins of the Second Temple Period,* n.p., 1967.

METCALF, D.M., *Coinage of the Crusades and the Latin Middle East in the Ashmolean, Oxford,* Oxford, 1983.

MILES, G.C., *The Coinage of the Visigoths in Spain,* New York, 1952.

MILES, G.C., *Early Arab Glass Weights and Stamps,* New York, 1948.

MILLER, D., *Coins of Roman Britain,* n.p., 1976.

MILLER ZU AICHOLZ, C. VON, LOEHR, A. and HOLZMAIR, E., *Österreichische Münzprägungen 1519–1938,* 2nd edition, Vienna, 1948.

MILLIES, H.C., *Recherches sur les Monnaies des Indigènes de l'Archipel Indien et de la Peninsule Malaie,* The Hague, 1871.

MILNE, J.G., *Greek and Roman Coins, and the Study of History,* London, 1939

MILNE, J.G., *Greek Coinage,* Oxford, 1931.

MILNE, J.G., SUTHERLAND, C.H.V. and THOMPSON, J.D.A., *Coin Collecting,* Oxford, 1951.

MITCHINER, M., *Indo-Greek and Indo-Scythian Coinage,* 9 Vols., London, 1975–6.

MITCHINER, M., *The Origins of Indian Coinage,* London, 1973.

MITCHINER, M., *The World of Islam,* 2 Vols., London, 1977–8.

MOESER, K. and DWORSCHAK, F., *Die Grosse Münzreform unter Erzherzog Sigmund von Tirol,* Vienna, 1936.

MONTAGU, H., *Copper, Tin and Bronze Coinage and Patterns for Coins of England,* 2nd edition, London, 1893.

MORRISSON, C., *Catalogue des Monnaies Byzantines de la Bibliothèque Nationale,* 2 Vols., Paris, 1970.

MOSSOP, H.R., *The Lincoln Mint 890–1279,* n.p., 1970.

MOUCHMOV, N.A., *Numismatique et Sigillographie Bulgare,* Sofia, 1924.

MULLER, L., *Numismatique de l'Ancienne Afrique*, Copenhagen, 1860–2, Supplement, 1874 (reprinted 1977).

MUNRO, N.G., *Coins of Japan*, Yokohama, 1904.

MURET, E. and CHABOUILLET, M.A., *Catalogue des Monnaies Gauloises de la Bibliothèque Nationale*, Paris, 1889.

N

NATHANSON, A.J., *Thomas Simon, His Life and Work, 1618–1665*, n.p., 1975.

NELSON, P., *Coinage of Ireland in Copper, Tin and Pewter, 1460–1826*, London, 1905.

NELSON, P., *The Coinage of William Wood 1722–23*, London, 1903 (reprinted 1978).

NELSON, P., *The Obsidional Coinage of the Great Rebellion*, London, 1907.

NESMITH, R.I., *The Coinage of the First Mint of the Americas at Mexico City 1536–1572*, 1955 (reprinted 1977).

NOE, S.P., *The Oak Tree Coinage of Massachusetts*, New York, 1947 (reprinted 1973).

NOE, S.P., *The Pine Tree Coinage of Massachusetts*, New York, 1952.

NOHEJLOVA-PRATOVA, E., *Krasa Ceske Mince*, Prague, 1955.

NOLAN, P., *A Monetary History of Ireland*, 2 Vols., London, 1926–8.

NORTH, J.J., *English Hammered Coinage: Vol. 1, A.D. 650–1272, Vol. 2, Edward I to Charles II*, London, 1963 and 1976.

NOSS, A., and HÄVERNICK, W., *Die Münzen und Medaillen von Köln*, 4 Vols., Cologne, 1913–35.

O

OMAN, C., *The Coinage of England*, Oxford, 1931 (reprinted 1967).

P

PAGANI, A., *Monete Italiane Moderne a Sistema Decimale (1800–1946)*, Milan, 1947.

PAPADOPOLI, N., *Le Monete di Venezia*, 3 Vols., Venice, 1893–1919.

PARSONS, H.A., *The Colonial Coinage of British Africa with the Adjacent Islands*, London, 1950.

PARUCK, F.D.J., *Sassanian Coins*, Bombay, 1924.

PECK, C.W., *English Copper, Tin and Bronze Coins in the British Museum, 1558–1958*, London (2nd edition), 1964.

PELLETIER, SERGE, *The 1980 Charlton Canadian Trade Dollar Guide*, 1st edition, The Charlton Press, Toronto, 1980.

PETROV, V.I., *Catalogue des Monnaies Russes*, 2nd edition, Moscow, 1899 (reprinted 1964).

PHAYRE, A.P., *Coins of Arakan, of Peru, and of Burma (Numismata Orientalia, Vol. 3, Part 1)*, London, 1882.

PHILIPS, M., *The Token Money of the Bank of England, 1791–1806*, London, 1900.

PICK, A., *Briefmarkengeld*, Braunschweig, 1970.

PINK, K., *Einführung in die Keltische Münzkunde mit Basonderer Berücksichtigung Österreichs*, Vienna, 1950.

PINK, K., *Die Münzprägung der Ostkelten und ihrer Nachbarn*, Budapest, 1939.

PLANT, R.J., *Arabic Coins and How to Read Them*, n.p., 1973.

PLATZBARDIS, A., *Die Münzen und das Papiergald Estlands, Lettlands, Litauens*, Stockholm, 1953.

POEY D'AVANT, F., *Les Monnaies Féodales de la France*, 3 Vols., Paris, 1858–62 (reprinted 1961).

POOLE, R.S., *A Descriptive Catalogue of the Swiss Coins in the South Kensington Museum*, London, 1878.

PRADEAU, F., *Historia Numismatica de Mexico Desde la Epoca Precortesiance hasta 1823*, Mexico City, 1950 (English edition, 1938, reprinted 1976).

PROBER, K., *Historia Numismatica de Guatemala*, Sao Paulo, 1954.

PROBSZT, G., *Oesterreichische Münz- und Geldgeschichte von den Anfängen bis 1918*, Vienna, 1973.

PROU, M., *Les Monnaies Merovingiennes: Catalogue des Monnaies Françaises de la Bibliothèque Nationale*, Paris, 1892 (reprinted 1969).

PROU, M., *Les Monnaies Merovingiennes: Catalogue des Monnaies Françaises de la Bibliothèque Nationale*, Paris, 1896 (reprinted 1969).

PURVEY, P.F., *Coins and Tokens of Scotland*, London, 1972.

Q

QUIGGIN, A.H., *A Survey of Primitive Money: The Beginnings of Currency,* London, 1949 (reprinted 1978).

R

RABINO DI BORGOMALE, H.L., *Coins, Medals and Seals of the Shahs of Iran, 1500–1941,* Hertford, 1941.

RAPSON, E.J., *The Coins of the Andhra Dynasty, The Western Ksatrapas, the Traikutaka Dynasty and the "Bhadi" Dynasty,* London, 1908.

RATTO, R., *Monnaies Byzantines,* Lugano, 1930.

RAVEL, O., *Les "Poulains" de Corinthe,* 2 Vols., Basel-London, 1936–48.

RAWLINGS, G.B., *Coins and How to Know Them,* London, 1935.

RAYMOND, W., *The Coins and Tokens of Canada,* 2nd edition, New York, 1947.

RAYMOND, W., *Coins of the World – Nineteenth-Century Issues,* New York, 1953.

RAYMOND, W., *Coins of the World – Twentieth-Century Issues,* New York, 1952.

RAYMOND, W., *The Gold Coins of North and South America,* New York, 1937.

RAYMOND, W., *The Silver Dollars of North and South America,* New York, 1939.

RAYMOND W., *Spanish-American Gold Coins,* New York, 1936.

RAYMOND, W., *The Standard Paper Money Catalogue,* 2 parts, New York, 1950–3.

REÍFENBERG, A., *Ancient Jewish Coins,* 2nd edition, Jerusalem, 1947.

REIFENBERG, A., *Israel's History in Coins,* London, 1953.

REIMANN, W., *Münzen und Medaillen Cabinet,* 3 Vols., Frankfurt, 1891–2.

REIS, P.B., *Precario das Moedas Portuguesas de 1140–1640,* Lisbon, 1956; *Precario das Moedas Portuguesas de 1640–1940,* Lisbon, 1957.

RENGJEO, I., *Corpus der Mittelalterlichen Münzen von Kroatien, Slavoniem, Dalmatien und Bosnien,* Graz, 1959.

RENTZMANN, W., *Numismatisches Legenden – Lexicon des Mittelalters und der Neuzeit,* Berlin, 1865–6, Supplement, 1878.

RENTZMANN, W., *Numismatisches Wappen – Lexicon des Mittelalters und der Neuzeit,* Berlin, 1896 (reprinted Halle, 1934).

RESCH, A., *Siebenbürgische Münzen und Medaillen von 1538 bis zur Gegenwart,* Hermannstadt, 1901.

RESTELLI, F. and SAMMUT, J.C., *The Coinage of the Knights of Malta,* 2 Vols., n.p., 1977.

RETHY, L., *Corpus Nummorum Hungariae,* German edition, Graz, 1958.

RIDGEWAY, W., *The Origin of Metallic Currency and Weight Standards,* Cambridge, 1892.

RIVERO, C.M. DEL, *La Moneda Arabigo-Espanola,* Madrid, 1933.

ROGERS, E., *A Handy Guide to Jewish Coins,* London, 1914.

ROLLA, M., *Fascio Numismatico sulle Monete Italiane,* Turin, 1947.

ROSA, A., *Medallas y Monedas de la Republica Argentina,* Buenos Aires, 1898.

ROTH, B., *Ancient Gaulish Coins, including those of the Channel Islands,* London, 1913.

ROTH, B., *The Coins of the Danish Kings of Ireland, Hiberno-Danish Series,* London, 1910.

ROYAL MINT, *Annual Reports,* 1870 to date.

RUDING, R., *Annals of the Coinage,* 3 Vols., 3rd edition, London, 1840.

RULAU, R., *World Mintmarks,* Sidney, Ohio, 1968.

RUSSELL, M. (ED.), *World Coin Almanac,* Amos Press, Sidney, Ohio, 1st edition, 1975.

S

SABATIER, J., *Description Générale des Monnaies Byzantines,* 2 Vols., Paris, 1862.

SALLES OLIVIERA, A. DE, *Moedas y Barras de Ouro,* Sao Paulo, 1944.

SALLET, A. VON, *Münzen und Medaillen,* Berlin, 1898.

SAMBON, G., *Recueil des Monnaies Mediévales du Sud d'Italie avant la Domination des Normands,* Paris, 1919.

SAMBON, G., *Repertorio Generale delle Monete Coniate in Italia,* Part 1, Paris, 1912.

SCHEMBRI, H.C., *Coins and Medals of the Knights of Malta,* London, 1908 (reprinted 1966).

SCHIVE, C.J., *Norges Mynter i Middelalderen,* Christiania, 1865.

SCHJOTH, F., *The Currency of the Far East,* London, 1929 (reprinted 1976).

SCHLICKEYSEN, F.W.A. and PALLMANN, R., *Erklärung der Abkürzungen auf Münzen der Neueren zeit des Mittelalters und des Alterthums,* Berlin, 1896 (reprinted 1961).

SCHLUMBERGER, G.L., *Les Bractéates d'Allemagne,* Paris, 1874.

SCHLUMBERGER, G.L. *Numismatique de l'Orient Latin,* with Supplement, Paris, 1878–82 (reprinted 1954).

SCHOLTEN, C., *The Coins of the Dutch Overseas Territories, 1610–1948,* Amsterdam, 1953, new edition, 1979.

SCHÖN, GÜNTER, *Die Deutschen Münzen 1700–1806,* 1st edition, Munich, 1983.

SCHÖN, GÜNTER, *Weltmünzkatalog 19. Jahrhundert,* 5th edition, Munich, 1982.

SCHÖN, GÜNTER, *World Coin Catalogue, 20th Century,* 4th edition, London & New York, 1983.

SCHOU, H.H., *Beskrivelske af Danske og Norske Monter 1488–1814, og Danske Monter 1815–1923,* Copenhagen, 1926.

SCHROEDER, A. ANNAN, *Études Numismatiques,* Paris, 1905.

SCHRÖTTER, F. VON, *Wörterbuch der Münzkunde,* Berlin-Leipzig, 1930.

SCHUBERT, T.F. DE, *Monnaies et Médailles Russes,* Leipzig, 1858.

SCHULMAN, J., *Handboek van de Nederlandse Munten van 1795–1975,* Amsterdam, 1976.

SCHULTHESS-RECHBERG, *Thaler Cabinet: Beschreibung aller Bekannt Gewordenen Thaler,* 5 parts, Vienna-Munich, 1840–67.

SCHWALBACH, C., *Die Neuesten Deutschen Münzen unter Talergrösse,* Leipzig, 1904.

SCHWALBACH, C., *Die Neuesten Deutschen Thaler, Doppelthaler, Doppelgulden,* 8th edition, Munich, 1915.

SCHWARZ, D.W.H., *Münz- und Geldgeschichte Zürichs in Mittelalter,* Aarau, 1940.

SEABY, H.A. *The English Silver Coinage, 1649–1949,* London, 1974 (revised edition).

SEAR, DAVID R., *Byzantine Coins and their Values,* London, 1974.

SEAR, DAVID R., *Greek Imperial Coins,* London, 1982.

SEAR, DAVID R., *Roman Coins and their Values,* 2nd edition, London, 1974.

SELLWOOD, D., *An Introduction to the Coinage of Parthia,* London, 1975.

SELTMAN, C.T., *Athens, Its History and Coinage before the Persian Invasion,* Cambridge, 1924.

SELTMAN, C.T., *A Book of Greek Coins,* London, 1952.

SELTMAN, C.T., *Greek Coins: A History of Metallic Currency and Coinage down to the Fall of the Hellenistic Kingdoms,* 2nd edition, London, 1954.

SELTMAN, C.T., *Masterpieces of Greek Coinage,* London, 1949.

SELTMAN, C.T., *The Temple Coins of Olympia,* Cambridge, 1921.

SERAFINI, C., *Le Monete e le Bolle Plumbee Pontificie del Medagliere Vaticano,* 4 Vols., Milan, 1910–28.

SEVERIN, H.M., *Gold and Platinum Coinage of Imperial Russia from 1701–1911,* New York, 1958.

SHEPPARD, T. and MUSHAM, J.F., *Money Scales and Weights,* London, 1975.

SIGLER, P.O., *Sycee Silver,* New York, 1943.

SINGHAL, C.R., *Bibliography of Indian Coins, Part I, Non-Muhammadan Series, Part II, Muhammadan and Later Series,* Bombay, 1950–2.

SKINNER, D.M., *Rennik's Australian Coin and Banknote Guide,* n.p., n.d.

SMITH, R.B., *The Anglo-Hanoverian Coinage,* London, 1970.

SOBIN, G., *The Silver Crowns of France,* n.p., 1974.

SPAHR, R., *Le Monete Siciliane dia Bizantini a Carlo I. d'Angio (582–1282),* n.p., 1976.

SPAZIANI TESTA, G., *Duatoni, Piastre, Scudi, Talleri e Loro Multipli Battuti in Zecche Italiane e da Italiani all'estro, Vol. I, Casa Savoia,* Rome, 1951; *Vol. II, Pontefici,* Rome, 1952.

STEVENSON, S.W., *A Dictionary of Roman Coins,* London, 1889.

STEWART, I.H., *The Scottish Coinage,* London, 1955, revised edition, 1967.

SUHLE, A., *Die Deutschen Münzen des Mittelalters,* Berlin, 1936.

SUTHERLAND, A., *Numismatic History of New Zealand,* New Plymouth, 1939–41.

SUTHERLAND, C.H.V., *Anglo-Saxon Coinage in the Light of the Cronhall Hoard,* London, 1948.

SUTHERLAND, C.H.V., *Art in Coinage,* London, 1955.

SUTHERLAND, C.H.V., *Coinage and Currency in Roman Britain,* London, 1937.

SUTHERLAND, C.H.V., *Coinage in Roman Imperial Policy,* London, 1951.

SUTHERLAND, C.H.V., *English Coinage, 600–1900,* London, 1973.

SVHULTEN, W., *Deutsche Münzen aus der Zeit Karls V.,* Frankfurt, 1974.

SYDENHAM, E.A., *Aes Grave*, London, 1926.
SYDENHAM, E.A., *The Coinage of Nero*, London, 1926.
SYDENHAM, E.A., *The Coinage of the Roman Republic*, London, 1952.

T

TAN, S., *Coin and Paper Money Catalogue of Malaysia, Singapore and Brunei, 1845–1977*, n.p., 2nd edition, 1978.
TAULLARD, A., *Monedas de la Republica Argentina*, Buenos Aires, 1924.
TAXAY, DON, *The U.S. Mint and Coinage*, New York, 1966.
TAYLOR, H.C. and JAMES, S., *A Guide Book of Canadian Coins, Currency and Tokens*, 2nd edition, Winnipeg, 1960.
TAYLOR, J., *The Architectural Medal, England in the Nineteenth Century*, London, 1978.
TEIXEIRA DE ARAGO, A.C., *Descripção Geral e Historica das Moedas Cunhadas en Nome dos Reis, Regentes e Governadores de Portugal*, 3 Vols., Lisbon, 1874–80.
THOMAS, E.R. and DALE, L.J., *They Made their Own Money: The Story of the Early Canterbury Traders and their Tokens*, Canterbury, N.Z., 1950.
THOMPSON, D.A., *Inventory of British Coin Hoards, A.D. 660–1500*, London, 1956.
THOMSEN, G.J., *Les Monnaies du Moyen-Age*, 3 Vols., Copenhagen, 1873–6.
THOMSEN, R., *Early Roman Coinage, A Study of the Chronology: I. The Evidence*, Copenhagen, 1952; *II. Synthesis I, III. Synthesis II*, Copenhagen, 1961.
TOBLER-MEYER, W., *Die Münz- und Medaillen, Sammlung des Herrn Hans Wuderly von Muralt*, 5 Vols., Zürich, 1896–8.
TOLSTOI, I., *Monnaies Byzantines*, (in Russian) 8 parts (unfinished), St Petersburg, 1913–14.
TOUR, H. DE LA, *Atlas des Monnaies Gauloises*, Paris, 1892.
TOYNBEE, J.M.C., *Roman Medallions*, New York, 1944.
TROWBRIDGE, R.J., *History, Coinage, Paper Notes and Medals of Edward VIII of Great Britain*, London, 1970.
TURNWALD, K., *Česke a Moravske Denary a Brakteaty*, Prague, 1949.

V

VALENTINE, W.H., *The Copper Coins of India*, 2 Vols., London, 1914–20 (reprinted 1 Vol., 1971).
VALENTINE, W.H., *Modern Copper Coins of the Muhammadan States*, London, 1911 (reprinted 1969).
VALENTINE, W.H., *Sassanian Coins*, Bombay, 1914.
VAN LOON, G., *Histoire Métallique des XVII Provinces des Pays-Bas*, 5 Vols., The Hague, 1732–7.
VERKADE, P., *Muntboek Berattende de Namen en af Beeldingen van Munten Gaslagen in de Zeven Voormalig Veneenigde Nederlandsche Provincien Sedert den Vrede van Gent tot op Onzen Tijd*, Schiedam, 1848.
VERMEULE, C.C., *Numismatic Art in America*, Cambridge, Mass., 1971.
VIVES Y ESCUDERO, A., *La Moneda Hispanica*, 4 Vols., Madrid, 1924–6.
VOGLHUBER, R., *Taler und Schautaler des Erzhauses Habsburg von 1484 bis 1896*, Frankfurt, 1973.

W

WALKER, D.R., *The Metrology of the Roman Silver Coinage*, 3 Vols., n.p., 1976–8.
WALLROTH, K.A., *Sveriges Mynt 1449–1917*, Stockholm, 1918.
WANG, YU-CH'UAN, *Early Chinese Coinage*, New York, 1951.
WARD, J., *Greek Coins and their Parent Cities*, London, 1902.
WEISSENRIEDER, F.X., *100 Jahre Schweizerisches Münzwesen, 1850–1950*, Bern, 1950.
WEYL, A., *Katalog der Jules Fonrobert, Schen Sammlung Überseeischer Münzen und Medaillen*, Vols., 1–3, Berlin, 1878–9; Vol. 4, Berlin, 1879.
WHITEHEAD, R.B., *The Pre-Mohammedan Coinage of North Western India*, New York, 1922.
WHITING, R.J.S., *Commemorative Medals, A Medallic History of Britain from Tudor Times to the Present Day*, Newton Abbot, 1972.
WHITTING, P.D., *Byzantine Coins*, London, 1973.

WILKE, J., *Daler, Mark Ogkroner, 1481–1914,* Copenhagen, 1931.

WITTE, A. DE, *Histoire Monétaire des Comtes de Louvain, Ducs de Brabant,* 3 Vols., Antwerp, 1894–9.

WOLLASTON, H., *British Official Medals for Coronations and Jubilees, A Commemorative Collectors' Guide,* n.p., 1978.

WOOD, H., *The Coinage of the West Indies with Special Reference to the Cut and Counterstamped Pieces,* New York, 1914.

WRIGHT, L.V.W., *Colonial and Commonwealth Coinage,* London, 1959.

WROTH, W., *Catalogue of the Coins of the Vandals, Ostrogoths and Lombards, and of the Empires of Thessalonica, Nicaea and Trebizand, in the British Museum,* London, 1911.

WROTH, W., *Catalogue of Imperial Byzantine Coins in the British Museum,* 2 Vols., London, 1908.

Y

YEOMAN, R.S.A., *A Catalogue of Modern World Coins,* 3rd edition, Racine, 1959.

YEOMAN, R.S.A., *A Guide Book of United States Coins,* 33rd revised edition, Racine, 1980.

Z

ZAY, E., *Histoire Monétaire des Colonies Françaises,* Paris, 1892, Supplement, 1904 (reprinted 1978).

ZEHNBAUER, HUBERT, *Moneta (Studies in Roman Republican Coinage),* 2 Vols., Paris & Athens, 1973.